The ENNEAGRAM *Symbol*

Mapping the Journey
of Personal, Social, and
Spiritual Evolution

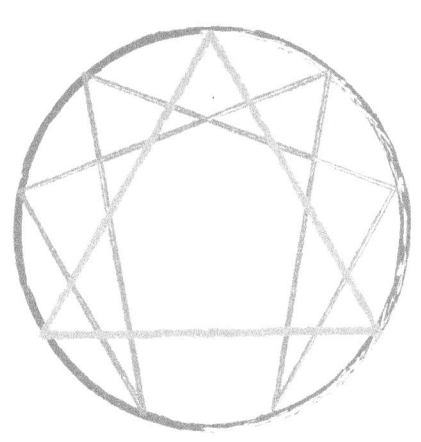

JENNIFER JOSS, PhD

JUMPING CURVES PRESS · ASHLAND, OREGON

*The Enneagram Symbol: Mapping the Journey of
Personal, Social, and Spiritual Evolution*

by Jennifer Joss, Ph.D.

Published by Jumping Curves Press

Cover and interior design by BookSavvyStudio.com
Author photo by: Tina Bolling Evoniuk

Library of Congress Control Number: 2023902324

ISBN: 979-8-9876640-1-8

Manufactured in the United States of America

For
Kate & Carly
My reason for everything

CONTENTS

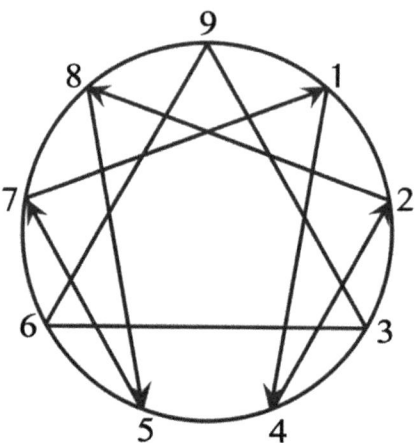

CHAPTER ONE

Introduction

I F YOU ALREADY KNOW THE ENNEAGRAM, you probably know it as a personality typing system describing nine "personality types," or patterns of thinking, feeling, and acting, arrayed around a circle, and connected through a curious collection of shapes and arrow lines. At this level, the Enneagram of Personality is used to improve self-knowledge and help us understand differences among people. Beyond this, the Enneagram can be used as a kind of developmental map: a guide to not only understanding, but also helping people grow from a fixed version of self (our personality type) to a more conscious, adaptive, and often more graceful and effective version. Applied in this way, the Enneagram can promote growth in people, teams, groups, and organizations. This was enough to capture my devotion to the system for many years. Little did I know there is more...

The Process Enneagram

I had been studying and applying work from various Enneagram teachers and schools for 23 years before I was introduced to the Process Enneagram by Uranio Paes, a Brazilian teacher and business consultant. The Process Enneagram is the study of the Enneagram Symbol and the "universal laws," or patterns of growth, conveyed by its geometric structures: the circle, triangle, and the hexad, representing the Laws of One, Three, and Seven.

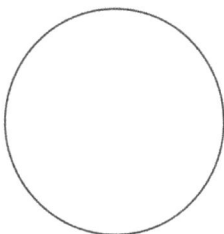
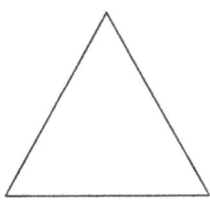
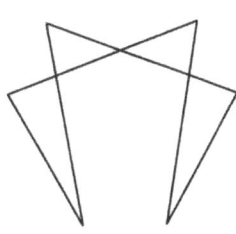

THE LAW OF ONE   THE LAW OF THREE   THE LAW OF SEVEN

In April of 2016 I was in New York City for a meeting of the Enneagram in Business Network (EIBN). While I had grown up in the Narrative Enneagram tradition, by that point in my life with the Enneagram I was using it almost exclusively to support individual coaching and large group development programs in organizations. This particular meeting, we had gathered to share ideas with other EIBN professionals working to help grow leadership, people, and teams. For a couple of hours one morning, Uranio spread a big Enneagram Symbol mat on the floor and introduced us to a unique way of using it—totally apart from "type"—as a map for a process of growth. He employed the arrow lines and movement around the Symbol to both reveal and work with various patterns and obstacles to development. When I was invited to step on to the mat, I felt my understanding of the Enneagram shift in an instant. I experienced the Enneagram not as a flat representation, but rather something more like a field. It felt like a field we can inhabit (perhaps *do* inhabit) that was animated by some kind of coherent pattern. I had a sense right then that has only deepened with time: that *we* are not teaching the Enneagram so much as the Enneagram is working through us.

Following that meeting, Uranio went on to partner with Enneagram author and consultant Beatrice Chestnut in creating a school that integrates their shared experience of the Enneagram of Personality with the Process Enneagram to facilitate psychological, spiritual, and professional development. Although it was highly experiential work in the early days, Uranio also dropped breadcrumbs of information about the Symbol, its esoteric history, and relationship to essential geometric shapes called Platonic or Pythagorean solids, the Seal of Solomon, and something called the Merkaba. And he referenced George I. Gurdjieff, the Greek-Armenian philosopher and teacher who brought knowledge of the Enneagram Symbol and its "laws" into the modern world in the early 1900s. Gurdjieff claimed that anything could be known and understood through this symbol, making libraries irrelevant. Anything? I was riveted.

My experiences with Bea and Uranio ushered me into a season of personal growth and deeper understanding of the Enneagram that resulted in a ravenous quest to further explore and explain the meaning of the Symbol. I felt like the ant whose brain has been populated by a certain kind of mushroom spore. The mushroom somehow compels the ant to climb a tree and then spread its spores widely by making the ant's brain explode! The problem is that finding clear and conclusive detail about the information depicted in the Enneagram Symbol is a challenge. People disagree on its interpretation. It's a *symbol*, after all. And Gurdjieff was a bit of trickster, intentionally shrouding essential truths behind a veil of complexity so we would have to work at understanding with our whole being. But he also said the laws are "eternal" and "universal"—they apply to every level of reality, from an atom to humans to the Universe itself, echoing the oft-quoted proposition from antiquity: "As Above, so Below."[1] If this is true, I thought, we should find evidence of these laws everywhere. So that's where I went looking.

Rather than sticking to the history of the Enneagram (which you can find elsewhere[2]) or draining the work of Gurdjieff's students, I went wide. I tracked the processes conveyed in the Symbol through three lenses: science—including general systems theory, neuroscience, psychology, and a smattering of physics; stories—our world's narrative tradition, in particular creation stories and the hero's journey myth; and spiritual wisdom—various religious and spiritual traditions with which I have some familiarity. While I am not an expert in any of these things, I tried to align Gurdjieff's teaching and writings with research and reflection from multiple diverse perspectives on the patterns represented in the Enneagram. And throughout this process I lived my way around the Symbol, using my own inner work to explore how the laws can help us in our relationship with ourselves, each other, and life in these chaotic times.

I have heard it said there is no new wisdom, and I am sure that applies to this book. I have tried to credit sources and people as possible, but I have been studying some of the ideas revealed in the Enneagram Symbol since I was a teenager. Because they set up camp in my brain somewhere long ago, my attempts to attribute and reference have surely fallen short. What I have aimed to add to the strands of wisdom collected here is my capacity for seeing patterns and weaving diverse threads into a coherent whole.

My heroes in that weaving process, whose ideas you will encounter throughout this book, include especially: Carl Jung, who integrated a massive body of ancient work in alchemy and mythic structure into his scientific understanding of psychology and the "archetypes" or objective patterns within the human psyche; Joseph Campbell, who digested the entire world of global mythology to deliver to us the central narratives used to light a heroic way through the chaos of modern life; Valentin Tomberg, the Christian Hermetic philosopher who illuminated the power of symbols not only to teach but to change us; Jordan Peterson, who employed the mythic imagination and archetypes, along with science, psychology, and religion, to map the sub-structure beneath all of western thought; and, of course, G.I. Gurdjieff, the one credited with bringing to life the laws of the Enneagram Symbol, himself a master of weaving diverse wisdom traditions, science, stories, and the arts into experiential teaching about eternal truths.

THE PURPOSE AND PROMISE OF THE BOOK

The purpose of the book is to help you, too, to explore the ancient wisdom handed down through the Enneagram Symbol, to apply it in your own journeys of growth, and to discover how it can help us all with personal, social, and spiritual evolution. In keeping with this, the book unfolds in three layers.

• It is, first, a theoretical exploration of the laws of the Symbol that weaves together diverse disciplines of study to try to answer the questions: *Are they really 'universal' laws? How do they work? How can they help us?* Rather than just tell you what I have concluded, I am inviting you into the learning process, to seat yourself at different perspectives from which to discern the meaning and value of the laws.

• Second, the book is designed to take you on a metaphorical hero's journey around the Symbol to experience the laws, how they interact, and to explore their application to psychosocial and spiritual transformation.

• Third, it is an attempt to integrate theory and metaphor into a developmental map, in hopes of providing signposts and sustenance along your own journeys of growth and renewal. In the end, your personal experience of the dynamics of the Symbol is required for true understanding.

And why would this sort of detailed inquiry into the Symbol matter? Given the complexity in the world—war, political unrest, global pandemic, economic and racial inequity, and natural disasters—why turn inwards and look at ourselves at all, much less take the time to reflect on ancient symbols and "universal laws," when there is so much to be righted in the world?

The Symbol itself is a map of the transition between unity and multiplicity. It shows how diverse, even polarized, parts of any system can re-member themselves as a unified whole. As such, the Enneagram has a lot to teach us about union and communion. This is an essential ethic and agenda for our times. Many of humanity's great teachers, both spiritual and secular, find the roots of our modern problems in how we know ourselves as separate from each other, the natural world, and *All that Is*—our shared Source and ground of Being. We are in need of a shared moral consciousness and pathway towards holding diversity in unity, in ourselves and within society as a whole. The Enneagram provides both, in a framework that accommodates diverse belief systems. Because it maps a universal process, knowledge of the Symbol provides a doorway into our common human experience, no matter our Enneagram type, gender, race, religion, culture, status, age, or political leaning.

Gurdjieff taught that we are all subject to the dynamic patterns of reality depicted in the Symbol. He said we are "mechanical beings," captive to unconscious and environmental forces that operate through us and tend to divide us, within and without. We are not at all "free," as we believe. But because these fundamental laws are universal, he said we could and should study ourselves to realize how they are expressed through us.[3] Rather than continue as naïve subjects of their influence, we can then learn to engage with the laws in doing the psychological and spiritual work that is the foundation for evolving a better world for all of us. He often referred to his method of working with the wisdom of the Enneagram Symbol as "building a soul," which he said is not inherent in humans.

I whole-heartedly agree with the idea that inner work is an essential foundation for peace and renewal in the world. Knowing ourselves fully and gaining the capacity to be more purposeful with how we show up equips us to live lives characterized by greater kindness, contribution, and dignity, aligned with higher principles. When we are fully present, aware, and integrated, we no longer act out our unconscious issues. We are less likely to blame "the other" in the world. The "better angels of our nature," as Abraham Lincoln called them, are free to act more consciously in service of who and what we care about, to observe the consequences of our impact, and adjust as needed. And when we face and integrate the previously hidden or shadowed aspects of our own hearts, we can transform them more skillfully in the world.

Some of this, for sure, we can do with a right application of the Enneagram of Personality (although this is not always how it is used). Beyond that, working with the laws of the Symbol can help us envision where we are going with those development efforts, show us why inner work is important when there is so much to be done in the world, and reveal how we might do it more fruitfully together, in service to our communities and to humanity as a whole. Using the laws of the Symbol in combination with the Enneagram of Personality can not only help us map our individual and collective journeys of growth, but also can help us shape more meaningful lives—something for which many of us are hungering in today's world.

King Arthur's Knights, setting out on their search for the Holy Grail—a symbol of the moral and spiritual development of the soul—entered the forest at the place that was "darkest" for each of them. The Enneagram of Personality helps us find just that place. Our type is like an entry point. It can also provide guidance about our gifts, as well as what is in the way of growth at specific points on our journey; a journey as potentially trans-formational as that of the Knights of the Round Table. But to find our way, we need a map—of who we are and who we aren't (yet). We need a map of the whole territory, and a plan. And wouldn't it be best if that map were one that has worked for generations of heroes and seekers transformed by their efforts to advance healing and unity in the world?

As fate would have it, my deep dive into the Symbol coincided with a descent into a very dark period in my own life. While I had been working on "ego deconstruction" in service of spiritual and psychological matu-rity, it was quite another thing to have life do it *for* me. Finding myself in the depths of the unknown, without the familiar buffers and signposts my prior identity and commitments had provided, was profoundly diffi-cult, humbling, and disorienting. I needed a map. And I found one in the Symbol. Its mysteries opened to me as much through dreams, meditation, inner work, and prayer, as through my studies. This gave me a thread to follow through the darkness, and it forged in me a commitment to weave all this into a guide to accompany other people on their own forays into the depths, chosen or delivered.

So if you are also on a psycho-spiritual journey and sometimes wonder where you are going and what it's all for, this book is written for you. If you are intent on changing the world, making it a more compassion-ate place, and realizing the harmony and interconnectedness preached and practiced by spiritual and secular heroes from all ages, you will find guidance from the heroes we follow here. If you are passionate about the Enneagram and curious to know more about the mysteries conveyed in the Symbol, you will discover more about them through theory, metaphor, and self-reflection if you go on this journey with me. And if you don't already know the Enneagram of Personality or your own type, you can learn more about that here too.

In fact, truth be told, despite nearly 30 years of Enneagra1 have not been able to confidently locate myself in one type. I have officially bounced around the types on the inner triangle (9-6-3), and strangely enough, I could also see my life unfold through the pattern of the hexad figure (1-4-2-8-5-7). Needless to say, this was discouraging and embarrassing for me as a certified professional, but it also motivated me to explore and compare teachings from different Enneagram schools. In that process, I found varying descriptions of types and subtypes, disagreement about the existence (or not) of countertypes, conflicting theories about instincts, the relevance of wings (or not), and the way to work with the arrows. Even whether or not we have only one type is debated!

This incongruity further fed my desire to look under the hood and make sense of the Symbol myself. I thought if we could understand the architecture lurking beneath the typing system, we might find an impartial authority to resolve some of the differences (which people defend quite passionately) within the global Enneagram community. I had to believe there was some kind of matrix of meaning behind the manifest teachings that could clarify not only my own issues with typing, but also how the system works to give rise to the core teachings about personality. It turns out there is! And we can uncover it by peering deeply into the Enneagram Symbol itself.

WHAT'S IN THE BOOK

While this is not really a book about the Enneagram of Personality, we will cover the basics and track the types throughout, as they provide essential points of perspective on our shared reality. Included in this introductory section of the book is a summary of the structure of the Enneagram of Personality and what makes a type a type. The rest of the book follows the three-part structure of the hero's journey described by Joseph Campbell as *Separation* from the everyday or "known" world, *Initiation* in the "unknown" world, and the *Return* to a renewed world. Because the middle section of the book (Initiation) follows the hero's journey itself, around the Enneagram, the book is a journey within a journey. And since "the journey makes the hero," and not the other way around, this book is a commitment for sure. It won't always be clear or smooth sailing, and if I did the job as charged you might be changed by your engagement with the material on your own soul's journey.

I have often thought the Enneagram should come with a warning. Stepping into its symbolic field inevitably leads to some kind of foundational undoing. While this is generally in service of evolution, that is not always obvious along the way. As Gurdjieff says it, "there is nothing worse than beginning to work on ourselves and then giving up and finding oneself 'between two stools;' it would be much better not to begin."[4] So while there is no particular prerequisite for the material in the book, consider yourself warned. The journey is always easier when we go by choice...and see it through.

Since people have different assumptions and associations with the word "hero," I want to offer here that the word actually means something like *a person of both divine and human descent*, and it derives from a Greek word that means "defender" or "protector." Joseph Campbell, who advanced our modern understanding of the nature of a hero, wrote that a hero is someone who has given his or her life "to something bigger than oneself." So to be clear, in the book I am using "hero" in this context, as one who is enlarged by a personally challenging and healing journey, and who applies the wisdom and gifts unveiled in service of the world.

That said, on this heroic journey, in Part 1: Universal Laws (Separation), we will travel far beyond the known world of the Enneagram and its history to reflect on universal patterns and their depiction in other disciplines: science, stories, and spiritual traditions. My own first encounter with the idea that the same patterns of growth could operate across very different levels of existence came in the way of another graphic representation, called *S-curves*, that I met around the same time as I learned the Enneagram. While the growth process shown in the S-curves is just one of many related patterns we will use to unlock the mysteries of the Symbol, it is one we will draw upon throughout the book. In the rest of Part 1, we will explore each of the laws of the Enneagram, from diverse perspectives, to see whether we can indeed say they are "universal." In some sense, this inquiry into the nature of the laws continues throughout the book, so if you prefer to learn first through experience and metaphor, feel free to skip to Part 2 and return when you have an appetite for theory.

In Part 2: The Hero's Journey (Initiation) we will follow the myth of the hero's journey around the Enneagram Symbol, using the symbolism of stories to reveal more about the laws and how they work together to realize the promise of re-union and renewal laid out in the Enneagram. To really understand this Symbol, we have to live our way around it. Like our heroes, we must face the *dragon*—the unknown, unconscious dimensions of our being; recover the *treasure* of our in-most selves; and tap into our own unique spark of imagination and creativity in order to serve and revivify our communities. Throughout the journey, we will track the qualities represented at each point of the Enneagram. Looked at sequentially, the particulars of "type" explain a great deal about the whole journey for all of us, how we can best navigate its challenges, and find our way "home." Ultimately, the "home" we come to is a signal of harmony and renewal in the kingdom as a whole, as well as in the hero.

The final section, Part 3: The Symbol (Return), aims to make the wisdom of the Symbol revealed along the hero's journey more concrete by proposing a sketch of how the laws work together to fulfill the "octave" of growth laid out in the Enneagram. This is where we get more specific about how the Symbol can help us with our inner work and service in the world. We will explore, as a key to the work, how to develop our own "inner triangle"—standing for our fully awake, present, and aligned mind, heart, and body as an integrated vehicle of higher intelligence. Then we will use the ancient science of alchemy (turning coarse matter into finer substance) to take a final turn around the Symbol, applying our inner law of three to the seven steps, to reveal more of the map of development.

While we will probably never fully fathom the mysteries contained in the Enneagram Symbol, validating its core patterns through many traditions yields "a" way if not "the" way to realization of some of its wisdom. Before we get there, however, we have some ground to cover. Step one: the Enneagram of Personality, where the journey begins for most of us.

THE PEACEMAKER
9

THE CHALLENGER 8   1 THE REFORMER

THE ENTHUSIAST 7   2 THE GIVER

THE LOYALIST 6   3 THE PERFORMER

THE OBSERVER 5   4 THE INDIVIDUALIST

CHAPTER TWO

THE ENNEAGRAM OF PERSONALITY

*There is nothing more confining than the prison
we don't know we are in.*

~ WILLIAM SHAKESPEARE

ALL OVER THE WORLD, people find themselves reflected in the nine personality types described by the Enneagram. They use the system for self-understanding, appreciating differences between individuals, and for personal and collective growth. While this is not foremost a book about the Enneagram of Personality, understanding the essential nature and challenge at each point of the Enneagram will support our exploration of the Symbol as a map to a transformational process that applies to all of us, no matter our type.

In some sense, we are all *all* nine types. As a consequence of being human, we navigate through many of the positions around the Enneagram. Looked at in this way, each point is like a mini personality (psychologists would call a "complex") that can rear its head in the moment we are possessed by its driving nature. We can all be hijacked by the Anger of Type 1, the Pride of Type 2, or the Fear of Type 6, for example. We are bound to observe at least a handful of the primary drives of type in ourselves. And yet there is one Enneagram type that sort of "captures" us. Thanks to patterns wired into our brain and behavior, we compulsively, automatically, and rather unconsciously, live from its particular orientation to the world, and the specific driving need that is running in the background.

This is why we say that our Enneagram type is *not* who we are. It is more like a strategy we developed to get our needs met and to protect ourselves from being hurt by life. A spiritual theory of the origination of type is that it is simply given; it is our soul's assignment in this life. Psychological theory suggests that type arises due to the combination of our inherent wiring, our *nature* or temperament, rubbing up against our early relationships and culture or *nurture*. As little kids we all have experiences that leave us not feeling secure enough, worthy enough, having enough autonomy, or otherwise not getting our "ego needs" met. To compensate for this, we each develop a very intelligent strategy for coping with, and trying to make up for, whatever we felt was lacking. Developing this strategy (our type structure) is quite a remarkable and adaptive process that unfolds in a young child, one that helps us survive and/or thrive in our early environment.

Our Enneagram type, then, is a kind of "operating strategy" that is running in the background, guiding our lives to ensure that we get our most important ego needs met. The word "ego" is often used as a stand-in for *personality* or *persona* in psychology. Ego does not mean "conceit" (as in egotistical) but rather something more like "deceit," in the sense of a false (because overly narrow) self we adopted to navigate our early lives. Even then, it's an unconscious deceit. We don't know anything other than this "self" we live out each day in an attempt to maintain a sense of security, control, and value in a challenging world. If we were to summarize those strategies by type, they might go something like this:

At **Type 1**, my strategy is to be good or "right," according to my own code.

At **Type 2**, my strategy is to be connected; to be liked and needed.

At **Type 3**, my strategy is to be impressive in what I do; to perform well.

At **Type 4**, my strategy is to be unique and authentic; to access depth and meaning in life.

At **Type 5**, my strategy is to be detached and objective; as little affected as possible.

At **Type 6**, my strategy is to be secure; to gain certainty and understanding.

At **Type 7**, my strategy is to be unlimited, have options, and to be excited by possibility.

At **Type 8**, my strategy is to be strong or powerful; to avoid being vulnerable.

At **Type 9**, my strategy is to be peaceful; in harmony with life, myself, and others.

These operating strategies are made up of consistent and largely unconscious patterns of perceptions and thoughts, emotional/motivational drives, and instinctual reactions—in other words: habits of mind, heart, and body. Over time, our type strategy leads to great strengths, because we get really good at certain things. Overused, however, or used unconsciously, these same strengths can get us into trouble. And eventually, our type structure becomes quite limiting, as a narrow expression of who we are, which is in some sense the whole circle—all nine types, and so much more.

Some people object to typing and personality systems as misguided attempts to put us complex people into simple boxes. However, the truth is that because of the habitual nature of our neural circuitry and emotional repertoire, each of us is already in a box—what my friends at the Enneagram Prison Project call "a prison of our own making."[5] The point of finding our Enneagram type and subtype is not so much to *put* ourselves in a box as it is to see the box we are in *already*, based on our mental, emotional, and instinctual habits—the inner programs we play out in our lives without really thinking about or choosing them. And again, while these programs may have served us well in our early years, their underlying assumption—that we must do or be something to shore up our sense of "self"—is precisely what separates us from experiencing the highest aspects of our nature and our interconnectedness with all life.

What makes an Enneagram Type?

Centers of Intelligence

Rather than detail the whole range of what each Enneagram type acts like, feels like, thinks like (which you can find elsewhere), I want to strip it down here and help you understand what really makes a type a type. To understand the make-up of type, we have to learn about intelligence centers. Each of the nine Enneagram types is located in one of three centers of intelligence, symbolized by the three points of the triangle 3-6-9. With point 6 as the anchor, types 5-6-7 sit in the head center; with point 3 marking the heart center, types 2-3-4 are located here, and point 9 anchors types 8-9-1 in the body center. The location of our type in a particular center says something about how our automatic patterns cause us to misuse, over-use, or distort the true wisdom of that center. We get a little stuck there. As Narrative Enneagram teacher Peter O'Hanrahan puts it: our type's main center is the one in which we have the most resources but *the least amount of freedom.*

BODY CENTER

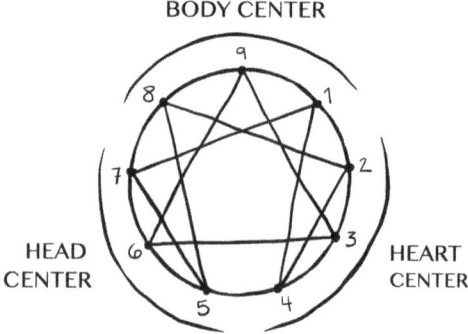

At the same time, it's important to remember that all of us have all three of these centers. For each Enneagram type, there are predictable ways that head, heart, and body intelligence play out. From this more general perspective, these three intelligence centers are zones in our being through which we take in and send out "intelligence" in the form of energy and information. Now this is quite literal. The world we experience is a massive and multi-faceted field of information. To make sense of all that, our brains must ignore some things, and zoom in on others to focus on what we believe is necessary. This is called *selective attention* and *value-tagging* in neuroscience. And it is guided by our type—our wiring and internal patterns as expressed through these centers.

In the head center, for example, if (thanks to my wiring and experience) I have a mental model that says the world is a hazardous place, I "select" and see threats in a setting. If your mental frame of reference is that the world is a place of endless possibility, you will "select" and see opportunity in the very same room. The way I "send" information to others is also framed by my head center through the way that I pay attention to people (or don't). This has a felt impact. People experience non-judgmental attention to be as rewarding as money or food, for example, whereas social judgment and pain registers in the same brain centers as does physical pain.

This sending and receiving of energy and information or "intelligence" ramps up in the heart center. The measurable field of the heart's electro-magnetic energy extends far outside the body and, by some accounts, is 100x greater than the field generated by our brain waves.[6] Emotional energy colors everything. We might interpret the meaning of a passing glance, for example, according to our mood, and we send energy and infor-mation to others (whether we mean to or not) through our feelings. There are structures in the limbic area of the brain that literally read and react to (and are changed by) *other* people's feelings about us. This explains why we often know how people feel about us...no matter how they are acting.

Finally, modern science is revealing more and more about the intelligence of our body center, sometimes called the gut or belly center, and how it reads and responds to information from our surrounding environment, as well as from within our own bodies, to help shape our emotional and cognitive perceptions. There is a good deal of evidence to suggest that our body language alone not only conveys information to others about our competence (or lack of it), but also impacts our self-perception. The habitual action of these three centers (mind, heart, and body), in each of us, makes up the "structure" of our ego and Enneagram type—meaning the actual wiring and patterning that has been laid down in the brain and body over many years of repetition.

Passions, Fixations, and Instincts

Once again, while our type may be located in a dominant center of intelligence indicated by its location around the circle, each type is also structured according to fixed patterns in *all three* centers. The first pattern, in the heart center of intelligence, is called the emotional habit or the *passion* of an Enneagram type. Rather than just a feeling state, this is something like a driving motivational force and orientation of the heart. It colors our experience by assigning value to information, people, and events based on past emotional memories and pervasive mood states, and it commands and compels us from within. Much as a fish does not see the water in which it swims, it can be hard for us to identify this pervasive motivational state underlying our conscious life. Below are the names of the passions by Enneagram point.

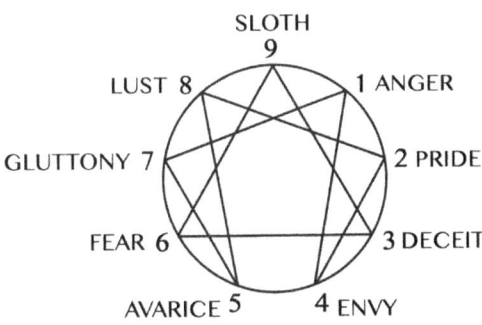

ENNEAGRAM PASSIONS

The second key identifier of type comes from the head center and is called the mental habit or *fixation* of type. It shapes how we see and understand the world and our place in it. Something like "a mental model," the fixation determines our experience according to our assumptions and attention choices. That's why it is "fixed" or "fixated." If I have a mental model of the world as a chaotic and messy place, for example, I will *see* things that need to be made orderly far more than someone who has a different frame of reference, and this will reinforce my worldview, keeping me trapped in it.

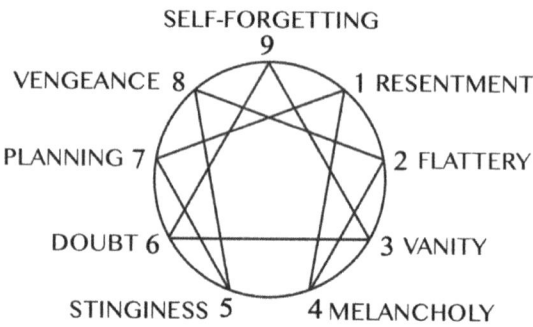

SELF-FORGETTING
9
VENGEANCE 8   1 RESENTMENT
PLANNING 7   2 FLATTERY
DOUBT 6   3 VANITY
STINGINESS 5   4 MELANCHOLY

ENNEAGRAM FIXATIONS

While the fixation and passion can be difficult to identify, embedded as they are in the very lens of your experience, if you cannot eventually find the passion and fixation of a particular type within you, you are probably not that type. That's how fundamental these two elements are in determining Enneagram type. And while we will explain them in more detail later in the book, for now it's good to know that the true meaning of each of these labels above is often a bit different than what we might assume based only on the word used.

Beyond habits of head and heart, there is third factor determining type, one that comes from the body center. This center also runs habitual programs, but to make matters slightly more complicated, those programs are based on not one but three instinctual drives. The instinctual drives of the body center are called the *self-preservation*, *sexual*, and *social instincts*. We all have *all* of these instincts. They are wired into our brain and nervous system as survival reactions handed down from our ancient ancestors. But one of them tends to be more dominant. It is another driving force that mixes with the passion of our type to constellate our particular Enneagram subtype, which is one of three variants of each primary Enneagram type (making 27 subtypes). The passion, fixation, and instincts are the primary defining aspects of an Enneagram type. But because they are inner habits, we can't necessarily see them in people's behavior. This means we can never say something like: "If you like to organize a lot, you are a Type 1." The same behavior can be driven by many different motivations. I might create order in my home, for example, because I can't tolerate disarray, or because my friends are coming over and I care what they think. Similarly, the same inner motivation can lead to significantly different behaviors. Two people with an emotional habit of Fear, for example, can act quite differently in the face of it depending on their dominant instinct and subtype: one retreating, the other moving toward what challenges her.

Thanks to this architecture, it is not always easy to identify type and subtype in ourselves, and it is nearly impossible when simply observing others. It can take many years of experience, on top of a deep understanding of the essential nature of these patterns, to reliably type someone else. And when it comes to your own typing process, while feedback from others and well-validated tests (which are rare) can provide data, the final confirmation should come from your own actual ability to see these patterns and map how they have permeated your experience. In other words, beware of typing based on Instagram memes and tests alone. It takes a good deal of inquiry, self-observation, and reflection to see how these hidden habits operate within you and to accurately identify your Enneagram type.

Moving from Ego to Essence: Virtues and Holy Ideas

While identifying our Enneagram type and the ways it operates in our lives is a path to growth, the understanding that we are whole people, not defined by a single type, is an equally important aspect of the system and distinguishes the Enneagram of Personality from other personality typing systems. Our Enneagram type illustrates how we are unconsciously blocking ourselves from knowing all of who we are, represented by the whole circle. Understanding ourselves as both the whole *and* the part can help us live more purposefully, aligned with not only our highest ideals and the unique gifts we were given, but also with the continuous process of growth and renewal that connects us with all the world. We call this *moving from ego to essence*, which is our higher, true, or "essential" self or soul, not bound by type, that knows itself as part of the unity of all things.

While we have this essence when we are born, it becomes obscured by the formation of personality. The developmental task of the "second half" of life is to uncover and further develop this essence that is both "ours" and reminds us of our inseparable connection to *All that Is.*

The Enneagram also maps the inherent qualities of essence, which are called the *virtues* and *holy ideas.* These are aspects of what is described as the "higher emotional center" and "higher mental center," respectively. They emerge when we are no longer run by unconscious patterns of type and can access a greater intelligence available through our integrated being. While virtues are said to arise from this "higher heart," they don't just come from our own hearts, and they are not really feelings. Virtues are more like *ways of being* when we are operating as an integrated whole being, or rather, qualities of the ground of Being itself that emerge when we know ourselves as not separate from Source and all of Creation.

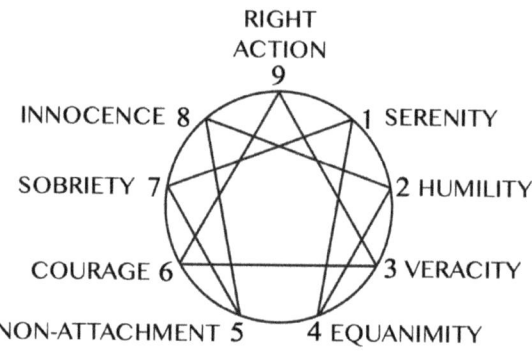

ENNEAGRAM VIRTUES

Similarly, the holy ideas from "higher mind" are not thoughts but rather different ways of knowing or seeing the world from a non-dual perspective, as whole or interconnected. Each type has a different angle on this direct perception of the nature of reality that was lost in the fall from union with Source that occurred when we were born into physical bodies. These perspectives, just like the virtues, can be regained along the path of growth.

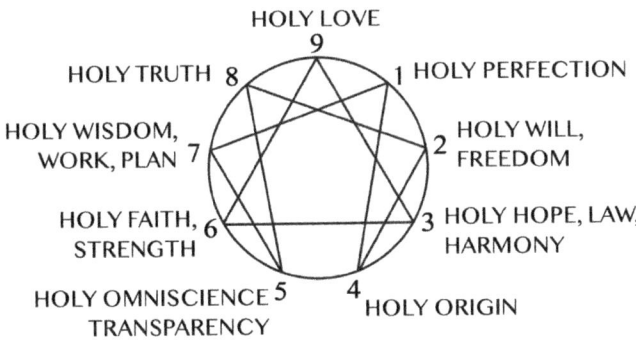

ENNEAGRAM HOLY IDEAS

According to the Enneagram of Personality, while you may identify with any number of the words listed on these two maps, one point will summarize a distinct orientation or doorway to growth for your particular Enneagram type. It will also allow you to be in touch with *all* possible higher perspectives (holy ideas) and qualities of Being (virtues) eventually, as they are all aspects of the same one interconnected reality.

We will explore these central Enneagram terms and concepts more fully as we journey around the Symbol in Part 2 of the book. Taken together, they will help us to experience the laws in action, and how they might inform our efforts to transcend our limited personality and realize our higher self or fully developed essence. Using insight from the Enneagram of Personality to observe and understand the patterns that play out in our minds, hearts, and behavior can be life changing. Understanding the universal laws, or the dynamic patterns depicted in the Enneagram Symbol can enhance our development work by clarifying how to do it more skillfully to help evolve our world as well as ourselves. But because this guidance is presented in symbolic form, we have some work to do to unlock the universal laws and the broader map embedded in the Enneagram Symbol.

PART 1:
Universal Laws

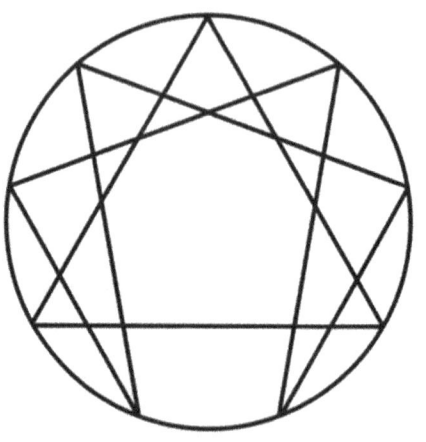

CHAPTER THREE

Universal Patterns

The Enneagram is a universal symbol. All knowledge can
be included in the Enneagram and with the help of the
Enneagram it can be interpreted ... A man may be quite alone in
the desert and he can trace the Enneagram in the sand and in it
read the eternal laws of the universe. And every time he can learn
something new, something he did not know before.[7]

~ G.I. Gurdjieff

I KNOW...THE IDEA THAT THIS SYMBOL we have been using to make sense of personality styles is also a map of the "eternal laws of the Universe" is mind-bending. Even the very existence of laws that comprehensively govern our collective experience sounds far-fetched, much less the notion that they could be explained in a symbol. And yet, in the ancient world, symbols, images, and stories were used widely to share "objective" knowledge about the nature of the universe gathered through careful attention to both inner and outer worlds. In some sense, this is not so different from what physicists do with their equations, which are essentially numerical symbols that model the Universe. Einstein himself was convinced we would someday prove that reality is a unified field, and we would find a unified theory to align and explain all that we know about how the Universe works and our relationship to it.

Seeking *Alpha*

While explaining our relationship to the Universe from a scientific perspective is generally a bit beyond my ken, I stumbled upon a mystery at the heart of physics that sets an apt backdrop for our quest to understand the universal laws of the Enneagram. I will introduce it here, and we will return to this mystery at the conclusion of the book...so stay tuned if you're curious! The *fine-structure constant* is a number in physics related to the motion of electrons spinning around atoms and the nature of the light emitted in that process. The "fine structure" pattern of the split lines of light (as you might see in sunlight coming through trees in a forest) is where the constant got its name. The fine-structure constant is a mystery because although it can be measured, no one knows where it comes from. Nobel Prize-winning physicist Richard Feynman (1918-1988) spoke of it as "one of the greatest damn mysteries of physics: a magic number that comes to us with no understanding by man."[8]

Known by the Greek symbol *a* or *alpha*, the fine-structure constant has some remarkable properties. For one, it is a "pure" or dimensionless constant, meaning the number will come out the same no matter the unit of measurement. This consistency is what makes it a "constant" or "universal" in nature. And *alpha* is made up of three more constants. One from each of the main domains of physics: the speed of light, from relativity; the electric charge of one electron, from electromagnetism, and Planck's constant from quantum mechanics, a number that determines the smallest possible measurement in the world.[9] *Alpha* is so precise that if it were to vary slightly, the structure of matter as we know it would not exist. This is one reason that some physicists (from the 1900s through today) believe the fine-structure constant might lie at the heart of a grand unified theory explaining the patterns of the whole Universe. Laurence Eaves, a physicist and professor at the University of Nottingham, said he thinks this number is so important that it would be the one you'd use to signal to other life forms that we have mastery of our planet.

What does all this have to do with the Enneagram? The number value for the fine-structure constant is oddly reminiscent of the dynamic laws of the Universe represented in the Enneagram Symbol itself: the Laws of One, Three, and Seven. That number, alpha, is:

$$1/137$$

S-CURVES AND THE ENNEAGRAM

Many years ago, and long before I knew about the laws of the Enneagram Symbol, I happened into another symbolic representation of a universal pattern from general systems theory: a graph made of S-shaped curves—in math, called a sigmoid function.[10] At the very same juncture, and right after a transformative experience I had as a graduate student, I also met the Enneagram of Personality for the first time. Given my inherent interest in what makes people tick, I was immediately intrigued by the Enneagram system, but I knew nothing about its deeper meaning. Instead, I became obsessed with the pattern of these S-curves and the process of transformation they revealed. While the coincidence of encountering these two symbolic depictions of growth may have been random, today I imagine they came together for a reason, calling me to the adventure of a lifetime.

In 1990 I entered a doctoral program in counseling psychology at Stanford's Graduate School of Education with a passion for understanding the psychological aspects of health, healing, and human potential. I wanted to know: Can stress really make you sick? Can your mind and emotions help you heal? What do we make of spiritual approaches and miraculous stories of healing? And what enables some people to excel beyond the apparent limits of human potential? With questions like these, I headed straight to the medical school, where psychiatrist and researcher David Spiegel was replicating a ground-breaking study he had done on the life-extending impact of psychosocial support groups for cancer patients whose illness had metastasized.

As part of this research group, I had the opportunity to observe (from behind a one-way mirror) support groups of breast cancer patients grappling with terminal diagnoses. Listening to them share their struggles, I learned many things about health, well-being, and life itself. I was awestruck by the ability of many of these women to grow through crisis. I was so affected by witnessing the apparent power of intangible factors on their health (emotional, spiritual, relational) versus more concrete physiological factors, that I experienced a small crisis of my own. It seemed to me these women were offering me a secret, and perhaps a warning. I was not exactly sure what I was seeing, but it caused me to question many of the assumptions upon which I had built my life. I had a crisis in faith, in myself, and in what I understood to be the entire western paradigm upon which a "good" life was built. I longed to understand more about the role of emotion and spirit, relationship, and meaning—things beyond the intellect and drive, grit and growth, that I had absorbed from my family and education. And I did not think I could learn about all this in an academic graduate program.

For months I flailed about, barely able to study due to agonizing over whether I should stay in school or join a monastery or something. My angst wore me down, disrupted my sleep, and made it hard to sort out what was happening. I had not made the decision to get a Ph.D. in counseling psychology lightly. I'd had a clear purpose and sense of mission that caused me to leave a good job to study behavioral medicine. And now I could not see how to continue. I felt torn in two by my competing desires to get the degree I had come for and to fulfill this inner drive for deeper and experiential knowledge of healing, the human spirit, consciousness, and myself. I did not think I had the strength to pursue both, with their contrasting paradigms, simultaneously. I was utterly paralyzed.

And then, just like that, the problem was resolved. My parents had taken my brother and me on a ski vacation for the holidays. One sleepless night, in an inn at the base of a large mountain, frustrated and fed up with my own suffering, I wandered outside into the deep snow with my walkman playing music. The moon was full in a clear sky, and the mountain, so rugged and majestic, was glowing. Somehow, under the gaze of that mountain and the moon, my pain and confusion were lifted. I moved from agony to understanding and then laughter in the space of a few hours, and I ended up dancing in the snow in the moonlight.

The revelation I had seems simple now. Then, it made all the difference. None of what I was agonizing about mattered. I got a very clear message: *How you are* is more important than *what you do*—a principle I would later work for years to understand and teach to leaders in organizations. And, for me, that *how* needed to start with being my own best friend, or something cheesy like that. The words were not as important as was the experience of feeling utterly lifted, loved, and transformed by something beyond myself. I was able to see my dilemma (should I stay, or should I go?) from a "higher" perspective that allowed me to work on my *being* while I was *doing* the work of graduate school...and to befriend myself through the process. Most important, months of agony resolved into a renewed sense of purpose and direction that would help me hold the tension of trying to knit together, both in myself and in my work, the diverse worldviews I was pursuing. Little did I know, this was my first experience of the Law of Three.

Not long after my revelation, although I had been quite sure I did *not* want to work in business when I left it to attend graduate school, I felt compelled to shift my research focus from medical applications of psychology to psychological aspects of leadership and organizational systems. I was learning to listen to that still, small voice inside me. I had begun to imagine that what I was learning about health and human potential, if applied in leadership and organizations, could make a difference not only in performance, but also in the health and well-being of people at work, in their families and communities. I was going to change the world one heart at a time! As it turns out, I was in the right place at the right time to meet the Enneagram and, eventually, change my own.

My newfound mentor in the business school, Michael Ray, had invited David Daniels to co-teach a full-quarter course on the Enneagram in the narrative tradition. David Daniels was a psychiatrist and adjunct professor who also started the Narrative Enneagram school in the California Bay Area with Helen Palmer in 1988. Every week in the class, we listened as David interviewed a panel of business leaders of a particular Enneagram type to reveal how type showed up in their work, leadership, and life experience. We had ample time for self-reflection and group dialogue. I loved the Enneagram but, despite many assignments and consultation with my teachers, I could not figure out my type (seeing myself in so many of them), and I had no idea about the universal growth map represented in the Symbol or the significant role it would play in my life.

My fascination with universal patterns was instead fulfilled by learning about "systems theory" and S-curves in another of Michael's classes on "new paradigm" business. The graphic representation of the S-curves explained to me the growth through crisis I had observed in the cancer patients and, on a lesser scale, in my own breakdown and breakthrough. I had always thought about growth as something that occurs in a straight line (like me, growing up, getting through university and into graduate school). The S-curves show how growth in nonlinear systems unfolds differently over time—in a discontinuous sequence of straight lines, breakdowns, and horizontal leaps (like me, falling apart, de-constructing my sense of self, and having a transcendent experience that changed the course of my life).

WE OFTEN THINK ABOUT GROWTH PROCEEDING IN A CONTINUOUS LINE

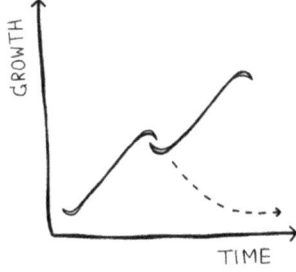

IN FACT, GROWTH OFTEN UNFOLDS WITH STOPS AND STARTS, AND SOMETIMES ABRUPT OR DISONTINUOUS LEAPS

A "system" is simply a collection of interdependent parts, and *systems theory* is an approach to analysis that focuses more on the complex relationship among parts than on the nature of individual parts. Nonlinear systems are those in which the collective behavior of the whole is greater than the sum of the parts. In other words, if you just study the pieces, this will not explain how the whole system functions. Something else, *something more,* arises from the relationship among parts.

A simple example is an ant colony building a complex anthill. There is no particular director, and no individual ant has the cognitive capacity to design and build such a structure, but somehow this surprisingly high-level collective talent "emerges" from what looked like individual ants running around chaotically. This system-wide capacity for intelligent self-organization is called an *emergent property* of the system. *Emergence*—when higher-level order seems to spontaneously appear out of chaos— is the closest thing to "magic" in the natural world.

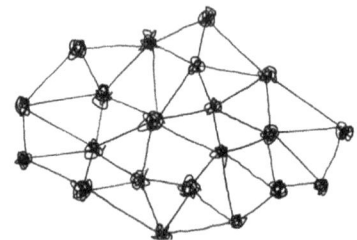

A NON-LINEAR SYSTEM
IS A COLLECTION OF INTERDEPENDENT PARTS
IN WHICH THE WHOLE IS GREATER THAN THE SUM

Systems are everywhere. In essence, *you* are a system, made of many moving parts and smaller systems that work together miraculously to let you think, breathe, move, and be you. Your family is a system and so is your place of work, although not all systems work together in a "coherent" fashion to evolve higher-level intelligence. Systems theory and S-curves have been used to map the growth of everything from organizations to fruit-fly colonies. At every major research university, institutes are springing up that bring together diverse fields to make sense of the dance of life within us, and in our Universe as a whole, through the study of nonlinear systems dynamics and the magic of self-organization.[11]

All nonlinear systems grow through a predictable process that includes what looks like chaos or disintegration. The type of growth shown in the rise of the first S-curve is incremental. It happens in a relatively orderly system where the parts work together and improve in gradual, and fairly predictable, small increments.

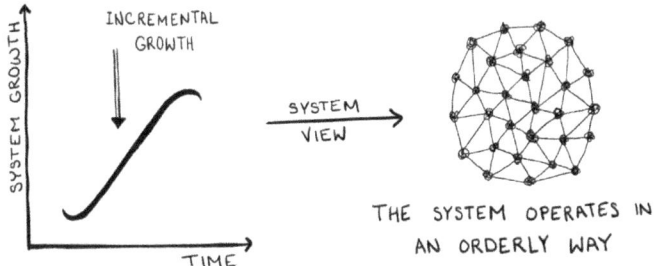

In all systems, over time, the growth rate slows and levels off (shown as the top of the S). Every system reaches a "limit to growth" in its current form—growth slows, and the system starts to break down. This is also called an *inflection point,* a point at which the growth curve reverses, and the system moves from orderly functioning toward decay and chaos, in which the system is fractured and the parts no longer "get along."

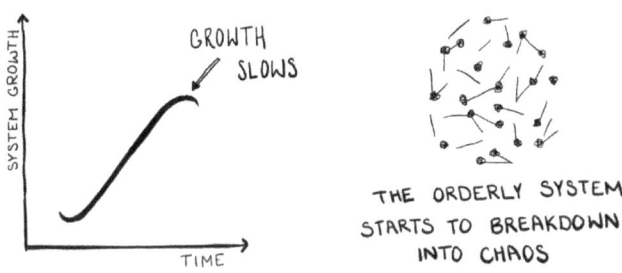

Isolated systems wind down over time, moving toward entropy. This is the second law of thermodynamics. The law of the natural world is such that the energy of what has been dissolved is eventually used in the shaping of new life, but at another level it just looks like chaos and death. From this view, the system is either growing OR dying.

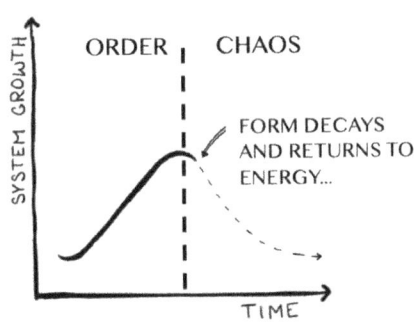

The S-curves show us a different view. Particularly in "open-loop systems"—ones that are open to feedback from their environment—chaos does not equal death. The inflection point and breakdown in the system opens things up a bit, creating an opportunity to integrate new information, parts, or skills from outside the system's boundaries.

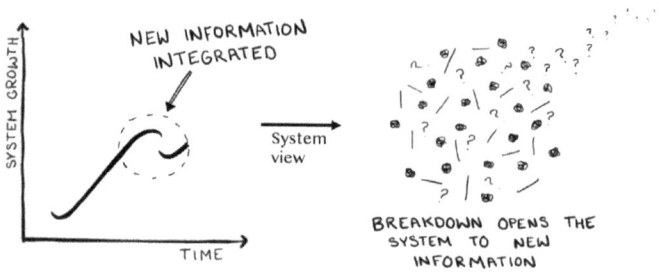

This influx of new and diverse intelligence compels the system to re-configure itself into something a bit different. As new organization *emerges*, the system reappears as a "higher-order" system, one that has enfolded the old aspects with the new to evolve into a higher-functioning system. As represented on the S-curve graph, the system seems to "jump" to a new, higher-level S-curve. Chaos subsides. There is a return to order, but it is a more adaptive and effective level of functioning at which the system can again grow in an incremental way.

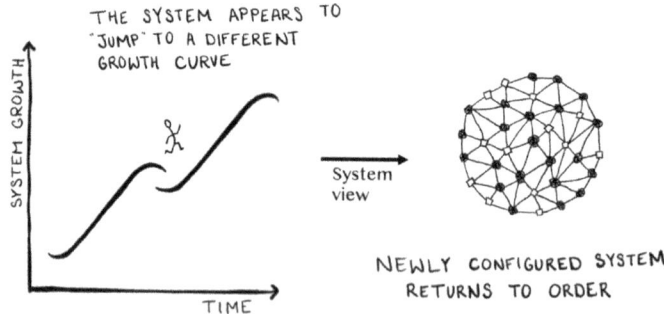

This pattern can be seen in systems as diverse as people, products, organizations, and other sorts of systems open to feedback. For example, incorporating new knowledge and skills for responsible self-sufficiency (among other things) allows a child to move through the chaos of adolescence and "re-organize" into an adult. An adolescent becomes an adult not just by aging but also by integrating new perspective and taking responsibility for life in a different way. The child doesn't disappear entirely; it manages to mix with an adult-ish part and transcend old ways of seeing and being in the world. The new perspective attained by a young adult is like "seeing" from a higher level how to integrate the old me with new understanding to evolve a more mature version of self.

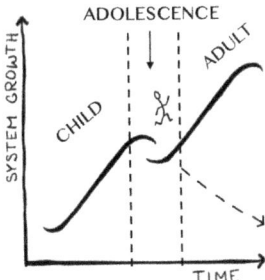

Similarly, when an individual contributor at work is promoted to become a manager, if she doesn't change how she understands her role and how to get work done through others, she will fail to make the leap... and likely fail to keep her job. Alternately, if she is able to redefine herself and what "good" looks like in this new role, she can integrate new ways of operating and *emerge* as a successful manager.

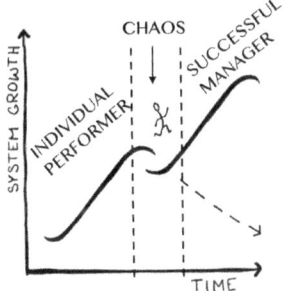

When the cell phone had become maximally slimmed down and efficient, the functionality of a computer was integrated into it, and the smart phone emerged ("jumped a curve") as a more complex device. And the most enduring organizations, while preserving their core values, know they must innovate to perform well across time. All growth of this kind requires embracing some degree of chaos. In fact, it is the inability or unwillingness to loosen up on the old pattern that actually guarantees dissolution. But unfortunately, resisting chaos is common. We cling to order! When things aren't working as well as they used to, we often hunker down and try to remain the same. Letting go of old patterns and perspectives means slipping from order into chaos—and the space between those two S-curves is often mysterious and confusing.

EMBRACING ORDER *AND* CHAOS

In nature, as in our own lives, two seemingly "opposing" forces—one that creates order and one that moves towards chaos—power change. An ordering force structures diverse parts so a system can function and grow in an incremental way. The drive towards chaos breaks down order to allow for the integration of new information. Systems are always both evolving and devolving, and what looks like devolving does not have to lead to death. When embraced as an essential process of coming apart so that new information, new perspective, new skills, and new energy can be integrated, chaos is engaged *in service of* evolution and growth.

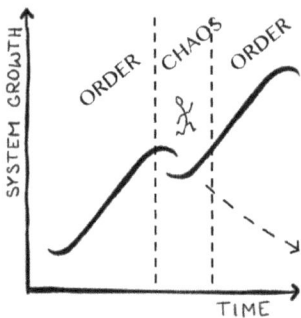

In fact, at the center of life itself, there is this continuous interplay of contraction (ordering into form) and expansion (chaos, flowing as energy). In addition to the Universe itself contracting and expanding, this pattern is present in the movement of your own breath, pulse, and heartbeat, as well as in the way a flock of birds in flight spreads out and re-assembles. Cycles of order and chaos (called synchrony) have been mapped by biologists, computer scientists, physicists, and mathematicians throughout nature, in people, and in matter ranging from electrons to planets. There are universal laws governing the transition from ordered to chaotic behavior in everything from electronic circuits to swirling fluids, chemical reactions, semiconductors, and many kinds of human systems.[12]

Start looking around you, and you will see this growth pattern everywhere. It suggests that we really can't evolve without first sacrificing something—some way of seeing or being—that we have held to tightly. This unraveling can be not only *not* terrible, but actually the source of adaptation, creativity, beauty, and new life. Understanding the growth process represented in the S-curves helped me in my work as a coach and consultant to guide the development of people, groups, and organizational systems for many years. Even as I worked with this pattern, however, I knew there was more to learn about that space between curves.

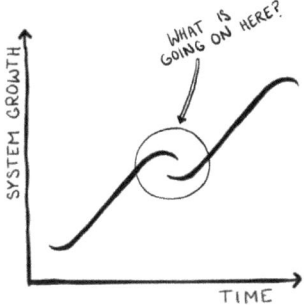

Understanding the dynamic process depicted in the Enneagram Symbol filled that gap for me. I was blown away when, after twenty-five years of studying and teaching the Enneagram of Personality, I finally learned something about the laws depicted in the Symbol and put that together with the S-curve graph. Both are symbolic representations of universal laws of growth. But the Enneagram Symbol lays out a far more detailed roadmap, especially for navigating that space between curves, to accomplish evolutionary growth.

By now you may be wondering about why we are deep in this rabbit hole. As we enter into the Symbol itself to explore its mysteries, these S-curves—or more specifically, the relationship between order and chaos, and the concept of *emergence*—will provide really important context for understanding the Laws of One, Three, and Seven that make up the Enneagram. With this information, along with additional detail from the sciences and enduring patterns from our world's narrative and spiritual traditions, we will first try to make sense of the individual laws of the Enneagram, and later we will track how they work together to renew life in stagnant and fragmented systems.

Universal Patterns in Science, Stories, and Spiritual Wisdom

Why would we turn to science, story, and spirituality to unlock the mysteries of the Enneagram Symbol? Well...it's a symbol. Like a story or piece of art, it can take some reflection and viewing from different angles, meditating on its underlying meaning, and integrating within your own life experience to arrive at understanding. The Law of Three, represented by the inner triangle of the Enneagram, shows us that everything in Creation is part of a triangle, whether we see it or not. The concept of triangulation in social science is borrowed from a method of navigation in sailing that locates a single point in space with the convergence of measurements taken from two other points. This approach is designed to overcome the potential bias inherent in using a single measurement so that we may more securely navigate to the desired destination.

And rather than a betrayal of something unique to the Enneagram, approaching a symbol from different points of view is something Gurdjieff advocated: "In expressing the laws of the unity of endless diversity a symbol itself possesses an endless number of aspects from which it can be examined and it demands from a man approaching it the ability to see it simultaneously from different points of view."[13] In truth, this may be the only appropriate way to approach such ancient and universal knowledge as is depicted in the Enneagram Symbol. And, even then, we may never fully grasp the mystery to which it points.

Science is the more obvious lens. Science provides an important perspective because it has a lot to say about universal laws and how things work in the observable world. A scientific approach has historically done a good job of helping us describe the universe of things, basically "matter" or the visible world. However, it doesn't do as well in helping us figure out the unseen aspects of human experience, or "what matters." In ages past, people turned to religious and spiritual traditions to answer big questions pertaining to what matters, like: *Who am I? Why am I here? How should I be when I don't know how to be? And how do I best deal with the inevitable challenge and changes in life?*

With regard to such questions, there is much to learn from our enduring wisdom traditions, particularly when we can find the threads they share. Exploring shared truths from widely different spiritual perspectives can tell us a lot about what is "universal" in the human family, especially as it pertains to unity with each other through our shared Source and ground of Being. And yet, I am aware that the differences among religious approaches to studying and answering these questions has sometimes led to more confusion, separation, and suffering. Being human, we can get very attached to our tradition's "way" to be, who belongs, and how to explain the nature of reality. So I have added a third way, balancing science and spirituality, to explore the laws of the Symbol and how they might be relevant to our human lives and longings: stories.

The fact that most of our enduring stories provide a "moral" points to their essential function as a compass for what matters and higher standards of being. Stories, and enduring stories or myths, in particular, are the perfect point of triangulation because they can give us the most detailed view of how things are, or perhaps could be, in the universe of human experience. At the same time, the word "myth" is almost synonymous with something that is *not* real. That is correct at one level. Cerberus, the three-headed dog that guarded the entrance to Hades in Greek mythology (and the entrance to the Chamber of Secrets for Harry Potter) won't be found in your local animal shelter. There is something very real, however, about the fears that "guard" or prevent us from doing what we are most afraid of in the name of growth, whether risking rejection to ask someone on a date, or honestly confronting our own anger or victimhood. As mythologist and storyteller Michael Meade says it, "Myth has a way of revealing truth that logic can't find."

Since the wisdom embedded in our narrative tradition is symbolic, it can be interpreted differently, for sure. But when a story continues to be told and to hold meaning for us, across cultures and generations, it must be "true" in some sense—even more true, one might argue—than some passing thing we observe in the world today. When stories are handed down, they are distilled, and the elements of story that continue to resonate with our lives remain. This is why we go again and again to the theatre, books, or to Netflix to experience our favorite heroes battling demons and prevailing. Mythic stories, fairytales and super-heroes, spiritual stories, dramatic and artistic stories, are all symbolic representations of life lessons handed down across time that can provide moral and human guidance. In some sense, they put us in touch with another world—a symbolic world of meaning just behind the literal one.

Beyond mere guidance, then, experiencing mythic patterns within ourselves *involves* us in the larger story of life. The underlying pattern of birth, death, and renewal that sustains Nature and the Cosmos itself is the inner secret process of human nature as well. Meade says that each time we engage with a story it can initiate us into a more conscious experience of ourselves, as well as the "living soul of the world" that is the underlying flow of intelligence in Creation, by connecting us within this shared symbolic realm. In this way, he says, myths go beyond time and our everyday subject/object dualism to awaken something essential in us—something unseen that helps us to know in ways that are creative, inspired, and imaginative. As a mythic story is told, we enter it as it enters us, opening deeper layers of consciousness.[14] As Gurdjieff described it, stories speak directly to the higher heart center.

In the presence of universal patterns, we can find the stories we came here to live. We are all living a story. In some sense, the unconscious and habitual patterns that make up our personality are stories. And they are true to human experience, clearly, when people from all over the world find themselves in the stories of Enneagram types. The question is whether you are living a story you have chosen? And if not, what would be a better story; one that might support you from surviving to thriving within life's travails? I hope you will answer this question and find something true about your own story in the context of the living story of the Universe as we make our way through the Symbol, starting with the Law of One. While we will consider the laws individually in this section, they are actually more like layers of a whole system, each of which reveals an aspect of a dynamic process governing the creation and continuous renewal of life in the Universe.

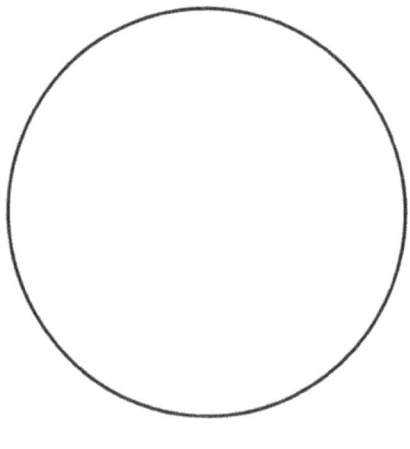

THE LAW OF ONE

CHAPTER FOUR

THE LAW OF ONE

You are not a drop in the ocean.
You are the entire ocean in a drop.

~ RUMI

There is no matter as such! ... Mind is the matrix of all matter

~ MAX PLANCK

W HEN WE MEET THE ENNEAGRAM SYMBOL, it is flat, two-dimensional on paper. What we don't see in this drawing is that the Symbol is actually three-dimensional—or it has the potential to be if we do the work, which is the point of this book. In full form, the Enneagram circle is a sphere. It represents the Law of One. Like all the laws of the Symbol, this law operates at many levels, through the nested systems that make up the Universe as a whole.

The Law of One speaks to the underlying unity of everything in the Universe. Everything in Creation evolved from *and is connected through* the same one Source that continues to reveal itself in the laws that govern the creation, evolution, and renewal of life at all levels. Because the Law of One, by definition, encompasses everything in Creation, the circle or sphere contains the other shapes, points, and lines of the Enneagram Symbol that exist in dynamic unity or "coherence." Within whatever "universe" or system you are examining—a brain, a self, a forest, country, or solar system—all the discrete parts are interacting at an unseen level.

It's easy to understand how diverse aspects of your body come together to make a whole being (you), but harder to see how your being is intimately interconnected with lives across the globe in a shared living system that is our planet. Each "whole" is also an expression of the Law of One at a different level of analysis. At the highest level, the Law of One refers to a unified field or shared ground of Being, both immanent and transcendent, that pervades the Cosmos. It is everything, everywhere; within, around, and between; transcending what we see and know; comprehensive but beyond comprehension.

The Law of One says that not only are we all connected, but we also share a common origin and fate. Aristotle, Plato, and other ancient Greeks explained this with the doctrine of "first cause," describing an initial cause of the Universe and continuing Source of all other causal phenomena. This was their version of the Law of One. Whether you understand that causal Source as God, the unified field of quantum energy, consciousness, or another name for the un-nameable, it is both the original source *and* a continuous creative impulse. As far back as we can know, people from diverse cultures have been drawn to connect with and know themselves as one with this original Source, as they understood it. The drive to transcend our sense of separateness and experience ourselves as part of something larger is reflected as much by passionate sports-team fandom and the use of plant medicine for healing through altered states of consciousness, as it is by participation in religious rituals and practices.

This drive is not so different from the movement we saw in natural systems (in the S-curve diagrams) to dissolve into a chaotic flow state and then to return to order after each period of dis-order. All of life seeks to realize itself, again and continuously, in a state of internal coherence, *and* as a part of even larger systems and the flow of life in which it is embedded. In fact, it is this dynamic tension—the relationship between the force that creates order and the force that leads to chaos—that helps renew life.

So in addition to a state of *being* wholly integrated and at one with *All that Is*, the Law of One refers to the continuous, creative process of *becoming* more whole—more whole within and beyond ourselves, and more in touch with transcendent Reality as it reveals itself through us, in moments and in cycles. The very nature of the different pieces of a system and their dynamic relatedness is what enables this *being and becoming*. Gurdjieff said that "a static Enneagram is a dead Enneagram," since it is meant to reveal a universal process, occurring within and around us, that is inherently creative and forwards evolution. We humans also have this potential for both being and becoming more whole, continuously. As we come into greater coherence with the whole circle of who we are, we may also resonate within larger circles of coherence and unseen dimensions of Being, as the expanding sphere implies.

THE LAW OF ONE IN STORIES

Many of our oldest known stories, creation myths, illustrate the Law of One. Whether mythic or religious, these narratives describe a created world emerging from a great primordial soup or matrix of energy. Just as we shape pots out of clay, Creation is formed out of this vast and dynamic field of energy that holds the potential for everything. The renowned scholar of comparative mythology and religion Joseph Campbell explains: "Briefly formulated, the universal doctrine teaches that all the visible structures of the world—all things and beings—are the effects of a ubiquitous power out of which they rise, which supports and fills them during the period of their manifestation, and back to which they must ultimately dissolve. This is the power known to science as energy, to the Melanesians as *mana*, to the Sioux Indians as *wakonda*, the Hindus as *shakti*, and the Christians as the power of God."[15]

From this undifferentiated force and flow of energy that contains all possibility, life emerges in diverse—even polarized—forms. And there is a pattern to this emergence, one (as we will see) that allows for continuous creating. In Greek mythology, three levels of the Universe (a realm of the gods, a realm of humans, and an underworld) were born from chaos. The word *chaos* comes from an ancient Greek word meaning "void" or "chasm," and referring to a formless, dark energy from which the Universe was created. Similarly, in Chinese mythology the Universe began as a formless cloud in an egg, holding the dual forces of yin and yang. The god Pan Gu awoke inside this egg and smashed it open, sending the lighter parts upward to form heaven and the darker parts downward to create the earth, while he stood between them to hold things in place.

There are many Egyptian creation stories, but among their common elements is the arising of the created world out of the waters of chaos too. And the first thing to be born from the water is a pyramid-shaped mound. The sun-god Ra emerges from the mound as the newly arisen sun (or son), with power to create through life-giving energy. Another formulation of this story includes a cosmic egg from which arises the sun-god, as primal creative power, emerging from the pyramidal mound set in the middle of the original chaos.[16]

According to the Judeo-Christian tradition, in the beginning, when God created the heavens and earth, the earth was a formless void and "darkness covered the face of the deep." Then God said: "Let there be light," and from there went on to create the world, in seven days.[17] The world unfolded in a cascade of opposites, as God separated light from dark, the waters above the firmament from those below, and sea from land. From those opposites came the capacity to create life, a pattern echoed in the (hu)man, "created as male *and* female." This male/female goes on to become a primary player in the second creation story involving the Garden of Eden and the subsequent fall from paradise that invites us to restore grace.

We also find in John 1:1: "In the beginning was the Word." Franciscan priest, author, and Enneagram teacher Father Richard Rohr weaves science into the Biblical story by teaching that the "big bang" was God's grace made manifest through something like a *blueprint*, an intelligent organizing force.[18] The Word (*Logos* in the original Greek) is akin to the first and ongoing cause, the light of God, and the creative principle that organizes the formless dark void of chaos into Creation. It is also a pattern (something like laws of the Universe) through which life continues to unfold, since God imbued all of the created world with Godself.

Kabbalah is said to be Jewish mystical tradition, although some Kabbalists describe it simply as a map and practice for fully receiving divine light and spreading it in the world (Kabbalah means "reception"). It teaches a detailed ascent of consciousness toward a "corrected state" of the soul; one that shifts us from a focus on self-gratification to the benefit of others.[19] In the Kabbalistic creation story, the infinite unknowable God created the Universe by first contracting His light to make a void or space (called *tsimtsum*) into which He could project just enough light to create the Universe. And yet, His light was so powerful that this vessel shattered into many pieces called "sephirot"—nine emanations of the Creator, all received or reflected in a tenth, as the manifest world we can see.

The sephirot are simultaneously manifestations of God, forces of Nature, *and* aspects of the human psyche or soul. They can be experienced at all these levels because they are something like features of a universal organizing *process* through which life unfolds at different levels.

The sephirot are laid out on the Tree of Life, a kind of ladder between the unknowable God and the manifest world, the Infinite and the finite. The sephirot are divided into three layers of three elements each, with the first three "higher" sephirot distinguished from the six lower (emotional) sephirot. The teaching suggests that humans have the potential to help put all these pieces back together; it is a process that restores this ladder and union with the Divine, repairing the world as it corrects the soul.

Our modern scientific story about the origin and structure of the Universe echoes many of these same themes, starting with a dynamic and expanding Universe born of one source at the moment of the big bang. The big bang has been described as the zero hour—the time at which the Universe emerged from the zero point, the void from which it exploded into existence. This empty space out of which all visible matter emerged is called the *zero-point field* because even at zero degrees temperature, the point at which all matter should theoretically stop moving, tiny fluctuations of energy are still detectable. This empty space (which is unseen or "dark matter") is quite alive; in fact, without its existence the visible Universe would collapse in on itself.[20] Remarkably, in science too, this dark matter or *chaos* is essential to the process of creation and the created world.

We don't completely understand what happened at the moment of the big bang because our physics breaks down at that point. The closest explanation, superstring theory, postulates that before the big bang, the cosmos was made of ten space-time dimensions: nine perfectly symmetrical spatial dimensions and one non-spatial dimension, time. The dimensions were packed into a tiny, tight ball at very high heat. Highly unstable at that temperature, this ball cracked first into two pieces, sending a shock throughout the cosmos.[21] In this first split, two separate space-times were created simultaneously: the manifest three-dimensional world we live in expanded, while a six-dimensional universe contracted further into hidden dimensions (dark matter/energy) that also govern the greater cosmos by preventing its collapse. Everything we see (and don't see) is a splinter of that original ten-dimensional Universe, which is still either expanding or contracting.

In this story, we hear echoes of not only the structure of the Tree of Life, but also the Enneagram Symbol: nine points situated in a circle, with three dimensions as revealed structure (signifying mind, heart, body) and six dimensions "hidden" but still helping to govern the cosmos. And both models start with the Law of One: that we are literally all made of the same stuff, seen and unseen, expanding and contracting simultaneously in a process of continuously *being and becoming* whole.

The fact that both seen and unseen aspects of reality exist simultaneously is as true on the tiniest scale of atomic particles as it is on the vast scale of dark and light matter. The principle of complementarity from quantum physics says that the sub-atomic particles that make up matter as we know it are seen as discrete particles (really, small packets of energy) and, *at the same time*, are part of an unseen continuous wave of energy. According to the quantum uncertainty principle, we can only observe one of these states at a time. In other words, the wave state and the particle state "oppose" each other. When a person, an intelligent observer, adds an organizing force to the situation (by just looking at the wave), this "collapses" the wave function, bringing the particle into being.

AN IMPLICIT LAW OF TWO

The process of creation in all of these stories, in which something visible is shaped out of a vast ocean of chaos, is then echoed in the created world itself by a first split into two "opposites" of particle and wave, seen and unseen, form and emptiness, matter contracting and expanding. This points to an implicit *law of two* in the Enneagram to which Gurdjieff referred but did not single out as part of the Symbol. Gurdjieff said: 'In studying the phenomenal world, we first of all see two opposing principles manifested in everything."[22] He taught that our entire lives are experienced according to this "law of duality," which he said is an objective law to which we are all enslaved.

The One, the totality of existence, manifests as particle and wave simultaneously, which are "opposites"—the matter we see (let's call *order*) and the unseen flow of energy and information still underlying and permeating it (known as *chaos*). The One becomes two to create in the world, as it takes two separate "opposing" energies to give birth...as we well know. These first two parents in the created world can be seen in the Enneagram Symbol as the circle and the triangle. We might label them as: chaos and order, yin and yang, spirit and matter, wave and particle, but all describe the dual nature of life which continually and cyclically contracts into form and expands into a wave of energy and potential.

The triangle is an echo of the original creative force that *makes* order from chaos, but—once fixed in matter—it represents the seen, known, and "ordered" or created world.[23] The circle represents the void from which order emerged, as well as all the aspects of life that we *still* can't perceive and know with our senses but are nevertheless present in energy and potential. The void is referred to as *chaos* because it is unformed, undifferentiated intelligence and "unknown" terrain. This basic proposition is hard to argue with: the One, totality of existence, consists of all that we know *and* all that is still unknown.

As humans, we are a collection of known behavior and experience that we carry out with mind, heart, and body, represented by the points on the triangle. But we are also made of vast potential, as yet unknown. By virtue of "choosing" to be in personality (which, of course, isn't entirely conscious), we simultaneously make a choice of *how-not-to-be*, which is part of that chaos outside the known order of our ego structure and Enneagram type. Keeping the "not me" outside our awareness shapes us just as much as our choices of how to be. While this is a good recipe for self-management, the larger circle is made up of both unseen impulses from the subconscious mind that derail us *and* all that we *could be* if we stretched beyond our conditioned patterns.

Viewing this from a spiritual perspective, an unknown spiritual reality is always present, hidden within the revealed world of matter as well as around, between, and enveloping it. At the heart of many traditions is this drive to know ourselves again as the unbounded *flow* of God, unitive consciousness, or the ground of Being. Spiritual growth is in one sense an expansion into this unknown terrain—a process of being and becoming more of the whole circle, more integrated within ourselves, and more connected with the larger "wholes" within which we exist. If Creation is a cascade from One to two opposing forces (order and flow, form and emptiness, known and unknown), and from there on into the diversity of the created world, then the path to knowing ourselves again as One must also engage these dual forces in the process of becoming more whole again.

This process of expansion has been memorialized in one of the story patterns that has stood the test of time: the hero's journey. Joseph Campbell popularized the hero's journey narrative as "the monomyth," or the ultimate mythological archetype, because of its appearance across cultures and generations. *Archetypes* are patterns in the human psyche and behavior that are like universal laws themselves, in that they represent enduring and pervasive patterns or "organizing structures" that can be found in people across time and within diverse cultures. The essential plotline of this pattern describes a hero leaving home (the *known* world of order) for an *unknown* and strange world where she encounters significant challenges that test and nearly destroy her. Profoundly and positively changed by encountering the chaos of the unknown, the hero then returns home to help create new order in the community.

Does this sound familiar? Of course, you have heard it in spiritual stories and myths, fairy tales and popular modern stories. But also, the hero's journey pattern follows the universal growth process we saw in the S-curves.

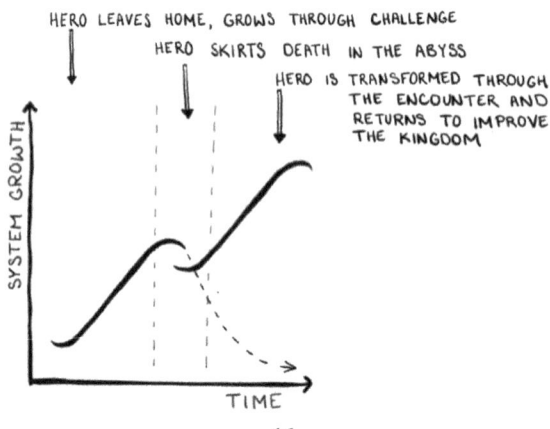

46

Influenced in part by psychoanalyst Carl Jung's depth psychology, Joseph Campbell taught the hero's journey as a metaphor for an archetypal process of inner development characterized by unearthing and integrating unknown, or "shadow," aspects of our psyche in pursuit of a higher, healthier, or whole self. Becoming more whole, making the unconscious conscious ("making the two, one") or integrating all opposing internal forces, constituted for both Jung and Campbell a "great work" that marked not only a path to psychological health and spiritual maturity for the individual, but also a way to transform culture and society for the good of the whole.

INNER WORK AND THE LAW OF ONE

The great work of becoming whole is akin to stretching beyond that fixed triangle into more of the circle, meeting and integrating more of who we are beyond ego. Modern neuroscience, with all its brain imaging tools, has illustrated what psychologists have been observing about the unconscious mind for years: that you are a rich mix of drives, mental constructs, and impulses, only some of which are conscious and purposeful. We may want very much to be in a harmonious relationship, for example, but our unconscious drive *to be right*, let's say, constantly disrupts the peace at home. It is necessary to bring these hidden driving mechanisms to consciousness so that we can be more in charge of how and when they are expressed. As Jung said, "Until you make the unconscious conscious, it will rule your life and you will call it Fate."

This process of integration, which Jung called *individuation*, is very like the nature of the psycho-spiritual development work we do with the Enneagram. The Law of One—both recognizing our inherent wholeness (vast unseen interconnectedness) and continuously becoming *more* whole by bringing more of the unseen to light—is central to many long-standing approaches to health and well-being. The word "health" comes from the same root as the word "whole," as does the word "holy." To heal is to make whole again, or holy. As a consequence of developing our ego ideal or Enneagram type, we cut off or repress so much of who we are. While this seems adaptive initially, the repressed material often comes back to haunt us. By bringing unconscious content to awareness, however, we can "own" and tame it, rather than getting triggered and throwing a fit or acting on impulse to eat the ice cream or have an affair.

Doing this kind of deep work resolves internal conflicts that have been sapping our energy, and it unleashes creative, often transpersonal, aspects of ourselves that have been bound up in the dark. Although Sigmund Freud (Jung's mentor) focused only on taming the subterranean drives arising from our personal unconscious or "shadow," Jung went on to clarify a deeper layer of knowledge and spiritual potential accessed through the unconscious unknown. He called this the "collective unconscious," and later the "objective psyche", to convey the universal or archetypal nature of this transcendent realm of intelligence available to all, beyond ego. Gurdjieff's map of "the work" also includes this idea of tapping into "objective" consciousness as a very high state of inner development from which we can see and feel the Unity of all things and gather true or objective knowledge about the nature of the Universe.

Horizontal vs. Vertical Growth

Taking a moment to distinguish between work to integrate our personal unconscious and work to access this "shared realm" of objective consciousness through the collective unconscious will help us make sense of the Symbol as the mystery unfolds. We might think about these domains as the human or "horizontal" plane of growth (in which our consciousness is still grounded in this material world, even when more integrated) and a spiritual, transpersonal, or "vertical" axis of development that reaches into a vast interconnected and transcendent realm. Both horizontal and vertical dimensions of inner work are mapped in the Enneagram Symbol.

First, let's consider the horizontal. Healing and becoming more "whole" at the human, psychological level involves integrating all the aspects of ourselves that were left in the unconscious unknown because they did not fit with the ego ideal of our Enneagram type. Today we understand the personal unconscious not as the shadowy and threatening place first described by psychoanalysts, but rather as hidden drives and habits from our past that shape our day-to-day behavior even when we aren't aware of them. Our early relationships to parents and our social environment contribute to unconscious patterns that drive our actions and reactions.[24] And the field of epigenetics reveals how some of our personal programming, including culture, beliefs, and even specific ancestral trauma, can be passed to us through genetic material and carried unconsciously as well.

A helpful metaphor to illustrate how this works in the brain is the image of a rider on an elephant from moral psychologist Jonathan Haidt.[25]

There is a big part of our thinking process (neuroscientists call "the low road"), symbolized by the elephant, that works very quickly, automatically, and unconsciously. It is driven largely by instinctual and emotional habits. The "high road" analytical function, symbolized by the rider, works more slowly, thoughtfully, and deliberately. It takes more brain energy for the rider part of the brain to interpret what is going on and choose a rational response than it does the for the elephant brain, so this thinking system is a bit slower.

ELEPHANT
- EFFORTLESS
- AUTOMATIC
- UNCONSCIOUS
- EMOTIONAL
- INSTINCTUAL RESPONSE

RIDER
- EFFORTFUL
- SLOWER
- DELIBERATE
- ANALYTICAL
- CONSCIOUS THINKING

THIS IS YOUR BRAIN ON AN ELEPHANT

As an example, imagine you are walking in the woods, and you see a snake. You react fast, jump out of the way, and perhaps feel a rush of fear. The quick-acting elephant brain has just saved the day! A moment later, the slower analytical rider kicks in, and you look more closely to see it's just a stick masquerading as a snake. To make itself feel more in control, the rider then interprets what happened after the fact, as if it *meant* to do it.

The elephant system actually drives far more of our day-to-day thoughts, feelings, and behavior than we know, while the rider sits there and *thinks*

it is in charge. The vast influence of unconscious programming is shocking to most of us who believe ourselves to be largely rational beings, masters of our choices and experience. In fact, we make all sorts of complex political, social, and moral judgments with the elephant brain. Juries excuse attractive people more often than unattractive people, for example. And when our *disgust* meter is triggered by a bad smell, we are more likely to judge harshly whatever is set before us. The automatic functioning of the elephant brain serves us because we don't have to *think* about jumping out of the way of an oncoming car, much less a snake, and most people are automatically moved to care for small children. But the strength of that same elephant brain also traps us in habitual patterns that don't work for us.

What this means is: we are blind to a good portion of ourselves. We know this because of how hard it is to simply set a goal (lose 10 pounds) and move purposefully toward it. Instead, most of us get hijacked by all manner of competing internal drives (*Oooh that cookie smells good!*). The aim of much psychological work is to unveil and make conscious use of more of the "unknown" aspects of our psyche by "integrating" them into consciousness. This not only lessens internal conflict, it also frees up energy that we can use to purposefully align with higher ideals and create a more meaningful or fulfilling life.

Remarkably, integrating the hidden aspects of our psyche creates neurological and biological change too. Thanks to the brain's "plasticity" (it is "plastic" or changeable), moving into unknown or unfamiliar territory by practicing new responses and reactions "turns on" whole new patterns and possibilities in our brain. When social anxiety inhibits us from making friends, for example, if we take the risk of extending ourselves into new situations, facing our fears, we might discover that saying hello to that attractive guy or gal in the vegetable aisle at the grocery does not cause us to crumble. With practice, we may stop feeling as much fear and will definitely stop being controlled by it. In this way, our mind and attention can literally re-shape our brain, cause new neural connections to grow, switch on new genes, and change our habitual responses. Greater integration across diverse aspects of the brain also leads to better, more flexible mental health, as well as the ability to have insight and empathy for others.[26]

Being and becoming more whole is a concept at the heart of what it means to be psychologically and socially healthy, but also more spiritually integrated in ways that transcend our individual personhood. Traditional approaches to mental and physical health, from Ayurvedic and Chinese medicine to various indigenous healing systems, have at their center an understanding of health as wholeness not only at the personal level, but in the transpersonal sense as well. They include not just harmonization of our own mind, heart, and body but also integration within the larger "wholes" of community, the natural world, and the spiritual realm through the shared flow of energy—chi, prana, consciousness, or Great Spirit—that pervades all of existence. Accessing this dimension of interconnectedness opens a "vertical" axis of development. It extends our forays into the unknown beyond merely our material existence (the "horizontal" plane) into the transcendent and spiritual.

In Chinese medicine, for example, great emphasis is placed on aligning the spine and opening the energy flow as a channel *between heaven and earth*, as well as enabling the free flow of energy or *chi* throughout the body and its basic organ and functional systems. The *wise (hu)man* is said to bring heaven and earth together by restoring this vertical integration both within and beyond oneself. In the Gospel of Thomas, Jesus is quoted as saying: 'When you make the two one, and when you make the inside like the outside and the outside like the inside, and the above like the below, and when you make the male and the female one and the same...then you will enter [the kingdom].'[27] The idea of linking "above and below" or *making two worlds One* is a concept at the center of the Enneagram. We will look further into the vertical dimension of growth later; for now, it's enough to hold onto the idea that, like the mythical hero, by journeying into unknown inner realms to become more "whole" at the personal and human level, we also access the One universal and transcendent reality through which we are all interconnected.

DIVERSITY IN UNITY

The Law of One in the context of the Enneagram of Personality suggests that while we may appear as one Enneagram type, our type or ego structure is simultaneously part of a much bigger internal landscape that is inherently seeking wholeness. Our type describes a relatively fixed pattern of how we use our centers of intelligence: instinct/body reactions, a dominant emotional drive, and mental habits of thinking and paying attention. If we look at the Enneagram Symbol as a map of ourselves, those three centers are represented symbolically by the three points of the triangle: body, heart, head. I say "symbolically" because thanks to the distorted use of these centers, most of us are not actually "home" in these centers when we begin inner work. Nevertheless, these points on the map call our attention to the fixed "structure" of our ego or Enneagram type.

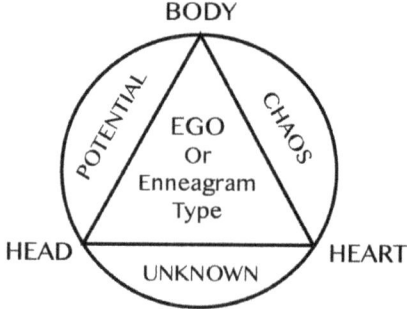

At the same time, we are so much more...represented by the unknown field of potential of the whole circle. Because our centers of intelligence work in a fixed and limiting pattern, they cloud the flow of information available within us but also outside of us—in relationship to others and within the natural and spiritual worlds in which we live. When we expand beyond our Enneagram type reactions and unbind our centers of intelligence, we access more of this unknown flow of energy and information, and claim more of our inherent potential, symbolized by the circle and the Law of One.

Because so much of that potential is outside our awareness, however, it arises first as disconnected fragments from the depths of our unconscious that distract and derail our best intentions. This is clearly represented in the Sufi explanation of the Enneagram. In this version, the space of the circle represents the soul that emanates from the zero point, the origin point of God, at the center. Our soul expresses itself in material reality along the circumference of the circle as nine fragments of the original primordial matter (chaos). Those nine aspects are derived from the three-fold division of mind-heart-body, and all nine (when governed by ego) serve to "attack" the spiritual heart, drawing us away from our center and connection with God.[28]

This characterization of the nine points is very like the Christian notion of "seven deadly sins" associated with the *passions* of type in the history of the Enneagram. As the story goes, the first naming of these "sins" arose from the experience of a group of Desert Fathers and Mothers, monastic men and women devoted to prayer and contemplation who lived in the desert in Egypt in the third century CE. One in their ranks, Evagrius Ponticus, identified seven distracting drives (*deadly sins*) that would pull them from meditation back toward their senses and into the material realm, keeping them from their desired unitive focus on God.[29]

As it turns out, like the meditating monks, all of us are wired for the passions revealed around the Enneagram. All nine passions are driving emotional/motivational states or "drives," embedded in our biological structure. They are more or less activated, more or less problematic for us, depending on our type, but we are all subject to these strong drives at times. Neuroscientist Jaak Panksepp has discovered seven primary emotional/motivational systems wired into mammalian brains: seeking, care, play, lust, fear, sadness, and anger.[30] Imbalance in these primary systems is linked to psychological disorders.

Another neuroscientist and psychiatrist, Tara Swart, cites eight primary emotions (related to our most common neurotransmitters: cortisol, oxytocin, and dopamine) that govern attachment and survival.[31] She lists five related to survival: fear, anger, disgust, shame, sadness; two related to attachment: love/trust, joy/excitement; and adds an eighth, surprise, that sits "between" and can flip the switch between survival-related and attachment-related emotions. While there is variation in the number and interpretation of these distracting drives, it seems that close observation of subjective experience by ancient peoples yielded something like what modern science finds through its more objective methods of scrutiny.

Modern developmental psychology also tells a story about the origin of drives and how essential they were, at one time, for our growth. The early stages of our life, from birth through the first few years, are described as a progression from a state of union, where we are undifferentiated from mom (and the ground of Being), to the dawning of a separate and independent sense of self called an ego structure (personality, or Enneagram type). While there is again variation among development theories, most describe similar themes in the formation of ego.[32] Below, I have mapped onto the Enneagram circle the first few development stages described by psychologist Jane Loevinger as progressive encounters with the dual structure of reality, expressed here as Nature and Culture.[33] These encounters draw out the emotional/motivational drives (passions) and help shape the ego. Perhaps most interesting is that, viewed in this way, these drives seem to illustrate a somewhat orderly and coherent *process* of unfolding in one direction.

Moving counterclockwise around the circle, we fall out of wholeness and union with *All that Is* into a body. Our first encounter in Stage 1, the Impulsive stage, is with Nature—our own impulses, needs, and the drive for their fulfillment through the archetypal mother energy. (Whether or not we have an actual mother and father in these roles, the structure of reality presents itself according to these archetypes of Nature and Culture, or *flow* and *order*.)[34]

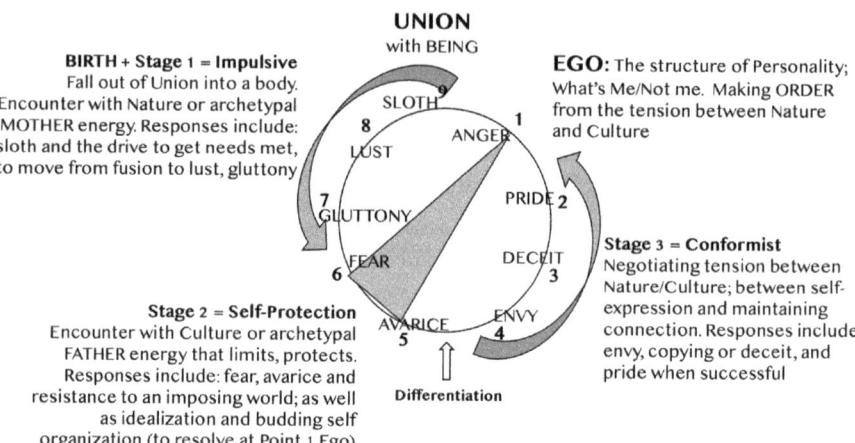

The Making of Ego Structure
(read counter-clockwise)

UNION
with BEING

BIRTH + Stage 1 = Impulsive
Fall out of Union into a body. Encounter with Nature or archetypal MOTHER energy. Responses include: sloth and the drive to get needs met, to move from fusion to lust, gluttony

EGO: The structure of Personality; What's Me/Not me. Making ORDER from the tension between Nature and Culture

Stage 3 = Conformist
Negotiating tension between Nature/Culture; between self-expression and maintaining connection. Responses include: envy, copying or deceit, and pride when successful

Stage 2 = Self-Protection
Encounter with Culture or archetypal FATHER energy that limits, protects. Responses include: fear, avarice and resistance to an imposing world; as well as idealization and budding self organization (to resolve at Point 1 Ego)

Differentiation

At birth we go from the comfort of fusion, in which all our needs are met immediately, to the shocking state of being in a separate body. As an infant, we don't even know yet that we are a separate being. All we know are impulses of hunger and needs for warmth and contact, and the distress of feeling need versus getting direct delivery in the womb. So the drive at Point 9 to return to the completely merged state of comfortable Oneness without effort (Sloth) makes sense. Lust, at point 8, dissatisfaction with things as they are and demand for fulfillment, is the avenue for satisfying impulses. And Gluttony, at point 7, the desire to seek and get more of the good things, and escape the pain of emptiness and limits, is also a universal drive.

The second stage of development, Self-Protection, begins as the child engages with "objects" outside of herself. It marks the dawning of the need for self-control through experiencing the "limits" created by the structure of the world, Culture or the archetypal father energy. We encounter the world outside us, and it sometimes objects to our initiative. Needs don't get met, things we want fall out of our orbit, sometimes we suffer when our expansive impulses bump up against the limits of our world and our caregivers. Fear and the desire for protection, at point 6, and the contraction into self-protection marked by Avarice, at point 5, are natural responses as our expansive orientation is thwarted. At the same time, the challenges we experience fuel our budding attempts at practicing and learning to manage ourselves in the face of this sometimes-hazardous world. Eventually, this practice results in an internalized self-control at point 1, way ahead.

Crossing the gap between points 5 and 4 on the Symbol marks the beginning of knowing ourselves as separate from our caregivers. In developmental theory this shift in consciousness is referred to as *differentiation*. The loss of connection with a shared sense of being presents an opportunity as well as a dilemma in stage 3, the Conformist stage. Ego psychologist Heinz Kohut taught that we need someone we can "idealize" in order to focus the expansive/impulsive energy of the first stage, self-manage our drives, and orient our practice as an emerging separate self within the bounds of our culture.[35] We conform by starting to apply our learning from encounters with the archetypal father energy—the ideals and limits offered by our caregivers and the world—by observing, learning, and modeling ourselves in response.

The dilemma at this stage is felt in the tension between wanting to gain connection, approval, or admiration from Culture, and wanting to express our Nature—our naturally expansive drives—in the process of becoming a unique, independent self. As a consequence of navigating this tension, three more emotional/motivational drives or passions unfold. Envy and longing for special skills and status observed in idealized others but missing in ourselves, at point 4, is followed at point 3 by Deceit—the drive to copy or model them, experience ourselves as competent, and prove our worth. Pride in successful attempts to please, perform, and draw the desired validation is a natural response for a child at point 2, passing through this stage.

The arrival at point 1 and Enneagram type ego formation on the map is a consummation of this development journey in early childhood, in which we sort out how to navigate between our own nature (inner gifts, drives, and impulses) and the culture external to us. Our sense of a separate self and our strategy for how to operate between these "opposing" poles is an internalized self-organizing pattern, our ego structure. In asserting our separate being, the passion of Anger (at point 1) is the driving need to distinguish *me* (who I think I should be) from *not-me* (all that must be repressed in the face of that), in defining our territory and realizing our ego's particular strategy.

Our Enneagram type, whether it centers on being safe, getting seen, or maintaining our autonomy, depends on our unique nature/culture context and where the struggles and disruptions occurred along the developmental journey.[36] This means that our type will often be found in the area where our needs were not met or where there was some conflict between our in-born wiring and the style of our cultural context. Because of this tear in the fabric, we become compelled to re-create for ourselves what didn't go so well in that stage. In doing so, we become more singularly driven by one of these guiding passions as a strategy of adaptation and an attempt to repair or compensate for what was lost. In the process, we also become more of a separate someone who believes our efforts (to be safe, seen, in control) are *essential* to our well-being...and our type strategy is born.

Although we may develop as one particular Enneagram type, at the same time, we have experiences and biological wiring that allow for *all* of the passions listed around the Enneagram. Even before the religious teachings about deadly sins and fragments that attack the spiritual heart were formulated, these emotional drivers were thought of as "demons," "spirits," or other animating forces. Ancients peoples personified them as gods who governed the Cosmos, which is an appropriate way to think about our emotional/motivational drives. Being possessed by Anger or Fear or Lust can feel similar to possession by supernatural forces! Powerful drives and emotional states always seem to act upon us before we can think things through, and they compel us to behave in ways we may not logically choose.

FORCES GOVERNING THE PSYCHE ARE REFLECTED IN THE COSMOS

At the same time, we would be remiss to reduce these powerful "gods" to only internal drives. Like the ancient folks seeing governing forces in the sky, more modern scientist-philosophers such as evolutionary paleontologist Teilhard de Chardin and physicist David Bohm offered theories about an organizing process of creation that is characterized by particular forces or qualities.[37] In mapping the evolutionary dynamics of the Universe to discover how it unfolded from the big bang, mathematician and cosmologist Brian Swimme observed 10 cosmological "powers" at play within the seamlessly interconnected universal field. These have rather "godlike" qualities, such as emergence, allurement, centration, and radiance.[38] And, just as we saw with the forces driving ego development, the relationship between these different qualities seems to point to a coherent process.

As constituent forces of an underlying ground of Being, the cosmological powers animate an unfolding narrative of creation, destruction, and transformation playing out on the macro scale of the Universe that is *also* reflected within the microcosm of the human psyche or soul. The ten sephirot of the Kabbalah Tree of Life and the *virtues* of the Enneagram are similarly regarded as universal qualities of Being that *also* arise within us when (having reconciled the "sins") we are more centered in a greater Presence that is connected to *All that Is*. In other traditions, such realized qualities that also animate the Universe are known as "Names of God." And while the names and numbers vary, the idea persists that the Cosmos and human character are governed by the same universal archetypes, collaborating in a unified process, that can be expressed as either deities or demons.

This idea that the psyche and Cosmos reflect one another is at the core of what Gurdjieff was teaching with the Enneagram Symbol, what Carl Jung was proposing with archetypes of the collective unconscious, and it is central to the Law of One. If every aspect of the Universe, seen and unseen, is part of the same One creative Source and Flow of Being, it makes sense to find parallel qualities, revealed through a coherent process or blueprint, unfolding at every level of existence. There is One shared fabric of reality. But far from pointing to an amorphous lump of One-ness, the Law of One represents the idea that all of the diversity we see, within and beyond us, is necessary to the collective process of creation and re-creation (becoming more whole) that allows us to know ourselves again as One with that unifying ground of Being. While it may look like chaos when not working coherently, there is rhyme and reason to the diversity; it is an essential aspect of the underlying order.

In this way, the Law of One reveals a paradox at the heart of the Enneagram: that we are simultaneously part and whole. We have within us all of the forces represented around the circle, *and* there is one Enneagram type that owns us. Our type—and the *passion* in particular—is more tenacious, more difficult to identify, because it is the water we swim in, and so we have less conscious awareness of and control over it than over the other passions. When we come to understand its operation and unravel its stickiest defensive ego patterns, we can unlock a great deal of growth within, and we often discover the particular gift of our unique expression of Being. At the same time, seeing our type as only part of our inherent wholeness allows us to access even more of our unseen *essence* and, through that, our interconnection with others, the natural world, and the underlying One field and flow of intelligence that is continually revealing itself through the pattern.

In our exploration of the laws of the Symbol and the map of growth they lay out, the Law of One reveals what it means to be whole or integrated at different levels of analysis that are relevant to our lives. We will discover what it means to be a whole self at the horizontal level, which includes more integrated centers of intelligence: mind, heart, and body. At times we will zoom in and reflect on what wholeness might mean as more flexible and integrated brain function; and at times we will zoom out to explore the larger wholes—the systems we inhabit through our relationships and communities. Throughout this process of discovery, I will keep pointing back to the vertical dimension and most expansive meaning of the Law of One as it relates to the dynamic Source and Flow of Creation, because the transpersonal or spiritual domain connects us all on this journey.

Finding a name for this One Source without alienating someone is impossible. In truth, words are poorly equipped to describe the ineffable, un-nameable Totality to which they point. As soon as we label it, we are separate from it, describing it, which is why the Taoists say that the Tao that can be named is not the Tao. I have used a lot of different words in my lifetime, so I'll ask your forgiveness up front as I point to the ineffable. And I hope you will use those markers to refer to your own knowing of the One as God or Goddess, the Tao, Brahma, Allah, Buddha-nature, the implicate order, matrix of consciousness, unified field of intelligence, or another word for our shared Source described by the Law of One. As Ram Dass said, "We are all just walking each other home." And, thankfully, the combined laws of the Symbol seem to give us a way to do that together.

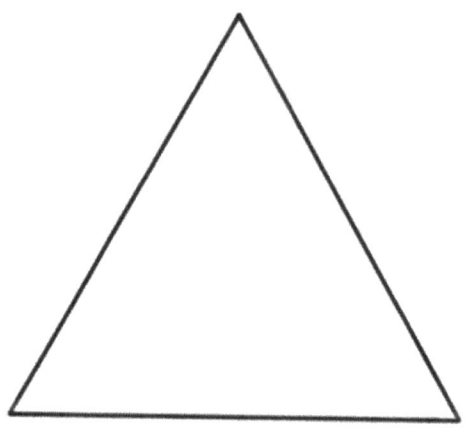

THE LAW OF THREE

CHAPTER FIVE

THE LAW OF THREE

*Everything in the world obeys the Law of Three. Everything existing
came into being in accordance with this law. Combinations of positive and negative principles can produce new results, different from
the first and second, only if a third force comes in.*[39]
*...This teaching of the three forces is at the foundation
of all ancient systems.*[40]

~ G.I GURDJIEFF

A S WE MOVE DEEPER INTO THE SYMBOL, it is helpful to remember
that the three laws are not separate, but rather like layers of a whole
system, each of which reveals an aspect of a dynamic process governing
the creation and continuous renewal of life. The foundational layer is the
Law of One. Everything arises from and is connected through the same
One Source that continues to reveal itself in the blueprint or the laws that
govern the flow of life at every level of the Universe. The second layer of
this unfolding process is the Law of Three, symbolized by the inner triangle
made by points 9-3-6 on the Enneagram Symbol. Gurdjieff also called it
the Law of World Creation. If we want to create something new, up-level
our growth or jump to a new S-curve, it happens through this law.

You can see the relationship between *one* and *three* in the Enneagram
if you imagine standing at the top of a 3D triangle or tetrahedron. As the
Source and birthplace of Creation, this single point represents the beginning and end of a complete process, the Law of One. The view from here
shows how the One Source "projects" itself into Creation through the
three points of the triangle that forms the base, like a spotlight or projector pointing downward. The three points of this flat or projected triangle
are still and always part of the One Source that is Everything, even if they
appear and act as distinct aspects.

If you think of watching a movie played on an old-fashioned film
projector, the movie that appears on the screen in front of you is a function of the light coming from way back in the projection booth as it is

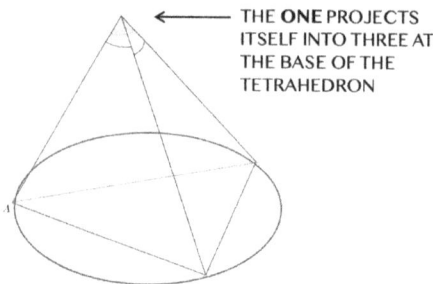

THE **ONE** PROJECTS
ITSELF INTO THREE AT
THE BASE OF THE
TETRAHEDRON

sent through the projector, through the filmstrip, to the screen. You can't see it when looking forward, but the world on the screen is *made* of this light. So while the triangle appears as separate, it is still part of the whole system, and projected from the same source.

Creation is set up this way so that it, too, can generate new life...albeit at a smaller scale. The three points of the projected triangle of new creation represent three elements or *forces* that work together in a cycle of continuous creating. Through this regenerative process, the One becomes three as manifest reality, and the three work (through a seven-step process) to know themselves again as the interconnected One, which can again split to create another three, and so on. We will explore the nature of these three forces, how they create together, and how they "return to One" and re-create, as we make sense of the Law of Three—the Law of Creation. Understanding the three forces of the Law of Three is key to unwrapping the mysteries of the Symbol as a whole.

The Law of Three can be engaged at every level of the Enneagram of Personality (there are three centers of intelligence, three types per center, three subtypes per type), just as it operates at every level of Creation. As Gurdjieff said, this law "manifests in everything, without exception, and everywhere in the Universe."[41] At one level, the circle, triangle, and hexad shapes that make up the Symbol represent the Laws of One, Three, and Seven.

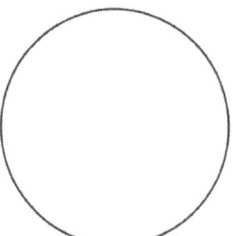

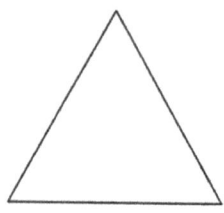

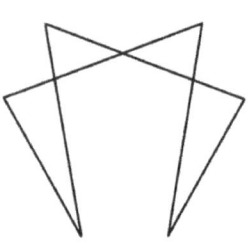

THE LAW OF ONE   THE LAW OF THREE   THE LAW OF SEVEN

At another level, these shapes illustrate one version of the three roles or forces of the Law of Three that are necessary for continuous evolution. When the One splits itself into three pieces in making the created world, those three parts are themselves an echo of the original creative dance that brought life into being. This sets up a Universe in which *as Above, so Below*; all levels of Creation are structured similarly, in a kind of holographic hall of mirrors.

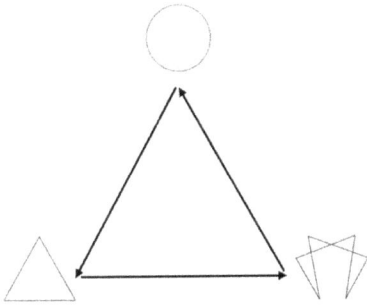

In the chapter on the Law of One we talked about an implicit *law of two* represented by the triangle in relationship to the circle. At the center of Creation are two "opposing" forces: one that contracts or organizes the underlying flow of potential into form (order), another that expands beyond form to re-connect with the primordial flow of energy (chaos). Their dance is represented by the hexad shape. It is often drawn with arrow lines to illustrate the continuous and cyclical dance between order and chaos that allows for the renewal and maintenance of life; one that unfolds with or without our conscious participation. This is amazing, and enables life to go on, but it is *not* an expression of the full creative potential possible through all three forces of the Law of Three.

In the flat Symbol, we have three elements working together in a fixed triad to maintain life. In this case, the manifest triad has been "caused" by forces outside ourselves. There is another kind of law of three process, however, that is "causal;" it engages the three elements in a purposefully creative way made possible by our inner work. This requires developing our own "inner triangle" and engaging the Law of Three *within* ourselves in order to evolve higher levels of being. The difference between a fixed triad and an "inner triangle" is key. Gurdjieff taught that "each completed whole, each cosmos, each plant, is an Enneagram," meaning that it follows certain natural laws of unfolding, but not each of these Enneagrams has an "inner triangle."[42]

As an example, again, the triadic relationship among our own three centers of intelligence when we are gripped by our type structure is fixed. We all have three centers, but because that triad was caused, and is controlled by, the habitual patterns of our past ("trapped in matter"), our true intelligence is limited. We live in reaction to things that happen "to us" instead of operating as conscious, integrated, creative, connected people. Alternately, when the Law of Three is engaged consciously, the three elements of a triad are able to relate in a particular way and create *something more* than they were before. To realize the promise of the Symbol as a whole, we need to learn more about what turns a fixed triad into that dynamic inner triangle to which Gurdjieff refers...which is *the third force.*

THE THIRD FORCE

As we saw in the creation myths, when *order* is carved out of the formless void of *chaos*, we get the first split of our multi-dimensional Universe into two major parts: the solid particle and the expansive wave, the seen and unseen dimensions. Usually, we think about these two states as entirely separate. Life emerges from energy (chaos) and is organized into form (order). Order then decays into energy, over time, only to be gathered again into form in a continuous cycle of order-chaos-order-chaos.

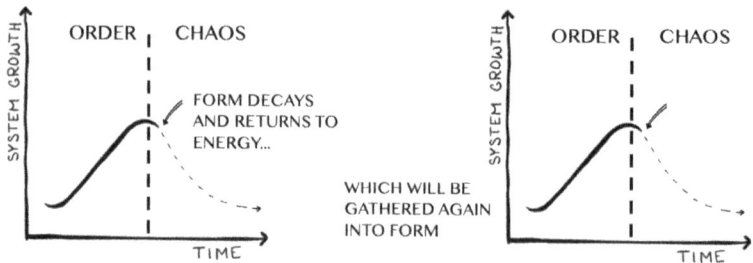

The polarity between the first two forces creates a dynamic tension in which, like two very different lovers who have found their way into relationship, they exist in a continuous push-pull cycle, alternately dominating the relationship. All of life is subject to this process that bounces between form and flow, particle and wave, in the eternal cycle of life, death, and rebirth. At least this is how we generally view things: growing or dying, good or bad, this or that. As Gurdjieff put it: "one part affirms, another denies. This is an objective law, and everyone is a slave to it. Only those who stand in the middle are free. If we can do this, we escape from this general law."[43]

What does it mean to *stand in the middle* and be free? This idea points us back to the S-curve diagrams and that mysterious space between curves. These same two forces, when harmonized or working together, create *something more* than the same old either-or pattern. Somehow, sometimes, before complete dissolution of the old order, something enables what seems like a magical leap (*emergence*) to a new S-curve of *higher-order* growth. The secret of that magical leap is found in the role of the third force, the one that *stands in the middle.*

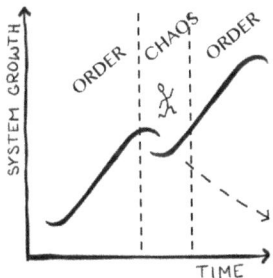

One of the clearest illustrations of the nature of this third force is in the well-known symbol from Taoism, the *Taijitu* or yin/yang symbol. The symbol depicts the first two forces as: 1) the white paisley shape as yang, or the "masculine" principle, that I am calling order or the ordering force; and 2) the black shape as yin or the "feminine" principle, which I am labeling as the force that drives towards chaos or flow. What most people don't recognize about this symbol is that there is a third element...the line *between* yin and yang.

The line represents a third force that mediates between the two polar forces, representing both, holding the paradox and *walking the line* between them. This force is an expression of the Tao itself, described as the source and natural order of the Universe. The Tao is the whole thing, the circle that just IS and created it all, but Tao is also the line or "the Way"—much like how God is God *and* Jesus Christ, the-Way-to-God. In this symbol, the Way refers to something like *the way to live well* within this ever-present and dynamic push/pull or affirmation/negation of inherently polarized forces. In Tao, order and flow are reconciled or harmonized. The Tao is also sometimes understood as "meaning," because it is on this line that one creates a meaningful life.

To be clear: the use of "masculine" and "feminine" in reference to polar forces has little to do with gender. Both forces are present within all of us, just as they operate at all levels of reality. Gendered terms provide a shorthand way of explaining that while the two primary forces are polar opposites, they are also "mutually arising," meaning they need and attract each other, and in fact, they represent the dual nature of the One reality. Just like the positive and negative ends of a battery, together these forces power life.

The "masculine" or yang principle represents an organizing, boundary-making force that creates life, but can be both protective and overly restrictive once its borders are established. It leads to order, structure, culture, and defines the territory, so it also represents the created or "known" world. Yang is often referred to as the "active" principle because imposing structure creates life and form out of energy. And yet, we need to understand that this principle can also constrict and deny the flow of life. Whatever is fixed in form becomes stagnant and begins to decay.

The "feminine" or yin principle represents the flow state, the primordial chaos from which the world is generated, and also the still-unknown aspects of the world and of ourselves. Yin is "feminine" by nature because it is "hidden" (being unstructured or wave-like, "empty" space), and because it is the stuff of Creation—the unknown potential that is organized into form. We call the feminine a receptive force because it "receives" yang, the cookie cutter that shapes it. And when order inevitably breaks down, it returns to or is "received" by chaos again (truly, the one becomes the other in a continuous cycle). Yin is often referred to as a "passive" force, and yet this principle can also be active, dynamic, and powerful as the constantly moving energy flow of Creation. Like water, it can both give and destroy life.

While we necessarily use words to describe these forces in the natural world, we really have to hold them symbolically. There are many ways to label them.

YIN	YANG
FLOW	ORDER
DARK	LIGHT
NATURE	CULTURE
MOTHER	FATHER
EXPANSION	CONTRACTION
CHAOS	TYRANNY
THE UNKNOWN	THE KNOWN

At the center of the Law of Three is this dance between the opposing forces of order and chaos. The third force shows us *the Way* to consciously mediate and participate in this dance to enable a better life, or to *integrate heaven and earth*, as the Taoists might say. *Walking the line* between order and chaos redeems life not only because either extreme leads to suffering, but also because the effort itself makes the suffering of life worthwhile in some way. This Way of being describes the continuous and creative process that is the third force and third role in the triangle of forces.

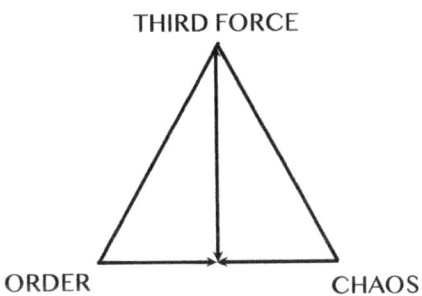

THIRD FORCE

ORDER   CHAOS

Serving as the key to a creative process does not make the third force better or more powerful than the other two forces. In fact, the third is "born" out of the dynamic tension between the original opposing forces. And, most importantly, all three forces are facets of the original parent, the One Source of All that Is. It's just that the third force is a key place for us humans to enter and collaborate in the Law of Creation because we don't generally operate this way or even understand how it works. A passage from the Tao te Ching succinctly describes the creative potential that arises when one can incorporate this third force: *The Way begot one, and the one, two; then the two begot three, and three, all else.* [44]

And three, all else. Something new—a fourth thing, if you will— emerges from this dance of three. Indeed, all of Creation arises through the relationship between order, chaos, and a true third force, which is the process of reconciling the tension of opposing forces that allows for the emergence of higher-level order. And because life is always changing (there is *always* more chaos ahead), imbalance occurs again and again in the dance between the two, calling forth the third in a continuous cycle of chaos, order, and reconciliation into higher-order growth.

Gurdjieff named these three forces of the Law of Three simply *force one, force two, and force three.* Other times he called them: the *active, passive, and neutralizing force,* or the *affirming, denying, and reconciling force.* From the labels it is clear that two forces act in opposition, and a third force serves to harmonize or reconcile the other two, neutralizing extremes and allowing collaboration.

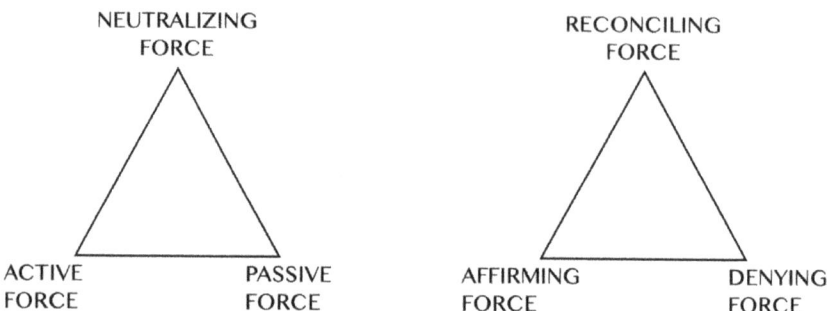

NEUTRALIZING
FORCE

ACTIVE
FORCE

PASSIVE
FORCE

RECONCILING
FORCE

AFFIRMING
FORCE

DENYING
FORCE

The wisdom of Gurdjieff's naming is that it leaves room for any element in a triad to serve as any force. The forces are more like roles exchanged among three elements in relationship. So while it's tempting to ascribe one particular role to the traditional masculine principle (active) and one role to the feminine (passive), this is not accurate. *Either* principle can be active or passive, affirming or denying life.[45] What's most important in understanding the law is that the first two are always in opposition, and the role of the third force is always "the spiritualizing and reconciling Source of every World formation."[46] As the "child" of the first two forces, the third is full of dual potential. When activated, since it is "made of" both of the other forces, the third force holds the tension of opposites purposefully, making "a Way" for new life to emerge from the dance. It helps to replicate the original creative process that brings order from chaos.

Because Gurdjieff's teaching is notoriously confusing, I turned to science, stories, and spiritual wisdom to reveal more about the nature and action of the three forces, as well as to verify whether the Law of Three is indeed a universal pattern. Once the three roles revealed themselves through other disciplines, I could return to Gurdjieff and make more sense of the way he taught about these forces with enough disguise to keep everyone seeking and doing the work of building our own inner triangle of creative forces.

The Law of Three in Spiritual and Mythic Stories

The idea of the One expressing itself through three elements that create together is a theme repeated across cultures and time. From a Hindu perspective, the supreme ultimate reality, Brahman (the One), gives rise to multiple gods, with the three principal actors being: Brahma, Shiva, and Vishnu. Together they make up what is known as the Trimurti. To sort the roles here, we have to know that Brahman, the One that gives rise to all form (and all three forces), is different from Brahma, who was once the embodiment of the creative force but became "an old man" over time, fixed in form.

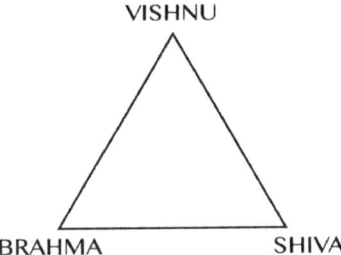

So we have the initial two opposing forces: Brahma who represents the ordering force but is now fixed and Shiva who is the unbound, creative/destructive force of chaos. The third role is carried by Vishnu, who is known as the preserver. He "preserves" through a dynamic third force process of reconciling order and chaos to maintain cosmic harmony.

In Christianity, God (the One) manifests through the creative vehicle of the Trinity: Father, Son, and Holy Spirit. If you have studied other formulations of the Law of Three, you may have found the Holy Spirit described as the third or reconciling force, mediating the relationship between the "opposing" forces of Son and Father. As examples, the virgin birth of Jesus is mediated by the Holy Spirit, as is Christ's ascension into Heaven following resurrection. At this level, the Holy Spirit reconciles the Son to God.

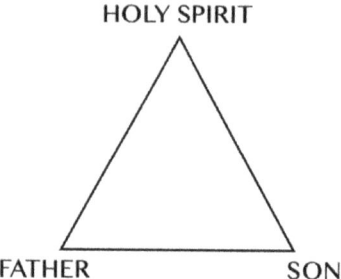

HOLY SPIRIT

FATHER   SON

And yet, the three forces are not absolutes (even if the Trinity and Trimurti are, as the highest expressions of the law). The forces are energies or orientations, three roles that can be assumed by the same entity at different times or at different levels of Creation. If we take the Law of Three down a few levels of the cosmological ladder and IN to the created world, things change. After all, once created, a thing has to be taken apart in some way in order to be made new. So the three elements change roles. In the middle of the Christian story—the life of Jesus in the created world—Jesus fulfills the role of the third force that serves to reconcile the created world (fixed form) with a (formless) spiritual reality, showing *the Way* to a Spirit-filled world. "In Christ God was reconciling the world to Himself."[47]

Through this lens, since God is not confined to one role but is the entire Trinity, the Creator and One Source of *All that Is* in triadic expression, we must consider "the father" here as the *order* of the manifest world, the result of *Logoic* action. Spirit is the "opposite" force, the *chaos/flow* of Being or the wave field of energy and information that continues to pervade what we see (with our limited vision) as fixed Creation. And the third force is the "son" as a dynamic manifestation of the original creative divine spark. He shows the Way ("Pick up your cross and follow me") to harmonize the first two elements, bring Spirit alive in the created world, and restore the fixed and fragmented parts of Creation to the "kingdom" (higher-level order) of the One, God. Jesus says, "I am the Way, the truth, and the life. No one comes to the Father except through me."[48]

Indeed, the life, death, and resurrection of Jesus Christ shows us the redemptive pattern of the Law of Three and, in particular, the Way and role of the reconciling force. This seems very like the Way of the Tao, the incarnated pattern or process of living that serves to harmonize order and chaos, restoring Tao. And like Vishnu in the Trimurti, Jesus is the one who preserves life through this continuous process of renewal (the

Way to "eternal" life). Each of them embodies (in the created world triad) the spirit of regeneration, an incarnation of the original *Logos* that made order out of the primordial chaos, or field of undifferentiated potential that still underlies the manifest world. And all of these representations of the third force are showing the Way we humans can engage opposing forces to renew the system and evolve a higher-order union.

As with the yin/yang symbol, the use of gendered terms here, however illustrative, can be misleading. As an example, both the Hindu and Christian triads are *masculine* according to their respective traditions, and yet they still have what some would call the yin, the *feminine* or unbounded "wave-like" role of chaos or flow (in Shiva and the Holy Spirit, two sides of a coin). Because the Law of Three operates at every level of Creation, both masculine and feminine forces (order and flow) exist *within* both feminine and masculine triads, persons, and systems. It would be better not to use gendered terms at all, but because the world's narrative traditions use them to distinguish and represent these mutually dependent but "opposing" forces, we can't discard this approach to conveying their nature.

There are other traditions that teach a Law of Three without personifying the forces as beings at all (and without a Supreme Being per se), but we can still see the three roles at work. Buddhism describes the process of awakening to Buddha-nature through the *trikaya*, three "bodies" or grounds of existence. There is: *nirmanakaya*, the solid, manifest ground of Creation (order); *sambhogakaya*, the unmanifest realm of perpetual change (chaos) that is "hidden" in plain sight; and *dharmakaya*, the as yet unformed space between these two, to be traveled by a third force, according to the teachings of the Buddha.[49] Similar to the Way of the Tao, the Dharma "reconciles" and establishes cosmic order through a Way of living (the Middle Way), on a journey of seven steps, along an eightfold path. The eighth step is the achievement of *samadhi*, which is complete meditative absorption before union with ultimate reality.

The good news is that it's not necessary to debate theology to understand the Law of Three. We can also learn a lot about the relationship among these three forces in the enduring themes of the world's narrative tradition. The Enuma Elish is one of the oldest known creation myths.[50] From ancient Mesopotamia, or Babylon, it is also known as *The Seven Tablets of Creation* (which tips us off to the importance of the number seven in the process of creation). In the beginning of this story, too, there is undifferentiated water swirling as primordial chaos.

Out of this swirl, the waters divided into the first two forces as bitter salt water and sweet fresh water. The salt water became the goddess Tiamat. She is a personification of the primordial chaos that manifests as a great dragon of destruction when enraged. The fresh water became her husband, the god Apsu. He represents the order that gives life and structure to turn the undifferentiated flow into something firm, but also, he is the "old man" who becomes stagnant in fixed form. Together they represent the dual nature of Creation.

Order and chaos create together through their dynamic tension. But they fight for dominance, one or the other always tipping the balance, so their creative process is often haphazard and does not always lead to "higher order." In this case, the union of Apsu and Tiamat resulted in the birth of a full complement of minor gods who were not particularly reverent with regard to their parentage. In fact, thanks in part to Tiamat's meddling, the minor gods end up destroying Apsu (or imprisoning him in a deathlike sleep). The kids (the distracting "fragments" of Creation) set up camp on Apsu's corpse and make a mess of the old order. Apsu's vulnerability to the minor gods is an indication that the old guy has lost his mojo and brought on his own demise. Order that is not continually updated grows stagnant.

Enraged by her husband's death, Tiamat takes control as the dragon of chaos, making life very unpleasant for all the gods (this is, of course, what happens when order breaks down). Having suffered enough at the hands of chaos, the minor gods elect a representative, Marduk, to face Tiamat, and they agree to make him king of the gods if he prevails.

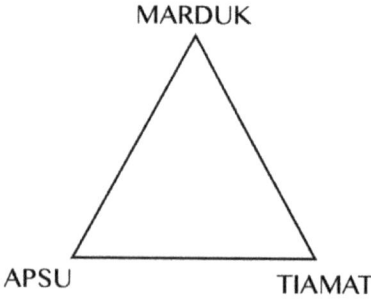

As the third or reconciling force, Marduk shows the Way to renew the world. First, he goes willingly into the underworld to battle the great dragon of chaos and her band of demons. He captures Tiamat in his net, an apt metaphor for placing some bounds around the vast chaos of Being. As

Marduk splits Tiamat in two, from her eyes flow the Tigris and Euphrates rivers, which signifies the necessity of preserving some of the *flow* of life within the created world. Marduk then uses the two pieces of Tiamat as a ceiling to push back the waters above, and a floor to stave off the waters below, establishing renewed order in Creation.

The Egyptian creation myth involving Isis and Osiris follows a similar storyline that also shows the affirming and denying aspects of each force. This story finds Osiris, once a great king (benevolent order), now sent to the underworld in pieces. (Don't we all fall to pieces in the face of tragedy?) In the case of Osiris, the fall was brought about by his brother Set (the controlling, tyrannical side of order), who betrayed him to claim the kingdom. In both this story and the Enuma Elish, the original representation of order, the masculine or father principle, falls into disarray (chaos) and a death-like sleep in the underworld below. In response, his wife Isis (the affirming power of chaos/flow), gathers up the essential part of him to unite with for the purpose of giving birth, and Horus, the son of that magical union between Osiris and Isis, is born as the third or reconciling force.

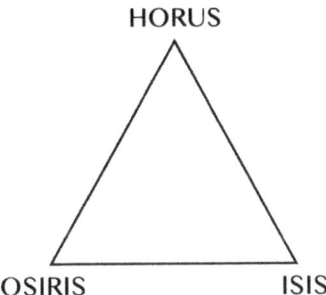

When he grows up, Horus fights and eventually overcomes the tyrannical Set, losing an eye in the process. As a symbol of consciousness and paying focused attention (the Way to navigate between tyranny and chaos), perhaps it is the single eye ("I") of Horus that helps him as he descends into the unknown below to find his father. Horus recovers his missing eye (or it was restored by the god Thoth, some say), and he uses it to heal Osiris, effectively uniting himself with his father. Together they return (or just Horus returns, depending on the version, but Horus, as creative consciousness in the present, is now imbued with the wisdom of the past). Their unity, in one form or another, represents an update and the renewal of benevolent order in the kingdom.

What Vishnu, Jesus, Buddha, Marduk, and Horus have in common is the ability to skillfully engage opposing forces (tyranny and chaos) and invite something different (*something more*) to emerge through opening up the battle and accessing new intelligence. This *something more* is something we could not fathom based on the way things were. It comes from the unknown; it is an emergent property of the system, called forth because the third force has made a Way to harmonize order and chaos, and help facilitate an evolutionary result. But the new result is not a return to the way things were. The dance of the three forces leads to a *fourth*, integrated, and higher-level outcome that *emerges* from the mix. Even if the hero of the story arises to be a new leader (like Horus), he is not what he was prior to the adventure. He embodies a higher order union of *all* the elements.

As a fourth and higher point of union, the outcome of the dance of three forces opens up a new dimension from the flat plane of the triangle in the Enneagram, creating the structure of a tetrahedron in the 3D Enneagram Symbol. For a moment, the three have become One again; the whole system (the kingdom) is renewed.

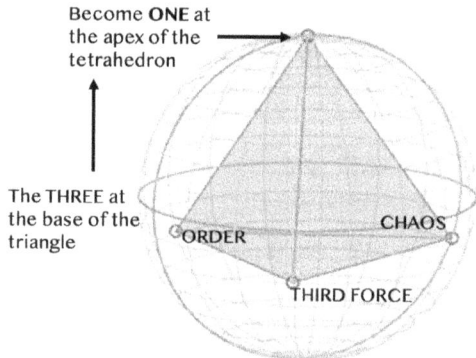

This pattern shows why the Law of Three is called the Law of Creation. A dualistic world, based on two polarized positions, stays locked in this-or-that. The two polarized forces, order and chaos, can create a third result together, but it is a haphazard process leading to a random third baby (like the children of Tiamat and Apsu), usually a reiteration of either stagnant order or total chaos that serves to keep the polarized world intact. To accomplish a new dimension or "higher order" growth, we need an awake third force that can *stand in the middle*. A true third force is able to invite some degree of chaos or flow (as new information and potential) without letting it completely overwhelm the benefits of healthy order. This creates a kind of alchemical process from which new growth can evolve as the fourth and higher-level outcome. The awake third force is *not* a simple synthesis of the first two positions (as in thesis + antithesis = synthesis). It is a point of conscious participation that allows for a fundamentally different fourth result. This formula of how the three forces create anew was so central to Gurdjieff's method that he called the entire body of his work the "Fourth Way." This is often understood as a description of how we must integrate all three of our primary centers of intelligence (mind, heart, body) into a unified fourth whole being that can realize higher dimensions of consciousness. However, that is just one manifestation of the Law of Three and how it makes a *Way* for the *fourth*. Gurdjieff's most simple and clear description of the Law of Three operation is: "A great dispute, if it is not purposeless, must give a result, a conclusion and an effect, and then **four** elements will be available: **yes, no, dispute, result;** that is, the transmutation of the binary into the quaternary."[51] Two forces create a third which, if it can hold an active and potentially *actualizing* dispute, yields a fourth new result.

If we have only *yes* and *no*, life swings compulsively between them, with a random winner, and the *either/or* polarity is maintained. When the tension between *yes* and *no* is held in conscious dispute by a third point, we embrace both but don't give in to either side. Holding the third force creates an opening (literally, through the open triangle created) to a field of greater potential from which a new outcome can evolve. This new outcome emerges from the mix of the forces for sure, but also from the self-organizing flow of intelligence that rushes into the open space. This unseen field of energy and information is always available. In duality we are closed off to it...experiencing it only as the dragon of chaos to be avoided. With the addition of a third point, that same chaos becomes a *flow* of potential.

Gurdjieff taught that a more conscious self (a Real "I" and a *permanent third* principle), not tossed about by our automatic reactivity of *yes* and *no*, can be grown through inner work. For this to happen, a certain fire is required—one lit by the friction of inner struggle inherent in holding the tension of opposites and welcoming the unknown. When we resist the trap of our personality that habitually demands *this* and rejects *that*, this *standing in the middle* creates friction and an opening. In that cauldron, old patterns are dissolved and transmuted into *something more*—a new dimension of being altogether. This capacity to engage the Law of Three, which I'll call third force consciousness, is the creative key to accessing new dimensions of consciousness all along the journey of growth.

Carl Jung spoke similarly of this process of holding the tension of opposites and arriving at a higher result, calling it the transformation of *binary into trinity, and trinity into quaternity.*[52] It was central to his concept of psychological development or "individuation," which occurs through the work of re-integrating *all* the opposing parts of the psyche into a whole and higher Self—with a capital "S" to denote its centrality and relation to a larger field of wholeness. The individuated self is, by definition, one who unites opposing forces, such as shadow and light, unconscious and conscious processes within oneself. It is akin to the concept of *essence* in Enneagram terms, sometimes referred to as the fully developed soul. We might imagine that Jung and Gurdjieff knew of each other's work, living and teaching in Europe in the same era. I don't know if this is true, and maybe it's irrelevant, because we can find this creative Law of Three everywhere. It seems to be a pattern embedded in the very structure of reality.

THE LAW OF THREE IS THE LAW OF CREATION

Just as today we use high-level math to map the contours of the Universe, ancient people from diverse civilizations also used numbers to describe the cosmos. Much of ancient Egyptian life, including the construction and placement of the pyramids, was based on sacred geometry, but it was Pythagoras, a Greek scholar who lived around 500 BCE, who is often credited as the first to link numbers and the Universe. Pythagoras believed that numbers are the fabric of reality and the keys through which we can "hear" the harmony of the cosmos. He proposed that the numbers 1, 2, 3, and 4 represent all known objects in the Universe because: 1 is a point; 2 points connected make a line; 3 points make a triangle and a plane; and 4 adds the depth dimension of the tetrahedron, a pyramid of four perfect triangles. The transition from one dimension to the next in the evolution of the tetrahedron is central to the process of creation, and the tetrahedron was one of the "Pythagorean solids" (later called Platonic solids) thought to form the constituent elements of the entire Universe.[53]

The idea that three forces are required for new creation continued into the modern era. The late Stephen Hawking, one of the modern world's most celebrated physicists, once wrote that you need three ingredients to make a Universe: matter, space, and energy.[54] In truth, these are different forms of force or energy. Matter is the created/revealed world of particles (order); space is the unbounded, unseen energy wave-field (chaos) from which form arises. Hawking's third force is the application of additional energy that shapes the wave-field into matter. This triadic dance results in a new (fourth) creative formulation of matter—an emergent property of the three forces—in this case, the Universe.

Physicist David Bohm tells a similar story of three roles that account for the process of evolution: the explicate order (the manifest world of form); the implicate order (the unseen field and flow of energy that underlies all, and from which all form emerges); and the super-implicate order, which is the intelligent pattern of self-organization that governs the unfolding process and brings new form to life. He associates this third force with consciousness and the establishment of meaning (which I understand as something like the Tao or "the Word" that creates). Both of these models from physics suggest that the pattern of three forces continually creating and renewing life is baked into the very structure of the Universe.

In chapter 4, we saw this creative relationship of three forces in the developmental journey of a child from birth to independent personality or ego structure, which is the "fourth" arising out of the tension between our inherent nature (instinctual chaos) and the culture to which we must adapt (order)...all thanks to a mysterious self-organizing intelligence. Nature and Culture are the two primary opposing forces that provide the constraints within which we all develop. Our nature lends the raw material and essential energy, and our culture creates boundaries within which we can act, learn, and still be safe and acceptable. But these two forces don't always get along. Somehow a third force guides development within the constraints. We could say that we are born with a divine spark that organizes all the information into a coherent strategy to do life, as we travel counterclockwise around the Symbol in the process of shaping a personality.

Although that ego structure is an adaptive strategy for a child, it eventually becomes more like a stagnant or tyrannical king—a fixed order that chokes off much of the flow of life, as well as the original creative spark. When we wake up to its limitations in adulthood, this process can unwind in the opposite direction—in a clockwise growth journey—to deconstruct the ego's tyranny and re-integrate the flow of unconscious instinct, spirit, and life force to re-create a more adaptive order. This is the process of realizing essence or developing a soul.

WIRED FOR THE LAW OF THREE

If the Law of Three can be found in the structure of Creation as well as in the formation of our ego structure, it makes sense that our brains mirror this same set-up. The human brain appears to be adapted for two modes of operation consistent with chaos and order. Right and left hemispheric coordination reveals a Law of Three process related to attention and learning. While many theories of left-brain/right-brain specialization have proven untrue or overly simplistic, there is indeed a difference between the operations of the two halves of our brain when it comes to modes of attention.[55]

Among other functions, the left hemisphere attends to the predictability of order or "the known" world. With a narrow, focused, and selective attention, the left hemisphere pays attention in a way that *fits* what we see into what we already know. It actively organizes the massive amount of information coming at us at any moment. The left hemisphere specializes in using language, linear thinking, positive action/feeling, and objective naming, to approach and categorize things within our already known understanding of the world. This is called *confirmation bias*. With selective attention we "confirm" information that supports our current understanding of things and deny information that contradicts it. We all have this bias.

This is very like the function of the mental habit or fixation of our Enneagram type. A fixed worldview at Type 2, that "I have to center others in order to get my own needs met," causes me to prioritize and selectively see other people's needs within the whole landscape of my life experience. If I have a Type 1 fixation with its need to constantly improve things, I selectively see things that are wrong. In performing this selective attention, our fixation guides us to be more efficient in processing, navigating, and re-creating the familiar (more of our type experience). In a very real sense, the left hemisphere helps us make and maintain *order* from our everyday experience by allowing us to perceive and structure reality today based on our past understanding. This all happens so easily that we can sort of sleep through it as our familiar world keeps on turning.

LEFT HEMISPHERE
- NARROW FOCUS
- PREDICTABILITY
- LINEAR
- SELECTS THE KNOWN
- ANALYZES AND NAMES BASED ON PAST EXPERIENCE

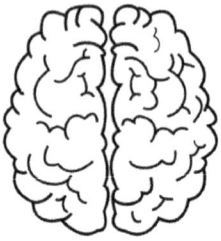

RIGHT HEMISPHERE
- OPEN FOCUS
- POSSIBILITY
- HOLISTIC
- ORIENTED TO NEW INFO
- SEES PATTERNS TO MAKE SENSE OF THE NEW

Until...something unusual happens and we are in new terrain. Here right hemispheric function dominates attention, adapted as it is for *chaos* and the "unknown" world. The right hemisphere is more possibility-focused, with a broad attention that is flexible and capable of orienting to new stimuli, changing frames of reference, and navigating encounters with the unknown. It processes images, thinks holistically, and looks for patterns as a way to make sense of new information (recognizing friend or foe, for example) so we can explore new things and expand our capacity without getting into too much trouble. Eventually, we *make new order out of chaos*, shifting back to left-side-dominant attention, integrating some aspect of the unknown into our new known world.

One modern theory of mind-brain health, also consistent with the Law of Three, is that it runs along a continuum between an overly ordered or rigid brain, in which disconnected parts operate in a controlled, habituated manner, and an overly chaotic brain, characterized by multiple and diverse cross-brain neural connections firing actively. Neither extreme is functional. An overly rigid brain leads to disorders such as anxiety, depression, and obsessive-compulsive disorder, while an overly chaotic brain manifests in problems like mania and psychosis. The science suggests that mental health lies in the space between extremes, where conscious awareness enables us to adaptively move within a healthy range of order and flow, mediating between rigidity and chaos to achieve greater coherence and integration throughout.[56]

In this example conscious awareness is the third force that enables us to actively navigate between these two modes, integrating, and sometimes walking the razor's edge between order and chaos. With this active engagement, remarkably, we can reshape our habitual reactions through rewiring patterns in our brain. As Dan Siegel, a psychiatrist, researcher, and pioneer in the study of the mind/brain, says it: "where attention goes, neural firing flows, and neural wiring grows."[57] Consciously applied awareness can break down fixed neural patterns and incorporate new information that changes brain structure and function. It seems that the creative power of the Law of Three is baked into our neurobiology, as well as into the natural world. And it starts young.

From the work of psychologist Jean Piaget in cognitive development, we know that babies grow the structure and function of their brains and bodies through exploring and continually updating their experience and understanding of the world around them. As babies, we literally have to go out into the "chaotic" world of unknown, undifferentiated information to encounter new things (a bathtub of water, for example) in order to expand our paradigm of what "the world" is made of. And maybe we even need to swallow a bit of water to learn that—unlike, say, getting into a mesh play tunnel—we can't breathe inside this stuff! In this way, we continually "create" ourselves and our world through encounters with the unknown. Literally, new genes inside us turn on and proteins wrap around neuron connections, changing our brains, as we integrate more of what is beyond the bounds of our past experience into a higher-order understanding of the world. And this process doesn't stop in childhood.

CREATING WITH THE LAW OF CREATION

Our experience of the known world, or life as we know it today, is based on our past. It is a function of our memories, wired-in habits and reactions, and what we expect. Our past creates order based on how we "know" things to be. Left to our own devices, we tend to perceive, feel, and act mechanically, consistent with this order. The combination of these habitual reactions, played out across time, is our personality type or ego structure. Let's say I *know* I'm shy, for example. Thinking I'm shy, I avoid or act awkwardly in social situations. People react in kind, so I keep finding these encounters difficult, and I keep understanding myself and the world according to my past expectations, labels, traditions, wiring, and history.

This is one reason Gurdjieff insisted that we are "machines" who act mechanically, without awareness or real choice. Most of us continuously create more of the past as we move into the future, reinforcing our Enneagram type. Who would we be without our knowns? If I gave a fork to an alien, she might use it to comb her hair, creating a radically different future with the fork. The rest of us would likely use it to eat in the present based on our past conditioning of what a fork is, thereby re-creating our past in the future. It's the same thing with "shy and awkward" or whatever habits and expectations define you according to type. Our type structure shapes our experience, we get more of the past in the present, and this scenario continues into the future.

PAST (*Order*)  More PAST in Future

But the future isn't a pre-destined place in time, like matter. It is actually more like space—a field of possibility where the potential for new experience, emotion, and belief awaits. In the creation stories, the future is more like the primordial chaos, full of undifferentiated potential out of which new life emerges, but also a scary place from which dragons and other *opposing* forces arise. It holds *both* the dragon of chaos *and* the treasure that changes our fortune. However, because we tend to see mostly the chaos of the unfamiliar, we cling to order. While safer and more conducive to mastery, certainly, the order of our past habits inadvertently limits the possibilities (treasure) of our future, like the old king who defends tradition.

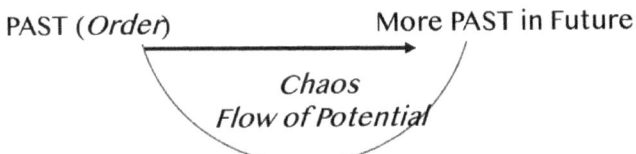

Until...order in the kingdom breaks down and all that potential really does feel like the dragon of chaos. We know this because of the chaos that ensues when something new—either terrible, like job loss, or wonderful, like a new baby—alters our world. Many of us experienced this state as COVID-19 descended. One minute life was orderly, predictable. We had a map. The next minute we were literally IN the unknown world...essentially a whole new "place."

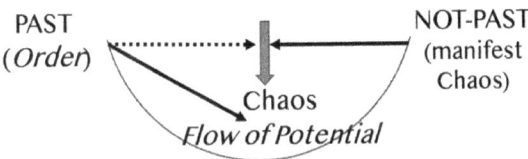

Our old maps for how to operate don't work in this place, so we are in chaos in a very real sense, figuring out how to cope, and facing some inner dragons as well (we would no doubt prefer stay in their cave). Sometimes we end up growing stronger or wiser through random life tragedies and opportunities; often we just get through them and return to the old order. Without awareness, we live through this continuous dance between rigid order and chaos, tossed about by people and situations that happen *to* us, as well as by our reactivity. As Gurdjieff put it, our entire lives are experienced according to this sort of duality, as opposing sides alternate power: "What is victor today is vanquished tomorrow; what is dominant today is subordinate tomorrow...all of these alternatives are equally mechanical, independent of our will and incapable of leading us to the attainment of any goal."[58]

However, if we understand the Law of Three and third force

consciousness, we humans have the unique opportunity to enter into this process, stop the mechanical madness, and partner in the unfolding of Creation. The entry point for this work is the present moment. In the present moment we can pause habitual responses of the past to see with fresh eyes (or a fresh mind/heart) what we might do differently with that "fork," or what we might do to have a relaxed and excellent time at the next social event.

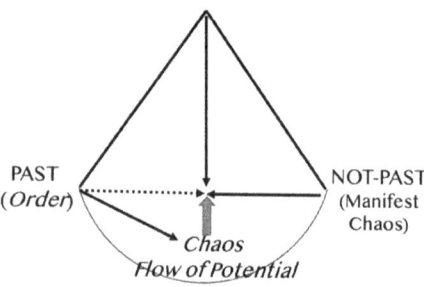

By countering and refraining from past habits in the present, we are actively choosing a "counterforce" (not-past, which is a little bit chaotic). We might fall into the primordial void of chaos for a moment (or two, or ten!), but if we can withstand the anxiety of not-knowing, and the discomfort of showing up differently, we can open the way for new information and allow ourselves to be re-shaped by the vast potential of possibility that is "future."

Our attention in the present moment is a key aspect of the third or reconciling force. It is an important aspect of the Way to intervene with the persistent past, and intentionally incorporate the flow of potential, to evolve a future that enfolds the wisdom of the past while improving upon limiting habits. The power of a third force that can hold the tension of not doing the same old habits and can tolerate not knowing what's ahead, enables a **fourth** point—an entirely new dimension of experience (new order)—to emerge from the access to new energy and information in the void.

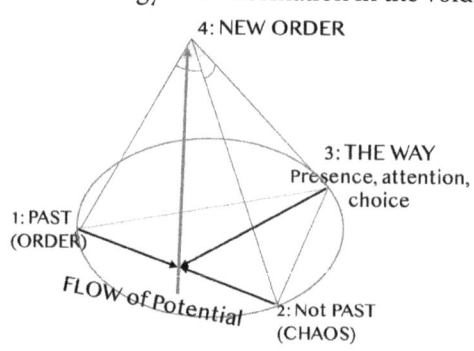

Sometimes the third force is inaccurately described as if it is only the result of the first two forces. Other times it is described as something that only comes from outside of us, as a gift from Source. This is not quite accurate either. When we consider the Law of Three from diverse perspectives, the third force is a conscious *process* of engaging the tension of opposing forces to create a Way for a fourth, integrated result to emerge. That fourth new arising is a "gift" for sure. It is beyond what we can imagine from the vantage point of our former level of consciousness. While we are not in control of the outcome, holding that third point, standing in the middle, opens the door for us to a partnership with Source as the underlying field of intelligence that flows in to lift us to new heights.

What Gurdjieff and other traditions with a version of the Law of Three seem to be showing us is that there is a dynamic Way to participate in Creation by consciously encircling the polarized positions and holding that third point—holding the door open between them, with patience, unifying kindness, and intention. This may explain why present-moment-based practices such as mindfulness meditation and contemplative prayer are central to most wisdom traditions, as well as to many disciplines for health and well-being that include creating new habits. Only in the moment can we simultaneously deconstruct our world, make new choices, and collaborate with the flow of potential to lift ourselves higher. The power of this creative process is profound.

Psychologist Ellen Langer, my thesis advisor at Harvard, devoted much of her career to studying what she called "mindfulness," referring not to the meditation technique but something more like the capacity to see with new eyes—eyes (or a mind) not biased by past conditioning.[59] This is akin to deconstructing past habits in the present to allow for a new future experience. Langer recognized, as Gurdjieff taught, that much of our thinking and behavior is "mindless," automatic or mechanical, and that waking up and altering embedded patterns is the pathway to growth. Her research revealed, across a variety of experimental situations, that the capacity to be mindful (think outside the box, beyond conditioning) leads not only to more creative engagement in the world, but also to physiological improvements in health and well-being.

In a remarkable illustration of this she called "the counterclock-wise study," in 1981 Langer invited eight men in their 70s to a five-day retreat at a monastery in New Hampshire. At the retreat, life was set up to exactly mimic the year 1959, from the artifacts and media to their clothing and conversation. The men were treated and asked to act as if it were 22 years earlier. They carried out the chores of younger men and chatted and acted as if they were currently engaged in the activities of their 50-something-aged selves. At the end of five days, the men had improved significantly on a number of physiological factors. Their grips were stronger, they sat taller, lost weight, their sight and hearing improved, and their IQ scores had increased.

This and other experiments hint at just how much the layers of our experience interweave. Mind, expectations, feelings, and beliefs can determine our experience both within us (biological and brain function) and outside of us, through our relationship to others and our environment. When we counter our conditioned responses, as laid out in the Enneagram of Personality, our possible futures open up widely. Awareness and choice, one moment at a time, reshape the self. Intentional conscious choice in the present is our way out of personality, and out of the unconscious processes that sustain our past and limit our future.

I had heard it said that "the smallest unit of existence is three," but it didn't make sense to me until I saw how life moves in this triadic dance that allows for continuous evolution. Whatever our Enneagram type, we are thrown into chaos and the unknown by life's challenges. It is very human to hunker down in stress patterns, pick sides, blame enemies, punish ourselves, or whatever else we do to attend to our ego needs and re-establish habitual order. It is also normal to dissolve in the face of chaos at times, suffering and enduring the natural consequences of disruption and loss. We automatically and habitually cling to certain responses and desires, and habitually reject and refrain from others. When those strategies break down under stress, we fall apart and then "get changed" by life's travails. But there is an alternative.

We can *choose* a voluntary encounter with both forces. We can look honestly at the terrain, willingly sacrifice old paradigms, and stretch into unconscious places in order to grow psychologically and spiritually enough to tolerate and integrate new information. This path of growth marks the path of the third force. It is the continuous work of staying awake, sacrificing ego, and choosing the courageous and creative process of renewal—a process that engages the friction of opposing forces to enable a fourth Way, a new way of being, more integrated and able to navigate the inevitable dragons that show up from both within and outside of us.

Life is continuously challenging and stretching us. It's hard. And that is how we grow. We are most alive when we choose the discomfort of engaging with the unknown, and then manage to make new order and meaning of it all. Indeed, our individual choices and commitments may be *all* that we have to redeem life in the face of suffering and hardship. I imagine this is what the Taoists meant with the idea that meaning is found on the line between order and chaos. Like Marduk, if we are brave and creative, we can face the great dragon of chaos directly. Then, whatever the outcome, through the process we find out what we are made of and regain some sovereignty.

Victor Frankl, who was a neurologist and psychiatrist in addition to being a concentration camp survivor, spent a good portion of his career refining a therapeutic approach built on his experience in the camps. Logotherapy centers on the human capacity to find higher meaning—whether psychological, spiritual, or both—in the face of breakdown and chaos. Many have repeated his famous words: "Everything can be taken from a man but one thing: the last of the human freedoms—to choose one's attitude in any given set of circumstances, to choose one's own way." And: "Between stimulus and response there is a space. In that space is our power to choose our response. In our response lies our growth and our freedom." [60]

This is part of what struck me deeply back in graduate school listening to those women with cancer grapple with the significant assault to their lives. I did not understand it then, but the growth I witnessed out of such a difficult encounter with the unknown arose from this dance between chaos and order, and the conscious third. Choosing to deal directly with chaos—feeling it, talking about it, and actively deconstructing *things as they had previously known them*—seemed to enable some sense of agency, and a degree of energy for the emergence of new life, whatever might be left of it, on their terms. Or, I should say, that is the meaning I made from the privilege of observing them.

Like Victor Frankl and the women in that support group, sometimes we are called into the cauldron between order and chaos by tragedy, sometimes we are called by opportunity, and sometimes we go there on purpose. Carl Jung talked about "the second half of life" not as a chronological age, but rather as the moment we decide to sacrifice and unravel the "false" aspects of ourselves that we developed in response to our upbringing, in order to discover who we truly are beneath the programming of the known. A map for this journey can be found in the Enneagram Symbol itself, and we can start on that journey by building third force consciousness.

BUILDING THIRD FORCE CONSCIOUSNESS

The Law of Three can help us understand many things about the Enneagram system, and about type and subtype. However, the most important way for us to understand the Law of Three is as a kind of internal creation machine, offering us a recipe and a way to lift ourselves from one dimension of consciousness to another. Gurdjieff reminded us often that we are *made in the image and likeness of God.* We are meant to build the laws *inside* us so that we can participate in the process of creation. Granted, we are working at a different level, but this suggests we can learn to employ our own little trinity of forces to catalyze growth beyond the limiting habits of type, to reclaim our inherent wholeness and, at the same time, restore some harmony in our world.

While the third force is not located within a particular center, waking up the heart center and working on emotional self-development is key to growing third force consciousness and advancing on our journey of transformation through the Symbol. Carl Jung said that the way into the unconscious is through emotion. Feelings seem to have a life of their own. Once triggered, they can quickly take us down a rabbit hole, but they also show us aspects of our unconscious that need to be integrated. Applying the Law of Three very specifically to the passions, or emotional habits of type, is a central leverage point for untangling the tenacious grip of personality and freeing us to create a different future. Since the Enneagram passions are also called "vices," this process is sometimes called "the vice to virtue conversion."

It can be confusing that this lower emotional habit is called both the *vice* and the *passion* of type, and yet together these labels explain the nature of the lower emotional habits. The word *vice* comes from the expression "capital vices," another name for the "seven deadly sins" of early Christian origin. There are nine in the Enneagram system because of the addition of Fear and Deceit.[61]

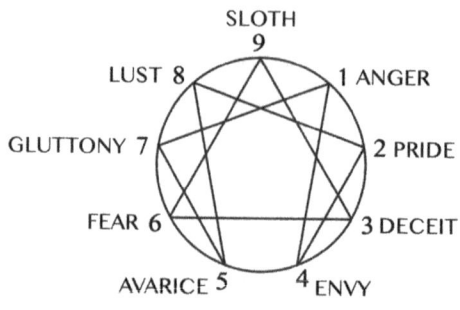

ENNEAGRAM PASSIONS

Vice is another word for sin, yes, and vice also describes *the next below* in reference to a hierarchy, as in *vice* president. It is, in this respect, "not quite there." The word sin is a translation of the Greek word *hamartia*, which also means something like *missing the mark*. So this sin or vice is a very particular way that, in personality, we are missing the mark of the true heart, only approximating (not quite there) who we really are—our essential self or soul that connects us to God or Source, the unified field of consciousness we lost touch with when we fell asleep to our true nature.

A consequence of this movement away from essence is represented by the word *passion*, which comes from the Latin *patiore*, meaning "to suffer." Applying both words, we can understand the full measure of the vices/passions of the Enneagram. They are driving forces that cause us to suffer by, paradoxically, pointing us just south of who we really are in essence. Hijacking our attention and energy, the passions effectively block us from our higher selves, expressed through the higher emotional center and its virtues. There is a reason that the meditating Christian monks singled out these deadly sins, and ancient people personified them as gods or planetary forces that possess us.

The architecture of this process through the Law of Three explains why some Enneagram teachers refer to *the vice to virtue conversion* as a process of "vertical" growth.[62] You don't arrive at the virtue of type by cultivating it directly. At best, this comes out as strained acting. Instead, virtues arise through that emergent process of reconciling "opposing" forces, through Presence and third force consciousness, to access that "fourth" point—in this case a higher level of being, the virtue of type and "higher" heart intelligence.

To counter the powerful force of a vice or passion, we often need to actively engage an opposite force to interrupt its functioning—something we really don't like, that goes against our ego ideal. Engaging the tension of opposites, in this way, invites third force consciousness. If we can hold the energy of both positions, without acting out our defensive habits, a doorway opens through which *something more* can arise. As an example: Type 1 and the passion of Anger. This Anger is resistance to things that are not as they *should* be. It is an anger that distinguishes right from wrong and aspires to make things right. For *all* of us, this is the energy that defines "me" and resists any and all assaults ("not me") to the fixated view of ourselves. But for a Type 1, in particular, countering the passion of Anger could be something like embracing mistakes, cultivating pleasure and ease, or otherwise coloring outside the lines or the rules. Can you imagine the tension this creates for a Type 1? If the Type 1 can interrupt the pattern and hold the "dispute" between force 1 (the control we want) and a counterforce 2 (cultivating "mess"), they can create a space within which *something more* can arise.

This new arising comes to us as a bit of a surprise from the sea of potential energy (chaos/flow) available when we don't do *the thing we always do*. In the case of Type 1, holding the passion of Anger with awareness *and* cultivating something opposite (without judgment, but without being consumed by it), opens the door to the virtue of Serenity. Serenity is the capacity to experience the ease and resilience inherent in Presence, *in the midst of* the messiness and injustice of life. From this state, it is possible to find an un-fixated way to engage with it all. We can't *make* ourselves experience this virtue, but if you trust the law, it comes as a natural unfolding of the higher heart center (connected to that underlying flow of potential) into the open space that has been created.

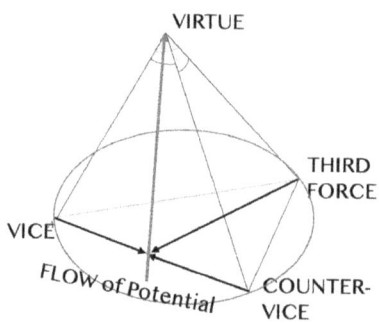

From this perspective, the virtue is not the "opposite" of the vice or passion, but rather an emergent property of the dance of three forces and the opening to higher intelligence. And because each time we work with the Law of Three in this way we build muscle for the journey of growth, it makes sense to bring the formula to bear not only on our specific Enneagram type habits, but also with all the other passions around the circle that arise and tie us to our separate, very human, and material world self, or ego. I imagine this is what the meditating Christian monks were doing in the desert. They were working with all the sins that caused them to *miss the mark* when pulled out of Presence by a temporary formulation of "self." It seems there was a method to their practice of working with all seven sins, as grappling with the paradox set up by at *each* point of the Enneagram maps a particular clockwise path of growth from ego to fully developed essence.

INTEGRATING THE LAWS OF THREE AND SEVEN

Just as the passions seem to reveal a coherent counterclockwise developmental path from birth to ego (we saw in Chapter 4), as we build third force consciousness and the Law of Three process in ourselves, we can advance along a journey of transformation (going clockwise around the Enneagram circle) that dissolves the habitual reactivity of the ego and develops our integrated essence and interconnection with *All that Is*. Making this journey requires that we learn to use the Laws of Three and Seven *together* in a complementary way. The integration of these two laws into one coherent process is another pattern that can be found by looking through diverse lenses into the process of growth

Integrating the laws of the Symbol along a longer journey is similar to a model of psychosocial development created by Erik Erikson, a renowned psychologist working in the US in the 1930s.[63] His model of eight stages of human development is eerily similar to bringing the Law of Three to bear at seven points, toward an eighth outcome (making an "octave" of growth). Each developmental stage is characterized by a "crisis" and paradox created by the tension between two "opposing" ego states. Erikson also named the new way of being that arises from the paradox a "virtue." Not a simple mix of opposing forces, the virtue is a higher-order capacity that, according to him, evolves from the creative cauldron of the two states *plus the capacity to experience and tolerate both extremes* of the life stage.

Stage	Psychosocial Crisis	Basic Virtue	Age
1	Trust vs. Mistrust	Hope	0 - 1 ½
2	Autonomy vs. Shame	Will	1 ½ - 3
3	Initiative vs. Guilt	Purpose	3 - 5
4	Industry vs. Inferiority	Competency	5 - 12
5	Identity vs. Role Confusion	Fidelity	12 - 18
6	Intimacy vs. Isolation	Love	18 - 40
7	Generativity vs. Stagnation	Care	40 - 65
8	Ego Integrity vs. Despair	Wisdom	65+

According to Erikson's model, as infants we grapple with the paradox of trust versus mistrust. A healthy resolution of these opposites transcends that duality and leads to the virtue of Hope. The successful resolution of paradox is also what enables an individual to move on to each successive stage of psychosocial development. Towards the end of life, holding the paradox of ego integrity versus despair leads to Wisdom in the healthy elder.

This pattern of how the triadic structure of Creation advances us along a developmental journey of specific steps is also one we can find in our narrative tradition. Beatrice Chestnut has made a complete study of Dante Alighieri's *Divine Comedy*, the 1321 Italian prose poem widely thought to be one of the greatest works of world literature. *La Divina Commedia* describes the afterlife, in keeping with a western Christian medieval worldview, as the soul's journey of the purgation of sin through hell and purgatory, and into the ascent towards paradise and God.

As Beatrice describes it, the progression of souls proceeds through a hierarchical process that is virtually the same as the "sins" or passions of the Enneagram. As with our individual Enneagram type's passion, one particular sin requires much longer and harder purgation for justice to be served. But it seems that each soul must still purge each sin, and find its related virtue, in order to ascend to the next level of work. Added together, these steps apply the Law of Three and move through a coherent pattern of seven steps to restore "paradise" or the integration of all parts as One. This progression leads us into to the third law of the process unfolding through the Enneagram Symbol, the Law of Seven.

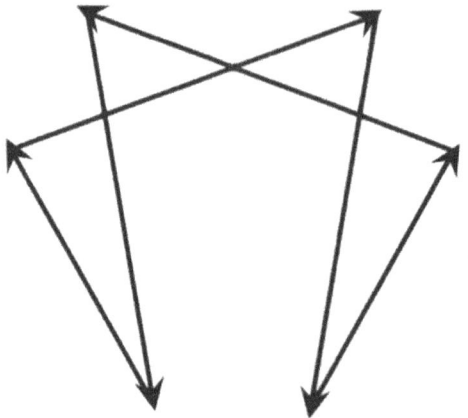

THE LAW OF SEVEN

CHAPTER SIX

THE LAW OF SEVEN

Everything in the universe, from solar systems to man, and from man to atom, is always either rising or falling, evolving or degenerating, developing or decaying. Nothing evolves mechanically, and that which cannot evolve consciously has to degenerate.[64]

~ G.I. GURDJIEFF

THE LAW OF THREE REVEALS the dynamic structure of the One original Source in the created world, and how that magical triad enables everything created to do its own creating, evolving into new dimensions. The Law of Seven is a law of process, a journey. It reveals the next layer of the Symbol—how something created can deconstruct and realign itself, over and over, in a process of continuous renewal and becoming more whole. It describes a more detailed version of what we read in the creation stories of Marduk and Horus: a dance of three forces that leads across dimensions toward higher being and the evolution of life.

Gurdjieff also called the Law of Seven the Law of World Maintenance because it shows how what is created maintains itself through continuous change. Gurdjieff's teaching arose out of a strong conviction that humans can play a particular role in not only the maintenance but also the *evolution* of the Universe through conscious engagement with these laws within ourselves. In this sense, self-development is our greatest duty. While we may just be trying to suffer a bit less, be better people, and find some meaning in this existence, in Gurdjieff's complex cosmology, our inner work and how we show up and engage in this life matters on a much larger scale. Learning how to do this requires that we understand the Law of Seven; it is not exactly as it seems.

The hexad shape in the Enneagram Symbol, often drawn with arrow lines to illustrate the dynamic flow of energy, is generally taught as a representation of the Law of Seven. If we divide one into seven equal parts ($1 \div 7 = .142857$), the result reveals the non-linear progression through the arrow lines that proceeds through six points (1-4-2-8-5-7) and resolves and returns at the seventh step of point 1, the start of a new cycle. However, Gurdjieff also referred to the Law of Seven as the Law of Octaves, and he mapped the numbers around the outside of the Enneagram circle, starting at point 9 with notes of the music scale or "octave" of music: Do-Re-Mi-Fa-Sol-La-Si-Do.[65] The path around the Symbol travels through seven points (9-1-2-4-5-7-8) making seven un-equal intervals, that resolve at the *eighth* step, point 9 again. Both versions—the hexad and the octave—skip points 3 and 6 on the inner triangle (more on this later).

THE LAW OF SEVEN – TWO WAYS

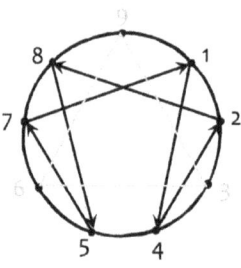

THE HEXAD

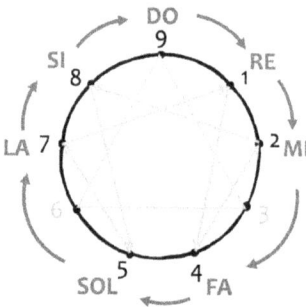

THE OCTAVE OF DEVELOPMENT

So why is the Law of Seven depicted in two ways? If the Symbol is a map, this seems like a really important issue to sort out. The short answer is that—just like two opposing forces in the Law of Three—these two routes represent two lines of effort in our inner work that are different but engaged simultaneously: "the line of knowledge" and "the line of being."[66] We often use the arrow lines to plan developmental steps when working with the Enneagram of Personality. However, a deeper look at the laws suggests that the hexad lines are not meant to be followed alone. Rather, they reveal a natural inner process that is meant to be heeded *while* we follow the octave of development around the circle. The result of that integrative journey combines the Laws of Three and Seven and culminates in the realization of Unity promised in the map. It also leads to a three-dimensional version of the Enneagram Symbol.

In the previous chapter we talked about the 3D triangle or tetrahedron as a representation of the way the One manifests in Creation via three roles or forces. We might say that as the One becomes three elements in the created world, the original creative divine spark gets "trapped" in matter, and this 3D figure is flattened into a triangle. Our job, then, is to build our fixed triangle into a creative vehicle that can help us realize our higher selves and interconnectedness with *All that Is,* and thereby elevate life on this plane.

This effort is made manifest through the "octave" of development in, not just one, but two tetrahedrons. The double tetrahedron or "star tetrahedron" is also known as *the Merkaba.* If you were again standing at the zero point, at the top of the sphere and looking down, you would see seven points—for a total of eight, including the point you are standing on. But we do not see this 3D shape in our flat rendition of the Enneagram Symbol because it represents dimensions of ourselves that are un-manifest at our current level of consciousness.

The Merkaba is described as a vehicle for ascending to higher consciousness. Threads of this idea extend from sacred geometry, ancient Egypt, Ezekial's vision of God's chariot in the Old Testament, even the Hindu *Rig Veda,* dating back to 1900 BCE. The word *Merkaba* means "chariot" in Hebrew. Some translate Mer-Ka-Ba as "light-spirit-body." From the Egyptian: "Mer" is a pyramid or place of *ascendence,* also associated with wisdom (*mer-rekh* is a lover of wisdom); "Ka" is an aspect of the soul close to the body, sometimes called the spirit twin that carries the spark of the divine; "Ba" is the celestial or traveling aspect of soul, most often understood as the soul itself, that connects the Ka to the body.[67] If we add that up, Merkaba means something like a temple of soul and spirit that "conveys" one toward wisdom, or a vehicle for ascension (a soul) that connects body and spirit with the Divine.

We work to build this "soul vehicle" or Merkaba by actualizing the Laws of Three and Seven within us. In doing so, we also realize (make real) the One Unity through our own higher being and consciousness in the manifest world. We can think of this figure as an expansion of the original mind-heart-body triangle into an integrated and embodied vessel for higher centers of intelligence (higher heart and higher mind) not yet available to us. In other traditions, this vehicle might be understood as a representation of body-soul-spirit that enfolds the lower centers of intelligence. We will explore how all this might come together in the coming pages.

SEVEN STEPS AS SEVEN LEVELS OF CONSCIOUSNESS

The concept of a "vertical" process of development, or ladder to higher consciousness, can be found across diverse wisdom traditions. Certain forms of Sufism, Hinduism, Gnostic Christianity, and Kabbalistic teachings all share a model of passing through increasing levels of consciousness on the journey to awakening or union with the Divine. This is similar to the progression depicted in Dante's journey in *The Divine Comedy* through hell and purgatory to paradise. While the number of levels varies, many spiritual traditions allude to there being seven stages or passages to higher consciousness (the eighth).

This coincidence of seven could reflect the fact that in symbolic language the number seven signifies a complete process. At the same time, the coincidence of seven reaches far and wide. Black Elk spoke of seven traditional Sioux rites or ways of union with the Father/Great Spirit and Mother Earth, that is at the heart of the spiritual life of many North American indigenous peoples. The Integral Yoga of Sri Aurobindo posits seven planes through which the consciousness of Brahman devolves into matter, creating seven stations of ascension or return to the Divine as the eighth step. Buddha took seven steps facing north when he awoke, foreshadowing his formula of seven steps to enlightenment along the Eightfold Path, the eighth step being arrival at pure or "non-dual" consciousness, a union with *All That Is.*

On pilgrimage to Mecca, Muslims circle the *Kaaba* at the center of the Great Mosque seven times, as did the prophet Mohammad, which parallels the pilgrimage to seek refuge in the inner *Kaaba,* an interior center that embraces the *Throne of God.*[68] St. Teresa of Avila described seven rooms of an interior castle one must pass through to reach the eighth central place, where the Divine dwells in the soul. Jesus lifted seven "demons" from Mary Magdalene, which scholar and priest Cynthia Bourgeault describes as seven "climates" through which Mary traveled to transcend ego and fully embody the teachings of Jesus. Jesus himself performed seven miracles and describes himself with seven different "I am" names. There are seven sacraments of the church. And, of course, in the Christian creation story God made the world in seven days.

A version of this seven-step process of transformation was laid down in the Emerald Tablet, a mysterious "document" supposedly etched in stone, and unearthed in ancient Greece (3rd century BCE) at a time and place in which major lines of religious thought intermingled.[69] The author is said to be Hermes Trismegistus, *the thrice great* Hermes. Hermes was a Greek god purported to move "between worlds" or dimensions of reality. *Thrice great* may be a nod to how the triadic nature of reality avails us of new dimensions. The Tablet is also linked to another such vertical way-shower, the Egyptian god Thoth, whose legendary existence extends back to pre-sand Egypt (circa 8000 BCE).

Whatever the true story of the Emerald Tablet's origins, most people have heard of its signature formula: "As Above, so Below." The full text of the Tablet is not only a statement of a Law of One premise—that all the laws of the cosmos can be found in a single atom—it also contains a recipe for linking the Above and Below, realizing spirit in the material realm...in seven steps. Those steps became the backbone of the "science" of alchemy.[70] Gurdjieff referenced the Emerald Tablet as a symbol of universal knowledge on par with the Enneagram, even calling the Enneagram itself "the philosopher's stone," which is the goal of alchemy and the vehicle for refining or *spiritualizing* matter and achieving eternal life.[71] Because of its overlap with the Enneagram and with many diverse wisdom traditions, we will use the alchemical formula to help us understand the mystery of this octave of development as we explore the journey around the Symbol.

One more way to think about the progression of seven comes from the Hindu depiction of seven *chakras* or energy centers along the spine and into the brain. Each center corresponds to a concentration of nerves, chemicals, and hormones, related to different body systems, and together they conduct energy and information through a central channel up and down our being.[72] If a center is undeveloped, intelligence of a particular frequency is blocked, which manifests as specific emotional, physical, and psychological symptoms, as well as a disruption in the flow of the intelligence and life energy (*prana* or *chi* in Eastern medicine) that connects us to *All that Is*. Releasing fixated patterns allows more energy and intelligence to flow, raising integration and health within the center and beyond. As more centers are attuned and aligned, increasingly higher-frequency energy moves through our system, gradually raising our consciousness and connectedness with higher-frequency realms.

Gurdjieff described the seven points up and down the spine as "crystallizations" of the original three forces trapped in matter. As fragments of our primary centers of intelligence, these seven crystallizations "deflect" and distort the natural flow of intelligence that would otherwise flow through us. At the same time, these fragments still serve as "receivers" and "transmitters" of energy, so they are responsible for much of the automatic reactivity that is literally wired into our bodies in what we call the subconscious or unconscious. In the Gurdjieff framework too, as we release old patterns and invite new intelligence, an increasingly higher vibration or higher frequency energy can move through the system.

MAKING HARMONIOUS MUSIC

Because Gurdjieff knew back in his day what modern string theory in physics has proposed—that all matter consists of tiny vibrating strings of energy—he described the seven step path of growth around the circle as a hierarchical progression of the speed of vibration, from low frequency to high frequency, using the music scale. The eighth and final note of the sequence "Do" is double the frequency of the initial "Do." It, in turn, serves to kick off the next octave and seven-step process of growth.

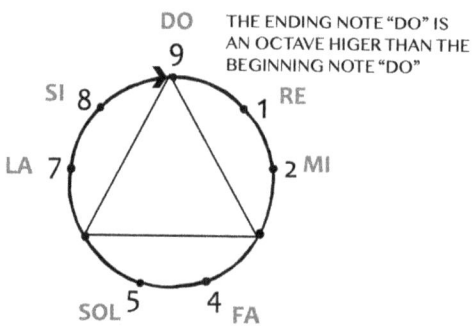

GURDJIEFF'S "OCTAVE" OF GROWTH

The Law of Seven marked around the circle, then, concerns the *rate of increase* in frequency or vibration across a period in which vibrations are doubled. On the continuum of materiality, the movement is from dense matter (low frequency) through increasingly less dense matter into energy (high frequency). This same sequence of change applies to all kinds of vibrations: light, heat, chemical, magnetic, and also sound vibrations.[73] So this seven-step progression in frequency should, theoretically, describe an evolutionary process occurring in any living system, whether through energy centers up the spine, dimensions of consciousness within, or across dimensions of the cosmos. This is one explanation, anyway, for how there could be a "universal" process of unfolding captured by diverse disciplines that occurs at various levels of observation.

Long before Gurdjieff was born, music was used to explain the "harmony" of the cosmos. Keeping in mind that evolution through degrees of frequency *might* be literal, it's also true that the *metaphor* of music is helpful in explaining the two lines of inner work: *the line of being* that proceeds around the circle and the *line of knowing* that unfolds through the hexad shape. The combination of these layers of work is necessary to "make music," or achieve harmonious development. In playing music, it's best to have access to all the notes of the music scale. More notes make for greater complexity and harmony. But we don't just play the notes in sequence up the octave. We need to mix them up to create an interesting and coherent musical story. If we use the notes in too orderly a fashion, the song is boring; if we mix them up chaotically, the music is intolerable. So in addition to "gathering" the notes for use, we need to work with the "theory," or rules for combining tones, that allows us to create something harmonious and moving.

With regard to our inner work, on the one hand, *seven* refers to points or fragments of our intelligence centers, as "notes" we must collect while moving *around* the circle of our being. Each of these notes is marked by a vice or sin—those unconscious passions that cause us to "miss the mark" of our essential self—so in moving around the circle, we are freeing, healing, and integrating these disjointed fragments of ourselves into a coherent whole that allows for a better flow of energy, health, and more conscious being. While the point of our Enneagram type will be the hardest to clear and collect, we also have to integrate all the other points to make good music.

On the other hand, as we are developing our *being* by reintegrating notes around the circle, the progression shown by the hexad figure defines certain built-in constraints (the "theory") we must heed in order to make meaningful music, so to speak. Knowing how and when to combine the notes is part of the art of the journey that helps to restore "harmony" to the dis-jointed aspects of ourselves and the world. This process of incorporating the lines of the hexad figure opens a "vertical" dimension of the Symbol related to a higher kind of *knowing*. At a certain point (when we have gathered enough notes), this aspect of making music can be layered in. Like the notes and the theory of music, these are two different but essential aspects that must be combined to create the symphony of our higher self or soul in harmony with the cosmos.

As discussed in the chapter on the Law of One, in the Sufi approach to the Enneagram, the hexad figure is called the "line of spirit." It is also the "line of change," the natural flow of life carving a zig-zag path, shaping something out of the void or space of possibility that is the area of the circle, our soul. When we are not aware and participating in this process, the line of spirit will carve that soul space according to natural law. Spiritual alchemy, on the other hand, unfolds when we do the work of consciously incorporating the line of spirit *along the soul's journey* to return us to center—the zero point from which all proceeds and to which all returns. In order to consciously engage in this way, we need to collect all the "notes" or fragments of soul around the circle, but we also need to know when and how to work with the "theory," the natural process of change depicted in the line of spirit. This evolutionary path does not follow the hexad line of spirit, but it prepares us to engage with that line along the circular journey.

This is where the inner triangle of the Enneagram Symbol comes in. The triangle penetrates the hexad lines at key places on the journey around the circle, creating "openings" and opportunity for new information (from outside the pattern) to evolve the system beyond the natural line of change. In the S-curves diagrams, we saw how integrating new information can change the sequential process of growing then dying by integrating some chaos at the right moment, which is in the gap between curves, or the point of greatest tension between the ordering force and the force that drives toward chaos and death. Because of this opposition, a third force is required to reconcile the tension between forces. When it is present, new intelligence can be integrated, and a Way can be forged, that changes course and leads to higher-order growth.

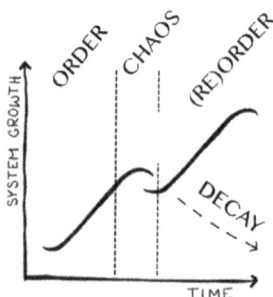

On the Enneagram, these moments of greatest tension between forces are represented by points 3 and 6 of the inner triangle (and 9, but we will get to that later). Gurdjieff called them shock points, and they are important places where the Law of Seven can work with the Law of Three. He taught that with specific inner work at these shock points (which requires developing an integrated three-centered Presence) we can take an evolutionary growth path around the circle, that engages the hexad line of spirit, to complete the "octave" of growth.

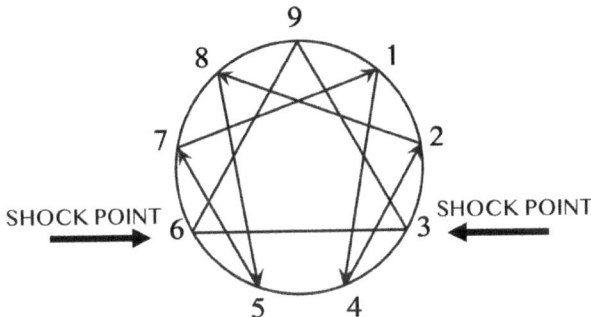

In part 3 of this book, we will further explore the two lines of development and how the laws come together to realize the promise of the Symbol. However, since a central premise of the Enneagram is that true *understanding* depends on our experience of being, we must first travel the integrative path on a journey of our own through part 2 of the book. Gurdjieff said: "In trying to understand the Law of Octaves, it is important to avoid too much theorizing. We have to understand and feel this law in ourselves. Only then will we be able to see it operating outside ourselves."[74] But because knowledge and being must grow *in tandem* to acquire lived understanding (wisdom), some theory has been necessary to orient you to the heroic journey ahead. I introduced the shock points here to help you imagine a very important threshold line on this journey that runs through the openings at points 3 and 6.

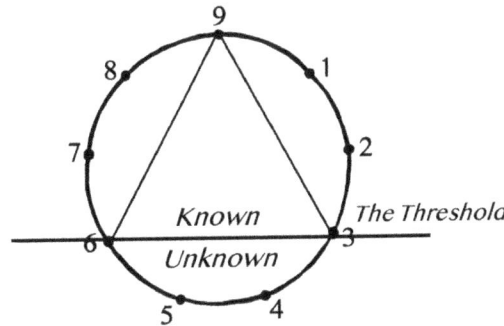

This threshold marks the points of greatest tension between the forces of order and chaos, in this case symbolized by a hero's descent from the known world into unknown terrain and back, as we move around the circle clockwise from point 9. Psychologically, this threshold crossing represents a movement from the known world of ego/personality, into the unknown aspects of our unconscious, and through a vast realm of possibility that we are missing in our devotion to habitual ways of operating. Spiritually the threshold signifies a transition between matter and spirit, between human and divine or transpersonal realms. Traveling between worlds is a concept shared across cultures, as it is the nature of life to move between *order* or the known world and *chaos/flow* or the unknown.

Joseph Campbell called this threshold "the existent non-existent line" between the everyday world and the world of adventure, across which a hero travels on the journey. Given the universal nature of the themes we are working with, perhaps it is not surprising that Campbell's summary of the enduring mythological pattern of adventure will be our guide to this process. And like the Enneagram Symbol itself, at the center of this narrative pattern is the Law of Three truth that transformative growth comes through paradox and sacrifice. We are meant to leave ourselves, our habits, and our cherished notions, at times, and embrace the unknown. On this journey, we meet "the other." We are seriously challenged. Some part of us is always sacrificed, but in that fire a hero is forged who can restore peace and unity in the kingdom. Now all we need is a potential hero to go on the journey of harmonizing order and chaos that is the work of a third or reconciling force, unfolding through the Law of Seven, to reveal the octave of growth.

PART 2:
THE HERO'S JOURNEY

THE ENNEAGRAM HERO'S JOURNEY

RETURN

SEPARATION

HARMONY IN THE KINGDOM

9

FREEDOM TO LIVE 8

1 TROUBLE IN THE KINGDOM

MASTER OF TWO WORLDS 7

2 THE CALL TO ADVENTURE

THE RETURN THRESHOLD
Rescue from Without 6

Known
Unknown

3 CROSSING THE THRESHOLD
The Road of Trials

APOTHEOSIS 5

4 THE ABYSS

VOID

INITIATION

CHAPTER SEVEN

INTRODUCTION TO THE HERO'S JOURNEY

The aim of 'myths' and 'symbols' was to reach man's higher centers, to transmit to him ideas inaccessible to the intellect and to transmit them in such forms as would exclude the possibility of false interpretations. 'Myths' were designed for the higher emotional center; 'symbols' for the higher thinking center.[75]

~ G.I. GURDJIEFF

THE POWER OF STORIES is that they point to the mysterious *unknown*—rich places beyond logic and *the known*—as well as to other ways of *knowing*. Along with Joseph Campbell, Carl Jung, and many ancient and indigenous cultures, Gurdjieff used allegory and symbolism to teach. He said both myth and symbol speak directly to essence. They convey concepts and layers of possibility that resonate with wisdom about reality that is already lodged deep in our being via our experience of universal patterns, within and around us. And because of this, they invite us deeper into ourselves to discover how these things actually work within us.

The hero's journey narrative, like the laws of the Symbol, maps such universal wisdom. It has been repeated in so many of our enduring stories: myths, religious stories, and creation stories, because it resonates within us as a true pattern at the heart of life; it is an *archetypal* pattern. An archetype is an "original pattern," meaning it was there in the first place and continues to shape the unfolding of life. Archetypes are considered aspects of "objective consciousness," as patterns most people experience that *also* endure beyond individual human consciousness. People across cultures, from adolescents to leaders of large organizations, can find their own stories reflected in the narrative of the hero's journey. While the hero used to be played most often by boys and men, today our female heroes range from Dorothy in the *Wizard of Oz* to Katniss Everdeen in *The Hunger Games* trilogy, Princess Belle in *Beauty and the Beast*, Wonder Woman, and Captain Marvel, perhaps the most powerful Marvel Superhero in the whole bunch.[76]

The myth of the hero, in a nutshell, is a symbolic portrayal of the idea that the world can be improved through a voluntary process of sacrifice and realignment of human attitude, feeling, and action. It is the incarnation of a redemptive pattern that is alive in the world and repeated by our wisdom traditions. The path of growth and the way to a meaningful life, both, are represented in the archetype of the hero's journey. This same path can be laid out around the Enneagram Symbol, it turns out, helping to reveal the nature of the laws of the Symbol and how they can be integrated into a dynamic and coherent process of evolving greater Unity in oneself and in the world.

Just as with my initial experience with the Process Enneagram, I was riveted upon first learning from Uranio Paes about a potential development process mapped around the Enneagram.[77] But it was not until I combined the study of mythology and mythic structure with Carl Jung's work on archetypes, alchemy, and individuation, that I started to understand Gurdjieff's writing about the laws and how they unfold through the Symbol. And truth be told, the initial mash-up of these disciplines came together for me in a flash, in the middle of the night, during a retreat with Beatrice and Uranio. I am quite sure that I would not have seen the laws operating in the broader world had I not lived them through experiential work in the Symbol with these teachers.

Since the interweaving of all three laws of the Symbol is complicated, we are going to first immerse ourselves in metaphor and learn from the characters and the stories themselves. In Part 3 of the book, I will return to the theory and structure of the Symbol to consider how we might apply what we learn along the journey to our own inner work. Fortunately, you already met the main characters of this narrative pattern in the brief rendition of creation stories involving Marduk and Horus. The archetypes of the king, queen, and hero will be with us throughout the journey ahead, as symbolic expressions of the three forces of the Law of Three that create together through their triadic dance across seven dimensions of growth.

As we know from the Law of Three, the One Source first splits itself into two forces that make a third, in order to continue creating. In the stories ahead, these three forces act at many levels (as does the Law of Three) so their specific expressions vary. At the highest level, the initial context or backdrop of the story, the One becomes three as: "the known world"—order, culture, or the father archetype; "the unknown"—chaos/flow, great nature, or the mother archetype; and "the Way" of the hero—the third force as the Way to harmonize and renew life between polarizing aspects of reality to help restore Unity. This Way, the hero's journey, unfolds around the Symbol as a battle between forces of light and dark, across the backdrop of the known world and the great unknown.

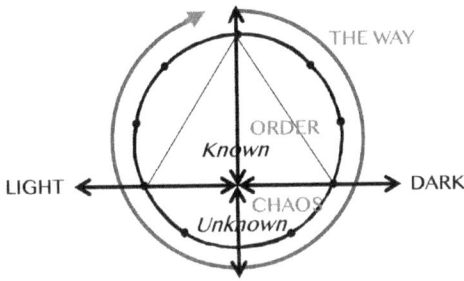

CONTEXT OF THE HERO'S JOURNEY

As we move from the backdrop into the content of the story, we will meet the three forces as actual characters: versions of the king, queen, and hero/adversary. Their dance through the Law of Seven unites the characters, transforms the protagonist into a hero, and restores harmony across the land. As the three forces materialize in the created world of the story, each is split into two parts. Creation is always a cascade into pairs of opposites. Every action has an equal and opposite reaction; every formation has its shadow. So in the myths and stories, each force has *both* a "light" and a "dark" version. Combined with the One ground of Being as the seventh aspect, this brings the total number of mythic elements to seven archetypes. They weave together throughout the journey, and they must be "collected" and integrated to restore the kingdom to Union. We will meet them as:

1. **The One.** The One represents the unity of *All that Is* in its continual dance of creation: culture/nature, spirit/matter, light/dark, conscious/unconscious, as well as the landscape behind the known and unknown worlds of the story. The One is the backdrop of the whole story and, once the kingdom or galaxy falls into disarray and polarity, it represents a future non-dual state of peace and well-being—a rest in the fighting among forces of good and evil, and between states of tyranny and chaos. The possibility of harmony is always there, but a hero is needed to help realize it. While realization of this state of coherence takes the entire journey, there is an access point through the Void at the bottom of the Enneagram Symbol. Like the original void or *chaos* from which the world was created, it is a place of utmost possibility, containing *all* the forces in their undifferentiated flow state, awaiting a divine spark of creation.

2. **The Benevolent Ruler.** The positive pole of the king or Great Father principle is the force that makes order out of chaos. It is the spirit of creation realized in a form that supports life. As territory that has already been explored—the known world—it incorporates culture, tradition, authority, and all "structures" of organization such as laws and traditions, the kingdom itself, and the walls around places like the Garden of Eden and the walled city in which the Buddha was kept safe as a boy. This element is a benevolent force that protects against the harshness and mystery of nature, chaos, and the unknown world. At another level, the positive or "awake" element of the masculine principle is personified by the wise king, father, mentor, or teacher (whether male or female), who helps the hero grow into a benevolent ruler herself.

3. **The Tyrannical King.** However, the king and kingdom can also become old and stagnant, or controlling and tyrannical, keeping out new traditions and people that might fertilize growth. Too much order, structure, and control—a rigid commitment to the known—can choke off the life and health of the community and restrict the growth of the hero. This is the "dark" or unconscious element of the masculine principle. It can be personified by a dead or worn-out king and deterioration in the kingdom as a whole, and his deterioration fuels the rise of an even darker rival, a tyrannical king, who is also often the adversary.

4. **The Dragon Queen of Chaos.** The unconscious aspect of the Great Mother is a manifestation of chaos and the unknown world that lurks outside the walls of the city (where the hero must go to grow). It can be represented as the elemental power of nature: drought and flood, a dark wood, desert, or wilderness. It shows up in specific incarnations as an evil queen, wicked witch, or another personification of the threats that arise from the Void of undifferentiated chaos (like Tiamat in the Mesopotamian creation story) when the known world has become rigid, dry, and controlling. The dark feminine is "dark" not because it is "bad," but rather because it represents what is unpredictable, unfamiliar, un-manifest, and unconscious—all things that *must* be integrated for growth. This force destroys stagnant order in service of new life.

5. **The Creative Flow of Being.** The positive pole of the Great Mother is a personification of the original chaos as the rich and fertile birthplace of all things—the ground or flow of Being. In the dark cauldron of

the Void, new elements, information, and perspectives are brewed together with the old to create a field of possibility. As it manifests in Creation, this aspect of the feminine is often symbolized by the hero discovering treasure, awakening a princess, falling in love, or otherwise integrating a divine feminine element that profoundly changes the masculine element after the journey through the Void, leading to the birth of a new level of integrative consciousness.

6. **The Adversary**. As the "child" of the king and queen's polarized dynamic, the adversary has *many* faces that attempt to keep the whole kingdom from coming into harmony, Because of this, the adversary can manifest as different characters representing the hero's involvement with either extreme of consciousness—tyranny or chaos. The adversary is often portrayed by a specific and central character, a dark shadowy figure that obstructs the hero's progress and threatens the kingdom throughout the story. But the adversary is also represented in the part of a young potential hero that refuses the call to adventure, staying comfortable at the expense of growth, and confining himself and the whole system to old patterns and the delusion that things are fine.

7. **The Hero**. The positive pole of the hero represents the awakening third force and the conscious, creative process of working with universal forces to help renew the world. The awake hero goes willingly on the journey. Aligned not with knowing but *learning*, she sacrifices herself in the chaotic unknown in order to help update what has grown stagnant in the kingdom. While the potential hero might start the journey somewhat brash and self-serving, or simply naïve, the challenges she faces deconstruct the ego kingdom and allow the emergence of a higher self, a true hero, who helps to restore harmony across the land. The hero is integrating aspects of herself and growing progressively with each new challenge (even when it looks like she's falling apart; that's part of the process), slowly making a Way to renew the kingdom.

While these are characters in the stories, our task is to hold them all as aspects of our own psyche and being. They are fragmented and polarized forces of mind, heart, and body that are initially working at odds with one another and will eventually unite under a new leader and higher self or fully developed essence. The points located at our main centers of intelligence are missing on this map because we are not present in them. They exist only in potential, or as a memory of higher forces lost. Although all of the mythic elements are constantly in play, there is one archetype featured at each point of the Enneagram and phase of the journey. It is helpful to think of them like the musical notes in an octave. Each is an important "note" that must be fully integrated to play the music that brings the One kingdom back to harmony.

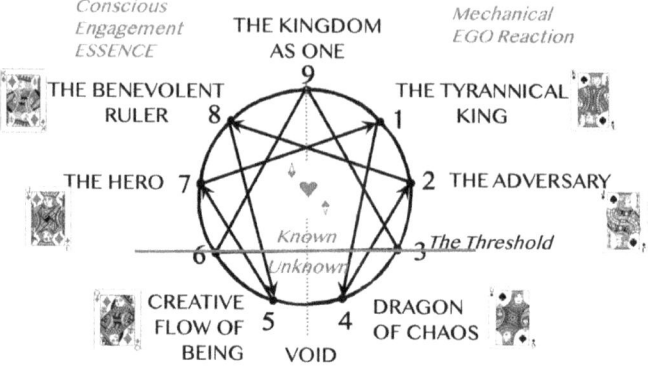

MYTHIC ARCHETYPES

Warning: by laying out the mythic elements around the Enneagram circle I am NOT saying that all Type 1s on the Enneagram are the tyrannical king and all Type 8s are the benevolent ruler, etc. First, we could easily flip the figure and place the "dark" characters on the left. And this is exactly what happens without the development of conscious being. Second, *this figure has nothing to do with personality types.* It represents fragmented aspects of one individual psyche, as well as forces that pervade all levels of life, within and around us. When thinking about the "positive" and "negative" aspects of the characters it is helpful to think about the +/- poles on a battery. Both are necessary to create energy, motion, and light. The "negative" pole of each element is just as essential to the formation of the hero and the evolution of the community. So as much as we might shrink from or rage at "dark" characters such as Scar in *The Lion King* or Voldemort in the Harry Potter series, we need them. Our heroes and kingdoms truly could not evolve without "counterforces" to help deconstruct the ego and cause growth and change.

As our stories unfold, we travel clockwise from 9 to 9, from dark to light, from ego to essence and conscious engagement. At one level, we will be tracking the hero and her adversary, particular passions she must encounter and integrate all along the way to become whole. This is the human and horizontal layer of work I call *gathering the notes*. At another level, we will be working with a non-linear relationship between the three forces (as king, queen, and hero/adversary) that is unfolding through the seven points of the arrow lines. On the first half of the journey (the right side), the forces are trapped in patterns that fuel the ego structure with a strong push-pull between them. On the second half of the journey, the forces are more able to harmonize within and between themselves to combine tones and open the spiritual or vertical layer of growth towards a fully integrated soul or essence in the Symbol.

As we follow these archetypes throughout the journey, it will be most helpful to let the characters unfold and reveal their dance, rather than trying to pin down their exact meaning. Their representations vary depending upon the level of analysis, because we are tracking ideas or energies for which the characters and story elements are merely symbols. In describing the symbolic nature of the mythic stories and characters, Joseph Campbell wrote: "And so, to grasp the full value of the mythological figures that have come down to us, we must understand that they are not only symptoms of the unconscious...but also controlled and intended statements of certain spiritual principles, which have remained as constant throughout the course of human history as the form and nervous structure of the human physique itself."[78]

Campbell believed that the power of myth was in helping our normally limited minds make the leap into the unconscious and through the transpersonal realm to reunion with a field of wisdom much greater than ourselves or any one moment in history. These characters and stories, as symbols, teach at many levels, some beyond our rational minds. Because of this, Gurdjieff taught that learning from symbolism requires a different kind of listening: "To be able to understand speech when it becomes symbolical it is essential to have learned before and to know already how to listen. Any attempt to understand literally, where speech deals with objective knowledge and with the union of diversity and unity, is doomed to failure beforehand and leads in most cases to further delusions."[79]

Ultimately, we have to turn within, where the stories and characters resonate with a deeper level of our being, in order to grasp the nature of what is being transmitted through these stories. So if you can enjoy the ride through story and symbolism without excessive analysis, listening to what resonates and noticing your own reflection in the mirror, you will gain greater understanding of the laws of the Symbol and how they might underlie your developmental journey.

STAGES OF THE JOURNEY

Joseph Campbell broke the hero's journey into 17 steps over three stages: Separation (from the known world), Initiation (in the unknown), and Return (to enable a new known). In order to stay consistent with the psycho-spiritual journey, including seven stages of development, the space between points 4 and 5 (the Void), and the shock points (at the threshold between worlds), I highlight 10 steps on this map of the Symbol: the 9 points of the Enneagram plus the Void, which is also an opening into the primordial chaos and singular ground of all Being as the background of the world.

THE ENNEAGRAM HERO'S JOURNEY

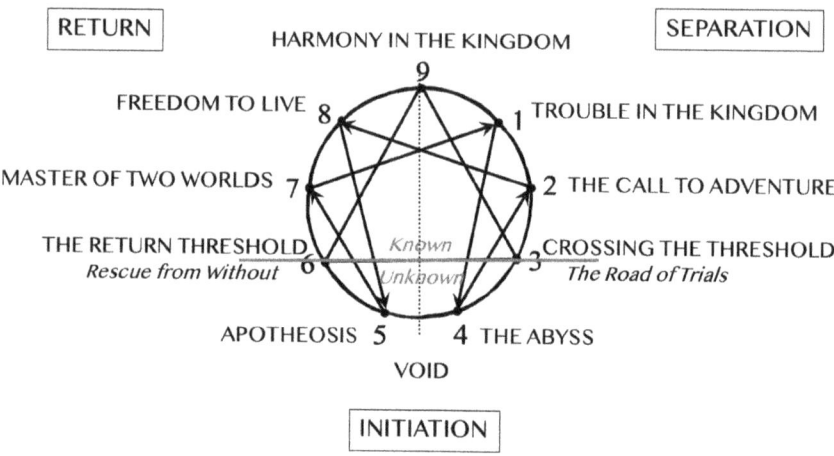

Because a story is a symbolic representation, like art, or the Enneagram itself, we may have different interpretations of its meaning, but the essential nature of the transformative journey shines through. And while I will walk through the stages sequentially, no journey follows a linear path. Each hero's experience is unique. The stories we will cover are the adventures of wizards and aliens, kings, and princesses, talking animals and superheroes, in magical and make-believe worlds. I will use relatively modern stories, from Disney favorites to *Harry Potter* and *Game of Thrones*, to show you how these patterns surround us and populate our adult imagination as well as our childhood fantasies. It won't matter if you don't know a particular story, as I will share enough detail to give you a sense of the character's journey, and I will use multiple examples at each stage in hopes that at least one might resonate with you.

While all the hero stories describe adventures in the world, they also reveal a pattern of inner work that maps to the Enneagram Symbol and has been described by many enduring wisdom traditions, depth psychology, and other consciousness-raising disciplines. At the same time, as we will see from our heroes, that work is in service of making not just our own lives, but also the world, a more peaceful place. As Campbell says: "The Passage of the mythological hero may be over-ground, incidentally; fundamentally it is inward—into the depths where obscure resistances are overcome, and long lost, forgotten powers are revivified, to be made available for the transfiguration of the world."[80]

SEPARATION

The separation stage of the journey is a preparatory stage before the hero heads into adventure in the unknown world. This stage features first an introduction to the known world and the shaping of the hero in response to his history, tradition, and culture. It marks the development of ego/personality in Enneagram terms. From there, we move on to the hero's dawning awareness that the bounds of her current world are both too tight and too vulnerable to the great mystery beyond the known. One way or another the hero comes to sense that the known world can never sustain her. As threats to the kingdom (the hero's known world) intensify, the hero faces a pivotal choice: to refuse the call to adventure and stay safe or go willingly into the unknown.

What we learn in this stage is that growth necessitates sacrifice. To sacrifice something of value today is always the price for achieving something greater in the future. The price of remembering our soul or essence is no less than our cherished ego, the part of us driven to be separate, central, safe, and in control. This is the very part of us that helped us survive or thrive as a child. For this reason, the separation stage is not always quick or straightforward. We often hesitate, preferring comfort and familiar personality patterns to heeding the growing split between *who we are* and *who we could be* and following the call to adventure. In this way, the separation stage can be a process of fits and starts, feeling drawn to change but missing the mark. We can go back and forth for years, or forever really, fleeing back to comfort, the small self, and what keeps our ego intact—until we find ourselves at the true threshold of the unknown.

HARMONY IN THE KINGDOM
The Everyday World

9
8   1
7   2
6   3
5   4

Known
Unknown

CHAPTER EIGHT

POINT 9:
Harmony in the Kingdom

At critical moments in life, we are called to remember who we are at
our core...It is easier to become lethargic and wind up sleepwalking
through life...not living the life our soul intends for us.

~ Michael Meade

ONCE UPON A TIME THE KINGDOM IS AT PEACE, THRIVING. There is an ease to the order of things. The land is fertile and plentiful, life abounds. From this richness, a baby is born to the king and queen. This is a state of Great Perfection where all is One in love—a state of equilibrium where order and flow, culture and nature, are in harmonious relationship and thriving. The potential hero both blesses and is blessed by this union, a spark of the Divine planted within it. The opening scene of *The Lion King* offers a vivid illustration of this state, as the sun comes up on a beautiful day, with Mother Earth in all her glory, and a great diversity of animals lined up peacefully, eagerly awaiting a big announcement. The scene represents the Law of One, expressing itself in unified diversity, and the Law of Three—the king, queen, and potential hero, responsible for all the diverse aspects of Being that make up the Circle of Life. Simba, the would-be hero, is both the product of the perfect union between king and queen and a key part of the solution when the kingdom falls into disarray.

At this point, the kingdom ruled by King Mufasa and Queen Sarabi, the Pride Lands, is a place full of potential, where nature's beauty abounds within the limits of the light (that creates order). Mufasa tells his son Simba that he will one day be king of this beautiful land that extends "as far as the light touches." The birthplace of the hero is often depicted as a walled garden or city, a place where the power of nature is alive but contained by the boundaries provided by culture—a harmonious balance of spirit and matter. This is in contrast to the place beyond the bounds where things are out of balance in some way. In *The Lion King*, the Outlands, a shadowy place where near drought conditions prevail exists beyond the harmony of the Pride Lands.

And yet, this point of the journey is less about the place or land itself, and more about the state of harmony between forces that characterizes it. This is the natural state of the newborn hero. Even when we meet our story heroes *after* things are out of balance in the world or galaxy, we still get glimpses of a lost state of harmony through flashbacks of their early lives. As readers, we learn before Harry Potter himself that he was born to loving parents, a Muggle (human) and a wizard, signifying the once harmonious union of diverse forces. Jon Snow of *Game of Thrones*, also unknowingly, was the product of a secret love union between historically oppositional kingdoms. Luke Skywalker lived in such balance before his mother was killed and his father fell to the dark side of the Force. All of these heroes were thrown out of a balanced "paradise" to grow up with relatives.

Point 9 on the flat Symbol represents undifferentiated consciousness and an original state of grace marked by the circle as a whole that emanates from the zero point, the point of origin at its center. Point 9 also stands for the imagined possibility of a future re-union of all parts at a higher "octave" or level of integration. In successive cycles around the Enneagram, point 9 might refer to a still point, an equilibrium in our lives after coming through a significant period of challenge and integrating new growth. When we have truly stretched into new territory, (whether behaviorally, psychologically, or spiritually) and dealt with the chaos of growth, we again rest in a balanced state—neither stagnant nor out of control.

Spiritually, point 9 marks a state of union with Source or consciousness itself, achieved after we are fully integrated and developed, in essence as our "higher" selves. It is the *alpha* and the *omega*, the point from which we arise and to which we return. It is a state we may strive for all our lives and which, paradoxically, can be experienced in a moment. This state calls to us just as "Home" calls to Dorothy when she is stuck in Oz: "There's no place like home." But to go the distance and then return Home, the hero first has to overcome Sloth.

THE PASSION OF SLOTH

The passion of Sloth at point 9 on the Enneagram is a danger to the hero at this stage. Sloth in Enneagram terms is not laziness. It is a resistance to losing inner ease, to being deeply affected by or engaged with life, particularly when it comes to unearthing our essence or soul. It is the *sin of omission*, to which we all necessarily fall prey in maintaining an ego structure rather than moving to discover who we really are. Gurdjieff named something similar, he called "self-calming," to be the number one evil and reason we don't engage in our evolutionary duty to wake up and be more on purpose with how we are operating.

The related mental habit or fixation at point 9, Self-forgetting, reinforces Sloth. Fundamentally, and for all of us, this is a forgetting of all of who we are beyond ego. We don't know and don't really want to know *who we could be* without this veil of protection. If *something more* stirs inside us but might be disruptive to our peace, we will put it aside and go back to sleep. And because we don't want to shake-up the comfort of the known, we rarely even look at our deeper self, priorities, and the necessary movement toward a higher aim. It is easier to go with the flow, stay harmonious, and stick with opinions and requirements learned from our culture and upbringing than to prioritize the journey towards essence— who we are at a deeper level.

Sloth has an adaptive function, certainly, enabling us to seem peaceful with others and with life; it leads to patience and prevents rash action. And yet, Sloth also seeds this dangerous temptation to stay fused with the known and not grow at all. The trap here is to masquerade as someone who has transcended to a peaceful or "spiritual" worldview, but never really goes on the journey to psycho-spiritual maturity. To get to Right Action and Holy Love—the higher emotional and mental gifts at point 9 that can transform life as we know it—we need to first differentiate out of this malaise. We need to have a self that is neither driven blindly by our nature, nor fused with our culture or family tradition. Some sense of self-and-other as separate is necessary, paradoxically, in finding a way to love that transcends "otherness" altogether. Somehow, we have to wake up and take action to separate.

This is not just a Type 9 thing, but a reality for all of us. In the journey stories we often find over-protective or controlling parents or relatives who want to prevent the hero from waking up and moving into an encounter with the mysterious and generative unknown outside the walls of the kingdom. In *The Lion King*, Mufasa warns Simba not to go to the shadowy place beyond the borders of the Pride Lands. Given that such a statement is guaranteed to stoke curiosity in any young would-be hero, one wonders whether the wise king understood that the making of a hero requires such a move into the dangerous unknown? His gentle discipline upon Simba and Nala's first trespass would suggest as much.

In contrast, the king and queen in *Sleeping Beauty* did everything imaginable to shelter their princess from the evil queen Maleficent (the personification of the dark feminine, chaos and the terrible unknown). As a result, a dangerous prophecy was made about spinning wheels and Sleeping Beauty's fate. And yet, the graver danger here would be for Beauty to stay fused with her parents, somehow hostage to living out their unlived lives instead of her own. So, since exactly what we avoid tends to find us, Sleeping Beauty manages to fulfill the prophecy by stumbling upon the one spinning wheel left in the kingdom (really!?). She pricks her finger and falls into a deep sleep. Tragic as it may seem, this is a step in the right direction for Beauty. Unprepared as she is to confront anything beyond her cloistered world, sleep is the way the childlike princess can pass into the mysterious unknown to grow.

Similar to Sleeping Beauty, in the story of Siddhartha the future Buddha, his father the king tries everything to keep Siddhartha behind the palace walls, safe from the harsh reality of the outside world. His father also received a prophecy: that Siddhartha would one day be either a great king or a great spiritual leader. Trying to ensure that the prince will succeed him in ruling the kingdom, the king goes to considerable lengths to make sure Siddhartha's home is filled with pleasure and comfort so he will not want to go beyond the known.

I imagine most of us contemplating the inner journey are past the point of protective parents and en-castled situations, and yet, upon closer inspection we can see how we also are defended by a mix of the forces of culture—our families, traditions, and heritage—and nature—our neuro-biological wiring, temperament, instincts, and genetics. Their initial partnership creates our personal walled garden of personality: comfortable, protective, and limiting. Limiting, because life can become boring and meaningless behind the walls. We are also at risk of committing the sin of omission, not taking action in a world where corruption haunts both within and beyond the walls. So, the hero has to grow up. And friction is essential for growth. Being thrown out of the metaphorical garden, and the subsequent development of self-consciousness, is an essential step toward our ultimate return. As the hero differentiates out of the comfortable state at point 9, the first step is to consciously inhabit her own personality.

In Enneagram terms, the virtue or higher heart center quality at point 9 is called Right Action. It is the ability of the heart to *sense* the most important action and take it, rather than avoid it and stay in Sloth. As undeveloped and unconscious potential heroes at this point, we are not yet in touch with Right Action—or rather the conscious awareness and ability it would take to choose this. All of the virtues become more accessible as we deconstruct ego later in the journey. But thankfully, the passion at point 1, Anger, can serve as a kind of antidote to Sloth in propelling us forward into the right action for us, right now, which is to become aware of the ego and personality pattern that will serve as our map back Home.

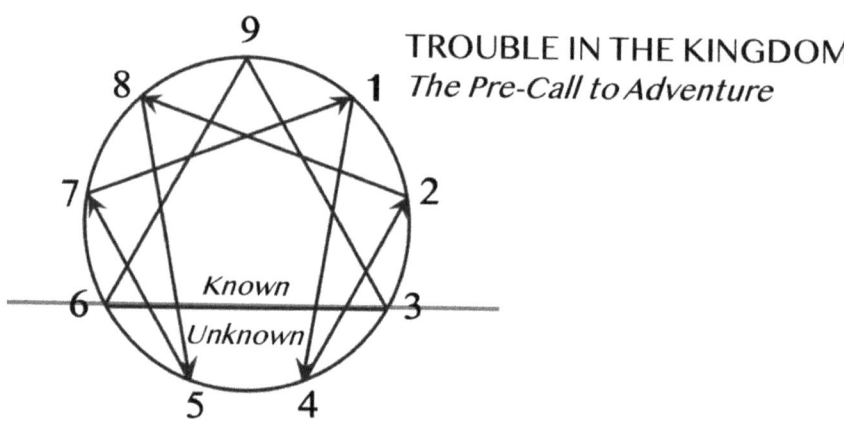

TROUBLE IN THE KINGDOM
The Pre-Call to Adventure

CHAPTER NINE

POINT 1:
TROUBLE IN THE KINGDOM

*The first half of life is devoted to forming a
healthy ego, the second half of life is going
inward and letting it go.*

~ C.G. JUNG

I N JOSEPH CAMPBELL'S ARTICULATION OF THE HERO'S JOURNEY, the first
step is the Call to Adventure where the hero experiences the draw to
leave home, often due to rising trouble in the kingdom. Starting there,
however, we miss significant aspects of the hero's early life that are relevant
for our understanding of ego development. Combining the Enneagram
with the hero's journey inserts an interim step: a prequel to the call to
adventure, or a "pre-call."

The distinction between these two steps becomes clear when we dig
into the Latin roots of the word "call." At point 1, the pre-call we receive
has its roots in the words *educare*—to train or to mold—and *educere*—to
lead out. Both are related to our modern word *education*. At point 1, the
hero is first "called out" from the state of sleep and "named" or molded in
response to his culture. In other words, he develops a personality. Later,
at point 2, the call to adventure experienced by the hero is more akin to
being "called forth," the Latin roots of which are *vocare*, which is related
to vocation or our calling in life. The hero is first called out (of undifferentiated malaise) and later called forth into the transformative adventure.
While two distinct steps, these calls are intimately connected.

We have to develop a personality type and a solid ego structure not
only to navigate the challenges of early life, but also because that personality type provides us with a map for our journey Home. Our personality
is something like our own unique version of the marriage between culture
and nature, conscious and unconscious drives. Personalizing and adapting to the forces that shape us is a necessary step in growing up. Perhaps
the ultimate example of this first call, the *call out* is the puppet Pinocchio.

He is literally created/carved out of nature (wood) by his father Geppetto, the personification of culture and the masculine principle of *order*. We quickly see that Pinocchio has a mind of his own, but it is one shaped by the constraints of both his raw material and his father's imagination.

This is easy to see in a puppet, but the dual forces of culture and nature that help shape us are revealed in people as well. The character of Jon Snow, one of the primary heroes in *Game of Thrones*, is forged in response to his genetic heritage for sure, but also is very much a factor of growing up as the (supposed) illegitimate son of Ned Stark, with five other children and a mother, Caitlyn Stark, who—while civil enough—is not happy about raising the child of another woman. Jon doesn't belong to his culture *or* his nature, given the mysterious factors surrounding his birth and heritage. And this impacts the kind of journey (through ice *and* fire) he takes toward heroism.

When we meet our heroes at point 1, their worlds are already in disarray. The shape of the hero's early losses and wounds, just like our own, figures heavily in ego development. Harry Potter, Luke Skywalker, Jon Snow, and Dorothy from Oz are examples of the many heroes who, when we meet them, are living with their uncle and aunt due to the loss of their parents (the loss of harmony at point 9). The Disney princesses Cinderella, Snow White, Ariel the Little Mermaid, and Belle from *Beauty and the Beast* were all defined in some way by the early loss of their mothers. And yet, the unique make-up of the hero's personality also serves to drive her forward, to shape the nature of the redemptive path, and it points to a central issue that will need resolution before the journey is out. So, difficult as these early circumstances may be, disorder, and the hero's response to it, is an important stage of the journey. Trouble in the kingdom fuels the passion of Anger.

THE PASSION OF ANGER

The passion of Anger at point 1 on the Enneagram is an energetic stance or orientation; an Anger *against* things that are "wrong;" a righteous resistance or movement against something that serves to define us in an alternate stance. Resentment, which is a dualistic worldview, splitting right and wrong, is the fixation or mental habit that reinforces Anger and positions us in resistance to things, both inside and outside of us. Holding fast to what's ok and not ok, "me" and "not me," is really quite stabilizing and adaptive for a kid. It helps us make choices and find our way. Having an ideal, a judgment about what "should" or "should not" be, helps the hero differentiate himself from forces that would keep him fused, and prepares him for the journey. As Carl Jung put it, the ego forms through experiencing itself *in opposition to that which it is not.*

At this pre-call stage, Anger leads to a specific "ruling principle" of character fixated on an idealized way of operating—an ego ideal represented by the archetype of the king. At the same time, the rigid insistence of *who I am* (or *should be)* causes us to disown a lot of *who I am not,* creating a "shadow" self—usually deeper feelings, memories, and instincts that have been repressed in service to the king. This shadow realm is the domain of the queen (which at this point feels only like chaos), the repression of which is depicted with the arrow line from point 1 to point 4. The tension between our inner king and queen, then, is our mini version of order and chaos. It is an echo of the original duality that emerged from the One ground of Being; the necessary paradigm of "good and evil" that got Adam and Eve thrown out of the Garden to begin the epic human journey toward re-union with God. There are two sides of every coin, and both of these forces serve to shape the hero's unique journey ahead.

The title of this step, *trouble in the kingdom,* featuring the tyrannical king, describes the unfolding of the would-be hero's development. Although developing an ego ideal is initially beneficial, its rigidity becomes limiting over time, its rules and protection against dark forces weaken. Threats start to circle. We might as likely use the words *rigid, fixed,* or *controlling,* as this aspect of the king is not always "tyrannical," but there is always a sense that what was once defining and protective is now too limiting. In some stories, the tyrannical form of order is symbolized by the adversary who sneaks in to try to disrupt or steal the kingdom from a king who is past his prime. King Mufasa's brother, Scar, has designs on the Pride Lands that are a threat to both Simba and Mufasa. In *Game of Thrones,* we can smell the sinister plans of the Lannister family as they arrive at the Stark family's compound with King Robert Baratheon, who is clearly in over his head.

As we saw in the S-curves, to stay the same is to eventually decay. In our stories, "the end of the world" or the deterioration of the kingdom is always just ahead, because what constitutes order right now is not sufficient for navigating the future. So at the same time that the old world stagnates and tyranny rises, chaos gathers outside the walls of the kingdom. Strangers and challenges arise from beyond the known as catalysts to change. A central truth of the Law of Three is that as one force (order) moves to its extreme edge (tyranny) it "attracts" the opposing action of the other force (chaos).

In *The Wizard of Oz*, the trouble brewing is similarly two-fold. Chaos is moving in as a tremendous tornado. Chaos is the natural response to a rise in tyrannical order symbolized by Almira Gulch. As the tornado moves in, Dorothy is about to run off with her dog Toto who has just escaped the nasty Almira Gulch. Mrs. Gulch tried to take Toto away and have him put down for biting her. Dorothy's personal moral code says this is wrong, and she will not sit idly by and let this happen. Of course, young as she is, this stance against tyranny puts Dorothy in conflict with her own drive to abide by the rules imposed. Asserting her personal order in the face of the adults' order calls up quite a storm in the unconscious unknown. And yet, defining herself in this way—separate from the known—indicates Dorothy's readiness to leave the kingdom and its outdated traditions and laws. She is preparing for the call *forth* to adventure coming soon.

Our heroes (as potential third force elements) arise out of this trouble and tension between tyranny and chaos to help restore the world. The "me" and "not me," defined by the passion of Anger fuels the hero's response to disorder or injustice in the known world. This resistance is vital to differentiating the hero from the normal everyday world, and it prepares her for the work ahead. Anger-against has a clarifying and defining function that does not have to manifest as "angry." Growing up with abusive relatives imprinted an inherent kindness and empathy in the likes of Harry Potter and Cinderella, while others like *Game of Throne's* Arya Stark, were strengthened and hardened by their early circumstances. It seems that everyone gets what they need to create the journey ahead.

The qualities called out of *The Hunger Games'* hero Katniss Everdeen by her early life circumstances shape her acceptance of the call forth to adventure and her journey as a whole. Due to the loss of her father (and her mother via grief), Katniss becomes a survivor: resourceful, fiercely independent, and irrationally brave. So when her younger sister Prim is chosen randomly to participate in The Hunger Games (an annual game-based fight to the death between 12 chosen young people), rather than send her sister to a sure death, Katniss volunteers herself to be the player or "tribute" and risk her life for her hometown, District 12.

It would be easy for our heroes to get stuck in the passion of Anger and then grow cynical and bitter. It would be tempting to resign and align oneself with the powers-that-be or to live a life defined by hardened opposition to conditions and people that hurt us. Really, the black-and-white thinking of our fixated ego is easier than looking into *who I am not*, in order to find out *who I could be.* But unresolved Anger-against keeps us locked into a victimized stance of blaming "the other" and resisting the journey to grow up and integrate the shadows in our *own* hearts. Katniss teeters on this brink throughout the series, given the intensity of her hatred and vengeance for her nemesis, President Snow. But the journey eventually does the work of deconstructing her ego, even as she pursues Snow, so that Katniss may eventually contribute to true healing in herself and her world.

This is not to say that Katniss's hurt, anger, and drive for retributive justice is not valid or necessary at all. Indeed, it contributes to important aspects of her character. And yet, we can see that the seeds of her ego structure also control, limit, and sometimes torture her. Even without knowing the full story, we can see that she will need something different within to sustain her work toward a better future (one she can't yet see). When we stay fully aligned with our ego at point 1, it does not occur to us that there is another way for us to be. We think life happens TO us. We have been shaped by, and are held hostage to, mechanical forces—unconscious, cultural, instinctual. The spark of our essential intelligence can get frozen by rigid patterns just when life needs us to wake up.

Creating walls defines a secure position, but it also walls off adaptive information (and people). Through our definition of a right way, we condemn others as well as aspects of ourselves; we reinforce fragmentation and separation. If health is wholeness, healing cannot proceed. And yet, at the center of life, there is this inherent drive toward union. So while the passion of Anger draws our heroes out of Sloth, none of them get stuck there...or they would not be heroes. The virtue at point 1, Serenity, is an aspect of being in the higher heart that arises from a sense of our fundamental wholeness and interconnectedness with all things. Serenity does not mean everything in our material existence is perfect, but rather speaks to being in touch with an unseen level of reality in which all diverse qualities intermingle as the same united ground of Being, or the *flow* of Creation. At some level, we are always and already whole. And when we relax into that, we become receptive to a greater intelligence, beyond our ego's limited perspective, that allows us to navigate challenge more calmly and skillfully.

However, since Serenity is not yet fully forged at this stage of the journey, what helps to drive the hero forward from point 1 is the passion at point 2, Pride. This is the hero's sense of their personal promise to become *something more* for others and the world. Eventually, Katniss, Luke Skywalker, and all our heroes follow Pride to experience the call forth to adventure and move deeper into the journey through which they are profoundly changed. In this process, they take themselves apart rather than only blaming the "enemy" and creating further polarization and pain. Following the heroic path, they eventually grow stronger or softer, more integrated, conscious, and less impulsive; they find "the Force" within or their magical ruby slippers that can help them save the kingdom and take them Home. But remarkably, the seeds for this transformative process are planted in the call out—the consciousness of our Enneagram personality type at point 1.

INNER WORK OF THE PRE-CALL TO ADVENTURE

When we arrive at point 1 on the Enneagram, we have fallen away from Source and have developed one of nine personality types described by the Enneagram of Personality. The ego/personality we develop is a defensive structure, a helpful but ultimately misguided attempt to mimic our essential selves and what we lost upon leaving the Great Perfection of our early life in Union. Because of our very specific loss, our personality type leaves an essence-shaped hole as a kind of road map back to this place of knowing ourselves again as whole, integrated in community, and One with Source.

As we saw in the developmental journey from birth mapped in chapter 4, the step from point 9 to point 1 on the Process Enneagram is a *counterclockwise* movement all the way around the circle. Along the way, we pass through our initial encounters with nature and culture to become separate little beings managing the tension of being a self, with its various drives and needs, and being in-relation-to others in a way that meets approval (or not). Somehow with our little divine spark, we navigate that tightrope to form an ego or personality type. We become a "me," a constellated point, formed out of the vast wave of possibility that is relegated to "not me."

The length of that journey makes sense if you consider all the biological and cultural forces that conspire to shape who we take ourselves to be in the early part of life. The long journey away from union with Source equips us with an amnesia about the pain of disconnection, and it prepares us to cope with life outside the comfort of point 9. For these reasons, it is easier to remain at point 1, rigidly committed to the personality—and indeed many people do. At point 1 we are not aware of anything other than who we take ourselves to be, and we will stay there until or unless we heed the call forth to adventure at point 2.

The development of a strong ego structure is an essential process for the first part of life. I have seen people open up to unconscious contents and higher states of awareness without this, and it can be very destructive. It is good to have a strong enough *walled garden* to run back to (like Prince Siddhartha had with his protected castle) when we first venture outside the walls. The ordering force of our personality structure is benevolent when it is flexible and allows new information and growth. As with the story heroes, appreciating our gifts—and how they have been shaped as an adaptive response to early life—is helpful as we begin the journey at point 1. As Susan Olesek and friends at the Enneagram Prison Project describe it, each Enneagram type, with its ego ideal, comes to teach us about important things:[81]

With their ego ideal of being right and good, **Type 1s** come to teach about goodness, truth, and how the world *could be* in their efforts to compensate for a lost goodness within and sense of perfection in our messy world.

With their ego ideal of being loving and giving, **Type 2s** come to teach about love and attending to others in their efforts to re-connect with a lost sense that love is always already available and needs will be met.

With their ego ideal of being valuable and successful, **Type 3s** come to teach about developing, improving, and shining in their efforts to re-create a lost sense of their inherent worth and that life unfolds as it should.

With their ego ideal of being unique and special, **Type 4s** come to teach about authenticity and what matters, beyond the obvious, in their efforts to discover a lost sense of significance—that we all belong and are all originals.

With their ego ideal of being knowledgeable and competent, **Type 5s** come to teach the value of non-attachment and a depth of knowledge, in their efforts to shore up energy and protect against a lost sense of the benevolence and abundance of love available.

With their ego ideal of being loyal and secure, **Type 6s** come to teach about awake attention, about loyalty and commitment, in their efforts to create safety and certainty in the face of a lost faith in life and their own inherent capacity.

With their ego ideal of being unlimited and ok, **Type 7s** come to teach about freedom, joy, and flexibility, in their efforts to create options for themselves and others in the face of a lost sense there is a wise plan and suffering will end.

With their ego ideal of being strong and invulnerable, **Type 8s** come to teach about aliveness, immediacy, and personal responsibility, in their efforts to assert control and justice due to a lost sense that there is an inherent balance in the cycles of life, and that they will be ok.

With their ego ideal of being peaceful and harmonious, **Type 9s** come to teach about peace, patience, and acceptance, in their efforts to maintain harmony due to a lost sense of being a connected and essential part of the unfolding of life.

Looked at through this lens, the development of ego structure and Enneagram type is a necessary process of creating order out of the chaos of being. The king or ordering force is that which brings structure and makes sense, an organizing principle. For us, it is first an affirming force, ruling our type's experience and expression in the world. We are constantly making sense of the chaotic nature of our existence through pre-existing frames of reference and ongoing narratives. With billions of bits of information coming our way, we have to organize and interpret them in some way. So, life happens, and then thanks to our type structure, we select and attend to certain aspects, we have reactions, and then we tell ourselves a story about it all. The nature of those stories, in large part, create our experience.

In fact, all three of our primary centers of intelligence (mind, heart, and body) are programmed by our wiring and patterns learned in childhood, and we remain controlled by their action. When we are talking about "habits" and "programming," it means that our past has become embedded in our present way of being and, literally, in our brain and biology. Our Enneagram style describes a particular way in which, deep in our wiring, we are automatically attached to some ways of being and reject others, confining ourselves to a dualistic code that is always agreeing and disagreeing, liking and disliking, moving toward pleasure and away from pain. And while this set-up evolved to protect us, it obscures our inherent wholeness and confines us to the land of duality and separation. We are like Pinocchio, a wooden puppet controlled by the "strings of the father" or the "ruling principle" of our ego structure.

Tyranny as top-down control is an apt way to think about the ruling aspect of ego when it is operating in us without awareness. In time, our type strategy becomes a "denying" force in that it limits our capacity to see reality as it truly is. It not only controls us, but also it obscures our essential self, who we really are (or could be) when we are *not* trying to re-create a false version through effortful egoic action. Ultimately, the king upon whom we relied for so many years—a symbol of our commitment to an idealized version of the small self that strives for significance, safety, or control—becomes the exact thing that prevents our growth.

The good news about the tyranny of ego is that it has a way of burning itself out. In alchemy this first phase in the process of transformation is called *calcination*. It applies heat to decompose the initial substance used in the work, and it is often symbolized by an old king turning to ashes. The landscape of the self becomes dry when too much of the elemental power of the instinct and spontaneity of the heart are locked out; tyranny always invites rebellion. As a consequence, we can become equally controlled by the disowned parts of ourselves that rise up from the unconscious sea of chaos below. This means the would-be hero is set up against the dual threats of possession by both the metaphorical Evil Empire seeking to control and the Beast within, seeking to devour him.

What do I mean by that? If I have a particular strategy for well-being, such as to be pleasing and needed at Type 2, this strategy will naturally have two allies who work to maintain it. There is an inner tyrant who will make sure I stick to the plan to be pleasing and helpful, and who will criticize any deviance. And, too, there is an inner chaos dragon who is actually "attracted," from time to time, by the over-control of the tyrant. I might rebel from discipline by over-indulging my own (unhealthy) needs or becoming really unpleasant with those who don't appreciate my efforts. So tyranny not only chokes off the exploration and diversity required for growth, but also it invites sneaky serpents within. Then this little vacation from my ego ideal serves to reinforce the king's drive, so the push-pull between order and chaos continues. We will look further into this dynamic dance just ahead on the journey.

For now, it is helpful to know that the ego tends to "see" any or all of our disowned parts (our inner chaos dragons) in the world and take up the charge to fix everything wrong "out there." This is called "projection," and it is a very common occurrence for all of us when we are stuck in personality at point 1. Without awareness, projection accentuates the split between right and wrong, a dualistic worldview that justifies discrimination and separation and is at the root of a great deal of suffering. I like Gurdjieff's metaphor for projection: "Every stick has two ends," he writes, and so "whenever I hold one end of the stick, the other promptly hits you in the head!"[82] Believing our internal splitting and projection to be responsible for much violence in the world, Gurdjieff (like Jung) felt that to avoid complete disaster, we must solve for this dualistic orientation to life that is fueled by our need to be someone or some way, in particular, and to simultaneously disown all the opposing parts. He said that we must immediately "find some means by which the two sides of man, and therefore, the two sides of the earth, can live together in peace and harmony."[83]

Knowing ourselves more deeply is the best insurance we have in a chaotic world that we may conduct ourselves in a manner consistent with higher values, rather than with this type of reactive response. No matter where we are in our development work, there are usually places we are still caught in reactivity and the Type 1 passion of Anger-against that keeps us in separation from our whole selves. While our attachment to "me" and reaction against all the "not me" parts certainly served us for a time, it eventually prevents us from being free, adaptive, creative beings. Worse, we perpetuate our own inner conflict, fragmentation; our disconnection from the ground of Being, from Source; and from our own lost essence or soul.

Unlike our heroes, we are not trapped in a story told the same way through the ages. We can, in fact, use the story of our type as a map for unwinding the key structures that keep us trapped in ego and the known world. If you choose to engage in this process of exploring new territory, this would be a good place to start to inquire into your type patterns. *What about your sense of self are you attached to? What aspects do you most dislike and hide about yourself? How did the state of your "kingdom" as you grew up, and your relationships, shape your idealized self?*

If you know your type, it is good to first reflect on the gifts of your type strategy; how it served you well in the past as a benevolent ruler in an earlier era. And then, as we turn up the heat and inquire into the more disruptive and limiting habits of type (the inner tyrant and chaos dragons), we also know there exists in us an inherently wise organizing capacity, capable of sensing, knowing, and adapting to life as it is, just as it did when we were very young. If we trust it, something of this divine spark can guide us through the journey ahead as we move beyond the limitations of type. While we must take apart the ego structure to grow, the point is not to eradicate it but to integrate it, along with all the archetypes around the circle, under the leadership of our higher self or essence, governed by higher values and ideas.

Part of the wisdom inherent in our inner organization of type is that it contains *within it* the seeds of its own discontent. This is a brilliant set-up because nothing rigid can survive in a changing landscape—adaptation is compulsory. As we see in our story heroes, some combination of tyranny in the kingdom and brewing chaos beyond the walls, creates unrest in the would-be hero. There is a growing realization that things cannot stay as they are in this precarious push-pull between forces, and more will be required if the hero is to survive the impending changes.

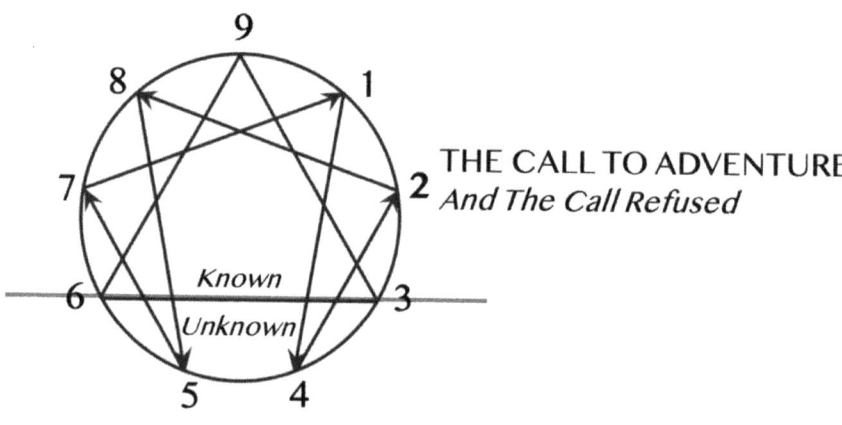

THE CALL TO ADVENTURE
And The Call Refused

CHAPTER TEN

POINT 2:
THE CALL TO ADVENTURE

For many are called, but few are chosen.

~ MATTHEW 22:14

AT THE SECOND STAGE OF THE JOURNEY, The Call to Adventure, the hero is feeling the growing split between who he is today and a different sort of possible future. Tension from both within and beyond the known world is calling something out of him. The life he is currently living no longer quite matches who he experiences himself to be on the inside. When we meet Luke Skywalker, he is clearly dissatisfied with his simple chores on the farm and the protected life his aunt and uncle have provided for him. He longs to leave Tatooine and join the Imperial Academy, but his uncle forbids it.

A similar story unfolds on the hidden island of Themyscira, home of the Amazon women and birthplace of Diana, the girl who will become Wonder Woman. Like all our heroes, Diana's character was shaped by her unique circumstances. In this case, she was sculpted out of clay by her mother Queen Hippolyta and given life by the god Zeus. As the story goes, Zeus created humans as good, but his son Ares, the god of war, corrupted them and created mayhem everywhere. Zeus managed to beat back Ares but knew he would return. In preparation, Zeus created the hidden island for the Amazons, who he decreed would one day restore peace to men's hearts and world. It is also said that he left a weapon powerful enough to kill a god—"the Godkiller"—which everyone thinks is a sword. Diana longs to train as a warrior and take up this sword and its quest, but her mother forbids it.

The call forth to adventure can arise from inside of the hero, in response to a growing disconnect between her inner nature and the decaying culture and tradition that wants to keep things just as they are. In the stories, this inner ruling principle might be represented by an actual person, like Queen Hippolyta, by walls and boundaries, or by whatever maintains security and order in the system. Like Luke and Diana, both Prince Siddhartha and Simba the Lion Prince become curious to explore the world beyond the safe walls of the king and the kingdom, sensing the possibility of growth inherent in a movement beyond the known.

Additionally, the call forth can be delivered by a mentor, often some-one from the world left behind when the hero's home was disrupted or parent(s) killed; someone, then, who also knows something about the hero's possible future. For Diana, it is her aunt, the great warrior Antiope, who (knowing Diana's true heritage and purpose via Zeus) pushes the queen to begin the girl's training. Ben "Obi-Wan" Kenobi, a friend to Luke's father before he fell to the dark side of the Force, pulls Luke forward into the journey when he shares Luke's true Jedi heritage. These calls from the old world foreshadow the promise of the journey as a process of recov-ering or reclaiming something of what was lost—for the hero and for the community as a whole.

It becomes clear to us quickly that Harry Potter's life is barely toler-able, as he is controlled, criticized, and taunted by his relatives. Nearing his 11th birthday, a letter is sent from the great Wizard Albus Dumbledore, inviting Harry to attend Hogwarts School of Witchcraft and Wizardry. This is also a call from Harry's past/potential future, as the boy knows nothing about his magical roots and wizard blood. Because his aunt and uncle conceal the invitation, more letters start arriving. As the letters are hidden, burned, or otherwise destroyed by the Dursleys, thousands more stream in by post, by owl, by fireplace, and other magic!

Finally, at the stroke of midnight on Harry's birthday, Dumbledore's messenger, the giant Hagrid, arrives to pry Harry from the grip of his tyrannical Muggle relatives. By then, the Dursleys had resorted to hiding Harry away in a high tower, in a remote place, to try to thwart his date with destiny. The tyrannical element of the psyche works hard to prevent change, but ultimately contributes to its own demise by calling up some-thing from the great unknown. It is often said that the call comes when the hero is ready, and yet we could also say (thanks to the Law of Three) that the hero is born when the system requires it. Tyranny attracts chaos, and the two opposing forces give rise to a third thing. While that third thing can be an adversary who works to maintain polarization, it can also be a potential hero and third force who might one day help to restore the peaceful existence of all the elements as One. And actually, it's both at once, two sides of the same coin.

Simba's forays to explore outside the Pride Lands betray an inner calling, but he is also "called" by changing conditions in the kingdom. Ultimately, he is caught in the evil plot of Scar, King Mufasa's brother, to kill the king. Luring Simba into serious danger, Scar knows Mufasa will go to save him, giving Scar the chance to cause an "accident." This is the inevitable rise of tyranny (loudly echoing the Egyptian creation story of Set and Osiris) in an otherwise peaceful kingdom. As the stories show, things grow stagnant in the known world when we are not paying close attention. Mufasa, like Osiris, did not understand the severity of the threat gathering right under his nose.

In the end, while the hero is ripe for change, the yin-yang dance between threats from outside the walls of the known world and corruption from inside it, together first shape and then call the potential hero forth, into adventure. In addition to Jon Snow and Arya Stark, many would-be heroes in *Game of Thrones* are "called" from the destabilization of warring factions within the Seven Kingdoms of Westeros *and* the threat of winter—with its frozen army of walking dead people—beyond "the Wall," the extensive wall of ice surrounding the kingdoms. Harry Potter's call comes from the deterioration of his life with the Dursley's and the need for his presence in the Wizarding world at Hogwarts School, due to the impending threat of Voldemort and dark forces. Within the hero, this formative tension between forces shapes the passion of Pride, a growing sense of her unique capacity to contribute.

THE PASSION OF PRIDE

At this stage of the journey, Pride, the passion at point 2, is a double-edged sword. On the one hand, Pride enables the hero to imagine *something more*—from herself, for the world—even if only vaguely defined. Pride can propel the hero out beyond the known world, as it did for Luke Skywalker. This Pride is not so much a puffed-up arrogance as it is a drive to know oneself (through others) as a needed and valuable person (like "I'm fine; I can help *you*.") Pride, and its reinforcing mental habit, Flattery, that places others at the center of one's attention, is an adaptive movement away from Resentment and Anger-against at point 1, because it pulls the hero out of her fixed position, defined by her past. For all of us, Pride is revealed in an investment in the control, safety, and shining up of our ego or material world self that—while often driving our version of "success" or fulfilling our "needs"—limits our connection with the vertical realm and the understanding of who we really are.

Like all the passions, unconscious Pride, a Pride that owns us, can be a dangerous trap. It is a good name for the adversary within us who believes our efforts to maintain an idealized version of self are "working" for us. With Pride we think we are more prepared to help, and more central to the world's well-being, than we actually are. And at this stage of the game, Pride can cause us to assert our personal will in ways that (however well-intentioned) restrict our growth and are destructive for the community. Surely Katniss has very little idea what she is doing, the brashness of it, as she raises her arm in the symbol of the resistance movement when she is named as tribute for District 12. This happens just before she is hurried out of the public eye toward the Hunger Games, while people in the crowd get beaten for reflecting back her gesture.

Clearly, at this point in the journey, none of our heroes are equipped to rule. While there is indeed an arrow line in the Enneagram Symbol pointing the way between point 2 and point 8, which symbolizes a future benevolent ruler, our heroes do not take this route directly. This would be dangerous for the hero and for the community—to advance immediately to heroic status. It is, instead, how the shadow wins and how the oppressed become the oppressors; it is the same old wine in new skins. As the saying goes: *you can't get there from here.*

When we meet another one of my favorite superheroes, Thor, the god of thunder, he is about to take that direct arrow line from point 2 to point 8 and be crowned king of his planet, Asgard. Although Thor is surprisingly good-hearted and a bit childlike, he is also brash and prideful, and manages to nearly cause a war on the day of his coronation (thanks to provocation by his adversary and corrupt brother Loki). So instead of crowning Thor, his father the wise King Odin, strips Thor of his supernatural strength (the massive hammer he uses as a weapon) and banishes him to Earth, where he will make the journey through the unknown and *around* the Symbol. From an ego-driven state, a direct move to point 8 risks turning Pride into a Lustful and immature power grab. And yet, at the same time, both Thor and Simba's sense that they have *something more* to offer is not wrong.

SUPERNATURAL AID

We can also say that the call forth comes from the hero's possible future: who we *could be,* and who we could be *for* our community, in the face of the changing landscape of life inside us and in our world. In the story of Pinocchio, Geppetto the puppet-maker wishes upon a star for Pinocchio to be a Real boy. That star represents the possible future, one that provides a *higher aim* and motivation for the journey. And it is constellated in the appearance of a magical Blue Fairy who promises to grant Pinocchio's wish if he can follow the Way of a Real boy. Along with the Blue Fairy, Cinderella's Fairy Godmother and Glinda the Good Witch are two more of many wise crones who both represent and point to the possible future for our heroes.

Dumbledore and Obi-Wan Kenobi each carry a future vision for their would-be heroes throughout the journey. Even as both of these wise old men pass into death, both Harry Potter and Luke Skywalker continue to have contact and guidance from the mentors who protect their destiny. Joseph Campbell describes the protective power of this sort of mentorship as *supernatural aid.* If we trust these age-old myths, this is an important statement about the support available to all of us from higher forces as we traverse the chaotic unknown ahead. When we heed the call and follow it courageously around the circle, Campbells says, "the protective power is always and ever present within the sanctuary of the heart, and even immanent within, or just behind, the unfamiliar features of the world."[84]

Both the hero's higher aim and the protective power are represented by that arrow line from point 2 to point 8. To follow the arrow lines directly is not the path of the hero. But if we use the arrow lines symbolically, they reveal a parallel internal process that can help us tremendously. On the hero's journey, point 8 represents the archetype of the benevolent ruler, the "awake" version of order that integrates flow, diversity, and allows for growth and change. The arrow points to the possibility of renewing the known world following the hero's transformation in the unknown, and it also gives us a clue about the nature of the "higher forces" guiding the hero's journey. The mentor stands in for this archetype until the hero can realize it in herself. And the fact that the mentor is represented as often by the good witch as it is the wise wizard gives us a preview of the non-dual world to come.

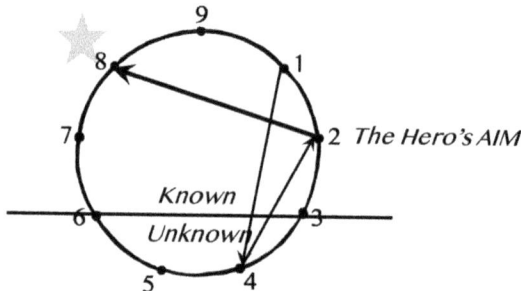

A CALL FROM THE FUTURE

If we use the arrow line from point 2 to point 8 on the Enneagram as a mental projection of what is possible, it provides fuel for the journey around the circle. Since our sins, our Enneagram passions, cause us to "miss the mark," then *taking aim* at a new target—our higher, more integrated self and its potential contribution to the whole—is an essential move. Having a vision, even if it is a Prideful one at first, serves to both focus and motivate the hero to leave the known world. We wish before we are able to *be*, but it's an important start. Gurdjieff says: "Wish is the most powerful thing in the world. Higher than God." But only if that "wish" is conscious, and from a unified will.

From a mind-brain standpoint, it matters less whether your aim is an external goal, such as to get an education or to address homelessness in the community, or whether it is an internal goal, such as to be a force for love or to uncover a unique purpose in this lifetime. What seems most important is that we aim "higher," meaning in alignment with something greater than our small selves. And in fact, it will require a sacrifice of that small self. As with Thor, if the "crown" for which you aim is being bestowed by the old king (ego ideal) or coming to you a bit too easily...think twice! The lesson from these stories is that the true way to heal the kingdom requires first surrendering the old. Or, more pointedly, Joseph Campbell writes: "The hero of yesterday becomes the tyrant of tomorrow unless he crucifies *himself* today."[85]

So the real hero has a long way to go around the circle, but the good news hinted at here is that *you* are the thing that can transcend suffering. And redemption is possible when we aim higher, beyond the known. A higher aim provides a different kind of supernatural aid. Having a meaningful goal organizes our behavior and provides motivation through the release of the neurotransmitter dopamine. Having an aim even allows our unconscious to work offline on our behalf, churning out ideas in our sleep. Even a vague wish or dream can shape our experience and serve as a call forth to help guide the journey. In fact, all we really have at point 2 on the psycho-spiritual journey is a sense or dream of what could be. We are not developed enough yet to know just what we are capable of when we move beyond our ego and its habitual ways of thinking, feeling, and being in the world.

And yet, isn't that what generations of spiritual and wisdom traditions, along with these stories, aim to provide? A "Way" to be when we don't know how to be? While each tradition has its own version, our universal maps agree that there is a Way of navigating the unknown that has promise. Life challenges us; we *will* be taken apart...or we can choose to take ourselves apart. Then what? A higher aim. Each spiritual tradition offers supernatural aid through a divine figure or figures of inspiration. The Enneagram provides us a view of what that aim might be as well. If you follow its map, you are aspiring to *virtues*, qualities of higher being and the sacred heart, and *ideas* that are *holy*, in that they have at their foundation a view that we are all whole, equal, and interconnected.

Aligning with a higher aim in the moral or spiritual sense is redemptive in that it can make the challenges worth the ride. As the Taoists imply, although order and chaos threaten in their opposing ways, *walking the line*, awake and choosing to weave them into a life, is inherently more meaningful because what you are spending time on, and how you show up for yourself and others, may itself redeem the suffering of the long road. Perhaps this is another part of the "protective power" available to us on the journey.

So while there are many layers of this possible aim—behavioral, psychological, relational, and spiritual—the ultimate star pointed at by that arrow is something like an integrated whole, developed essence, or our highest expression of self that is simultaneously in alignment with Source and in service to community. For Dorothy, this is the *"Somewhere" Over the Rainbow* where dreams come true. Pride would have us go there directly. But unless and until we go on the journey to deconstruct ourselves and align with more of who we are, there is no place like Home.

Refusing the Call (The Adversary)

When we get the call forth at point 2 on the Enneagram, we are at an important choice point: shall we stay safe or go further towards this surely hazardous encounter with chaos (that we can almost smell across the threshold ahead)? Refusing the call is an exit strategy that can go on throughout the entire journey, as it represents the ego's Prideful resistance and *all* of the passions that dog us throughout the process. The adversary has many faces and will not give up the game easily.

As potential heroes, we are by now really feeling the split that comes when something inside us no longer matches up with our actual life. Maybe we are longing for *something more,* or just sense that some part of ourselves is missing? Paradox starts to form: "am I this or am I that?" We don't always feel like "ourselves," and aspects of our "old" life become unsatisfying. But we still have this implicit driving need, our Enneagram type passion, to maintain our idealized and fixated view of who we are in the known world. Point 2 can be a confusing and painful place. With Pandora's box open a crack, unwelcome emotions and impulses claw at us with their vague but persistent demands from the shadows below. The old ways aren't working as well to keep the lid on. Some people will have the desire to flee into distracting pleasures or numbness here, others will escape back to the anesthesia of the ego's strong control at point 1. It is common to rock back and forth between points 1, 2, and 3, only periodically sniffing out the unknown terrain ahead.

Prince Siddhartha makes three forays beyond the walls of the palace before he decides to heed the call. Encountering first old age and then disease outside the Palace, Siddhartha is content to retreat and reflect each time. Despite the king's efforts to increase the pleasures and distractions within the walls and to station guards around the palace, Siddhartha goes out again and comes upon a dead man. Struck by the stark reality of death, Siddhartha considers leaving the known world of his childhood, but again he stays put. Finally, when he meets a monk, Siddhartha follows the call into the unknown to explore the universal problem of suffering and how to deal with it—the journey that makes him into the Buddha.

The internal split inside the hero can also be personified by another character or characters, which is why the adversary sits at point 2. The journey's hero is identified with the spiritually and morally courageous process of updating the deteriorating order of the kingdom. She does this by first transforming herself, her character and ideals, through the encounter with chaos, and then she helps to renew the kingdom as a whole. The adversary is both fighting and fueling that process all along the way.

At one level, the adversary represents the destructive aspect of Pride we all have when ego is our guide and compass (whatever the type structure). Some say that Pride is considered the highest in the Christian hierarchy of sin because Pride's refutation of need means: I don't need help, I don't need to grow, and ultimately, I don't even need God. In fact, I will play God by asserting my will and serving in His stead. In Milton's version, *Paradise Lost*, Satan was originally God's highest angel. Filled with Pride, he could not bear to not be God, and so fell from grace and sought to impose his rule. The danger here is that Pride not only aborts the journey of growth, but also it can cut us off from whatever collective wisdom and higher guidance might otherwise be available. This prideful adversary is often a major dark figure, literally shadowed or shrouded like Voldemort and Darth Vader who hide their distorted forms behind masks and other objects.

But the adversary has other faces too. As a symbol of powerful internal forces that keep us attached to our small self and habitual ego patterns (and for which we betray our highest spiritual truth), the anti-hero has multiple ways of coaxing the hero off his path (all the deadly sins). Some adversaries seem less threatening, like Fox and Cat who led Pinocchio astray; some masquerade as friends who claim to "help" or do what is for our own good, like Almira Gulch and the Dursleys. But all are significant forces that influence the hero under ego. They may tempt us to stay aligned with the known world, tyranny, and the rigidity of *things as they are*; and they can lure us, in a pathological way, to distraction, indulgence, and chaos. And, like the passions, the adversary both threatens the hero *and* drives him forward, helping (in a seemingly sinister way) to lay out the path of adventure.

Pinocchio's early adversaries lead him to experiment with both extremes along the first half of the journey, much to the dismay of his conscience, Jiminy Cricket. Pinocchio knows the path to becoming a Real boy is to be brave, truthful, and unselfish. But he gets side-tracked when, on his way to school, his "friends" Fox and Cat convince him to join Stromboli's puppet show. Of course, Pinocchio becomes a big star as the only puppet who can perform without strings! We, too, resist the call by clinging to ego, like Pinocchio, who is still acting out the strings of the father principle. And yet, like the puppet master Stromboli, this aspect has a tyrannical side that just might lock you in a cage and threaten to turn you into firewood if you don't perform.

The same silly friends next lead Pinocchio into the opposite pole (chaos) by tricking him into a visit to Pleasure Island, where all sorts of delinquent and indulgent distractions occupy him. On Pleasure Island all the little boys are turned into donkeys before being sold into slavery. We too can make a "jackass" of ourselves with addictions, distractions, and impulsive indulgences that offer only temporary escape from the internal split we are feeling: *am I this? Or something more? Should I stay or should I go?* This is very serious business, as revealed by the evil intent of Pleasure Island's owner, the Coachman. And it means that some part of you is quite capable of killing off the best in you—if you remain asleep.

In addition to attempts to derail the hero's journey, the adversary plays a pivotal role in the transformation of the hero. Although it seems at any point this figure could bring about the premature death of our hero, the adversary goads the hero on through the initiatory process by threatening her and the entirety of the kingdom. Voldemort and Darth Vader, the Wicked Witch of the West, and President Snow from *The Hunger Games*, all lay out a map to growth for our heroes that keeps them on the journey. And, in the end, we find that this figure has bound up a particular piece of the puzzle the hero needs in order to fully release himself from ego. This is most literal as the piece of Harry Potter that got exchanged for a piece of Voldemort in their first fateful meeting. When Harry was a baby, his mother foiled a deathly spell from Voldemort. Instead of killing Harry, the spell killed her, and resulted in this sharing of matter between "good and evil," spark and sin.

Somehow our sin and our divine spark are two sides of the same coin. This is an interesting dilemma. If the adversary were simply destroyed, the journey might end rather abruptly. All along the way, adversity contributes to the learning and growth of the hero. In *Wonder Woman*, the adversary Ares, god of war, masquerading as Sir Patrick Morgan, a leader in the British War Council, actually supports Diana with money and guidance to pursue her plans, drawing her deeper towards her destiny. Even when falling prey to the adversary's foolery causes the hero to temporarily lose her way, the diversions expand awareness and teach important lessons.

All forms of adversary, but most especially the likes of Voldemort or Darth Vader, serve an important function of providing friction for the hero. We would do well to remember this truth that without adequate friction we cannot grow. We must challenge ourselves and choose discomfort at times, in order to develop. So while our adversaries might threaten and waylay us, going *towards* them is a far cry better than refusing the call by staying asleep. And really, what kind of hero story would we have without the dark forces that call out of us capacity we did not know existed?

INNER WORK FOR THE CALL FORTH

The Pride of our individual ego keeps us striving toward our type's fixated ideal self and convinces us that we have no personal need to question this set up. Instead, we believe we have the answers for what the world needs. We are ready to deliver the kingdom, just like Thor, and unfortunately our efforts to insert ourselves before we are ready can sometimes, unwittingly, bring down the house. Even though we are starting to feel the tension of competing factions within, this prideful stance keeps us in the trap of seeing what is broken outside of ourselves. In a most colorful passage, Campbell writes:

> *The crux of the curious difficulty lies in the fact that our conscious views of what life ought to be seldom correspond to what life really is. Generally, we refuse to admit within ourselves, or within our friends, the fullness of that pushing, self-protective, malodorous, carnivorous, lecherous fever which is the very nature of the organic cell. Rather we tend to perfume, whitewash and reinterpret; meanwhile imagining that all the flies in the ointment, all the hairs in the soup, are the faults of some unpleasant someone else.*[86]

When we feel the uncomfortable split that forms at point 2—the sense of confusion or dissatisfaction with things as they are—we can easily double-down on our personality patterns and ego needs, and simply apply them towards shaping the world to our designs. This is so human. The ego structure is comfortable, familiar...and exactly the trap that prevents our growth. It is fueled by our passion, our version of refusing the call, into a return to tyranny (the idealized ego, with its often-controlling inner critic) and/or dissolution in a sea of emotion, reactivity, or indulgence (chaos) when we slip. This dichotomy is consistent with modern research into mind/brain functioning that indicates many forms of psychological suffering are the product of either too much chaos or too much rigidity in our brain function and in our lives, and the inability to wake up and mediate between these extremes.

While it may seem safer to refuse the call forth, avoiding the dragons and dark night ahead, the journey line says that this is a losing game. Like Bill Murray in the movie *Groundhog Day*, if we stay in the known world (rigidly attached to old patterns), we are destined to live out the same stories, feelings, and experiences over and over, unconscious of our impact on the world around us, all the while sacrificing our greatest potential. This is the promise of our Enneagram type, lived unconsciously.

And it's not comfortable. Says Campbell of the refusal, "What formerly was meaningful may become strangely emptied of value."[87] The split at point 2 remains lurking at the edge of consciousness, like the minotaur at the center of the mythical labyrinth. Once you have been called, once aspects of truth at the center of your being have been awakened, refusing the call makes life more difficult. As with Harry Potter, the letters keep coming, one way or another, chipping away at our fortress of fixed habits, ideals, and affinities. A slow disintegration is inevitable, as the necessity and capacity for creative adaptation is at the very core of the gift of life we are given. In alchemy, this second stage of the work is called *dissolution.* It marks the start of a process of dissolving the dried-out ashes of the old structures (that are burning themselves out) in something that will return life-giving moisture. But even if we are not yet ready to dive into the unconscious unknown across the threshold (and a sure dissolution of the old order), we can stir the pot with some reflection.

The first point of inquiry involves that internal arrow from point 2 to point 8 signifying a higher aim and supernatural aid. What would it mean for you to aim higher? Let me qualify that... Because we have not yet accessed higher being and consciousness, the wish from point 2 across to that future state at point 8 requires some imagination, dreaming, or meditation to see from beyond ego. Time spent dropping into a present-moment, relaxed state in all three centers of intelligence opens a doorway beyond the fixated habits of our mind, heart, and body. It forwards dissolution by welcoming the watery darkness underlying our fixed form and tiptoeing towards the necessary sacrifice of Pride that "knows" the answers. In moments of presence, we can "jump out" of the ordinary world structures into a state of greater *flow.* That is the place from which to ask or imagine what *could be.*

This does not have to be complicated. Time spent in quiet contemplation, with relaxed and grounded body, clear and open mind, receptive and nonjudgmental heart, awaiting inspiration, will suffice. Ask for your aim to become clear. Don't try, wait. The mind being what it is—like a puppy— you will have to notice when it's wandering or has its nose in something it should not, and gently direct it back: sit, here, now, good puppy! And since our higher centers of intelligence speak to us in symbols, metaphors, and stories, don't be surprised if in your open awareness you get a download of images, shapes, feeling states, or other clips of possibility from your higher self or essence. With the invitation, this process may continue into your dreams at night. Write them down somewhere. It may take time and reflection to decode these symbolic offerings from the unknown.

In a period of dissolution in my own life, I kept seeing in my meditation on "the future" a huge triangular window that is the entire back wall of the sanctuary of a church in California I had been to only once, over 25 years prior. The window opens onto a glade of redwood trees, with three trees situated front and center. At first, I thought I should move to the area. I did for a time, and I was blessed with the support of a wise pastor and companions on the journey. Some time later, I figured out that I was being offered a vision of how the Law of Three "creates." How else could my soul convey what it might be like to walk *through* the triangle (through the triangular church window) to a higher fourth point, realizing the tetrahedron? So while it may be helpful at this stage to look for an actual mentor—some external form of *supernatural aid*—we can also look for guidance from the messages and metaphors offered from within. This practice of presence and listening for whispers from beyond the known world can provide much-needed companionship and holding for the challenges ahead.

The second thing we can do in our inner work at point 2 is to bring kind attention to the inner split arising, noticing and feeling the "warring" forces within that are conspiring to keep us in our limited Enneagram type structure. The adversary works in a tricky way to keep us asleep to the potential of third force consciousness that would interrupt the status quo. So just seeing this silliness in action—how the little triangle of forces keeps us fixed—can further the dissolution of ego and ignite a desire to take more concerted action toward change. Looking honestly at our very human struggles is also a good way to seed the growth of Humility, the virtue at point 2 on the Enneagram.

Like our heroes, we too are a product of the dynamic tension symbolized by the arrow lines between point 1 and point 4. The split we are feeling at point 2 that heralds the call to adventure is created by the tension between an unknown, unconscious, and undifferentiated "watery" chaos calling from below the threshold line (at point 4), and the increasing tyranny of our fixated ego ideal (at point 1). Surprisingly, perhaps, both of these forces are allies of the passion and inner adversary who would like to prevent the journey. We might even say that together they birth him (and his counterpart, the potential hero), and then they all work together to keep our type structure intact when we are not awake.

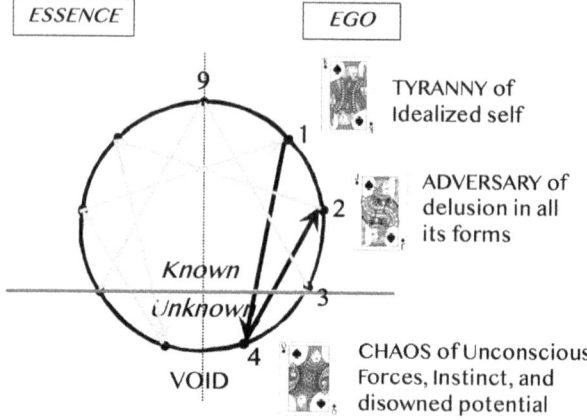

Our inner intelligence *ordered* the confusion of early life into an ego structure that could navigate the demands of both our nature and our culture. In "choosing" our type, however, plenty of instinctual reactions, feelings, memories, and beliefs had to be sent down into the unconscious unknown, as "not me." This terrain presents as undifferentiated *chaos* until some particular dragon gets triggered. The rumblings of these hidden counterforces to ego call to us at point 2, because some part of us knows they must be addressed and integrated in order to reach the higher aim and wholeness pointed to in the potential future represented at point 8. However, to avoid this mess now, the conscious ordering principle of ego can turn into a rigid and critical tyrant who asserts its dominance over deviation from approved ways of operating. The interesting twist here is that this tyrannical force actually "attracts" more opposition and rebellion from the chaos dragon.

Both of these forces (as characters) are working to "protect" the hurt child hiding somewhere below it all, who developed a driving passion to be someone, to be safe, and in control. The tight hold of our mental model and rigid protection of who we are "supposed to" be, however, causes the instinctual life force to rise up in resistance, at times, to give ourselves a break. Chaos creates an opportunity for the adversary, strongly motivated to take over the kingdom, which fuels the tyrant who doubles-down to maintain the status quo. Dragon emerges, tyrant locks down, and we stay fixed in the delusion of this ego structure that believes its driving need and efforts to fulfill its desires and avert opposition actually "works" for us in the greater scheme of things. Without an awake third force there is no one to interrupt the fixed dance of three that captures, distorts, and deploys our centers of intelligence in service of the ego structure.

I have heard Russ Hudson, a long-time Enneagram teacher, consultant, and author, teach the two polarizing aspects of personality as the inner critic and the inner rebel.[88] Bringing awareness to the masterful way these two characters partner with the adversary to prevent the journey (a form of Pride for all of us), can inspire compassion for ourselves and a great deal of Humility, the virtue at point 2. While you should definitely consult your personal version of this unconscious triangle, these examples can give you a sense of how the dynamic dance works.

At **Type 1**, the tyrant is quite clear, asserting itself to make sure we are right, responsible, and maintain tight control on any wayward and impermissible feelings and instincts. All this pressure can give rise to an inner chaos dragon that might range from clear deviance (i.e., acting out the "unacceptable" thing you campaign against), to a mischievous rule-breaking, to playfulness previously forbidden. When we get too far afield in chaos, the driving need to go against anything "wrong" kicks in to restore the ego's equilibrium.

For **Type 2**, the tyrant locks down when we even think of being selfish, or bring attention to our own needs, or when we have been less than pleasing. This force can give rise to a chaos dragon that feels justified in indulging with treats, spending money, and finding other ways of "serving" our own needs that may not serve us. When we get too far afield, the driving need to re-focus on being valuable in the eyes of others kicks in to restore the ego's equilibrium.

The **Type 3** tyrant comes out to drive us when we are not on top of things, not productive, not enough (even on vacation), or heaven forbid, have actually failed in some way. In response, the inner chaos dragon might lead us to withdraw into "failure," resigned and exhausted, or refuse competition altogether. When we get too far afield, the driving need to get up and earn our worth kicks in to restore the ego's equilibrium.

At **Type 4,** the tyrant's job is to keep us in this defensive strategy that involves comparing ourselves and noticing how we don't measure up, what is missing, and how we don't fit in. In response, the chaos dragon bounces back and sometimes makes us feel superior, except this move maintains the sense of separateness that sets us up for feeling broken again later when the driving need to compare ourselves unfavorably kicks in to restore the ego's equilibrium.

For **Type 5**, the tyrant is behind the drive to be the most knowledgeable one that protects us both from feeling lost and having to deal with people, feelings, and needs that deplete our energy. When the chaos dragon is tired of all this, it might compel us to dominate others instead of ourselves, or make stuff up in a scattered and ultimately more draining display. When we get too far afield, the driving need to retract and contain energy kicks in to restore the ego's equilibrium.

The **Type 6** tyrant keeps us safe, especially when it comes to fulfilling our duty and responsibility toward others so we won't get in trouble. This tyrant can have a lot of voices and opinions that are paralyzing, so the chaos dragon just throws up its hands and heads into action, sometimes in a risky way that causes the fear-driven tyrant to react with criticism and "I told you so." When we get too far afield, the driving need to stay secure kicks in to restore the ego's equilibrium.

At **Type 7**, the tyrant is a little paradoxical. It comes in when we are not having enough fun or freedom, or not positive and optimistic enough. Instead of classically rebellious, then, this chaos dragon can be quite strict and critical, like taking his ball and going home. When we get too far afield, the driving need to throw off limits kicks in to restore the ego's equilibrium.

The **Type 8** tyrant has to be strong and handle *everything*; stay in this big energy so that we don't get taken advantage of. The chaos dragon can be like the bear pulling into its cave. We are out of energy, crash, and may numb out or blow off steam. When we get too far afield, the driving need to be strong and make big things happen kicks in to restore the ego's equilibrium.

For **Type 9**, the tyrant assures that we can go along and get along, and don't assert ourselves in ways that will cause conflict and disconnection. The chaos dragon can surface, however rarely, as the Hulk who really can kick ass and take names. Sometimes it acts out, but sometimes just the anxiety about all that power on the inside is enough to kick in the driving need to subdue our agenda and intensity again.

Two opposing forces (tyranny and chaos) call in a third element, but their dynamic tends to keep the system intact versus the transformational process that can unfold through the triangle with an awake third force. In type structure, the forces have crystallized into mind, body, and heart operations distorted by past experience. Since we are not present and choosing our thoughts, emotions, and reactions when fused with our personality, time spent in intentional and non-judgmental awareness of fixed patterns can start to loosen things up a bit. If we can bring kind attention to the crazy marriage between the first two opposing forces that fuels the adversary and keeps our particular passion and Enneagram type structure intact, we may gain appreciation and motivation for the necessary journey of deconstructing the ego across the threshold ahead.

Once we are on to the ego's games, in addition to humbling, it can get kind of old. One way to activate change, says the poet David Whyte, is "to arrange to become really tired of ourselves." And then, funny enough, we may find that this rebellious inner dragon of chaos, can be a great ally when engaged directly, with purpose. But we have work to do still, if we are to heed the call to greater adventure and hazard the dragon's lair. I am reminded of a passage from the Gospel of Thomas: "If you bring forth what is within you, what you bring forth will save you. If you do not bring forth what is within you, what you do not bring forth will destroy you."[89]

The only way out is through.

INITIATION - *Descent*

The Initiation phase of the journey starts with the transition across the threshold and the descent into the unknown, beyond the bounds of the kingdom, to confront the great dragon of chaos (metaphorically speaking). The hero literally leaves home and heads into unfamiliar territory that will test and try him. While the challenges ahead serve to deconstruct the immature, self-oriented and dualistic worldview that characterizes his early life, they also strengthen the hero in some way. Picasso said: "Every act of creation is first an act of destruction." Before being initiated into a new way of seeing and being in the world, there must be a sacrifice of the old structures.

With only a vague vision of possibility and no guarantee of what is ahead, crossing the threshold into the initiation process is not easy and often resisted. This is because, first of all, upon dipping into the unknown we really start to see the truth of who we are: previously unconscious patterns of thinking, feeling and acting are revealed through the challenges we encounter. The ego has spent a lifetime keeping us from the shadows and lost parts of ourselves. It wants nothing to do with this revelation! A new kind of bravery is required to face the truth and sacrifice who we thought we were.

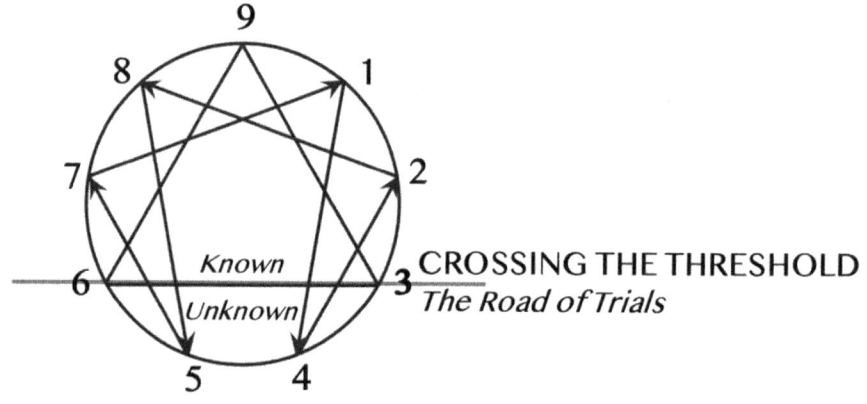

CHAPTER ELEVEN

POINT 3:
CROSSING THE THRESHOLD

But whether small or great, and no matter what the stage or grade
of life, the call rings up the curtain, always, on a mystery of trans-
figuration—a rite, or moment, of spiritual passage, which, when
complete, amounts to a dying and a birth. The familiar life hori-
zon has been outgrown; the old concepts, ideals, and emotional
patterns no longer fit; the time for
the passing of a threshold is at hand.[90]

~ JOSEPH CAMPBELL

At POINT 3 ON THE ENNEAGRAM, we reach the threshold, the door-way from the known into the unknown world. This is mysterious terrain where order and the old rules, culture, and operating assumptions, don't apply so well. Things as we knew them, including our sense of self, no longer make sense; we are on the verge of chaos. Joseph Campbell describes this threshold crossing as a form of self-annihilation in "the belly of the whale"—the worldwide womb image. He characterizes the entire unknown world as feminine, representing the Great Mother prin-ciple. At the same time, the Great Mother, as the primordial chaos from which Creation was formed, contains within her all possible elements as the undifferentiated flow of potential. "Woman, in the picture language of mythology, represents the totality of what can be known. The hero is the one who comes to know."[91]

So while crossing into the unknown can be scary, chaos is not inher-ently "bad." Like dark matter, it is dark because it is "hidden," given its undifferentiated state, and represents what is unseen, unconscious, and unknown to us. And like a woman's womb, close to the source of creation, it is also a birthplace of possibility. "The temple interior, the belly of the whale, and the heavenly land beyond, above, and below the confines of the world, are one and the same."[92] So the unknown Great Mother is not only the belly of the whale, or a place inhabited by the wicked witch and devouring queen—"the death of everything that dies"—she is also "the world creatrix, ever mother, ever virgin…the life of everything that lives." She is both "the womb and the tomb."[93] The hero goes inward to be re-born.

The unknown is, at the end of the day, a place we *must* go to grow into our heroic capacity. In most stories this movement across the threshold is represented by a passageway from the everyday world into a challenging and unfamiliar place: Dorothy is delivered to Oz, Alice goes down the rabbit hole to Wonderland, King Arthur's knights enter the dark forest, and Katniss Everdeen is shuttled away from District 12 to the Capitol threshold and then into the labyrinth-like arena of the Hunger Games. Standing at the threshold, the hero has a little more sense of the dangerous terrain ahead than she did at point 2.

THE PASSION OF DECEIT

Because of the awareness of potential danger, we actually need a strong enough ego to cross into the unknown. So, Deceit, the passion at point 3 on the Enneagram, serves as an animating force. The passion of Deceit is not like lying, but rather a closing off of the heart and one's true inner experience (the good, bad, and ugly) to take on the role and image of the hero—whatever works to forward the mission. We pretend that we are already *who we could be* and so, up for the challenge of the journey. And then, deceiving ourselves chiefly, we have more courage to proceed and try to prove it.

Deceit drives *all* of us when we are in personality, as it is the very nature of ego and Enneagram type. We have all taken on an approximation of our essence in developing our ego. That is the real deceit that must be sacrificed to unveil our true heroism and relationship with *All that Is*. And yet, at this stage of the journey Deceit has a bit of an adaptive function, allowing us to hazard ourselves in the unknown. I mean, consider Pinocchio—he's a wooden puppet, mentored by a tiny cricket, and he sets off to face the world outside his father's workshop. The odds are not exactly in his favor! Thank goodness for Deceit in this moment. It fuels and is fueled by the mental habit of Vanity at point 3, of seeing ourselves as central to making things happen—in this case, to saving something, someone, and renewing the world.

Deceit and Vanity—knowing more of the threat but maintaining an image of competence—leads to what Joseph Campbell calls "threshold bravado" on the part of the hero. Having grown up on a sheltered island, our brave Wonder Woman, Diana, is convinced that she can cross the threshold, into the center of World War I, and save the humans from destroying one another by finding and killing Ares, the god of war. And Simba, still a teeny-bopper lion, leads his friend Nala beyond the boundaries of the Pride Lands, bragging all the while that he will soon be "king of everything." Of course, his bravado gets them in over their heads and surrounded by a band of menacing hyenas from which they need rescue. Eventually, curiosity (and bravado) gets the cat, and the next time Simba strays beyond the bounds of the Pride Lands he does not return. Caught in Scar's plan to execute Mufasa, Simba crosses the threshold for good after Scar tricks him into thinking he is responsible for his father's death. Essentially, Simba banishes himself to penance in mysterious lands far beyond the kingdom.

RESISTANCE, THRESHOLD GUARDIANS, AND ALLIES

As Harry Potter crosses into the Wizarding world at Diagon Alley, it is clear that he too is in a strange and different place full of magic. But the most colorful threshold scene may be from the first *Star Wars* movie: Luke Skywalker's stop into the cantina populated by all manner of odd and potentially unsavory aliens. All those freaky characters are a harbinger of coming to know our shadows and the truth of what drives us from the unconscious unknown. Still in Deceit, Luke scoffs at Ben Kenobi's warning to "watch yourself," by proclaiming: "I'm ready for anything!"

When Deceit gets the hero in over his head, he meets threshold guardians and attracts allies. Threshold guardians are sentinels at the gate that challenge the hero in some way. Their purpose is to test and strengthen the hero to make sure he is ready for the journey, or to turn him back if he is not. Campbell writes that threshold guardians "ward away all incapable of encountering the higher silence within."[94] Both bullies inside the cantina and military-like Storm troopers outside it are provoked by Luke's carelessness. But thankfully, by this time Luke has allies in Han Solo and Chewbacca, in addition to his mentor Ben Kenobi, to save him from himself and facilitate his movement across the threshold.

For us, threshold guardians can be internal or external. There may be people in our lives who caution us from change or from engaging in the "crazy" and out-of-character explorations we begin on a therapeutic or spiritual path, a new health kick, or other attempt to break out of our current malaise. There is something threatening about someone in the group getting their life together in ways that differentiate them. Sometimes with good intentions, sometimes not, people may try to hold us back. Certainly, the Dursleys worked very hard to keep Harry from his date with destiny, and without the help of Hagrid, Harry might have stayed stuck with them—a misfit in the everyday human or "Muggle" world.

Often, however, the threshold guardians in the stories symbolize the resistance that comes from inside us in the form of fears, insecurity, guilt at leaving others behind, or the desire to stay comfortable and in control of our ego needs. These threshold guardians can be formidable, because it is their job to make sure the overbold adventurer, driven by Deceit, is not beyond his or her depth. If we really knew what was ahead, most of us *would* choose to stay home! The ego is not a fan of the deconstruction it can sense just beyond the threshold, where it will see the truth of its own shenanigans. But when those internal guardians appear, if we welcome them, they can be an opportunity for growth. If we can look honestly at the habits that dissuade us from relaxing our ego patterns and going deeper into the journey, it can make our passage across the threshold less shocking. The Enneagram points directly to threshold guardians that aim to hold us back in the defense mechanisms of Enneagram type.

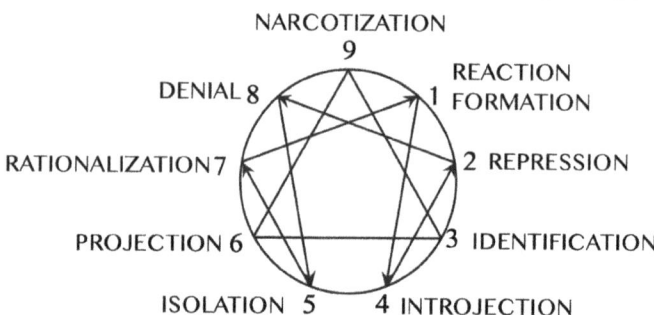

ENNEAGRAM DEFENSE MECHANISMS

These are complicated words, but their action is simple in that each defense mechanism amounts to a very sneaky and precise way that an unconscious habit keeps intact our ego structure—particularly the dance between the inner tyrant and the chaos dragon that is maintained by the driving passion of our type. Directly blocking the awakening heart at this access point between worlds, these sentinels at the gate are designed to keep us in the delusion that our attachment to certain ways of operating and avoidance of others (our type) is actually working for us.

At Point 1, **reaction formation** is acting the exact opposite to what we feel, for example, being overly nice to someone when the critic is raging, thus maintaining the internal stance of being "good" or "right."

At Point 2, **repression** serves to keep us away from our own needs and feelings so that the ego can continue to strive for being liked and needed by others.

At Point 3, **identification** describes how we imagine the most admirable way to be in a situation and then manage to inhabit that character, keeping ourselves from knowing and being who we really are.

At Point 4, **introjection** is a process of taking inside ourselves an imagined critical "other." This lets us control it but also keeps us down, ensuring we stay with the longing to be something more.

At Point 5, **isolation** refers to cordoning off feelings (and sometimes ourselves, entirely) so as to stay detached from feelings, people, and situations that might be draining or overwhelming.

At Point 6, **projection** describes a process of imagining that we see in others what we are actually feeling inside ourselves, which serves to keep us fighting or feeling insecure and anxious about imagined threats.

At Point 7, **rationalization** is the habit of putting a positive spin on everything that could be seen as sad or hurtful in order to keep ourselves upbeat and moving, avoiding limitations.

At Point 8, **denial** describes the inability to see our true impact and intensity which serves to keep us feeling like we still have to be bigger and protect something or cause change.

At Point 9, **narcotization** refers to the various habits, routines, and behaviors we use to stay comfortable and peaceful on the inside, so as to avoid dissatisfaction and the necessity of becoming who we really are.

Upon reflection, you might find that you use more than one of these defense mechanisms, but there is usually one that works rather constantly and diligently to defend the passion, the driving orientation of your type, and keep the whole ego system intact. It helps us avoid unacceptable thoughts and feelings, internal or unconscious aspects of ourselves that might cause disruption. One sure way of helping ourselves across the threshold, then, is to simply refuse to carry out defense mechanisms as we wade into challenging territory. Good luck! Just this move might be a bit shocking to the system, but we can use this very struggle for growth.

The First Shock Point

Point 3 is the first shock point in Gurdjieff's formulation of the Symbol. This is a point of maximum tension between opposing forces—order and chaos (here represented by known and unknown worlds)—that invites a third or reconciling force. The dual threat of the rise of tyranny and the chaos driven by nature out of balance has reached its pinnacle. This point marks a potential change in direction, down and in, to a strange land with different rules. Things can't continue as they were, and yet it looks pretty messy ahead.

As opposing forces approach their extremes, a specific kind of third force is needed to hold the tension of polarized forces and help accomplish some degree of harmony and a higher order result. We saw how this works in the Law of Three. This space between stagnant order and total chaos, when held, creates an opening for new intelligence from outside the system. Remember that when new energy and information enters between S-curves, the alchemy of it all can spur adaptive change. It's the same for us.

As we hover at this threshold between known and unknown, we have a chance to engage the tension of opposing forces and invite possibility. This brave and difficult move can keep the journey's momentum going forward around the circle, into the unknown, and on an evolutionary path. Gurdjieff's teaching suggests that we can *give ourselves* the shock of this crossing. And yet, most potential heroes aren't awake enough at this point in the journey, and they end up getting tossed over the threshold by life, and often abruptly. This represents the truth that forces outside of ourselves often throw us into chaos, inviting our unconscious responses. But we have a map! By choosing to step into this place between forces, we can smooth the process a bit. Going consciously into paradox, the hero chooses discomfort and opens the way for higher intelligence to enter through this interval and opening between worlds.

This is not an easy choice, and in fact this crossing is often portrayed as a narrow passage or gate. It is much easier to stay in the world where things are clear and we know how to be—generally, against "this" and for "that." As Joseph Campbell describes it: "The pairs of opposites (being and not being, life and death, beauty and ugliness, good and evil, and all the other polarities that bind the faculties to hope and fear, and link the organs of action to deeds of defense and acquisition) are the clashing rocks that crush the traveler, but between which the heroes always pass."[95] Gurdjieff taught that we can lessen this shock with "conscious labor."

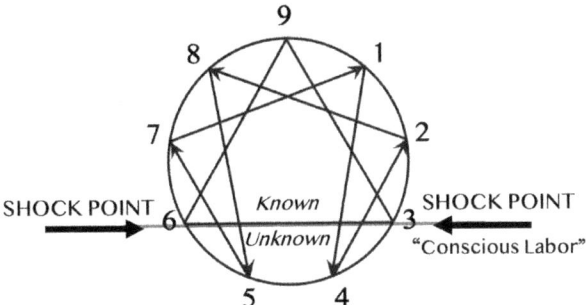

Conscious labor is, for one, a *voluntary* departure and encounter with the unknown that begins to "take apart" the ruling aspect of ego and the known world. And while it is surely "laborious," if we avoid the work and retreat to the safety of a more coherent self at point 2 or point 1, life often steps in and provides a "motivational" shock anyway. Crisis, loss, divorce, death, illness, betrayal, and injury all have a way of unraveling our fixated attachment to ego. Who we think we are and how we thought the world was supposed to work can get stripped away in a moment when we are thrown into chaos in the unknown world. Cycles of order and chaos occur with or without our participation.

Some of our heroes experience shocks by getting thrown across the threshold into mysterious and challenging territory. This isn't all bad. Who is to say whether Dorothy would have ever learned her lessons without the tornado that whisked her out of Kansas? Simba's loss of his father at the hands of Scar similarly launches him across a threshold, away from the forces that have both shaped and protected him. While this is indeed a tragic loss (who wasn't devastated at that point in *The Lion King*?), the departure from the known world advances Simba along his own heroic path.

Other heroes are sent into the unknown by the mentor, and prodded and coaxed by allies. The presence of new allies in this crossing also supports the idea that there is something deeper than our past patterns and stories that we can trust in, if we go. Han Solo (engaged by Obi-Wan) plays this role for Luke Skywalker and Hagrid for Harry Potter, at Dumbledore's bidding. In the passage between worlds, Katniss finds an ally in Peeta Mellark, the baker's son, and meets Haymitch, their deceptively hapless mentor. If we are humble enough (think Harry, not Luke) to admit when we are entering difficult terrain, we can find friends on the path who help smooth the way.

The third way our heroes cross the threshold is the eyes-open, conscious choice to risk oneself in the face of hazard in the deep unknown.

This is rare. Some heroes flop around a bit and then choose, but some do go straight away. Diana takes this path after the US pilot Captain Steve Trevor crash-lands off the coast of her island. She pulls him from the water and saves his life, just as a battalion of German soldiers that were pursuing him descend on the island. While the Amazon warriors prevail in the fight, Diana's mentor Antiope is killed protecting her from a bullet. Perhaps it is this sacrifice that drives Diana to her own? Soon after, Diana leaves the magical island with Steve to seek out and destroy Ares, who she believes is orchestrating the destruction of humanity through this war.

Many of our great spiritual leaders illustrate this *third way* and conscious labor—the voluntary encounter with the unknown that comes with the understanding that in times of great tension and confusion, the thing that will save us does not exist in the "world" of what we already know. We saw this in the story of the Buddha, Prince Siddhartha, who deconstructed his world and himself by choosing to leave the comfort and privilege of his life behind the palace walls. And there are many Old Testament heroes, such as Noah and Abraham, who heed the call directly, however difficult the road ahead seems. Since Abraham was about 75 years old when he was called, the good news is that it is never too late!

CHOICES AT THE THRESHOLD

The five legitimate children of *Game of Thrones'* Ned Stark, Warden of the North, illustrate the different options for the would-be hero at the threshold. All of the Stark children have their known world altered when their father Ned is called away from the Stark home at Winterfell to serve King Robert Baratheon in King's Landing. Since King Robert is really a pawn of Queen Cersei's family, the power-hungry Lannisters, he is a symbol of the deterioration that sets in when order is not periodically renewed. Ned Stark (once a hero in his own right) is no match for the growing corruption and tyranny that turns everyone's world upside down. Eventually, King Robert is killed and Ned is executed, as the Lannisters take the Iron Throne and assert their power over the Seven Kingdoms of Westeros. This rise of tyranny, set against the threat of an encroaching ice age and army of dead "White Walkers", marks the threshold for Ned Stark's children. When the forces of both Nature and Culture are fraying, we are at a shock point.

Each of the Stark children navigates the shock point differently. The youngest, Rickon, essentially stays unconscious or undeveloped at point 9. Since that may be the fault of the writers who chose not to develop his character, we might throw him a bone here. Still, it's a good example of one choice we have—to not wake up or change at all, while tyranny and chaos unfold all around us.

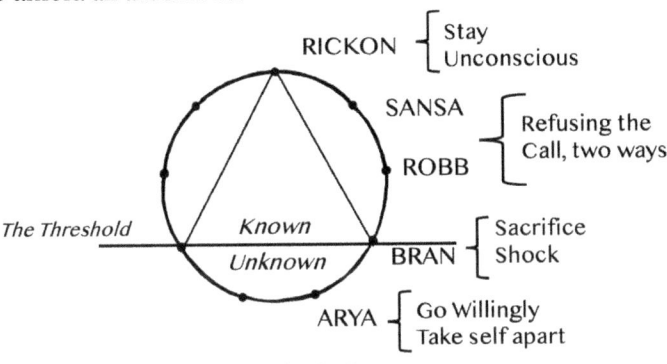

CHOICES AT THE THRESHOLD

At points 1 and 2, Sansa and Robb Stark represent the two different ways we adapt to change with our ego still intact. Young Sansa sides *with* the tyrannical aspect of the known by naively aspiring to marry prince Joffrey Baratheon (actually the child of two Lannister siblings), who is destined to be king. Robb reacts reflexively *against* the Lannisters and mounts an army to avenge his father's death and restore order directly. Robb is killed, and while Sansa becomes a heroic figure in many ways as the series unfolds, she stays more aligned with the known world and past traditions of power and control, even though she is more benevolent like her father.

The other two Starks cross the threshold. The middle son, Bran, is shoved (literally) into the unknown by the malevolent act of Jamie Lannister who pushes him out of a tower window—a fall that results in Bran's paralysis. This is an example of an "inferior" external force that can rise up and have its way with us at a shock point not chosen. To his credit, however, Bran takes up his cross and forges deeper into the mystery beyond the expansive wall of ice at the far north of Westeros that separates the Seven Kingdoms from threats beyond, and into his own profound transformation as a seer and leader in his own right.

Of the five Stark children, only Arya chooses conscious labor at the outset, blazing her own trail into the unknown. It may be that her special relationship and additional time with her father at King's Landing helped her. In a very unorthodox move, Ned facilitated her training in a "water dancing" style of sword-fighting that was essential to her journey through chaos. After Ned's death, Arya establishes an aim and pursues it:

Vengeance. While hers is not yet a "heroic" or higher aim, it is one that guides and keeps her focus on the journey. Because the journey makes the hero, the important thing at this point is to go, even in Deceit.

Tyranny eventually descends into decay and chaos anyway. But to choose the unknown willingly reframes the context, making the journey seem easier, more adventurous, less traumatic. Arya hazards herself at every turn, attracting significant allies in the Hound and the Faceless Man. These and other external forces both challenge and shape her along the way so that the impulsive girl, possessed by Vengeance, is slowly transformed. From this perspective, we might predict Arya's surprising and pivotal heroic act of destroying the Night King—the leader of the army of frozen dead beings, White Walkers, that inhabit the land beyond the Wall.

The Case of Jon Snow

I left out Jon Snow, the supposed illegitimate son of Ned Stark, because he is not actually Ned Stark's son and because Jon's threshold does not come upon leaving Winterfell like the others. *Game of Thrones* is derived from a series of novels by George R.R. Martin called *A Song of Ice and Fire.* Jon Snow's journey is worth tracking, as it takes him deep into the heart of each of these elements, ice and fire (perhaps a symbol of the extremes of the two forces at the center of Being). As the events unfold that lead to the downfall of House Stark, Jon Snow leaves with his uncle Benjen Stark to join the Brotherhood of the Night's Watch, a band of men stationed at Castle Black located at the ice Wall and charged with protecting the realm from the Night King's army. For Jon, this move is a further identification with the principle of order and the father archetype.

Jon Snow's ego has been shaped by his experience of not being enough in the eyes of the archetypal father and culture in which he has grown up as a bastard son. Going to the Wall for Jon is like Pinocchio joining the puppet troupe, aligning with the father principle. Attached to traditions and outdated codes of honor, the Brotherhood of the Night's Watch and the Wall itself represent culture at the edge of order, frozen against time and change. Like Siddhartha, Jon's first encounters with the unknown forces that will undo him happen as he ventures beyond that threshold, beyond the Wall, on various missions. He finds there a world populated by Free Folk, also referred to as "wildlings," who live free of the restrictions of the known.

THE THRESHOLD CROSSING AND THE LAW OF THREE

You may recall that point 3 is not one of the points that make up the Law of Seven as seven "notes" (Do-Re-Mi-Fa-Sol-La-Si) that mark the journey around the Symbol as 9-1-2-4-5-7-8-9. Point 3 is a "shock point" and an interval or opening between points 2 and 4 (Mi and Fa). If you know the musical scale on the piano, you know that between these notes (E and F) there is no black key. So it is literally a space between notes and, from the perspective of the story, a space between worlds. It is in such "between times," when the known world (order) is no longer working, and the future is scary and unknown (chaos), that new energy and information can enter (indeed "seeks" to enter) a decaying system.

In the stories, the new intelligence that comes through this opening is symbolized as an external force (often the mentor; sometimes a tragic event) that "helps" the hero across the threshold into an unknown territory that "opposes" and will further deconstruct her former understanding of things. This intervention is "shocking" in that it changes the direction of what *might have been* if the hero had followed the arrow line that goes away from the unknown (from point 4 to 2 to 8) when chaos and change came calling.

The interval through which new information arrives also marks the penetration of the inner triangle (points 3-6-9) and the Law of Three into the Law of Seven. Normally, we don't properly inhabit that triangle because our centers of intelligence, hijacked by ego habits, are distorted and don't work together well. But at point 3, the hero who crosses the threshold is making a separation from ego and the known world. The choice to "jump out" of the fixed use of centers and into the *flow* of Being is a beginning effort of third force consciousness that can hold the paradox of opposing forces (order and chaos) without reverting to defensive habits. I like to imagine that when we are finally present in our centers—the three points of the triangle—they are more open and aligned, and so create a "doorway" through which higher intelligence can flow. The hero is still governed mostly by ego here, but this active movement into chaos is an embrace of the opposite and a willingness to *stand in the middle* (in the not-knowing) that creates an opening for that *something more* to emerge in the Law of Three.

THE ROAD OF TRIALS

Crossing the threshold, the now-more-alert hero moves into a series of challenging encounters in the unknown that Joseph Campbell named the Road of Trials. This road is the territory between the threshold at point 3 and the Abyss at point 4 that marks the edge of the Void space between points 4 and 5 on the Enneagram. It further explains Gurdjieff's assignment of conscious labor. In addition to voluntarily choosing the challenge of stepping into the unknown, conscious labor includes the essential work of inner development called *self-remembering.* This is a particular kind of self-awareness in which we honestly observe our body, feelings, and thinking while they are happening. It requires that we fully inhabit our being/body, so that we can actually *sense* what is going on during our observation.

Self-remembering is a process of remembering that we are far more than our personality. Because self-observation creates a separation between one part of yourself who is *watching* and another who is *being,* through this process we also come to know an aware part of ourselves that is not fused with our experience. Separating from personality to align with awareness itself (jumping out of the distorted use of centers with real-time awareness) paves the way for more conscious being through aligned centers of intelligence. When we can observe an automatic thought or feeling as it arises, we create a tiny separation and opening, as well as a measure of choice over what's next. The alchemists called this entire phase of the work between points 2 and 4 *separation.* The first separation is leaving the known by cleaving this "inner observer" aspect of consciousness from the embedded patterns of the ego

Along the road of trials, we can use this growing capacity to direct our attention, observe, and sense, in order to further differentiate and name aspects of our type that have been unconscious. Unlike simple self-analysis, inhabiting and re-membering our deeper self (literally, inviting it into awareness as a "member" of our whole self) introduces us to both shadows and hidden potential. No amount of reading about your Enneagram type creates growth. Only with conscious labor can we accurately sense, see, feel, and free ourselves from the habits and unconscious forces that block our true nature. In this way, conscious labor contributes directly to the development of our essential and whole self with access to higher centers of intelligence.

From a psychological perspective, crossing the threshold marks a turn inward, away from the ego's various strategies for defending us from potentially uncomfortable, previously unconscious contents. It is a *road of trials* because this turn of attention inevitably offers up repressed feelings and desires, fears and judgments, memories not dealt with, and other aspects of our unconscious we developed ego strategies to avoid. They tend to arise when we start practicing any kind of solitary reflection or meditation. But also, if we are choosing this encounter and developing an inner observer on purpose, we are going to see and feel how our ego works habitually to defend us from all this stuff. The road of life, walked with awareness, shows us the structure and function of what we have been up to in personality if we let it.

Our heroes' ego habits are revealed through a series of tests that show their strengths as well as where they have work to do if they are to survive the graver danger of the abyss and Void ahead. Campbell noted that the challenges of the road of trials often come in threes. In the first *Harry Potter* movie, Harry (with his allies, Ron and Hermione) faces a giant troll in the bathroom at Hogwarts, tames a wayward broomstick during a quidditch match (while simultaneously catching the snitch to win the match), and is saved by a centaur from his first brush with death in the dark woods outside the school grounds. All of this from an 11-year-old boy! We see both his character and his Deceit in the naivete with which Harry pursues heroism. This string of adventures serves to reveal issues, but also to prepare him and strengthen alliances before the defining face-off with his nemesis Voldemort in the cavernous basement below the school. That's the point of the road of trials; it illuminates the truth of what the hero is made of *and* the unconscious habits blocking him from his higher self and Source—or the Force, in the case of Luke Skywalker. When Obi-Wan Kenobi first teaches Luke about the Force, Luke is still too reckless and arrogant to understand and sacrifice his ego. He starts to get clearer after he is tested and humbled in the rescue of Princess Leia and events that unfold on his visit to the Death Star.

Simba's road of trials seems pleasant in comparison. He is rescued from solitary shame, depletion, and circling vultures in the desert by a couple of misfits: Timon, a wise-cracking meerkat, and Pumbaa, a somewhat dense warthog. They teach him their signature *hakuna matata* "no worries" approach to life. This doesn't seem like a road of trials, until you consider that Simba is a descendent of the kings of the jungle. His Deceit consists of the gluttony of singing and dancing, laying around, and eating bugs. While Simba surely needed a dose of Humility, this is humiliating. Nala (by then a beautiful lioness) makes haste to reflect as much when she finds him in this state. She challenges Simba to take back his pride in the form of their homeland, the Pride Lands, which has dried up and deteriorated under Scar's tyranny. Not yet ready to look honestly and take the leap into *who he could be* as a more integrated hero, Simba refuses her initially.

Dorothy crosses the threshold into the strange land of Oz and immediately has to surrender conceptions of the known to see the truth of her nature. She first comes to see the truth of "mind" when she meets a talking scarecrow with a head of straw. Her road of trials continues to illuminate the forgotten and rusted heart of the Tin Man and the repressed instinctual energy of the Cowardly Lion. This is a direct reflection of our own assignment as we cross the threshold: to look honestly at our habits and how they obscure our centers of intelligence. Dorothy's work is cut out for her now, as she goes on with the journey of healing and aligning mind, heart, and body on her way Home.

Jon Snow's trials beyond the Wall are equally revealing. While he spends time with the Free Folk and even succumbs to the sexual advances of the powerful and spicy wildling woman Ygritte, he is dabbling, insufficiently humble in the face of the power of chaos to deconstruct everything he knows about himself and the world. Ygritte embodies what Campbell would call "the temptress," a bit of a diversion or false flag in the encounter with the unknown Great Mother principle. And still, it is a near lethal engagement, and a premonition of his future undoing. When Jon returns from his first threshold crossing to Castle Black and the Night's Watch Brotherhood finally, he is half-dead with three arrows in his back courtesy of Ygritte.

It is not clear that Jon Snow, even after surviving these serious wounds, has been changed by his encounter with chaos. He goes on to throw himself recklessly into further death-defying missions to subdue "the wild" on behalf of the brotherhood—a metaphor for wrangling his own disruptive unconscious nature. This "works" for him to some extent, as after bravely leading the defense against a wildling attack on the Wall, Jon is elected to be Lord Commander of the Brotherhood of the Night's Watch. Like Pinocchio as he masters the puppet stage, Jon Snow has somehow "made it" in the eyes of his culture. In truth, this is a return to ego as the "less than" feeling of Envy that drove Jon to the far edge of the father principle (ice) flips into superiority. One of Jon's first moves as commander is to personally execute one of his own former oppressors, Janos Slynt, who resists Jon's order.

As the road of trials reveals the truth about our hero's ego habits, we can start to identify the core issues driving them. In Enneagram terms, one of these is our emotional habit or passion. Working with the passion is key to unlocking greater possibility that has been kidnapped by our unconscious habits. Carl Jung taught that emotion is a bridge to the unconscious, because our reactivity shows us where we are hooked by our past beliefs and wounds. In doing the conscious labor of self-remembering, we come face-to-face with lots of expressed and unexpressed feelings that drive us, shape our attention and perception. If we follow those feelings and our reactivity deeper, in time we may find a driving theme defined by one of the Enneagram passions.

We can see this kind of motivational theme in each of our heroes, and it is sometimes even embodied as a primary adversary or ally. Arya Stark faces her passion in the form of Sandor Clegane or "the Hound," who is himself consumed by Lust for revenge. Fittingly, the Hound teeters on the edge between ally and persecutor for Arya. While he is a very difficult companion at times, he protects as well as challenges her, and ultimately shows her the way to healing her ego's commitment to Vengeance. Snow White takes this idea even further, as her allies across the threshold come in the form of the seven dwarves: Grumpy, Happy, Sneezy, Bashful, Dopey, Doc, and Sleepy. While it's a stretch to map these exactly to the seven deadly sins and the passions of the Enneagram, the metaphor is an apt one. Snow White serves, supports, and gathers these disparate drives (parts of herself) who can then act in service of *her* when she eats the poisoned apple and descends into the Void in a death-like sleep.

While the particular passion of our Enneagram type is generally the hardest to unravel, Snow White reminds us that we all have *all* of the passions to contend with and to integrate as we travel the journey. Facing, feeling, and yet <u>not</u> acting out the emotional intensity of our lower heart center starts to develop in us third force consciousness. When we can hold the tension of strong drives, without either letting them take over *or* repressing them, we break down the ego structures and build more of this very important capacity to integrate paradox and open the door for a higher, more inclusive way of being and seeing the world. We will explore this further at the edge of the abyss ahead. For now, we must travel our personal road of trials and unmask the truth and exploits of our own ego adversary.

Inner Work on the Road of Trials

As we consciously cross the shock point between worlds and choose the voluntary encounter with our own depths, we will first face the aspects of our type that drive us. Easing up on those will later reveal what is lurking deeper in the unconscious, under the ego's protection. By design, this work challenges our cherished sense of self and attachment to ways of being we think work for us. Joseph Campbell describes the road of trials as a process of "dissolving, transcending, or transmuting the infantile images of our personal past." [96] But because the hero who steps into the adventure is also "covertly aided by the advice, amulets, and secret agents of the supernatural helper," when we pass through the narrow gates into the unknown places of our soul, we will be carried by our own mentors and unseen forces. Whether the intelligence of a greater consciousness, the Holy Spirit, the generosity of Mother Nature in her ever-present unfolding, or all of the above, the stories suggest that we can trust the process of this undoing.

Our road of trials begins what we call "shadow work." Everything we don't like and don't want to see about ourselves gets thrown downstairs into unconscious or "shadowed" terrain. But we don't actually get rid of that stuff. Father Richard Rohr says: "Our shadow is often subconscious, hidden even from our own awareness. It takes effort and life-long practice to look for, find, and embrace what we dismiss, deny, and disdain. After spending so much energy avoiding the very appearance of failure, it will take a major paradigm shift in consciousness to integrate our shadow in Western upwardly mobile cultures."[97] We come to full consciousness, he says, by making friends with our failings. Truth sets us free.

For all of us, whatever the Enneagram type, conscious labor begins the movement from Deceit to Veracity—the virtue at point 3. Deceit describes the identification with our separate ego. When we believe this is who we are, there is no observing self to reflect on what is driving us and what might be the costs and benefits of our habits. That's why the first step across the threshold requires *separation* from ego—freeing a part of us that can observe, sense, and experience the ego's patterns. We cannot transcend ego until we first see it clearly: how it operates, what drives it, and what it serves to hide from our awareness. Veracity is becoming present to the truth of our whole being and the interconnected flow of Being as it arises continually through our centers of intelligence, undistorted by ego habits. We have some work to do to get there.

Our centers of intelligence are perceivers and transmitters of energy and information that flows into and out of our mind, heart, and body. We receive and make sense of experience with our beliefs and expectations, as well as our emotional and instinctual reactions to it. Similarly, we "send" information through our emotion, attention, instinct, and body language, as well as with our words. In fact, social scientists suggest that only a very small percentage of the messages we receive, and that people get from us, are verbal. Our presence speaks louder than our words. Gurdjieff used the metaphor of "buffers" or organs that prevent humans from being in contact with the truth and flow of reality, which is an apt way to think about how our centers cloud or distort the full measure of energy and information, coming and going. They are preoccupied with their own unconscious agendas.

We might, for example, see and feel criticized by a distracted face if we are sensitive to judgment. Or we might unconsciously convey judgment of another person with our body language, even though we tell ourselves and them "it's nothing." With our thinking, feeling, and instinctual reactions, we are tossed about by the automatic operation of our dual nature, our *yes* and our *no*. By habit, we like and dislike, agree and disagree, seek pleasure and avoid pain. We are effectively "owned" by this kind of compulsive reactivity, continually creating more of our past personality in the future and keeping ourselves hooked to the material world and a sense of self as separate.

But we don't see all this. This is the Deceit—our limited way of seeing and being in the world in ego. Of course, we are not doing it on purpose. But it's still happening, which is why some teachers specify the passion here as Self-Deceit. Veracity grows for all of us as we courageously look first at the "shadow" programs driving our ego habits of thinking, feeling, and reacting (our own versions of Scarecrow, Tin Man, and Lion). We come to see and sense these aspects of our character that, while seeds of our great strengths, also are limiting and sometimes thwart our best intentions or, worse, manifest in destructive forms. Most importantly, we uncover the ways they keep us from fully inhabiting our centers of intelligence (also like the Scarecrow, Tin Man, and Lion) so we can be in touch with all of who we are.

Like laboring in our jobs or our gardens, conscious labor is an effortful and continuous process, not an event. Self-remembering as we carry out habits and patterns is challenging not only because it is unpleasant, but also because it takes more brain energy to activate that conscious system, the "rider" part of our brain that does the observing. And yet, *not* doing the work is also labor—just in a different way, one that perpetuates the same problems in our lives, and the same polarization and conflict in the world. Our goal as we move into the unknown, then, is to be as open-minded as possible in noticing the ways our habits work automatically to obstruct the well-being of ourselves and others while we also notice the strengths they have developed in us.

WHAT EXACTLY IS SHADOW WORK?

Shadow work is a term that gets thrown around easily but not often described. The reason we dig deep and look for the unconscious patterns and disowned parts of ourselves is not because we enjoy seeing this messiness. We do it because these patterns are what prevent our autonomy and growth, our healing and wholeness. Our unknown habits prevent our three centers of intelligence from working clearly and working together, as a singular "I" or will, intentionally directed in the true manner of their design.

We also do shadow work because (thanks to our ego) we have given away a lot of power and energy by disowning the things we learned that we "shouldn't be" and things about ourselves that are too scary for us to allow into awareness. It takes a lot of energy to keep this stuff repressed. And when we repress and push feelings and whole parts of ourselves out of awareness, they are *more* likely to sneak up on us and cause problems or prevent us from being free and aligned with our higher aim. Yes...more likely. Remember how the tyrant attracts the chaos dragon? It is precisely the pressing down that spools up tension and the drive for unconscious material to rise. So as we consciously face the impulses and energies hiding behind our defensive patterns, not only do we calm their need to make themselves known, but also we can use the energy freed up for further growth.

Finally, we do shadow work to take back the projections we met at point 1. Carl Jung taught something like "you spot it, you got it" to describe the defense mechanism of projection that causes us to see in (or project on to) others what we can't or won't look at in ourselves. If you've ever wondered why a certain quality or type of person bothers you immensely while your partner doesn't react at all, that has everything to do with your shadow and its *projection*. Why do you react to *this* person or quality, and not something else? We are all capable of projection. It is one way our fixated head center can distort information and shape our experience according to the particular concerns and attention-focus of our Enneagram type. Here are some examples by type, but as always, please consult your own experience to discover what it is that you project on and react to in other people.

Type 1s often see what is "wrong" in others and the world, because they try so hard to disown their own imperfections.

Type 2s may see needs in other people and in the world, because they won't see their own.

Type 3s often see how things are not good enough and can be better and faster, rather than own what does not feel worthy inside.

Type 4s can see others as abandoning or judging them rather than seeing how they do this to themselves.

Type 5s imagine that what drains them is out there versus seeing the persistent way they cut themselves off from life energy.

Type 6s can see what is threatening or unreliable outside themselves versus owning their own fear and self-doubt.

Type 7s may see potential limits or dampers to their well-being outside themselves rather than seeing the persistent way they limit themselves with their compulsive avoidance of pain and suffering.

Type 8s tend to see oppressors out there and move to right the scales rather than finding the internal bully.

Type 9s may see conflict and pressure as coming from others rather than seeing how they are constantly in internal conflict, pressing down their own strength.

No matter what your Enneagram type, you can look at what triggers you in others to identify an internal issue that controls you from the shadows. While this may be incredibly annoying or shame-inducing, re-owning our projections is one of *the* most effective ways that Carl Jung taught to reveal our shadow and restore energy, heal our divided self, and repair our conflicts with others. Bringing more of the unconscious into conscious awareness, we gain choice over it. For example, if I know that I am so self-critical that I tend to imagine others criticizing me, I can let go of those thoughts when they arise and stay present with a person to experience reality as distinct from my projections. When you understand how this works, it's fabulous, because you can use the irritating (or infuriating, or shame-inducing...) "other" as a teacher or a flag for you to unwind what is triggering you *from the inside.* Pretty much everything we see *out there* exists as a seed, at least, in us. This can be tricky to own, however, because sometimes a shadow is very hard to see.

If I react strongly against "selfish" people, selfishness is probably in my shadow. Now there are two ways this can go next. I might be able to acknowledge my selfishness, own and forgive it as part of my messy humanity. With this internally generous stance, then, I more easily forgive others in their missteps (and no longer get so triggered). That's called "integrating" a shadow. I think it's like digesting it. Somewhat paradoxically, we disempower its control over us by "owning" it, or at least its possibility. Then we are free to set a boundary (or whatever else is needed in relation to that other person), without all the tension, reactivity, and fanfare that generally fuels the fire of blame and polarization.

However, I might *not* see my selfishness. If I hold myself to very high standards of unselfishness, as a rule, how could I be selfish?! How could I be projecting? Well, when I am having the reaction to selfishness out there (a big "no, not me"), *it is still controlling me* from the shadow. I am tense and reactive when I see it. And because of my judgment of the potentially selfish part of myself, I compulsively hold myself to an opposite extreme standard. This rigidity will make my own life difficult, as well as the lives of the "selfish" others who continually trigger me.

Unexamined, our shadows drain us. I recently asked a leader if she felt like she had to contain herself often. Her voice cracked with emotion as she said: "All the time." I knew immediately that this was both a tender spot and a place we must go to unlock energy. While it was not comfortable to touch into this pattern, and where it came from, when we hung up the phone she already felt more free. We also set her up to watch for the times and circumstances in her day when she was "managing herself," and to learn what exactly she was managing. That's shadow work. Without shining a light and rooting around in this previously hidden and painful pattern, she would continue to be drained by the automatic way it grips her life and leadership.

The Enneagram of Personality can be very helpful in pointing us toward what to observe. For us the road of trials also comes in threes, as in our three centers of intelligence. Our road of trials work is to observe and experience instinctually driven reactivity (from our dominant instinct), the emotional and motivational drive that most defines and derails us (our passion), and the fixed ideas about self and others that shape our limited view of reality (our fixation). We are trying to become conscious of what owns us.

Just observing the conditioned habits that keep us bound to the past, distort our centers of intelligence, and obscure the potential of who we could be, starts to take apart the ego structure. This will not be comfortable as, again, feelings, thoughts, and memories kept out of our everyday awareness by these habits will arise. And yet, it is a necessary step on the way to greater health and wholeness. Like our heroes, it is not a bad idea to go with allies, as well as to learn to be an ally to yourself. As we collect our awareness, bring light to what was in the dark, and learn, without judgment, we strengthen our integrated presence and the conscious third force that will eventually help reconcile dark and light, the unconscious with the conscious mind, and make order out of the chaos within.

OBSERVING THREE CENTERS

The Body Center and Instinctual Drives

While mind, heart, and body obviously tangle together as we live our lives, it serves us to describe and try to observe them separately in learning how they work together in personality. The old alchemists would say that only what is separated can be re-united. So not only is this cataloging work stabilizing, giving us at least some structure in murky terrain, but also sifting and separating what's useful from what is not—the old tyrant king from our heroic potential—prepares us for the sacrifice ahead.

Starting with the body, the work of self-remembering requires that we practice sensing our body, energy, and movement from the inside, not just with our minds alone. Again, without this work we can never progress, because our ideas about type structure are only that—ideas. We can change ideas, but that doesn't change the essential reality of the feelings, impulses, and thoughts as they arise *in* our bodies. We will have to get to that level of reality to disempower conditioned habits and unlock new intelligence.

It's surprising to realize how little we are in touch with when we start observing and sensing from within. I know for myself, I can't say I really felt feelings until I worked on experiencing them as they arose through sensations in my body. Before that, they existed as agitation that was caught up and perpetuated by the mind's need to obsess or repress with thinking and distraction. There is no real chance to capture, process, or shift the various expressions of our ego structure until we fully inhabit them. Because all of our automatic programs (whether expressed through mind, heart, or body) arise from this body as a record of our past conditioning, a body scan or mindfulness-based practice for inhabiting and sensing through all three centers of intelligence is an essential vehicle for the work.

But there is also more specific self-observation work to do in the body center. The Enneagram system names three instinctual drives: the self-preservation instinct, the social instinct, and the sexual instinct.[98] We all have all of them, or the basic wiring for them, as they are part of our human inheritance. There is disagreement among long-time Enneagram teachers as to the specifics of how these instincts show up in humans, and also how they mix with the passion to make three distinct subtypes within each Enneagram type. Because the Enneagram describes universal laws, I again turned to other disciplines to see if I could understand the instincts through a broader lens.

John Bargh is a cognitive scientist from Yale whom some consider to be the utmost expert on the workings of the unconscious. As he describes it, we all come "factory installed" with three drives, inherited from our ancient past, that significantly shape our automatic actions and reactions.[99] This means they work with or without us, often driving us to behave in ways counter to our best intentions. These three unconscious drives correspond with the three instincts described in the Enneagram system. Importantly, they are also aligned with the three forces at the center of Creation and organized in the triadic pattern of the Law of Three.

Bargh describes the two survival drives that evolved first as: the drive for safety and the drive to reproduce. At the most basic level, we could think of these two drives as contraction and expansion. We have the drive to survive by conserving resources and repelling threats (maintaining order), and the drive to survive by extending one's reach and genetic material beyond current boundaries (moving into flow/chaos). Even single-celled organisms exhibit these two drives as impulses to avoid and approach. In the Enneagram system these drives are aligned with 1) the self-preservation instinct: a drive to contract, conserve, repel threats, and stay safe; and 2) the sexual instinct: a drive to explore and compete to create and extend the species.

The third instinctual drive, which Bargh describes as "cooperation," arose a little later in history as a result of gathering in groups to live better. We have an innate drive, facilitated by the presence of emotion, to adapt with, help, and cooperate with others. Cooperation also served as a mediating force in its initial arising, as it likely inhibited extremes of either the sexual or self-preservation drives that did not go over very well in a group context. Cooperation is still a survival instinct, but it forwards survival through adapting to others: belonging to, sustaining, or directing the life of the group in order to also preserve and extend the self. This drive corresponds with the third instinctual drive described in the Enneagram, the social instinct.

As you can imagine, each of these instincts can play out in affirming *and* denying ways. They are essentially animal instincts after all. Animals can be driven to compete and kill for resources in the name of preservation and survival, compete and kill to acquire a mate and extend the species, and compete and kill to take power and defend the tribe in responding to the social instinct. While our human version may be (a little) better behaved, it is important to remember that these are strong drives. And because the instincts are part of that automatic elephant system in our brain, most of us aren't very aware of how they work in us.

While we all have all three, one of them tends to be more dominant, another repressed. Both the dominant and repressed instincts can strongly influence our unconscious habits. Repressing or "going against" a shadow or drive can create just as strong a hook as "going with" a dominant drive. With careful attention and sensing on our road of trials, we can start to experience the way each of the instincts operate in us. Again, we would do well to notice the actual experience of these essential survival drives to contract and create boundaries, to expand and destroy boundaries, and to adapt our own needs within a broader social context.

Ideally, we would have all three instincts working in balance, and we would be at choice with how they play out in our lives. We actually need to be *more* in touch with our most primal instincts, as this is an important source of life energy and higher intelligence, but they too get distorted and mixed up with other centers of intelligence. In particular, our emotional habit or passion of type mixes with our dominant instinct; this combination makes up a powerful underground force and unique Enneagram subtype expression. Because there are three instincts, there are three distinct ways that the dominant instinct engages with the passion in each type: one in which the instinct moves against the passion (a "countertype"), one in which the instinct moves with the energy of the passion, and one in which the instinct goes either way according to context. These three versions of the passion/dominant instinct relationship make up the three subtypes of each Enneagram type. As you might imagine, they can look a bit different from each other.

So there is more granular self-observation work required to learn how all this works in you. Again, it is important to discover your own experience, especially because of conflicting information about the nature of the instincts and subtype expression across Enneagram schools. My belief and hope is that applying a deeper understanding of the Law of Three to type and subtype could resolve the discrepancies, but that is a subject for another time. If you have not gotten to this subtype level of complexity of the Enneagram of Personality, no worries. Just observing the instincts in yourself will be enough to help you begin to see how your ego structure results in conditioned reactions that defend but also limit you.

Passions—The Heart Center

The Enneagram passions are the realm of the heart center. These emotional and motivational drives also run their own programs that capture and control us. In contrast to the ancient instincts, these unconscious influences are rooted in our more recent personal past: our early relationships with caregivers, as well as our inborn temperament. If you are like me and Snow White, you might find that you also "live with" all of the emotional habits listed around the Enneagram Symbol. However, most people find one passion that is not just a passing feeling but rather a constant, compulsive state of the heart that dominates their experience. It provides the fuel for the ego structure's particular worldview and operating strategy. The passion can be hard to resist, as it works to maintain a core sense of self, safety, and ego strength. It takes a lot for Arya Stark, for example, to give up her Lust for revenge or for Jon Snow to transcend Envy.

And yet, the other label we talked about for the emotional habit, the vice, describes how this passionate drive causes us to *miss the mark* of our higher self and essence as One with Source and *All that Is*. The irony of this situation is that, in an errant attempt to "be ourselves" and to compensate for what we felt was missing as we grew up, we prevent ourselves from being fully present in all of our centers of intelligence—through which we might actually experience what it is that we have been looking for! It turns out that we are punished *by* our sins, not *for* our sins. On our road of trials, we aim to root out this sneaky source of suffering by experiencing its exploits.

As you gear up your inner observer to experience yourself in moments you can see for yourself: *What is my most powerful motivating drive...the one I can't NOT do? What is my knee-jerk reaction to challenge? What passion derails my higher aim or gets in my way of being the person/parent/ leader I want to be? What passion am I most powerless to avoid, calm, or recover from? What quality do I most often get feedback about, or do those closest to me have trouble with?* Mostly likely in this reflection you will find something new and something true about your Enneagram type passion. Here is what I have gathered from my teachers and experience about the central drives and how they cause us to miss the mark of our true self:

Anger, at **Point 1**, is an anger-against things that are not as they *should* be—in myself, others, or things in the world—and the related drive to fix or improve them. It is fundamentally a drive that defines and separates. This prevents me from experiencing the essence and perfection of myself, others, and things as they are, continually unfolding at a deeper level of Being.

Pride, at **Point 2**, is a driving need for self-elevation through being pleasing, likeable, and seeing and fulfilling others' needs without having needs of my own. While I'm sure I need this connection, it prevents me from being present to experience the love that is always already available and freely given from the ground of Being itself.

Deceit, at **Point 3**, is denying the truth of my being while over-identifying with qualities and characteristics that will allow me to earn my worth and be valued in whatever situation I find myself. Absent from my own heart, I can't experience the inherent worth of my own being without effort, in relation to greater Being, in a Universe harmoniously unfolding on its own.

Envy, at **Point 4**, is a pervasive drive to see what's beautiful and good outside myself that leads to a painful sense of longing, or to sometimes compensate by feeling superior. This prevents me from inhabiting and knowing the ground of my unique being as, simultaneously, an equal part and one with the ground of Being.

Avarice, at **Point 5**, is a holding back and holding in of myself, energy, time, space, and knowledge out of a fear of being depleted; it is a resistance against feeling and flowing with the life force of Being itself. This prevents my receptive wisdom and the energy that comes from being present to the continuous flow of intelligence available.

Fear, at **Point 6**, is the reaction to danger that may or may not be an actual threat. Because I am not inhabiting my own being, I cannot trust my inner authority. I make great effort to gain certainty. This prevents me from experiencing my inherent knowing and a strength accessed through Being in connection with *All that Is*.

Gluttony, at **Point 7**, is the pursuit of what brings pleasure and enables me to avoid pain; it is a desire to sample many things and not be limited. When I am out striving, however, I am not home in myself to experience the simple and essential joy always available through being present to the depth and flow of Being as it moves through me.

Lust, at **Point 8**, is a drive of excess and intensity to help me experience my impact on the world. It fills my inner emptiness through physical gratification, provocation, and expansion of energy. When I am not present, however, I can't experience the inherent aliveness of this moment, nor relax into the innocence and pleasure of Being itself.

Sloth, at **Point 9**, is a drive to avoid being in touch with my own sense of being; it is an inattention to what's going on inside me that could be in service of my growth. When not inhabiting my full presence, I cannot experience the true power and sense of belonging inherent in my connectedness to *All that Is*.

The passion can be very difficult to see, as it is fundamentally an unconscious stance toward life and oneself. It takes time and real-time self-observation and self-remembering, experiencing your internal process in the moment. And there is always the chance that you may be the "countertype" of a particular Enneagram type, whereby the energy of your dominant instinct pushes against the passion, creating a distinct variant.[100] In any case, it will help you to also pay close attention to your head center, as our habits of head and heart work together to reinforce our ego structure.

Fixations—The Head Center

The head center is where we find our particular Enneagram fixation, the limited way that we see the world and define how to be in order to get our ego needs met. The fixation and passion work together to reinforce each other and embed the personality pattern in our very body and being. All fixations are the result of an underlying sense of self as separate from *All that Is* (a "dualistic" worldview). This sense of a separate self arises as we fall away from Union at the beginning of this life. Because of the loss of a particular perspective on Unity (our holy idea), we think we can't trust in the Universe, much less ourselves and, in order to deal with our loss and fear, we develop a set of implicit beliefs about *how to be* that correlates with our passion or driving need.

At **Point 1**, the fixation is called **Resentment**. It is a duali
splitting right from wrong, good from bad; a mental habit
resistance to chaos, both inside and outside of us, and re
against all that *should* not be.

At **Point 2**, the fixation is called **Flattery**. This worldview arises with the
Prideful drive of needing to be liked and central in the lives of others. It
centers on the belief that I can, through my efforts, get you to see, need,
and like me.

At **Point 3**, the fixation is called **Vanity**. The core of this worldview is the
belief that I am central to making things happen for others, for the world;
indeed, I earn my worth through this "heroic" action. It is reinforced by
the Self-Deceitful pattern of becoming whatever character I need to make
sure things happen.

At **Point 4**, the fixation is called **Melancholy**. With this worldview, I see
myself as uniquely outside the ordinary human flow of life. This leaves me
feeling disconnected from a lot of basic goodness, noticing what is missing
in me and experiencing Envy towards what seems superior out there.

At **Point 5**, the fixation is called **Stinginess**. With this view of being cut
off from the interconnected flow of life, I see a world and others that
will overwhelm me. Focused on the risk of being depleted, I experience
the Avaricious drive to control and contain my resources of space, time,
energy, and feeling.

At **Point 6**, the fixation is called **Doubt**. This worldview arises from a
divided mind. Because I do not trust myself to navigate, the world appears
unpredictable and unsafe. I focus on questioning, testing, and finding
information from external authorities in order to assuage the Fear, or
potential Fear, related to my divided loyalty.

At **Point 7**, the fixation is called **Planning**. At the center of this worldview is the idea that I can avoid pain and limitation if I am in charge of
the manner in which life unfolds. I focus on creating options and finding
escape hatches, and fulfilling my Gluttonous driving need to bring about
more and more of only the good in life.

At **Point 8**, the fixation is called **Vengeance**. With this dualistic worldview, I notice the unfairness and injustice in the world and experience
the Lustful drive to assert myself in a big way to balance the scales, bring
retribution, and otherwise compensate for what has been damaged.

ₐt **Point 9**, the fixation is called **Self-forgetting**. This worldview hinges on seeing myself as separate and my effort as less important to the greater unfolding of life. It is fundamentally a forgetting of my essential nature. Minimizing my higher self with Sloth, I go with the flow of my material needs and instincts, maintain harmony, and avoid having to assert myself.

To uncover your own fixation, you might ask yourself: *What is my fundamental belief about how to be ok in the world? What do I believe about other people in general? What about the world and how it operates? And how do I respond due to those beliefs? What assumptions or beliefs underlie my most compulsive patterns, identified via my passion? How does the passion reinforce my beliefs or stories about myself, others, the world? What do I react strongly to in others (our projections always reveal implicit beliefs)? And what does that say about my assumptions and priorities, and my entire worldview?*

Caution: Do not lose the forest for the trees. We have to walk deep into the details of these components of functioning to sort out how the ego has been operating and learn what it is that we no longer want to rule our lives. It's easy to get lost in there, however, and spend years detailing every aspect of our Enneagram type. If we are not mindful, this can strengthen our attachment to self and self-focus. So it's always good to climb up a mountain and get some perspective on where we are now, what we are doing, and where we are going with our inner work. Right now, the most important thing is to practice staying present and open to experience in all three centers of intelligence.

Just the practice of sensing and observing starts to change us. What we really want to know is: *What closes my heart, to myself and others? What clouds a clear and present mind? What moves me to compulsive action and reaction?* And we can bring these questions into our own everyday life and work (our road of trials). Whether you are triggered by your partner's late arrival, or struggling to be influential with your peers, ask: *What am I thinking, feeling, and doing or not doing? And how is it working for me?* Stay focused on your own contribution to the dynamic; use it to sift, separate, and learn. You will find themes over time: common stories you tell yourself, assumptions and projections, feelings and an emotional tone that is typical, and rapid instinctual impulses that get the best of you at times.

All of this requires that we extend to ourselves a great deal of kindness, empathy, and courage, since we are looking at things we may not really

want to see. But if we stay in the game, we will find that consc
brought to bear on unconscious patterns serves as an essentie
to their operations. It allows us to pause, wake up, and gain
perspective. Seeing the programs that drive us and maintain our sense
"self" brings light to shadows and advances the journey. It counters Deceit,
the fundamental delusion that our efforts to maintain a coherent sense of
self are "working" for us. This counterforce helps to develop the virtue of
Veracity, which is something like *being* truth, in presence, aligned with the
flow of Being itself. This simple but powerful shift awakens the hero and
starts to develop a more conscious third force capacity to reconcile the
dualistic dance between the king and queen, order and chaos.

We build the muscle of third force consciousness by *standing in the
middle*. When we can hold what we see in the light of awareness, instead
of automatically reacting, we are holding that third point between reacting *with* and reacting *against*. In doing so, we start to break patterns and
open the way for new energy and information—a different kind of capital
"P" Presence—to come through us that is beyond what we have known in
personality. Also, learning to take this third role will be a lifesaver as we
head into the abyss. When the exiled child within us (the one that needed
those ego patterns to be safe, in control, and worthy) knows we are strong
enough to stay present in the face of all manner of monstrosity, we will
be drawn into the lair of the dragon that hides and protects him or her.

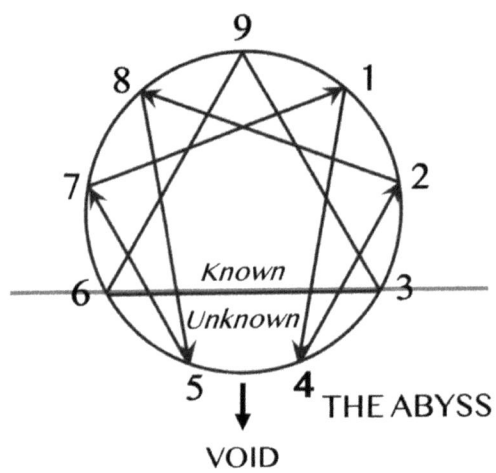

CHAPTER TWELVE

POINT 4:
THE ABYSS

But when it suddenly dawns on us, or is forced to our attention,
that everything we think or do is necessarily tainted with the odor
of the flesh, then, not uncommonly there is experienced a moment
of revulsion: life, the acts of life, the organs of life...become intoler-
able to the pure, the pure, pure soul.[101]

~ JOSEPH CAMPBELL

WHILE THE ENTIRE JOURNEY through the underworld radically transforms the hero, nothing defines the Initiation stage more vividly
than the Abyss at point 4, and the Void, the space between points 4 and
5 that is created by the hexad figure in the Symbol. This passage is very
dangerous for the hero. It is the darkest point on the journey and includes
the actual sacrifice of the ego's habitual, self-oriented and fixated strategies, everything we came to see along the road of trials. This is "the odor
of the flesh" in the above quote, that the emerging soul finds intolerable.
Campbell calls this "the crisis at the nadir...at the edge of the earth...or
within the darkness of the deepest chamber of the heart." The ordeal here,
he says, "constitutes a deepening of the problem presented at the first
threshold: can the ego put itself to death?"[102]

THE PASSION OF ENVY

Envy, the driving passion at point 4, draws us to the edge of the abyss.
Envy is not jealousy but rather a drive that sees the ultimate good and
beauty outside of us, and often finds ourselves lacking in comparison.
That comparison creates a pervasive longing for what's missing that we
call Envy. This longing is something we all taste due to our separation at
birth from unitive consciousness, and from a specific aspect of the ground
of Being that characterizes our individual soul. Having already endured
threshold guardians and the road of trials, the hero is now far more in touch
with her small-minded ego defenses, shadows, and the limiting aspects of

her psyche, and she has some sense of the threat ahead. Yet, she is drawn still deeper into the unknown...to seek! What could compel one forward in the face of danger other than the longing for *something more*, for a deeper, more sublime experience that characterizes the passion of Envy?

As Lord Commander of the Night's Watch now, Jon Snow travels beyond the Wall in another reckless mission to try to coax the wildlings to join forces in the fight against their common enemy. It is during this foray that Jon comes face to face with the immensity of this enemy: death, personified by the Night King and his army of the frozen "undead" or White Walkers. Jon survives this encounter only because the sword he was given by the former Lord Commander is made of Valyrian steel, which turns out to be one of few things that can kill the undead. Jon Snow's road of trials has revealed this hidden gift, as well as many of his limitations, and it has brought him face to face with the real enemy. But because Jon is still under the sway of his own ego needs, he cannot serve as a reconciling force. He can neither convince the Free Folk wildlings nor the Brothers of the Night's Watch (who have always been in opposition) to unite in the fight against the Night King.

At the edge of the abyss, the hero faces off with whatever has the most power to destroy her, often embodied by a central adversary and an even darker landscape that symbolizes the shadows of the collective unconscious. The collective unconscious is that part of our psyche or soul that goes beyond our personal history, connecting into archetypal patterns from a vast lineage of human experience. This realm also puts us in touch with the rhythm of life and the pattern of birth, death, and renewal that has been present since the beginning of time. *As Above, so Below*—the laws uncovered within us govern the world around us—and so, at the edge of the Void we are on the verge of touching into a vast and transpersonal realm of Being. But moving toward it is not an obvious choice!

Dorothy gets captured by the Wicked Witch and separated from her companions. The hero is often alone, with only her emerging inner wisdom to rely upon as she faces the depth and breadth of her character embodied in these scenes. Dorothy gets separated from her companions when she is captured by the Wicked Witch and trapped in the castle, surrounded by the witch's guards and those horrific flying monkeys that gave me nightmares as a little girl. The Wicked Witch creates a terrible bind for the girl by threatening to drown her beloved dog Toto if she does not give the witch her ruby slippers, a gift from her mentor Glinda that Dorothy knows she is not to relinquish under any circumstances. Even Toto runs off when he wrestles free. Things do not look good for Dorothy.

After facing some serious hazards (like a human-sized chess board with knights and pawns carrying deadly weapons), Harry Potter is also separated from his companions Hermione and Ron. He is alone in the deepest chamber under the school when he meets his anti-hero, the crippled soul of Voldemort (aptly portrayed like a puff of smog) hiding under the turban of Professor Quirrell. Being forced to look into a mirror that reflects back one's inner-most desires somehow causes *the sorcerer's stone* (thought to offer eternal life) to appear in Harry's pocket. As this is exactly what Voldemort needs to re-fashion a body of his own, Harry also finds himself in quite a crisis. Refusing Voldemort's offer of an alliance in exchange for the stone, Harry faces sure death.

Thor's moment of choice comes after he has come to care for the humans who are studying the black hole through which he fell to Earth. Like Simba, he is enjoying his time in exile, and even starts to fall in love with the astrophysicist Dr. Jane. And yet, thanks to his brother Loki, chaos calls to awaken Thor to his true destiny. It turns out that Loki is not even Thor's blood brother, but the son of the leader of the Frost Giants, King Laufey. King Odin adopted Loki after a war between Asgard and the Frost Giants...which explains Loki's perpetual scheming and trying to win his father's approval over the golden boy Thor. When Loki learns his true heritage, he causes mayhem. He offers his real father Laufey the chance to kill King Odin, and then sends a massive, indestructible robot called "the Destroyer" to Earth to kill Thor and his buddies from Asgard who have gone to retrieve Thor.

These tense moments represent an encounter with the most shadowed aspects of our character, and what they hide: the deepest chamber of the heart. The strategies of our Enneagram type are our emotional defense system. Our ego grew up to protect us from the wounds, fears, and feelings that we could not deal with. But the potential hero must face it all, the ego defense system, the ugly and disowned parts of himself, and his core wounds, to get in touch with the vast potential that makes a real hero. Harry would never become the hero he is without Voldemort, nor Dorothy without that Wicked Witch. Their willingness to face the dragon, all that unconscious chaos, and prevent it from wreaking havoc on the rest of the community, is fundamental to their heroism. For this, however, all heroes pay a price.

SACRIFICE IN THE ABYSS

Death and rebirth is one of the oldest ideas of humankind, whether the mythical phoenix rising from the ashes or the crucifixion and resurrection of Jesus Christ. Our modern stories don't shy away from this metaphor either. Both Sleeping Beauty and Snow White fall into a death-like sleep after their first real encounters with malevolence in the world. And before Voldemort makes his smoggy escape from the chamber beneath Hogwarts, he flies right through Harry Potter's heart—a move sure to kill. Death or near-death is a common theme at the edge of the Void, and the moment is often associated with water, a metaphor for the depths of the unconscious shadows we must face within as well as for the baptism into a new way of being.

By the time Pinocchio has caught on to the deadly curse unfolding for all the boys on Pleasure Island, he is already half donkey, with ears and a tail. Pinocchio watches in horror as his buddy Lampwick turns completely into a donkey and runs off screaming...or braying, really. In arguably one of the darkest Disney movies ever made, through Lampwick we gather the full consequence of the ego's endeavor to ignore facing the shadow. There seems to be some hope still for Pinocchio, however, as he is able to escape the island with Jiminy Cricket by diving directly into the ocean to brave the treacherous waters surrounding his pleasure prison.

Arya Stark, once again choosing the true Way, is willing to give up her eyesight and her identity to become "no one" (literally, that's what they call her) in training as an assassin with the Faceless Men in Braavos. As with Horus, the loss of sight symbolizes the necessity of a change in consciousness—one's way of seeing, and with the loss of identity—one's way of being. The Faceless Men is a society committed to carrying out the work of the "Many-Faced God of Death," and the members often do this by using the literal skinned faces of their previous victims as disguise. After "facing" Deceit in this way, Arya's heroic path drives her even deeper into the abyss, and the Void ahead. When her trainer decides to turn on her, Arya sustains a serious stab wound, and to escape her persecutor she dives into the waters of the canal...which seems like sure death given her woundedness.

While death is the ultimate symbol of sacrifice, our heroes represent the sacrifice of ego here in other ways too. Dorothy destroys the Wicked Witch, the embodiment of her ego's Fear and self-limiting ways. Simba is moved to give up childish avoidance and distraction when Rafiki, the wise shaman figure, crashes his *hakuna matata* party. Thor's exile parallels Simba's to an extent, but at this point in the journey Thor gets the harder lesson. He and his buddies engage in a courageous battle with the Destroyer, but it becomes clear to Thor that there is no way to defeat this machine with force (perhaps an apt metaphor for the strength of our ego structure?). In an effort to save the people he cares about, Thor lays down and gives himself up to death at the hands of the Destroyer, knowing that he is the real target for this messenger sent by Loki.

Our stories tell us that we must always sacrifice something of who we are today, maybe even the something most precious to us, in jumping curves to *who we could be.* The laying down of old strategies is required to open a new Way. The most brutal example of this to my mind (as a parent) is the story of Abraham in the Old Testament who is asked to sacrifice his own son. This is his only son, mind you, the one he and Sarah waited nearly a hundred years to have. Abraham does not have to go through with it in the end, but by then the symbolism has seared into our hearts the lesson that we are called to sacrifice our small self, and what it clings to, in order to grow into a higher aim.

Resisting the Sacrifice—the Special Case of Jon Snow

The long story of Jon Snow in *Game of Thrones* affords us the chance to see what can happen when we don't sacrifice ego willingly. Jon's leadership as Lord Commander of the Night's Watch has only accentuated the division in the brotherhood—rooted, as it is still, in his own divided heart. Soon after returning from his encounter with the Night King, Jon is lured out of his quarters late at night by Olly, a boy he rescued after some wildlings brutally murdered Olly's parents. A product of war, Olly can't see beyond his own hurt and becomes a pawn for the tradition-bound faction of the Brotherhood of the Night's Watch who are alienated by Jon Snow's leadership. Jon follows Olly into the courtyard and walks into an ambush of a handful of brothers standing by a "traitor" sign. They all take turns stabbing Jon, but the boy deals the final blow to Jon's heart.

Olly's role in the murder underscores the fact that our ego habits develop for good reason. They are adaptations to early childhood wounds; they are strategies to cope with and defend ourselves from pain and earn love. The strategies are not "bad." They are "shadows" because we don't see them clearly as largely unconscious products of our unremembered past. As an illegitimate son, it makes sense that Jon Snow was struggling to prove himself in the eyes of his culture. Order, culture, and traditions are important, even necessary, to harness and organize energy for useful ends, but these forces deny life when they become rigid and frozen against change. This is the threatening "death by ice" symbolized by the Night King. Like Pinocchio, Jon got tied up with the strings of the (dark) father principle in attempting to become a Real boy, and the ego-shattering work of facing deeper shadows awaits him.

That Jon is brought back from death by the Red Woman, the Priestess Melisandre, and her invocations to the "Lord of Light," is an indication of a big shift in his journey. Because Jon was killed by the brothers, and did not sacrifice himself, his revival does not mark the illuminating revelation achieved by other characters who sacrifice ego and face or visit death via bravery. On the contrary, it seems to kick off further trials that test and shape Jon Snow. Melisandre is a dark character, the embodiment of chaos (the dark feminine) that deconstructs ego. Melisandre leads Jon deeper, into the collective unconscious, to face greater demons. He is dark and brooding upon his revival, more aware of the challenges ahead.

Jon finally chooses his journey into the deepest part of the unknown by executing Olly along with the adults who betrayed him. This lack of compassion for the boy is uncharacteristic for Jon Snow, particularly given that Olly saved Jon's life at one point. But Olly is the sacrifice of Jon's ego personified. It is with this gesture that the part of Jon's ego attached to earning his worth within the realm of the father principle is killed. We can surely put it off, but the character we developed in response to our early relationships and culture must eventually be sacrificed (at least for a time) to do the difficult work necessary for the true hero to rise. This shocking act ushers Jon Snow into the transition from ice to fire, deeper into the unknown.

INNER WORK FOR THE SACRIFICE

Along with our heroes, our work at the edge of the Void is to sacrifice what is most precious to us: the automatic habits that make up our ego ideal and Enneagram type, everything we came to see along the road of trials. Gurdjieff described this as: "the death of the tyrant from whom our slavery comes, the death that is a necessary condition of the first and principal liberation of man."[103] For us, "the body" we sacrifice refers to the ego habits that are literally embedded in the wiring of our brain and biology. To accomplish this sacrifice, we must refuse to believe the same stories and perceptions, resist indulging the same emotional habits, and refrain from acting out our primary instinctual demands. Instead, we stay right here, present to what these habits are hiding. Stripping the veils that have protected us from old wounds might be painful, but if we can bring our ever-deepening capacity for compassionate, integrated presence to what we witness, *something more* can grow.

The ego is a tenacious adversary, however, so we may need creative strategies to break its grip, make the sacrifice, and fully enter the primordial chaos below. Like all our heroes who move deeper, into dark waters, deep woods, and towards the life-threatening encounter, we also can do this by approaching the dragon (of chaos). In Enneagram terms this would be something like calling in the opposite of our Enneagram type ego ideal. Chaos can become our ally when consciously engaged. This practice breaks down the rigid ego structure by virtue of that paradoxical process at the heart of the Law of Three. If we use a conscious third force capacity to hold the tension of "who I think I am" with "who I think I am not" *and not act out* our habitual type-based defensive responses, that clash takes us deeper into the "belly of the whale"—the furthest reaches of the Great Mother, a tomb but also a womb, as it unites "bad" and "good."

Working with opposing forces and the Law of Three also takes us into the terrain of the great mystics. Mysticism is simply experiential understanding of spiritual things.[104] At its core, mysticism is about paradox too, for example, that we can find faith, hope, and love, amid shadow and great pain. The tension of holding strongly opposing positions is not only difficult to tolerate, it serves to scramble the brain. This is the same idea behind *koans*, teaching questions from the Zen Buddhist tradition like "What is the sound of one hand clapping?" It is a strategy for pointing us at the mystery beyond the known and our rational minds. In the space of not-knowing, *something more* can arise that transcends the level of prior understanding.

The mystical journey is a journey of stages, divinely given, that takes one fully into the heart of Oneness/Love/God through deconstructing the preoccupations that separate us from that wholeness. There are a variety of ways to characterize the stages, but sacrifice is always part of the transformative process. The idea of *dying before you die* is at the heart of every mystical path. The Christian mystical journey holds that the first step to *theosis*, or to being filled with God, is *kenosis*, which means "empty" in Greek. The work is less about attaining something and more about getting something out of the way, creating an inner emptiness that allows for direct contact with the flow aspect of the Divine, the ground of Being. Like Arya Stark, when she was with the Faceless Men in Braavos, here *a girl has no name*, which is precisely the state that can lead to emergence. From an inner work perspective, we sacrifice ego because our centers of intelligence need to be unclogged of biases, patterns, and other personal stuff, to work freely as clear receivers and transmitters of information and energy from the flow of Being as it continuously arrives through us. Using the Law of Three to grow—deconstructing a thing by engaging its opposite—is a strange formula for the rational mind. If I have spent much of my life being strong as an Enneagram Type 8, why in the world would I want to practice being vulnerable? That is likely the A#1 quality in my shadow, the bag of qualities I most abhor and disown. Or if I have been a passionate guardian of right and wrong at Type 1, to now seek play and pleasure!? Scandalous! As Carl Jung describes it: "Then the true way does not lead upward, but towards the depths, since only my other leads me beyond myself. But acceptance of the other means a descent into the opposite, from seriousness into the laughable, from suffering into the cheerful, from the beautiful into the ugly, from the pure into the impure."[105]

Using an inner chaos dragon as a conscious means for interrupting type patterns is very different from acting it out unconsciously. The point here is not to identify entirely with what we have previously disowned, but rather to use the voluntary encounter with "the other" to deconstruct type and fall into the deepest realm of chaos (*all* the disowned and unknown aspects of being kept at bay by the tyrannical aspect of personality) in hopes of unlocking new life—the treasure within. When we own *both* sides of a dilemma, with our integrated presence and attention, it can't help but disrupt the dysfunctional power politics of either/or that keeps forces polarized (trapped as they are in ego) and the type structure intact. This conscious engagement of opposites with third force consciousness forwards the necessary process of ego dissolution.

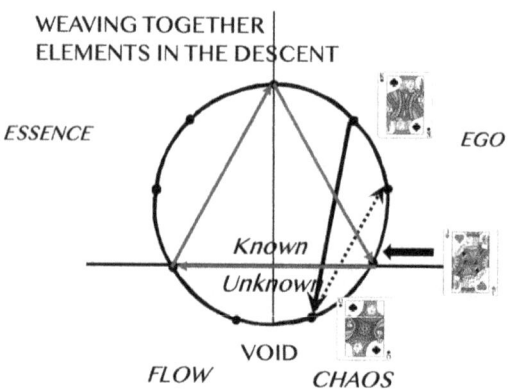

You can design your own counterforce out of your greatest avoidance. Or look to the next point along the arrow line forward from yours (e.g., if you are Type 1, look to Type 4) to find your stress-growth point. Or, since the arrow lines show us an archetypal pattern, you can also imagine your own type at point 1 and look to what would then be "your" point 4 for a secret special opposing force (that for some types is not the usual forward arrow point). Use the following only as ideas.

Type 1s can practice ease and relaxation, play and pleasure, in the face of all that may not be going according to their plans and sense of rightness.

Type 2s who focus on fulfilling the needs of others and taking pride in their capacity, can practice owning their own needs and caring for themselves.

Type 3s who earn their worth by achieving, can practice being still and feeling the truth of emotion they keep at bay.

Type 4s who are accustomed to seeing their deficits and suffering, can practice taking in the good and enjoying ordinary beauty.

Type 5s can risk spontaneity, opening themselves to elemental energy and to being touched by the watery flow of life.

Type 6s who are gripped by doubt, can take a strong stand and move into action; those who are "too sure" (the opposite of doubt) can practice staying present with the fear that compels counteraction.

Type 7s can practice being in this moment, with no plan, satisfied with the unfolding of life.

Type 8s can practice being open and in touch with their child-like nature, capable of receiving life vs. reacting.

Type 9s can risk taking up space and stepping into their power to bring about heartfelt action.

Now, just a warning...if you engage the dragon of chaos directly to deconstruct ego patterns, the prize at the bottom of that cereal box is not immediately accessible (rather more like those ones you had to send away for). The more we disidentify with ego, the more we are going to see additional aspects of ourselves that it was hiding in the shadows. We inevitably find the hurt child for whose protection this entire defense system was forged. The dragon was fierce for a reason! And we will find further impulses and thoughts we are not proud of, feelings we long ago disowned, and powerful instincts previously repressed within the myriad of disowned and exiled parts. All of this surfaces to be integrated—without fighting, fleeing, freezing, feeding, fawning, or otherwise reacting in habitual ways. This is next-level shadow work.

Jung said that "the shadow reaches all the way to Hell" as a way of conveying that at the edge of the abyss we may contact not only our personal shadows, but also when we do this work honestly we come to understand that, at some level, we are all capable of *all possible* manner of darkness and vulnerability—the collective shadow. Jung goes on:

> *It sneaks up like a fever, like a poisonous fog…Here you would gladly stop feeling across to your beyond. Startled and disgusted, you long for the return of the supernal beauties of your visible world. You spit out and curse everything that lies beyond your lovely world, since you know that it is the disgust, scum, refuse of the human animal who stuffs himself in dark places, creeps along sidewalks, sniffs out every blessed angle…Everything odious and disgusting is your particular Hell. How can it be otherwise?…Your Hell is made up of all the things that you always ejected from your sanctuary with a curse and a kick of the foot.*[106]

Gurdjieff said simply, "So long as a man is not horrified at himself, he knows nothing about himself."[107] In the end, this IS the sacrifice of ego… seeing the collective ugliness and potential for evil within.

Owning "the other" in ourselves is necessary and serious business on the road to our higher aim; we must reconcile these split-off energies to move ahead. Without this work we will remain caught in the conditioned and repressive habits that defend our ego, drain our energy, and keep us asleep to our true nature. We must also own our particular hell because we project on and fight in others what we don't face in ourselves, causing more division and pain. Richard Rohr makes it simple: "People who accept themselves accept others. People who hate themselves hate others."[108] Seeing your collective shadows and hurt requires owning your place in the messiness of humanity. And it just might break your heart, but then…that's the point. Breaking your fixated heart, defended by ego habits, prepares it for a higher heart—the sacred heart that can hold *all* that humanity in divine embrace. And it is precisely such enlargement of the individual heart that has the potential to transform us.

A most vivid example of conscious surrender to paradox and transformation is Jesus on the cross. The psychological significance of the crucifixion is the sacrifice of ego and the known world for a higher aim. His example says we are meant to go open-armed and willingly to this place of tension. "Take up [your] cross and follow me."[109] The cross is a symbol of paradox and the Law of Three, holding opposing concepts: "In him all things hold together."[110] But this process takes you apart. How in the world do you love your enemies *while* being crucified by them?! How do you hold good and evil in the same circle, in love...without blaming someone, fleeing to one pole or the other, and without turning away from the pain and confusion of that seemingly impossible stance? This is the kind of paradox that can "kill" the ego. It can send us into a dark night, raging against the pain of loss or despairing of the possibility of resolution. But ultimately staying right there ("x" marks the spot) and surrendering to the Unknowable, is the thing that makes way for the arising of a higher perspective, a fourth way and a consciousness SO MUCH LARGER that it can transmute the inner war of opposites.

Indeed, the emergence of a *vertical* dimension of growth, modeled by Jesus, is what we make Way for when we access the part of ourselves that can hold both dark and light in a broader field of awareness. It's important to call out that we extinguish the ego by *not acting it out,* <u>not</u> by denying its existence or by punishing it. In following this evolutionary pattern, we are not shaming and subjugating our sins. We disempower sin and shadow by refusing the separation, holding it all with love. In becoming the third force between deeply conflicting ideas, we hold the door open for *something more* from the flow of Being to arise through us in that opening between wanting *this* and resisting *that.*

Fighting and resisting fuels opposition, drains the energy of willpower, and traps us in duality, in an internal war. From a mind/brain standpoint, self-criticism and resistance don't work well as a strategy for change. When we are gripped by shame, creativity and learning shut down. And the science shows that simply repressing urges is not a successful path to habit change either. We need to deal directly with impulse, shadow, and sin, and hold it with acceptance and compassion, to find a new Way. Even more radical, perhaps, is the necessity of sacrificing our need to "suffer" as we do all this, as it only keeps us attached to an old identity and sense of self as separate.

This teaching of sacrificing our suffering and *welcoming it all* applies as equally in the outer world as it does in the inner world. Fighting fuels opposition and polarization. This may be why the Bible verse about "turning the other cheek" is common knowledge even across non-church-going populations. "I say unto you, Love your enemies, do good to them which hate you. Bless them that curse you and pray for them which despitefully use you. And unto him that smiteth thee on the one cheek offer also the other."[111] To change the world, we too are charged with holding paradox, which means continually sacrificing *ourselves* to that very difficult place in the middle.

This is not easy, holding both sides, embracing darkness, refusing to turn away, but it is redemptive in some way we can barely fathom. The potential promise in these stories is that in sacrificing ego—with its desire for knowing, safety, pride; its addiction to power, lust, control; its attachment to all our old stories, the blame and shame, and *all* of the passions that cause us to choose sides, suffer and *miss the mark* of the One integrated whole—by owning it all and surrendering to the process, we are given the promise of new life. Outside the habitual, fixated constructions of our mind, body, and heart, we access both the shadow *and* the transcendent. As Gurdjieff said it, "The way up is at the same time the way down."[112]

The sacrificial act that results from the full embrace of opposing forces is the last move of the alchemical process of separation. With this sacrifice of the "body" of the hero, the king and queen are separated too—the forces are released from their dysfunctional dance, freed from their imprisonment in matter to evolve into more expansive versions of themselves. Having previously lived mostly under the domain of the king and the known world, the hero then falls completely under the spell of the queen in the Void ahead. No longer bound by the body, the chaos in the domain of the Great Mother reveals itself to be the vast and undifferentiated flow of the primordial Void that awaits the light of Creation.

In our own practice, we accomplish this sacrificial movement not by leaving the physical body but rather through deeper contact with our bodies. Here's the idea: if we can tolerate and care for painful thoughts, feelings, memories, and all the discomfort that arises when we don't act out ego patterns, we can transmute the actual energy they bind up into new form (thus "freeing the king and queen" to fulfill higher-order functions). By dropping our awareness and presence deeper into the body center, we can experience these disturbances as sensation. If we can maintain enough observing consciousness in the face of those sensations to stay present and avoid repressive or distracting cognition, we can practice grounding and regulating our nervous system's reaction to relax in the face of repressed content and the stress of discovery. This sort of "bottom up" processing can help us "digest" the material and rewire old responses over time.

I learned something about this when I started practicing qigong, which is both a healing art and a meditative movement practice from Chinese medicine. As with many other body-based transformative practices, qigong guides us to *invite* discomfort (which is a literal energy block), hold still, open to it, and relax. I had done a lot of yoga before, and I would often distract myself and disconnect from my body when it felt hard to stretch and hold a difficult position. Thanks to my qigong teacher, I learned that cultivating the encounter with discomfort is really the whole point. Direct and patient presence with these knots of energy unleashes flow, health, and well-being. A new dimension can open up in a moment. To get the treasure of health and new energy, we have to meet the dragon *and* create a kind of spaciousness around it. We have to *increase* our capacity to tolerate (even welcome and love!) the intensity that arises when we move into the mystery beyond ego.

You might feel a lot more. But you likely won't die from it (only your defenses will). And not only will you realize that you can tolerate a lot more than you thought, but also this process changes something. Neuroscientist Jill Bolte Taylor experienced this passage through the Void during a prolonged stroke that took her left brain hemisphere offline. Among many revelations in this Void, she discovered that when you truly experience emotion as it arises, it lasts only for 90 seconds and subsides. That is...if you don't ruminate, leap to action, analyze and engage your past emotional memories. I can't say that's exactly true (the 90 seconds) but if you know feelings are like a wave that passes, it is easier to invite sensation without reacting and creating further suffering.

This sort of presence practice is a third way; it is neither trying to "figure out" and control our experience with our minds nor getting swallowed up by the contents of our newly accessed feelings and impulses. When we break the dualistic stand-off in *each* center of intelligence by not acting out habitual patterns, our three centers (mind, heart, body) can start to work *together* as a coherent vessel of presence with access to a greater flow of Presence that brings new energy and information. The intensity of a particular disturbance (dragon) can then be integrated, and its gifts incorporated into our increasingly more aligned intelligence centers. The result is an entirely different kind of intelligence.

TAMING THE DRAGON

So far, we have talked about three centers of intelligence featuring mind, heart, and body. Here's a twist: the body center comes in three parts (which maybe you grasped in considering the three different instinctual drives). These are called: the moving center, instinctive center, and sex center—making five total "lower" centers of intelligence. You don't have to understand all the details to use this information. What is helpful to know for now is that the moving part of the body center represents all the ways our body has "remembered" past habits, including automatic ways of thinking and feeling that are embedded in our hormones and nervous system. What we imagine to be our own free thinking and reacting are "trapped in matter," trapped in these patterns, when we are not aware. Instead, the moving center runs the show, imitating the past, keeping our ego structure intact.

When we wake up to its patterns and become willing to sacrifice them, this "body" is no longer in charge. The "king" and "queen" are then freed to evolve toward "higher" and non-polarized versions of themselves, and the body center overall can become a conduit for new intelligence. Some of that new intelligence comes from the instinctive part of the body center. In addition to the reactions that come from instinctual drives, the instinctive part of the body center contains much wisdom. First, it runs all our complicated brain and body systems without conscious participation. But also, deep in the body, beneath waves of reactivity and pain, we can sense a flow of energy and information that is part of our collective unconscious and inheritance from animals and people who lived closer to the earth. Here we tap into an aspect of the interconnected nature of reality—a knowing in our whole being that is tied to being in relationship with the natural world.

As we practice being present in all centers, relaxing the tension of embedded ego patterns, and deepening our awareness of the body center in particular, we begin to sense this connection to a greater flow of intelligence (energy and information) that animates the world around and through us. The more attention we pay to this flow of energy beneath emotional waves and personal material, the more it wakes up. You might feel it as an electric or bubbly surge; it can feel like a warm coat, or a friend, enveloping you; at times it may come to you as a sense of tension or dread, if the energy of the world around you is in disarray. Either way, when we sense that we are an integral part of the vast network of life, spirit, and energy that makes up the flow of information surrounding and penetrating us, our hearts open in a different way. Maybe you've felt it in the stillness or awe of nature? In the nave of a great cathedral? Or in the stirring of your heart when the cat or dog sits quietly on your lap?

In some sense, every time we come to an open and collected presence in our body, heart, mind, and drop through personal distraction and suffering, we "tame a dragon" and harness its elemental power as food for our developing soul. There are many ways to tame a dragon, but it is essential to have a practice that takes us into the heart of emotions as actual body sensations, and then helps us calm our nervous system and relax the reactive patterns so we can accept and integrate what is difficult. Integrating "dark" and "light" across brain hemispheres in this way, we are effectively pairing new resources with old disturbing memories and states of arousal, diluting their power by washing them in the larger field and flow of awareness.

There are many ways to do this kind of work. I like the "RAIN" meditation practice taught by mindfulness teacher Tara Brach, because it highlights another very important aspect of the greater Presence toward which we are aiming, which is the capacity to link intentional kindness with our pain and woundedness.[113] Below is my short version of Tara's practice, which begins once you are comfortable, focused, and have turned your attention inward. Remember, you can always use the breath as an anchor to come back to when you notice you are lost in a story or feeling overwhelmed.

R—Recognize what is going on inside you: observe thoughts, beliefs, feelings, impulses, and sensations—all of it. It is stabilizing to observe and name what is present, especially what is bothering or activating you.

A—Allow the experience, whatever it is. Accepting (without judgment) the actual thoughts, feelings, and sensations creates an ease that deepens awareness. You don't have to like them but do accept *what is*. Our resistance or criticism of *what is* just perpetuates the hook to it. Paradoxically, softening around the nugget of tension or pain can loosen things up.

I—Investigate by zeroing in on what is most activating. Bring attention to the felt sense of experience in your body. Where do you feel it? What is the sensation? Does it have a color or image associated with it? Don't try to explain it or tell a story about where this came from in your past, but do inquire about why it's here now: *What is the need here? What is it* *trying to tell me?* Allow insight to come. If you're prone to overanalyzing things like I am, staying present with sensation is most helpful. You will find that it often changes, moves, dissolves, and as you follow it you can investigate further what is behind the suffering. You're not really trying to solve anything, but rather to dis-solve—to allow feeling and analysis to drop away and enable the body's deeper wisdom to offer you something.

N—**Nurture** yourself with an intentional gesture of kindness, maybe something as simple as putting your hand on your heart. You can also call in the compassion and energy of another loving being or spiritual figure if it is hard to offer kindness to yourself. Even just a simple acknowledgment that it's hard to be human and navigate all this complexity is a good start.

Tara then recommends something she calls "after the RAIN," which is to rest in the more generous and expansive space of Awareness itself and the flow of life, beneath the waves of reactivity, that connects us all and sustains us. Fully aware in the present moment, when we are no "one," not separate, not attached to our familiar stories and feelings, we sense ourselves as part of this more expansive Presence within and around us. To tap into this, the Christian mystic Meister Eckhart taught that the seeker must "unknow" everything she thinks, including her definitions of God. At some point, I think, we must unknow everything we think about our Enneagram type as well. All explanations stand in the way of this opening.

Envy, the passion at point 4, has allowed us to see the insufficiency of who we have been so that we can embrace the immensity of who we are beyond the known. The hero's next move is deeper into the unknown and into the Unknowable. We have to go further, beyond Envy, because focusing on suffering or what's missing, analyzing our fixations and patterns can become another version of attachment to ego. For me, struggling to nail my type when my life experience played out all around the Symbol, this was a pivotal realization. Any version of "self-ing" takes us from Presence. All the stories we tell ourselves about who we are and who we should be are a distraction and protection from the risk of opening to the mystery of death and rebirth at the heart of life itself.

While we are also working on a longer psychological process to more permanently free our centers from old patterns at each step of the journey, the spiritual disciplines teach a direct path to this opening through various contemplative practices like RAIN. All of these practices aim at an immediate, present-moment movement beyond the known, beyond ego and its obstacles, to access the ever-present flow of life and spirit, always available through and around us. If we are willing to sacrifice ego's attachments and aversions and drop deeper into our experience in this way, we strengthen the third force that can hold the door between rigid order and uncontrolled chaos to make way for *something more* to arise from the unified field of potential accessed in that opening.

When we get better at holding third force consciousness in *each* center of intelligence, we can more often inhabit all centers. When the mind and heart drop into the body, three become One, catalyzing a Law of Three process that invites higher intelligence and results in the emergence of a fourth outcome—integrated being and a new dimension of consciousness. While we do not originate the information that comes through from the field of greater intelligence, we facilitate it by heading into the unknown, staying open, holding the tension of chaos without fleeing back to old patterns, and sensing what wants to arise. Our collected Presence then becomes like a container or vessel that allows us to welcome and integrate all that we meet in the unknown with curiosity and compassion.

Gurdjieff describes the formation of a second "body" he called the "kesdjan body," a "higher being body" that is part of our developing soul or essence. Thanks to the influx of new intelligence, the flat "trinity" of the three lower centers we were using as "mind," "heart," and "body" is turned into a "quaternity," or four-pointed figure. We can imagine it as an actual field of energy around our physical body in the shape of the lower tetrahedron.

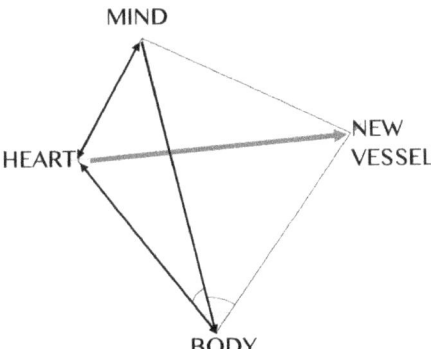

The friction created from welcoming feelings, reactivity, impulses, instincts and more, *and not-acting-out our defensive pattern*, "sacrifices" the ego and feeds our soul simultaneously, helping to form this additional energy body that connects us to a "higher" heart center. The result is a more stable center of gravity and intentional Presence that is essential for our inner work, for tolerating discomfort, and for accessing new growth. This vessel will continue to solidify into our fully integrated soul, in communication with higher intelligence or spirit, but for now it is our boat across some potentially stormy seas. Exploring the deeper realms of the unconscious and collective shadow can be challenging, and we need to do it with all the graciousness, receptivity, and compassion possible; and often with a therapist until the container is strong enough.

In my mind, this is one of the most important teachings of the work. If we stopped here, we would still make a great leap in well-being and growth. But also, if we don't build this grounded vessel, the rest of the work is not only not sustainable, but not advisable. Developing the capacity to hold our inner experience with kindness and nonjudgment (whatever it is, whether it's "acceptable" or not to our ego) is a vital foundation. Diving into deeper inner terrain without this vessel can be destructive. We can get lost in the watery realm of the Void ahead, swallowed up by unconscious contents. It is possible to get stuck. On the other hand, with a strong enough vessel of Presence, we can access a new kind of insight and guidance through this crossing.

INITIATION—*Illumination*

When the hero is still deep in the mystery of the unknown, the darkest leg of the journey resolves into a process of illumination and consolidation of learning. And, while many challenging encounters remain, we see the spark of something different start to form. The descent into the initiatory realm was about consciously engaging chaos to break down old egoic patterns of being, thinking, and feeling. We had to see them clearly to be able to sacrifice the ways we sabotage who we truly are. Deconstructing what was most precious to us and facing the repressed and rejected parts of ourselves, we find that the "other" in us leads us into an "other" dimension of being entirely.

In Taoist mythology this dimension is ruled by *Xi Wang Mu*, a very dangerous version of the dragon queen, with tiger's teeth and a leopard's tail, who sits on a three-legged stool in a deep, dark place with no beginning or end. Xi Wang Mu is also the goddess of life, death, and rebirth, however, and this "Mysterious Pass" is where death returns to life.[114] So while the emptiness of the Void is potentially frightening and definitely disorienting, it is also a source of vast potential. And as we integrate the depths of our own being, we remember more of who we are and what we know as part of the vast ground of Being that permeates the Void.

The realm of the Great Mother has many names: the Mysterious Pass, the belly of the whale, the river of Great Memory or the Cave of Knowledge, the *prima materia* ("first matter" and primordial *chaos*) from which the world was created, and the *anima mundi* or living soul of the world. Whatever we call it, traversing these waters reminds us of a current of wisdom pertaining to the interconnectedness of all things—our shared patterns of life, death, and rebirth—and it puts us in touch with a different kind of intelligence. Somehow in the depths of our being, as chaos turns into the *flow* of potential and we access a higher heart, the spark of a higher mind can take root as well. Because *the way down is simultaneously the way up*, we find the door to a vertical axis of growth through which this illumination will continue to unfold along the second half of the journey.

REVELATION IN THE VOID

CHAPTER THIRTEEN

THE VOID:
REVELATION IN THE VOID

The secret is that only that which can
destroy itself is truly alive.[115]

~ CARL JUNG

HALFWAY THROUGH THE VOID, the space between points 4 and 5 on the Enneagram, there is a profound internal change. Joseph Campbell referred to this moment of the journey as an "illuminating revelation." The dictionary describes revelation as a communication of divine truth—something revealed to humans by a greater intelligence. What is illuminated is, first off, how the two (the hero and the thing he is fighting) are actually One. Having faced all shadow within, the hero finds that *all* polarity is deeply, mutually interdependent. As the ego dissolves and the heart expands, the hero experiences no distinction between self and other, good and evil, darkness and light. As Campbell describes it:

> *The hero, whether god or goddess, man or woman, the figure in a myth or the dreamer of a dream, discovers and assimilates his opposite (his own unsuspected self) either by swallowing it or by being swallowed. One by one resistances are broken. He must put aside his pride, his virtue, his beauty, and life, and bow or submit to the absolutely intolerable. Then he finds that he and his opposite are not of differing species, but one flesh.*[116]

The hero has sacrificed ego by seeing "the other" in himself and embracing all this complexity with Equanimity, the virtue at point 4. This initial revelation kicks off further operations through which the hero will come to terms with all opposing forces. In alchemy, the integration of polarity that proceeds from the Void occurs through the process of *conjunction*; it marks a "sacred marriage." The word *marriage* is apt, because only the unifying force of love has the capacity to hold the various and conflicting parts of us, and all of life, together. At one level, we are uniting consciousness with formerly unconscious aspects of ourselves. As we face the realm of the collective unconscious, however we find that this way "down" opens out *and* up into another dimension of being entirely, one that brings light into the darkness of the undifferentiated Void. The primary revelation and focus of this transit is the creative possibility that arises from the unification of *all* opposing forces in the Void. This idea is at the heart of the Law of Three and the entire Enneagram Symbol.

UNITING OPPOSITES THREE WAYS

Campbell traces the growth through opposing forces ignited in the Void in three ways, in keeping with the three forces of Creation (chaos, order, and third force) as they act through our three mythical elements of queen, king, and hero. He defines this work as *meeting the goddess, atonement with the father,* and the *hero recovering treasure.* These are threads that will continue to unfold on the journey up the left side of the Symbol. It all starts here in the Void, however, because as the ego is dissolved all of these characters intermingle as the vast undifferentiated chaos/flow of potential—the *prima materia* from which Creation originated out of the primordial Void.

This is an important tipping point in the journey. When enough of our lower centers of intelligence have been cleared and connected, they allow for a different kind of energy and information, a greater Presence, to arise through a "vertical" dimension of intelligence in the Symbol. We are still making the very personal human and "horizontal" journey around the circle, dealing with the various faces of the adversary, and "collecting" the fragments of our energy centers. As we do this work, we are opening to virtues of the higher heart and gradually refining the coarseness of our being so it can sustain higher levels of collective being and consciousness. This work on higher *being* opens the door to the second layer of work and vertical dimension of growth—the transpersonal and spiritual aspects of higher *knowing*. Of course, the door was there all along. We just learned how open it.

The ancient Greeks referred to this shift as a change in the dimension of time, from ordinary clock time or *chronos*, to *kairos*, an extra-ordinary dimension of timelessness (the eternal) rooted in the depths of our lived experience. It is a qualitative shift or opening that happens in the moment. This dimension may or may not be connected to the idea of a Supreme Being. The "Middle Way" of the Buddha lands one in a still point, between attachment and aversion, through which we move out of duality and see anew the nature of Reality as it unfolds without our striving. During her journey through Wonderland, Alice asks the old white rabbit, "How long is forever?" His reply: "Sometimes, just one second," betrays both the immensity and the curious nature of this dimensional shift.[117]

Up to this point, the central forces of Creation symbolized by king and queen have been "trapped in matter," meaning order and chaos have been playing out their oppositional dynamic through the material concerns of a separate self. The king represents the tyranny of the conscious dominant of the psyche, our fixated ego ideal, and the queen stands for the more chaotic unconscious realm of repressed feelings and instinct, as well as hidden potential. Both are embodied as programmed habits expressed through mind, heart, and body. As we saw, the sacrifice of the hero at the edge of the Void changes things. With the release of the ego "body," the forces are freed from embedded patterns, untangled from each other, and free to evolve into higher forms. We will come back to the king's movements shortly (how the fixated conscious mind *aims higher*). For now, we will follow the hero as his sacrifice leads deep into the now un-bounded realm of a "higher" queen or *meeting the goddess.*

Thus far we have been more focused on the destructive element of the Great Mother—wicked witches and monsters of the deep, dark forces and forests, the dragon of chaos in all its forms. Part of the "illuminating revelation" in the Void is that chaos is also the source of new life, and a fundamentally new dimension of being and intelligence. The Blue Fairy who eventually turns Pinocchio from a dead puppet into a Real boy, Cinderella's Fairy Godmother, and the three Fairies who help the Prince in *Sleeping Beauty* when he is trapped in the dungeon by the evil queen, are all representations of the revivifying power of chaos. When we face chaos directly, through the sacrifice of ego, the flow of Being or the generative element of the unknowable realm is revealed.

Following his revival by Melisandre and sacrifice of the boy Olly, Jon Snow heads away from the "ice" of the controlling father principle (that melts into the water of the soul) and into the "fire" that is ignited within the terrain of the Great Mother. Jon leaves with a noble aim to unite the kingdoms against the Night King, and his journey takes him into alliances with the feminine principle. In this part of the journey, each of his sisters, Sansa and Arya Stark, work together and separately to save Jon's life and ensure the future of the Seven Kingdoms. Sansa shows up to the battle at

Winterfell with an additional army, just as Jon is about to be crushed in a brutal fight with the Bolton's army. The two sisters together conspire to eliminate a threat from within their ranks, Lord Baelish. And later, Arya deals the defining blow to the Night King just when it looks like Jon (and all the living) will be overtaken.

Also during this time, Jon unites with Daenerys Targaryen, the "Mother of Dragons," whose resources are critical to defeat the Night King. Dany's story is complex, but for Jon's journey she symbolizes the extreme feminine polarity, chaos, and the fire he must contend with and transmute within himself. Hesitant at first, Jon finally decides to "bend the knee" to Daenerys and her ambition to reclaim the Iron Throne of the Seven Kingdoms for House Targaryen. Jon is freed from ice and directly aligns with fire, illuminating the way polar forces vie for control. While subjugating himself to the Mother of Dragons may seem a detour for Jon Snow, bending the knee is a representation of the proper attitude of humility required to face and "tame" the elemental power of the dragon at the gates of the Great Mother.

Most of the Disney Princess stories portray the inner marriage of opposites as the union of the princess and a rescuing prince. This is always a transformative moment in the story, and in the consciousness of both characters who become One. People rail at these tales as anti-feminist, but they are telling of the integration of opposites that live inside each one of us. In Hunger Games, Katniss Everdeen plays the heroic part while Peeta Mellark, the sensitive baker's son, is the complement she needs to grow her true heart. And surely, Simba would not have returned from exile beyond the Pride Lands if Nala had not come to rouse him.

Carl Jung named the part (of a male or a female) that actively confronts the dragon, the *animus,* our inner masculine element. *Animus* means "spirit" in Latin. But the future of the kingdom is still very much dependent on union with the princess, our *anima* or inner feminine (in both genders). *Anima* means "soul" or "psyche" in Latin. She is accessed in the depths of our being and through integrating what is most "other" in ourselves. The "negative" aspect of the *anima* is that which remains "hidden;" it possesses us and surprises us from the dark through our passions, drives, and entanglements. The "positive" *anima* or soul awaits the right moment of integration with the illuminating principle of consciousness or spirit to awaken. So while Sleeping Beauty and Snow White appear to be sleeping, they are playing an important role of receptivity by transiting the depths of soul and the "other world" with the potential to connect us with spirit. The ancient alchemists differentiated soul and spirit too. The soul, represented by a feminine figure, is closer to the body and feelings, preferring depth and imperfection as the poetry of everyday life, versus the spirit king that strives for truth and higher realms. Symbolized by the mentor or benevolent father figure of the past, the king in our stories is generally absent or sleeping (existing only in potential or *spirit*) as the hero enters the deepest realm of the unknown to recover his soul. Eventually, a renewed king and queen will unite again *within* the transformed hero, but that is a second-level conjunction enabled by the hero first uniting with his own soul and, through it, the soul of the world (*meeting the goddess*). I believe the idea of a "higher heart center" in the Enneagram is related to this goddess figure and the idea of a universal soul or ground of Being.

Without this first conjunction, in the depths of the Void, the hero would not be able to handle the power of higher intelligence—the renewed spirit king symbolized through *atonement with the father*. The vessel of Presence and new "body" formed through "marrying" one's soul in the Void is the vehicle for the reunion of king and queen, and the birth of integrative consciousness (the hero's *treasure*) across the Void. By facing chaos directly, the hero harnesses new intelligence, vital life-force, and great potential. We see a literal representation of this as Jon Snow discovers, to his surprise, that he is able to ride the dragons of Daenerys Targaryen, which symbolizes a leveling-up in *being* that makes way for higher consciousness.

The idea of an inner vessel that unites opposites and allows us to receive and sustain ever greater degrees of spiritual light is central to the teachings of Kabbalah. In this tradition there is a division between the transcendent, un-nameable, concealed aspect of God (*Ein Sof*) and the aspect of God revealed in Creation. This latter aspect of God is in fragments because the light that the One God poured into Creation was so powerful that it cracked the original vessel into fragments—the sephirot, that are also considered "opposing" or complementary energies of the Divine. In this story, God needs *us* to put the broken pieces back together, through virtuous action, so the vessel can hold His light. This teaching of *tikkun olam* is another version of the Way; it is the Way to bring divine light and love into the created world.

In the tradition of Christian Hermeticism, Catholic mystic Valentin Tomberg describes a downward facing triangle as the "Luminous Trinity," representing Mother, Daughter, and Holy Soul. Just as in the Holy Trinity of Father, Son, and Holy Spirit no one comes to the Father but by Way of the Son Jesus Christ, no one comes to *know* (Real-ize) the Word of God but by Mary-Sophia. One must prepare as a vessel to receive divine truth, just as Mary receives and conceives the Word incarnate, Jesus Christ, who brings the pattern of Creation to life in the world for us.

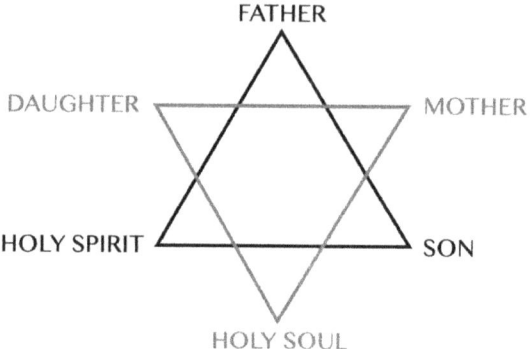

In this philosophy, the symbol of the hexagram is not a representation of good and evil as is sometimes thought, but rather of the three-fold pure act of "fire" and the three-fold reflective and received action of "water." Tomberg explains that the water is the conscious *yes* to the Divine. It is a reflection of divine light, and an essential opening for the reception of a divine Presence within that leads to the realization of the Word in Creation.[118] Biblical scripture reads: "Except a man be born of water and of the Spirit, he cannot enter the kingdom of God."[119]

Jung also related the soul and *anima* to *eros* and the creative force of the unknown that gives birth to possibility. As we deepen our Presence in the body center through this vessel, the final aspect of the body center, the sex center, opens in a new way. The sexual instinct in all of us is the vital life force that propels us out to explore, and into this re-combinatory relationship with opposing energies that "gives birth" to new possibilities. While using the word "sex" to describe this may narrow our view (just as using the gendered terms male and female to symbolize opposites is limiting), it is hard to think of another way to represent (with metaphor) how the *sacred marriage* between polar forces brings rebirth.

What is born out of the hero's union with the goddess is symbolized as some kind of magical elixir, boon, or *treasure* lifted from the Void. Really the hero recovers himself—his soul child who was hidden in the dragon's lair—and, with it, his creative potential as an indestructible spark of the

Divine. This is the treasure that will be used for transformation ahead. The soul child is the essential self or essence (aware of its interbeing with all of Creation) that will grow up through the back half of the journey, guided by the spark of higher mind or spirit. Often the hero already had this treasure, received from a mentor goddess or the lost benevolent father figure, but only "discovers" its power and meaning through the sacrifice of ego and re-membering all of who she is. Dorothy had no idea the power of those ruby slippers, and Jon Snow carried the Valyrian steel sword for some time before he realized its powers to kill the "undead" (a great metaphor for how the shards of our egoic past cling, as well as the need to cut them away).

Harry Potter finds treasure in the sorcerer's stone he finds in his pocket during his lethal encounter with Voldemort in the chamber under the school (in the first book of the series). J.K. Rowling seems to know a great deal about alchemy. Harry travels the seven steps through seven years at Hogwarts and seeks to destroy the seven *horcruxes* or fragments of Voldemort's soul (the eighth, unfortunately, being Harry himself and a symbol of their interdependence). And "the sorcerer's stone" was originally written by Rowling as "the philosopher's stone," the ultimate goal of alchemy. As the "gold" created from the "lead" of coarse material, the philosopher's stone represents enlightenment and "eternal life" achieved by the alchemist engaged in transforming his own soul from earthly toward spiritual concerns. This *spiritualized matter* is the true elixir, the gold and treasure derived from the alchemical process. In facing darkness directly, Harry acquires this treasure as a symbol of his potential to renew himself, and the community as a whole, by the end of the series. He can acquire the stone (and so prevent Voldemort from using it to create a new body for his mangled soul) because he is the only one with a pure heart. Acquiring the treasure requires a different kind of heart, clearly, the higher heart of a hero who has faced the dragon and reunited with his essential self or soul.

An exception among Princess stories, *Beauty and the Beast* highlights the last of the conjunctions sparked in the Void that Joseph Campbell calls *atonement with the father.* Campbell writes this word often as *at-one-ment* to make obvious the idea of transcending the ego to experience union with the benevolent ruler within (fully developed essence) and Source beyond. In this story, Belle pledges her life to the Beast so that he will release her aging father, whom the Beast has imprisoned in the dungeon.

In addition to "marrying" her opposite and owning the "animal" instinct within, Belle's pledge is a commitment to revivify the "dried up" kingdom (symbolized by her own ailing father) and channel a renewed spirit king within her. With this act she claims her true character and destiny as a more integrated being who can help renew the world as well.

While the full realization of Belle's *atonement with the father* principle occurs much later in the story, it is sparked in the depths of her captivity, and by the first marriage with her own soul and "higher" heart. By facing the Beast within, Belle places herself smack in the middle of a very difficult paradox, like Jesus, to learn to love her enemy—her hideous and destructive captor the Beast (representing the full complement of collective shadow). Thanks to Belle's very large heart a curse is broken, and the Beast is transformed into the positive masculine archetype of her prince. This is Belle's version of re-uniting spirit and soul that leads to *treasure* and will resolve in a higher degree of *at-one-ment* ahead as both face the fractured community. Only together can these two renewed forces accomplish the heroic journey to vanquish prejudice, revivify the castle, and restore life to the surrounding kingdom.

Wonder Woman lives out a similar story after she opens her heart to Captain Steve. Following their union, Diana has an epiphany about love that helps grow her capacity and see what it will really take to save humanity. Simba's ego defenses have hidden the pain of his loss, guilt, and shame, but they have also obscured the immense potential of his essence and birthright as the son of a long line of lion kings. It is the reunion with the future queen, Nala, that opens the way to his revelation of truth and spark of higher consciousness. His atonement with the father (spirit king) comes after Rafiki, the shaman figure, leads Simba deep into a cave to see his reflection in a pool of water. Simba sees that his father "lives in him." Soon after, Mufasa appears to Simba in the clouds and urges him to "Remember who you are, Simba!" We will pick up this inner marriage of king and queen, soul and spirit, and the resulting *treasure* lifted from the unknown at point 5, as our heroes emerge from the Void.

Overall, the stories show us how facing and integrating the previously rejected aspects of ourselves is the Way to "free" ourselves from them. The illuminating revelation here is that they actually free *us*...and bring gifts at the same time. Somehow our gifts, and that divine spark of potential, are activated through this most difficult traverse through our shadows and wounds, the depths of our being, and the "maternal" ground of Being.

Carl Jung describes this experience as "a restoration of the original state of the cosmos, the divine unconsciousness of the world," and ties it to revelation of the "vertical" axis of growth. Joseph Campbell writes that the hero endures the crisis in the Void "to find, in the end, that the father and mother reflect each other, and are in essence the same."[120] We learn that there is nowhere that the light of consciousness and love cannot reach.

INNER WORK IN THE VOID

The Hindu goddess Kali is a striking embodiment of both the hazard and the possibility of this transit through the Void. As chaos, she is the disorienting force with which we must contend on our journey through the unconscious. If you have seen her image, with outstretched tongue, a necklace of heads, skirt of arms, brandishing a knife dripping with blood, you know what I mean. And yet, Joseph Campbell notes the power and place of the dark feminine in our destiny: "As change, the river of time, the fluidity of life, the goddess at once creates, preserves, and destroys. Her name is Kali, the Black One; her title: The Ferry across the Ocean of Existence."[121] Kali is both the terrifying chaos and "the ferry" or way through that great river of potential between points 4 and 5. Facing her is the hero's crisis at the nadir *and* its solution. The fact that she is at once creator, preserver and destroyer explains the various threads of work initiated through this transit.

Michael Meade, an expert on mythic stories from all cultures, describes two rivers that we access beyond the known. One is the stream of forgetfulness that runs into oblivion. The other is the river of Great Memory—a well of deep memory and rejuvenation that leads us back to Truth. When we re-member our souls (having collected the pieces of ourselves) we connect into the greater flow of Being, the soul of the world, and remember essential things about ourselves that we knew before birth. These things seek to be revealed through our individual souls when the structures of culture and nature are in disrepair.

An important aspect of what is re-experienced and remembered in the Void are the laws—the core patterns of life, death, and renewal at the heart of Creation—that connect us with both the natural world and the spirit world.[122] This seems to be essential wisdom for the road ahead, as it increases both our capacity for empathy and our understanding of the Way to catalyze the emergence of new order in a fragmented world. However, since the ego's strategies do not work in the deepest recesses of the unknown, we have to draw on something we don't understand or even know is possible to survive the Void and access this well of wisdom earned. We can't grow ourselves working within the limited self and context defined by our personality. That just makes sense. Ego can't develop essence, our higher self. Our willingness to sacrifice constricting patterns and enter the Void is what changes our entire center of gravity, somehow turns chaos into flow, and sparks new life. At the center of this mystery in the Void is the brain's Default Mode Network (DMN). The DMN is a system of connected brain regions thought to be the neurobiological basis for a sense of "self"—the brain's egosystem! This network is active when our minds are either fully resting or wandering, using memory and imagination to think about ourselves, remember our past, and imagine our own future. Similar to how we think about ego, the DMN is running in the background nearly half of our waking hours, shaping our experience based on our individual biases. Despite its considerable influence, this kind of mind-wandering does not make us very happy.

The DMN does *not* operate when we have either single-pointed, focused attention, or open awareness, which is a very broad attention encompassing the vast world outside our small self. Either way, "getting out of our heads" by taking the DMN offline seems to be conducive to well-being and positive changes in the brain over time. Interestingly, both of those modes of attention correspond with two main types of meditation and prayer: receptive, open-focus states, like mindful awareness or centering prayer; and one-pointed-focus, as with mantra meditation or focused prayer.

Suppressing the DMN with open-focus awareness results in the brain making wider and more complex connections. It is the neurological correlate of Campbell's *sacred marriage* in the Void. Our everyday consciousness and sense of a separate self dissolves, and we are absorbed in Awareness itself. Buddhist teacher Thich Nhat Hanh says that in contemplating emptiness (no self) we find a new fullness, a state in which nothing is separate, a state of interconnected flow that he calls "interbeing." Dan Siegel describes entering this state as accessing "the plane of possibility," a place of timelessness (eternity), of maximal diversity (infinity), and maximal possibility (potential choices). The subjective experience is an ego-less, boundaryless, timeless consciousness that eliminates borders within the self, between self and other, self and the natural world. We can see why this state is often experienced as transcendent or mystical. Beyond the arrow of time (*chronos*), a door to the eternal (*kairos*) opens.

Just as particle dissolves into wave from the perspective of physics, the self dissolves into the mystical union, wherein we are one with the great flow of Being behind the multiplicity of the created world.

Making connections between disparate brain regions like this also shakes up rigid patterns and resets the brain in significant and often adaptive ways. It may be like scrambling rigid synaptic connections all at once, rather than pruning them slowly, preparing the way for a re-set. More and different energy and information becomes available. Unconscious material emerges from within, and more raw data is incorporated into consciousness from outside of us. We access a collective field of intelligence (the river of Great Memory) from which new possibility (in-sight and imagination) can emerge. In long-time meditators, this flow state is characterized by very high-frequency gamma brain waves related to a high degree of neural integration, as well as to moments of insight, where something new leaps into awareness.[123]

Dissolving ego in the Void may be part of the mystery I started inquiring into many years ago whereby great suffering can lead to significant growth. While we would not wish tragedy on anyone, the science and stories seem to say that allowing, even cultivating, the unraveling of the known can lead to a different kind of healing, if not curing, what befalls us. Free from the confines of ego identity, we come to a broader sense of who we are, in relationship to *All that Is*, and often gain a new sense of why we are here. This is the *illuminating revelation* Campbell describes. Revelation is key, because simply knowing those things doesn't change patterns embedded in the structure and function of our brain/body. We have to first UN-do old neural connections to make room for new possibilities, new energy and information, that can re-route neural pathways and allow for insight and evolution.

I incorporate the neuroscience here not to reduce transcendent states of consciousness or mystical experiences to biological phenomena, because I do not believe they can be. I am using the science to illustrate how the laws operate at many levels of experience: from the biological to the psychological, the spiritual and cosmological. There are many ways to enter this timeless ocean. And from a neuroscience perspective, a healthy mind-brain requires the flexibility of *flow* as much as the support of *order* (structure), *and* the third force consciousness to access and integrate these states of awareness and being by choice.

The good news is that, beyond tragedy, there are many psychological and spiritual methods for stepping outside the DMN to access the flow of Being and the illuminating revelations that seem to arise from there. From practicing three-centered Presence to Siegel's Wheel of Awareness meditation, as well as other forms of meditation and prayer, to engaging in deep inquiry work and dream analysis, ecstatic dancing and drumming, and psychedelic-assisted therapy, dropping into the Void and experiencing oneself as intimately part of *All that Is*, can be personally healing and transformative. It increases our capacity for empathy and connection with others and the natural world, and it gives us an experience of universal patterns that can help us piece ourselves and our world back together. It's true: the chaos we were afraid of becomes the ferry through this great ocean of possibility.

FROM NOTHING COMES EVERYTHING—THE HIGHER HEART

Dropping in, to the primordial chaos, we find that the absence of self is not nothing; it's everything. From *kenosis*, emptying out, comes *theosis*, that divine filling-up. This place beyond ego turns out to be restorative and supportive of its own accord. But also, from this plane of possibility, we access new sources of healing and growth. A quantum sea of potential energy awaits its realization in form. In the *kairos* of a moment, between impulse and action, we can allow new images, emotion, and wisdom for *how to be* bubble up from a wider plane of possibility. And in doing so, like the Grinch who stole Christmas, we might find that our hearts grow a few sizes.

A central teaching of Buddhism is that meeting suffering with compassion and a spacious mind leads to the arising of higher qualities of the heart called "divine abidings" or *Brahmaviharas*. God (Brahma) is said to dwell (vihara) in four faces of the heart: loving-kindness, compassion, appreciative joy, and equanimity.[124] These qualities are very like the nine virtues of the higher heart center described by the Enneagram that flower in the Void. And, as with the *Brahmaviharas*, we don't "practice" them and become virtuous so much as we cultivate the soil through our willingness to open the door to Presence and align ourselves with the field and flow of possibility—interbeing, the *anima mundi* or soul of the world. From that fertile ground, virtues sprout.

In the Void, after we sacrifice Envy and the stories and habits related to our personal suffering, we all unlock the virtue of Equanimity. Equanimity is a quality of the higher heart that enables composure and psychological stability even in the midst of great stress. The root words in Equanimity (*aequo animo*) refer to a "level soul or mind." It is the very definition of what it means to *stand in the middle*. When we have sacrificed the ego's yes/no grip that distorts our centers of intelligence, there is an equalizing of shadow and higher self that means *everything* has the potential to call forth more from us and through us. Equanimity is not a numb or forced peace, nor a compromise between shadow and light. It is a continuous dynamic balance, enabled by a third force that can open a Way for the emergence of qualities from beyond our current level of being. It's a funny recipe, but as we empty ourselves of ego and fulfill the marriage of opposites, we become full of the vast expanse of Presence and potential from which new life arises.

I had a dream while writing this section from which I awoke with the phrase "the higher heart is made of dances." From this I gathered that rather than something we find in a particular location, the higher heart "center" is our thread into the vast flow of interconnected intelligence, the ground of Being accessed through our own, now integrated, "vessel" of Presence. When all lower centers of intelligence are clear and aligned, we are "dancing" with and in this flow of Being. I thought of Gurdjieff's description of himself as "a teacher of dancing," and that it is often said that the virtues are gifted to us. I imagine they arise from this new way of *being* in the flow of the "higher" or universal heart (soul), without the constrictions of ego, in the Great River of re-membering where opposites unite and insight arises. While we can gain access to all the virtues through this point, our individual Enneagram type virtue gives us each a doorway and connection with the "heart" that equalizes and infuses all Creation.

At **Point 1**, the virtue of **Serenity** describes an extremely calm and relaxed heart, at peace with the way things are. There is a complete lack of the judgment that creates separation, which allows one to sense into the deep flow of grace underneath the complexity of the world.

At **Point 2**, **Humility**, puts us in touch with our insignificance in such a vast Universe. And yet, when we are no one special, we are everyone. Already worthy, love flows without need for distinction or approval in the receptive vessel of Presence. My will becomes Thy will.

At **Point 3**, **Veracity** describes the Truth that arises when we are present in grounded body, open heart, clear mind; integrated and in alignment with *All that Is*. There is nothing to be done, nothing to adapt to, only the harmonious and radiant unfolding of Creation through us.

At **Point 4**, **Equanimity** is the balance point between attachment and aversion, the still point of Presence, and an opening to the eternal now. It enables composure and psychological stability, even in the midst of great stress. There is an equalizing of shadow and higher self. We have met "the other" in ourselves and taken him or her in. With no more "opposition," we experience the flow of the higher heart.

At **Point 5, Non-attachment** describes a heart that is open to the conversation, the continuous give and take with Creation. As a conduit of energy, we experience the immensity of Source energy without needing to grasp or constrict, define or control, any of it, because there will always be more that comes and goes through us.

At **Point 6, Courage** is the willingness to move into life with an open heart, relaxed presence, without waiting for anyone or anything else to take the lead. We know no one else creates safety, and someone has to *stand in the middle*. This strength of heart allows us to trust and collaborate with Creation.

At **Point 7, Sobriety** is a commitment to take seriously what life is bringing us, just as it is, one thing at a time, in this moment. The addiction to ego is gone, so we can stay focused on a higher aim. But sober is not the same as serious. With the purification of personal desire, a great joy can arise from simply flowing with what is ours to do, without distraction or creating more options.

At **Point 8, Innocence** is the capacity to respond to each and every moment with the freshness and wonder of eyes that make all things new. There is no need to judge, defend, or react, because an open heart is resilient and strong. Innocence renews our capacity to choose in each moment to play with Creation by both *being* and *knowing* the Divine in *All that Is*.

At **Point 9**, Uranio describes **Right Action** as the heart's compass. In touch with the flow of Creation, it knows the one thing that needs to be done, right now, for the whole of life, to bring things into harmony. This may (paradoxically) require disruption, confrontation, and challenge to act AS, and on behalf of, Holy Love.

You'll notice that these virtues of the higher heart center are not really feelings, but more like ways of being, and ways of being *in communion with* a shared sense of Being (interbeing) that does not have our separate self and ego needs at the center. The Kabbalah speaks of a *point in the heart* of every one of us that is a fragment of the light of the creator. When this point wakes up, its first movement is to *receive* spiritual sustenance and a different kind of intelligence from the collective flow of Being. Accessing the higher heart gives us a different compass for the rest of the trip, and its navigating forces are these virtues that give rise to true conscience and moral leadership. This is not the same as applying the morals and rigid commitments of subjective traditions. It is based on a felt sense of being One with *All that Is,* and it opens a Way for higher guidance to co-create the reminder of the journey.

Experiencing our birthright and shared nature as the universal heart or soul of the world is the understanding of Holy Origin, the holy idea at point 4 that connects us with the wisdom of Creation through interbeing. This wisdom has nothing to do with our intellect, however, as logic fails in the land of the Great Mother. For alchemy to unfold and a transformed hero to emerge from the Void, we still need to listen for the whispers of the soul. As we discovered before, she speaks through deeper stirrings in the body, through that felt sense of connection to all of life inherited from animals and ancestors who lived closer to the earth, but also at this point she starts to become the vessel for intuition, dreams, and imagination—the language of the higher mind or spirit. The *anima mundi* is the gateway to what was previously unknowable through the *axis mundi*, the vertical pole or "tree" that connects the earth with the heavens. For us, that means that when our centers are no longer distorted by unconscious contents, and we have access to the sea of potential beyond the known, a fundamentally different way of seeing and knowing becomes possible as well.

In addition to developing a practice of dropping in to a relaxed and receptive state of listening for the rest of the journey, to keep the small self out of the center and hone this connection with higher consciousness, we can reflect on: *What still needs to be owned so that it does not own me—so that there is no "me" to be owned?* When we are no longer in resistance to what *is,* nor grasping at what we think *should* be, we are free...and ready for an even higher aim. Arya Stark, *the girl with no name,* somehow rises from the baptismal waters and manages to regain her sight, kill off her persecutor, abandon her trainer, and leave for Home. She still has her special sword *Needle* and list of targets to assassinate, but we can also see that Arya is changed: more skillful, mature, and increasingly aware of a mission far bigger than she is. She has a new compass. When we are no-one, no longer only a separate self, we begin to realize our purpose, our gifts, and our place in the destiny of the kingdom.

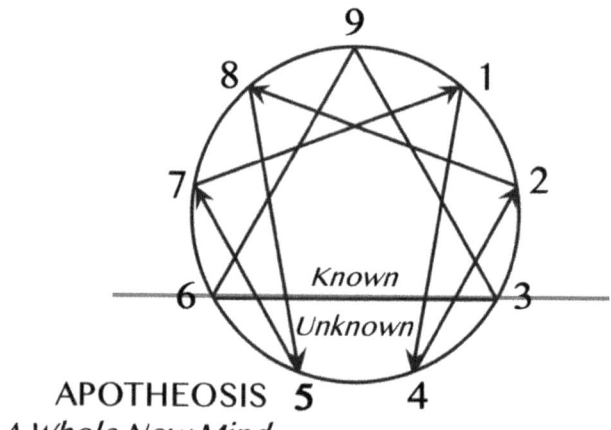

APOTHEOSIS
A Whole New Mind

CHAPTER FOURTEEN

POINT 5:
APOTHEOSIS

Something in you dies when you bear the unbearable.
And it is only in that dark night of the soul that
you are prepared to see as God sees and to love
as God loves.[125]

~ RAM DASS

A T POINT 5 ON THE JOURNEY, the hero has survived the worst of ego deconstruction and faced the full depth and breadth of her character. She emerges from the Void with greater heart, humility, and the grace that comes with no longer feeling as internally divided or separate from oneself and *All that Is.* And yet, she is not finished with her work in the unknown. Apotheosis, the name of this stage, has to do with a shift in consciousness that occurs as a result of the marriage in the Void. Campbell writes: "When we quit thinking primarily about ourselves and our own self-preservation, we undergo a truly heroic transformation of consciousness. And what all myths have to deal with is transformations of consciousness of one kind or another. You have been thinking one way; you now have to think in a different way."[126]

The dictionary explains *apotheosis* as the highest version of something, or the elevation of a person to "divine status." Obviously our heroes have not leapt to divine status simply by surviving the Void, so what's going on here? As a result of the surrender of the ego that separates and divides, the hero has integrated a vast field of formerly unconscious being—"the other" in all its forms—and had a heartfelt experience of Being or *interbeing* far more than she thought she was. More integrated within, she has opened to a new dimension of consciousness and remembered herself as soul or essence, an integral part of the flow of energy and information that runs through all of Creation. With this lived experience of sacrifice and expansion, the hero learns something essential about universal laws and the process of growth that will serve both her and her community upon her return. Joseph Campbell says that *apotheosis* comes from "unity with the ultimate mystery of being." He writes: "With the wall between opposites shattered, the hero is admitted to the vision of God."[127]

While encounters in the Void might literally include an experience of the Divine, we can also understand *vision of God* as a change in perception, something like "seeing as God sees," a mind that is "higher" or a non-dual awareness in which nothing is outside the light and love of Source, nor exempt from the patterns of birth, death, and renewal. The hero's transcendent experience of being One with the Source and Flow of Creation, has sparked new understanding about Creation itself and her role in it. She has a new sense of purpose and ideas about how she can contribute to the revivification of the kingdom. But a profound shift in consciousness takes time to unfold, in contrast to the emotional epiphany.

This order of growth makes sense from a neuroscience perspective. The brain is remarkably malleable or "plastic." The internal wiring of enduring thought patterns can be transformed and new neural connections can be laid down. A life-long habit of anxiety approaching novelty, for example, can be re-wired in the brain…but it takes practice. Changing our minds can not only rewire our habitual patterns of thinking and perceiving, it can even change how our genes express themselves over time.[128] It is not the transcendent experience alone, but the ability to process and live these glimpses of *something more* that creates a sustained experience of higher mind through all centers of intelligence. Point 5 marks the birth of higher consciousness through integrated being, and the beginning of the second half of the journey to grow into a fully developed essence or unified soul-spirit-body.

THE PASSION OF AVARICE

The passion of Avarice is both the mover and the trap at point 5. Avarice is not greediness, but rather like closing the doors against the "intrusive" flow of life. It is the desire to retreat from impact, to grasp and to preserve one's self and resources (time, space, energy) from being depleted. It is a fundamental drive to defend, contain, and conserve, and it reinforces separation like all the passions of the Enneagram. While the hero is no longer fully under the sway of the ego that separates one from awareness of *interbeing*, the impulse to contain is an appropriate movement coming out of the Void. A literal separation from the world might be merited here. It takes time to solidify a tectonic shift in being.

One might not even want to return to the everyday world.

After reaching enlightenment, Siddhartha—now the Buddha, meaning simply "the awakened one"—spent many more weeks near the Bodhi tree where he had his awakening (actually 7 x 7 days in different states of repose).[129] He spent them sitting, walking, and contemplating his new state, the nature of life and death, and sorting out what he would teach upon his return to society. Like the Way of the Tao and the Way of Jesus, this was also to be a Way—a "Middle" Way—to be realized on an Eightfold Path, walked with "right" mind/heart and effort. Buddha's example and time for reflection illustrates not only a profoundly changed perspective, but also the continued ripening and consolidation of higher mind (which is also a mind not separate from heart and *All that Is*) that can take time.

Most of our heroes don't get stuck in this containment phase, as that would mean the end of the journey. At point 5 the path of the mystic and the path of the hero diverge. The mystic stays with an ever-deepening process of unity with the ultimate mystery of Being touched in the Void. This is a legitimate choice, but according to our mythic tradition as well as some of our spiritual heroes, there is another way forward. Buddha considered staying on this path of retreat into a solitary life of further contemplation and more profound states of awareness. But he didn't. Neither did Jesus. Or Muhammad. What makes a hero is the willingness to venture back across the threshold ahead, from the unknown world back into the known, in order to complete the transfiguration of being, embody the change, and share oneself to help revivify the kingdom.

In the Beast's castle it takes time for Beauty to see the Beast as a beautiful soul in his own right (although she has help from the household objects). Despite her growing understanding, Belle must eventually cross back into the known world, save her father, revive the Beast with her love and, together with him, fight the oppressors and prejudice in their community to rebuild lives. The full realization of who we are as One (*seeing as God sees*) is not complete until the end of the journey. The journey makes the hero. And we are not done. Seeds have sprouted, roots are growing, but there are more formative steps ahead.

A courageous and noble adventure gives significance to life partially because of how we come to understand ourselves and the world in its wake—how we make meaning from it, and eventually live it. When we allow space for not only our hearts but also our minds to be altered by our experience in the unknown, our entire worldview can shift. Or maybe it's fair to say that our entire mind is lifted, since the higher mental center is not limited by the analytical mind that categorizes and divides. On the way of the hero, higher mind arrives from an integration of all centers of intelligence into an embodied way of *knowing* in partnership with the higher heart and flow of Being.

Prior to the initiation in the Void, the hero's ruling principle or *ordering* function was rooted in the known—the ego's fixated way of experiencing life based on the past. Unaware of how much we are controlled by unconscious patterns, we can't grow. Avarice, the conservation of being and energy, cuts us off from the continuous fountain of energy and information (intelligence) available within and around us that is necessary for the renewal of life. And Stinginess, the mental habit at point 5, fuels the fire by compelling us to hold tight to past ways of perceiving and interpreting life as a separate self. The truth is that *all* patterns, rules, and systems decay over time and need to be updated. This idea is represented in our myths and stories by the absence or death of the old king, the rise of tyranny, deterioration of the kingdom, and the need for a hero to renew and revivify the old order.

The Pride Lands become dry and dark after Mufasa's death, subject to the tyrannical rule of Scar. Belle, resigned to living her life in the castle, sees in the Beast's magic mirror that her father Maurice is sick and alone in the woods, looking for her. Pinocchio, having survived the dangerous swim from Pleasure Island, heads home to Geppetto's workshop determined to make things right and behave once and for all, only to find that his father is missing. The Blue Fairy, as a dove, reveals that Geppetto has been swallowed into the belly of the great whale, Monstro, after a failed attempt to find and rescue Pinocchio. And Thor's father, King Odin, has fallen into a death-like "Odin-sleep" on Asgard, while Loki carries out his treacherous plans.

At the heart of what these stories are about is this lesson about decay of the old order, the regenerative role of chaos, and the necessity of renewing our "authorities," culture, and systems of control (inside and out).[130] The idea of the old king of the psyche being released as the hero travels through the darkest passage of the unknown is a necessary separation for facing chaos. Not even the mentor can go with the hero through the Void. We can think about it as a temporary split, whereby the lower mind as the dominant (but insufficient) ruler of consciousness must be let go for a time.

As the hero emerges from the Void, however, we see a new sort of guiding light start to flicker from within her, symbolized by a growing internalization of the mentor's wisdom—in Luke Skywalker's case: the Force within. This guiding light is a fundamentally different kind of "mind" or knowing, more like intuition or *gnosis* that "arrives" within when we are in Presence. The stories suggest that while our narrow minds take a break, we can trust that something of a higher mind or spirit is over-seeing this whole production. In contrast to the dogma and tyranny of decaying ego systems, the second half of the journey requires a new ruler: a consciousness awakened to the gifts of the unconscious but no longer dominated by it; an integrated consciousness, a heart-mind that sees from the perspective of the Unity of all things and can participate in the renewal of community.

Making Order from Chaos

An intelligence that is "higher" in this way does not just discern and define, but also receives, relates, and *participates* in the creative unfolding of life with imagination, vision, and inspiration. As the hero confronts the dragon and traverses the Void, she helps to "turn" chaos into the *flow* of potential in Creation that enables new growth. *Making order from chaos* is the active work of re-perceiving the world with a new "ruling principle." It is possible because of the hero's choice to leave the old king and king-dom, and meet the vast power of chaos with respect and humility. And it is actualized because of the hero's receptivity and expansion of being that allows her to identify with all of humanity. Having acknowledged in herself all manner of shadow and ugliness, the hero knows both what she is capable of (to watch out for) and how to rise above the polarized egoic thinking that fuels it all to *aim higher*.

Stripped of his super-human strength, Thor grows in maturity, heart, and humility during his time with Dr. Jane and the other scientists on Earth. A new conscience is revealed in Thor when he lays down his life in hopes of saving everyone from the Destroyer that Loki has sent to Earth to kill them all. With that decision, seconds from being crushed, Thor's special hammer (source of his superpowers, he thinks) comes flying back to him. His powers are restored just in time, and the renewed god of thun-der destroys the Destroyer. When King Odin took away Thor's hammer, he put some magic on it to ensure that "only one who is worthy" could wield it. Freed from his former bravado, acting from a higher heart, Thor can use his weapon once again to draw down thunder and lightning (energy and intelligence) from beyond his small self.

The intelligence that Thor draws on comes from the vertical dimension in the Symbol that opened in the Void. The arrow from point 8 to 5 indicates a new connection from the hero's higher aim, the higher mind or spiritual intelligence of our fully developed essence—a new and benevolent ruler of consciousness. If we consider again that the Symbol illustrates two lines of development—around the circle and through the hexad figure—their coming together again across the Void at point 5 is a significant moment.

To see how this works, let's go back to point 4. Alchemically, both the king and queen were *freed from matter* (from their limited roles) by the hero's sacrifice of ego. The hero then united in the Void with the unbounded soul queen, which opened a door beyond the personal unconscious and into a vast dimension of Being. At the same time, the spirit of the old king or mentor was released to travel the arrow lines (4->2->8) and unify with a higher aim at point 8. In the process of ego death, the narrow mind that judges and separates is transmuted into something higher. As the hero marries her soul and experiences herself as One with Being itself, she opens a mysterious door to the vertical dimension of growth. At point 5, the ensouled hero can receive "from above" something of a higher mind (8->5), marking a reunification of king and queen and a new kind of integrative (third force) consciousness in the hero. This is the real *treasure* the hero lifts from the Void. It is symbolized by the queen of diamonds in the figure below as a representation of new life, but we might imagine this as the "king" of the queen's domain. In fact, we are in a different world on this side of the Void, where the distinctions are not so clear, and the forces harmonize more readily.

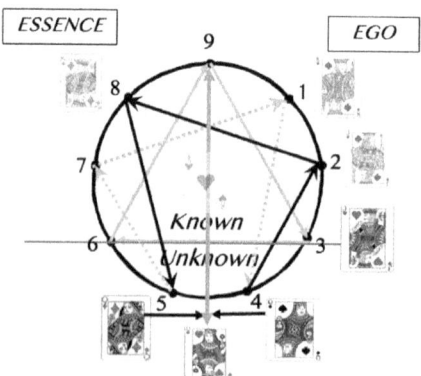

Becoming One with the flow of Being opens up the
vertical dimension, engaging higher forces.
Integrated consciousness is born.

Luke Skywalker's story is similar to Thor's here. After facing death in a massive water-filled trash compactor and losing his mentor Obi-Wan Kenobi, Luke emerges from the rescue of Princess Leia on the Death Star with far less of the bravado and recklessness that characterized his prior approach. Luke has a long way to go to be a Jedi Master, but the shift in his perspective is evident as he controls his panic and focuses his mind while fighting off Storm troopers with Han Solo. He is more collaborative with others, and with the higher guidance of the Force he now accesses from within.

Non-attachment, the virtue at point 5, describes a capacity to grasp nothing that, paradoxically, allows access to everything. Relinquishing the attachment to ego fixation is something like finding the Middle Way that the Buddha taught, and another version of third force consciousness. This is the Way between the two central forces (chaos and tyranny) that pull our strings and keep us attached to the material world where separation consciousness is primary. In personality, our mind, heart, and body are too often owned by the strong reactions to what our ego needs (or needs to resist) in order to feel secure, important, and in control. At point 5, no longer controlled by our lower centers, we are free to *re-know* our experience.

When the mind is not fixated by the known, we can see things differently—maybe, *as they are* for the first time. This is the beginning of a different way of knowing for the hero, higher mind, and it is also something like a "beginner's mind" described in Shunryu Suzuki's classic teaching on Zen Buddhism.[131] In ego, our personal reality is an artifact of our personality. What we "see" is a projection of our internal process, distorted perceptions based on personal history, memories, and embedded brain patterns. Having seen through the exploits of ego, the hero can now refuse to take her initial assessments as "real." We don't have to believe the old stories. When we know that *we* are making the movie we see "out there," we can inquire directly into the true nature of things.

At point 5, the hero adopts a *process* of continuous learning and creating (staying on the journey, or the Way) that requires staying open to guidance from beyond the fixated mind in the face of changing conditions. Without the attachment or aversion to this or that, there is no judgment. Without judgment, anger, fear, and shame fall away. This is a very different way of operating that neither shuts out nor is controlled by old patterns, shadow, and unconscious contents. Freedom from inner preoccupation, combined with the awareness of *interbeing*, allows for a different kind of intelligence and the possibility of truly moral behavior. It takes time and practice, however, and the hero has miles to go still before sorting all this out. So we often see another character serve for a while as her conscience and a conduit between the hero's now-more-integrated-being and truly higher heart-mind.

Kansas, and its controlling adults, symbolize the tyrannical aspect of ego that Dorothy must leave behind to find reliable higher guidance within. In the interim, her little dog Toto serves as a stand-in. Toto plays a pivotal role in getting Dorothy in to and out of various scrapes, as well as finding her allies. As she proceeds through the journey, gathering mind, heart, and body intelligence, however, we see Dorothy's own inner guidance starting to grow. When we last saw Dorothy, she was trapped in the Wicked Witch's castle and the witch was threatening to drown Toto. Toto was able to escape the witch's evil designs (for the second time...since she looks suspiciously like Almira Gulch) and round up Dorothy's three friends (and centers) just in time to get her some back-up.

In a pivotal moment, the Wicked Witch makes a move to ignite the Scarecrow (Dorothy's lower mind) with fire/fear. Responding spontaneously in the moment, Dorothy has enough Presence to save the day. She grabs a bucket and throws water on the Scarecrow, splashing the Wicked Witch at the same time. This act melts one of Dorothy's key adversaries and transforms the flying monkeys of fear and delusion into free and friendly beings. Having accomplished her assigned mission, Dorothy can make her way back to the innermost sanctum of the Wizard, the supposedly all-knowing mental controller of Oz. Because Dorothy is still intimidated by old power structures, however, Toto is the one who pulls down the curtain to unmask the Wizard. All that supposed knowledge and bombast is nothing but an old man from Kansas! The Wizard is a representation of the fixated mind with its limited view, old stories, and inner critic to whom we were addicted. When Dorothy discovers that the all-powerful Wizard of Oz is not so, finally, it frees her to be in touch with higher mind.

Pinocchio's mind is personified by Jiminy Cricket, who grows up alongside the puppet-boy. Initially Jiminy's guidance is like that from our fixated mind, with its particular way of being right. After failed attempts to keep Pinocchio on the righteous path, however, Jiminy gives up and leaves the puppet to his undoing. When he returns to help Pinocchio, it seems that Jiminy has changed. He guides Pinocchio with a more compassionate and collaborative approach, even risking his life to dive into the sea with Pinocchio to rescue Geppetto from the belly of the whale. When Pinocchio dies in the process of saving his father and escaping Monstro (who turned into an underwater dragon), Jiminy mourns as much as Geppetto does. Fortunately, the Blue Fairy arrives to resurrect Pinocchio as a Real boy, due to his unselfish and heroic effort to save his father. While there, she awards Jiminy Cricket a gold badge, noting that he is now an "official" higher conscience.

At first Simba resists any guidance from Rafiki (the mandril that doubles as a shaman), just as he arrogantly shooed away Zazu, who served his father. But after Nala weakens Simba's resistance, Rafiki finds a way to influence Simba by revealing to him that Simba and his father are One. Like many of our heroes, Simba cannot trust himself, cannot find his Way, until he faces a defining issue from childhood. Simba has been resisting his true heritage as a lion king, due to unresolved guilt over his father's death. Simba's *apotheosis* here is a step towards full *atonement* with the father principle. With Rafiki's help, Simba will eventually find guidance from the stars and "higher aim" that led his father Mufasa and all the great lion kings of the past.

Jon Snow has three advisors that lead him through apotheosis to atonement and higher guidance on the back half of the journey: the gentle, bookish Samwell Tarly, the weathered, loyal Ser Davos, and the third, rather unlikely one: the ill-behaved dwarf Tyrion Lannister, shrewd son of the enemy Lannister King. Samwell seeds the awakening of Jon Snow to his destiny by revealing Jon's heritage. Not long after Jon's pledge to follow Daenerys Targaryen, Sam tells Jon that he is the child of Ned Stark's sister and Daenerys' brother. As the child of House Targaryen and House Stark, Jon is the embodiment of fire *and* ice, and the true heir to the Iron Throne. This is a spark of new consciousness that awakens Jon Snow, but it is not fully internalized. Instead, it is Tyrion who gets to Jon in the end.

All of Jon's advisors are "misfits," marginalized by their culture and the archetypal father element like Jon himself, but perhaps none so much as Tyrion Lannister whose own father is so openly hostile toward him. Tyrion (interesting name...he surely could have succumbed to tyranny, embittered as he was by his father's rejection) redeems his past by executing his tyrannical father Tywin Lannister. And despite Tyrion's many issues, we see him grow in wisdom and heart throughout the series. Finally, with the future of the Seven Kingdoms hanging in the balance, Tyrion is the one who opens Jon's eyes to his true calling and role in saving the realm at point 8 ahead.

The reunion with a "higher" king or ruling principle indicated here starts to resolve a central issue at the heart of the hero's ego or personality structure that was left behind at the beginning of the journey. Instead of a puppet controlled by culture, the hero will ultimately align with higher guidance to become something greater: a hero, like Princess Belle; a Lion King; or a Real boy. That part of the journey (at-one-ment) is not complete until we get to the end, but it is made possible through the hero's union with the higher heart field of potential in the Void that opens a new dimension in the Symbol and a Way for apotheosis—a higher mind.

Weaving Together Elements in the Ascent

Locating the hero's conscience and connection to transitional higher mind gives us a bird's eye view of the work to be done along the second half of the journey. Down the first half, the potential hero differentiates from the adversary to address the polarized dynamic between the fixed program of the king and kingdom at point 1 and the repressed chaos (queen) below, at point 4. He furthers the deconstruction of the known world of ego by crossing the threshold and integrating the vast power of the unconscious, thereby recovering his soul and connection to higher intelligence in the Void. When he emerges from the Void at point 5, he is "reborn" as a Real hero with all his lower centers of intelligence aligned. He has a new compass of more integrated being, guided by conscience and the higher heart, and has had at least a glimmer of a different kind of knowing that comes from creatively participating *in* the vast power of the Universe.

Point 8 ahead stands not only for a fully realized higher mind but also for the fully integrated hero in service of much greater Truth than he could anticipate at the outset of the journey. It is marked by the positive aspect of the Great Father, benevolent *order*, but it is "positive" because it is not only internally integrated with shadow but also One with the Great Mother, *chaos/flow*. In practical terms, that means we *know* with our hearts and our whole *being*, without squeezing out the adaptive flow of spirit, love, lifeforce, and other gifts from the unknown realm. Having stepped through the door that accesses the vertical dimension in the Void, the third force challenge on this side of the journey includes integrating the Above and Below at a whole different level.

WEAVING TOGETHER
ELEMENTS IN THE ASCENT

ESSENCE
Conscious
Engagement
"LIGHT"

Known
Unknown

EGO
Mechanical
Reaction
"DARK"

This time the call to move ahead on the journey comes from above. It's like the arrow line from point 8 to point 5 attracts the divine spark within the hero's awakened essence or soul child lifted from the Void. Richard Rohr says there is a divine spark of love in all of Creation waiting to be unleashed. It is an aspect of the original creative force that brought the Universe into being out of the primordial waters of the deep. When cultivated, it knows its purpose (higher aim) in bringing that creative love alive in the world. A Taoist story about this spark describes its genesis at the moment of conception as due to an invisible hand that scoops light from the Milky Way and delivers it into the egg in our mother's womb. This starlight organizes the form of the growing child and stays with us throughout our lives. During life, it lives in our hearts, connecting us to messages from the heavens through a point at the top of the head. At death, this spark is released through that point, as spirit, to return to its home.[132]

We see the heroes in our stories also beginning to know through "messages from the heavens" or from a "higher" perspective that includes not only the whole self but also the whole of humanity. Although through much of *Game of Thrones* Arya Stark remains gripped by her ego's need to exact revenge from those who destroyed her family, having survived near-death, we see her fixated quest start to morph into something higher. When the Red Priestess Melisandre reminds Arya of a vision that she will kill many, including "those with blue eyes" (indicating White Walkers), Arya can take in this "intelligence" from Melisandre—an emissary from the depths of the feminine principle—and integrate it without either being controlled by it or dismissing it. It draws her onward. In time, with Presence, she will also understand (higher knowing + higher being) what it means.

We can literally see the spark of awakening in Arya's eyes as she makes sense of Melisandre's prophecy during the epic battle between Westeros and the Night King's army of the blue-eyed frozen dead. It seems like everything Arya has trained for in the unknown comes to fruition with a shocking and precise ninja-like maneuver that enables her to kill the Night King while suspended in mid-air, still trapped in his deathly grip. This is organized chaos, or *flow*, in a moment. It takes your breath away. Still, there is more journey ahead, and Arya does not give up Lust, Vengeance, and fully realize higher mind until the end of the series.

THE INNER WORK OF APOTHEOSIS

While we have been practicing Presence and third force consciousness, point 5 marks what Gurdjieff called "a more permanent line of will" to engage the struggle between opposing forces and make integrated autonomous choices. This is the beginning of what he calls "Real I." It grows out of the sacrifice of the many false "I's" of ego and its temporary manifestations of attraction, aversion, and self-centered thinking that distort our intelligence. Real I is an indication that the ego is no longer needed to defend against unconscious material, and so marks the emergence of a unified will and permanent third force consciousness. From here, we can further develop this single "I" (or eye, like the eye of Horus) and higher master, and use our aligned three-centered Presence in a purposeful and generative way to align with higher intelligence. From biblical scripture: "The light of the body is the eye: if therefore thine eye be single, thy whole body shall be full of light."[133]

In the realm of the timeless, undifferentiated Void, we found the door to the vertical axis of growth (the *axis mundi*) that links the spiritual with the material world. When all five lower centers of intelligence are aligned and free of egoic distortion, we access two higher centers of intelligence that connect us to *All that Is*. Simply put, we must be one, internally, to experience ourselves as One with the higher heart and uncover that divine spark that connects us with a higher mind. On this side of the Symbol, "Above and Below" have taken on greater meaning. The Taoists might say we have found the Way between heaven and earth. To a Christian Hermeticist, all five senses (material existence) have been "nailed to the cross," enabling a way for vertical or spiritual knowing to open from its center. And from the lens of alchemy, we have "squared the circle." When the four earthly elements (earth, air, fire, and water) have been dissolved together into the *prima materia*—the chaos out of which life is formed—a formless ether or *spirit* rises as the fifth element (the *quintessence*) to draw the soul upwards.

There are many ways to describe the process of ego dissolution and inner integration that builds the soul and opens a door to spirit or higher intelligence. But they all clearly point to a new dimension of transpersonal work on this side of the Symbol that marches further towards Campbell's *at-one-ment with the father* that the hero tasted in the Void. The inner experience of unity is a prerequisite to this greater union. We might imagine that the formation of the lower tetrahedron (our vessel for accessing the higher heart) enables the reception of information from above that calls or lights the inner spark, giving birth to conscience and a different sort of consciousness, which is the beginning of a more enduring connection to higher mind for the hero.

SPARK LIT FROM ABOVE

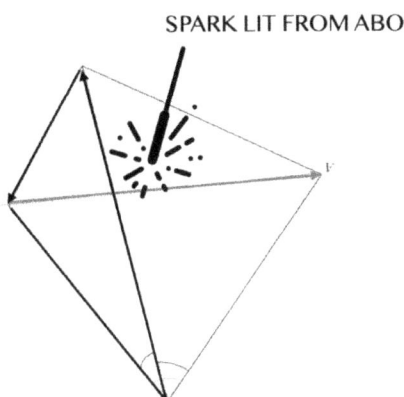

Just as we gathered the first four points (fragments of our being) around the circle to create a "quaternity" arranged as a tetrahedron, at point 5 we have a "quinternity" of five points with this connection to higher mind. The containment of this five-pointed symbol in the larger whole of the Enneagram shows us that a further evolution of essence or soul must be governed by a higher mind or spirit, and not by ego.[134] In Gurdjieffian terms, we "lock up the pentagram" by bringing the lower five centers into union with the higher centers of intelligence. This process, the architecture of the philosopher's stone, the Merkaba, or fully developed essence or soul unified with spirit, is laid down throughout the second half of the journey.

In the alchemical process, point 5 represents the reunion of (now evolved) king and queen in the birth of "the lesser stone"—the baby version of the philosopher's stone. It represents the emerging essence of the hero who is liberated from internal drama and can align this spark of new intelligence in service of higher things. Gurdjieff called this stage of the work reaching *self-consciousness*, but he was referring to a higher "self"—a state of awakened purposeful being without the small self at the center at all. No longer assailed by internal contradictions, our collected intelligence is more of a "Real I" that can perceive and use attention in a generative way, but this is only the start of a connection to higher mind that will be fully Real-i-zed at point 8 with what both Gurdjieff and Jung called *objective consciousness*—a kind of universal wisdom—that ensures we use our creative powers for good.

As with the higher heart, I think the higher mental center to which the Enneagram refers is not entirely "ours." There is an ever-present universal mind and heart that we can connect into via our own developed and integrated being, heart, and consciousness. This is more akin to the Source and Flow of Creation or the transcendent and immanent dimensions of the Divine. Having the potential for "higher" centers indicates there are values (virtues) that transcend our personal interest, rooted in our interbeing with *All that Is*, and there are (holy) ideas to guide us from the realm of objective knowledge which transcends our individual minds and allows us to see and know the Unity of all things. While we connect into these higher "centers" via the two tetrahedrons of the Merkaba formed from the integration of all of the energy centers, they are neither entirely separate, nor entirely ours.

We must remember, however, that we are trying to name the un-nameable. Different traditions have different names for the concepts to which we are referring. That said, the connection to higher mind sparked at this point of the journey is captured in the Enneagram by the idea of Holy Omniscience, the holy idea at point 5. This is received wisdom, *gnosis* or knowing that arrives to us without effort, unfolding from the virtue of Non-attachment. Non-attachment describes our ability to *stand in the middle,* to stay open in each center of intelligence, and come to the combined center of our whole being that is the portal between worlds. With the door between the Above and Below open, our formerly narrow valve of knowing opens out to allow much greater understanding of life, ourselves, and what the journey is about. And it's not about us.

For this reason, the expansion of consciousness at point 5 can bring additional suffering. Every new emergence brings its shadow along. With apotheosis, a perspective of the wholeness and holiness of all Creation, we feel the longing for at-One-ment in a much keener way. Seeing more clearly the nature of Reality, and our role in it, can cause a great deal of remorse as well. Like Pinocchio, our developing conscience reveals how off-course we have been, and we are more sensitized to the inevitable missteps of our personality, and the shame and horror inherent in human-ity. We see the consequences (to ourselves and others) of having lived so far from the truth that we are all connected at a deeper level of being. We can see that how we show up, how we treat ourselves and others matters, a lot. Our wish upon the star has greater meaning. This is a good thing, however, because that wish can provide additional fuel for the difficult crossing of the return threshold and the challenges that come with heading back into the known world (with all its triggers).

The alchemists called this stage in the process *fermentation*. Chem-ically, fermentation is an internal boiling or burning that occurs when a carbohydrate is turned into an acid or alcohol—*spirits* or the quintessence. It results in a further purification of the "lesser stone" that here relates to the remorse of a conscience that sees the gap between *what is* and *what could be* and intensifies the soul's desire to amend the situation. The fire applied at this stage is gentler than the fire of calcination that burned off the ego king. It is an inner boiling of a soul that longs for more, a smol-dering that motivates and chips away at doubts and distractions related to one's purpose and higher aim, newly clarified. In our stories, the hero transformed by her encounters in the Void has brought new order to the flow of potential within. But she still needs momentum to proceed across the threshold to revivify the kingdom, which is by now a complete mess.

Another purpose of cultivating this inner secret fire is to burn off any spiritual materialism that may arise here. This may include thinking we alone know the truth, or that our morality is better than any other, and contributes to the very smelly nature of ego-remains (the *ferment*) left behind here when we are diligent in our work. What we started by recov-ering our soul's essence and divine spark in the Void continues to flower and connect into higher mind as the journey unfolds. On a practical level, this means that our lower centers may still get hijacked by old patterns that arise from our sense of being a separate someone.

The practice of Non-attachment enables us to recognize and cut through any leftover ego stuff with that divine spark that *knows* from a higher perspective. It's like a sword of creative consciousness that can trans-form those dragons into the broader flow of vital energy and information in, around, and through us that sustains our higher aim. As soon as we claim we are "someone" we separate ourselves again. With Non-attachment we observe the inevitable arising of self-focus (even if it's about our fear and unworthiness for what's ahead) and let it go, without judgment. Staying aware, bringing shadowed patterns into the field of light, without aversion or attachment, is the essence of en-light-en-ment, which has nothing at all to do with being special or wise and everything to do with being no one.

FROM EGO DISSOLUTION THROUGH VIRTUE TO HIGHER MIND: THE HOLY IDEAS

At point 5, the more integrated human soul is filled with Real information from our connection with others, with the natural world, and from the vertical dimension of objective knowledge and spirit as well. In Shamanic traditions this channel within is likened to a hollow bone. Since we are empty of self, transparent, truly higher mind can arrive through us. This is related to the second holy idea at point 5, Holy Transparency. Detaching from personality patterns that distort our intelligence we can *know*, not with the ego at the center, but rather Real, real-time, energy and information. As Joseph Campbell puts it: "The two—the hero and his ultimate god, the seeker and the found—are thus understood as the outside and inside of a single self-mirrored mystery which is identical with the mystery of the un-manifest world. The great deed of the supreme hero is to come to the knowledge of this unity in multiplicity and then to make it known."[135]

The Enneagram gives us a more nuanced view of this process of realizing the Unity in multiplicity through the holy ideas. The holy ideas are unobscured perceptions of the nature of Reality attributed to the higher mental center. While some people interpret the word *holy* as designating something different from ordinary human life, the words *holy* and *whole* come from the same old English root that means undivided, complete, and healthy. So each holy idea is a way of understanding the whole of Creation with our whole self that allows us to see ourselves within the Unity of all things, including our particular gifts and purpose in helping to restore this vision to the world. This is in contrast to our Enneagram fixation, the lower mental habit that confines us to dualism and blocks us from knowing our purpose and our true nature as One with *All that Is*.

As with the virtues, "we" don't work at the holy ideas, so much as they arrive in the open field of integrated awareness we prepare through surrender and integrated Presence. The existence of these transcendent ideals implies that there is an aspect of Reality that is objective, that arrives to us, and can impact and even rearrange our being. It gives us a little faith in the future of our hard work. And it can help us with the sometimes-inhuman task of reconciling opposites we have given ourselves. The holy ideas are also "holy" because they are "of God" or *seeing as God sees* with the unifying intelligence of Creation—which is Holy Love. So if you don't understand the intelligence pervading the Universe as God, substitute Love, non-dual consciousness, Source, the implicate order, or whatever works for you. Surely, any attempt to describe the holy ideas reduces them to mental constructs which are far too small to house them. But while the map is not the territory, sometimes maps are useful.

The holy idea at **Point 1** is **Holy Perfection**. Holy Perfection is the understanding that, at one level, everything is always and already perfect just as it is—part of the great flow of Being. It is a hard one to digest in a world that guarantees suffering and inequality, but Holy Perfection realizes that *we* don't know the truth, and are not in charge of judging, fighting, and making the world conform to our personal sense of perfection. We are charged, instead, to take ourselves apart and align with the perfection of the continuous unfolding of Being and Becoming. From there we may know our role more clearly and proceed to bring more of the inherent perfection of the Divine to life through lifting others.

At **Point 2**, **Holy Will** is the understanding that the Will of the Absolute is enough, and we don't need to make things happen for others; and indeed, it is sometimes best not to interfere. This leads to **Holy Freedom**, the understanding that we are free to have our own needs, know they will also be met, and no longer have to compulsively earn love by being for others. Ultimately, we are free to live the unfolding of our own particular journey—which is always in service to something beyond ego.

Point 3 has three holy ideas. **Holy Harmony** understands that life unfolds as it should, without our efforts, and we need not create or force or do much of anything on our own. Instead, we attend and align with **Holy Law**—knowing the law-full universal pattern through which life unfolds in a discontinuous process that integrates opposing forces. And **Holy Hope** refers to the possibility that if we align with this pattern—hold the tension of opposing forces that leads to *something more*—and aim higher, then we have reason to believe a Way will emerge in which to engage meaningfully in the evolution of a new future.

At **Point 4, Holy Origin** is the understanding that we all came from and are part of the same One Source. We are always and already part of the whole, the divine ground of Being. We don't need to do anything to be better or compete with anyone, because no one can ever be better or worse than anyone else. We are all special as we have a particular journey to fulfill; one that requires us first to be *not* special, no-one, to know ourselves as the vast expanse of interbeing.

Point 5, Holy Transparency is the ability to know the whole Universe and how it operates through our own experience of being "filled" with interbeing as it unfolds continuously. The embodied experience of *All that Is* enables profound understanding without the analytical mind. And **Holy Omniscience** further describes this access to objective knowledge, through our open Presence, like a direct download from higher mind.

At **Point 6, Holy Faith** arises when our being, our eye and "I," is single and in union with higher mind. As there is nothing bad or good in Being, there is nothing to fear or doubt. With **Holy Strength** we understand that we are immeasurably strong in spirit (as opposed to personality), and we can do what it takes to hold polar forces together. We know that *something more* comes from holding the center. And even when it seems like we are furthest away from Source, that effort to *stand in the middle* will always reveal a higher-order and unified outcome.

Point 7 has three holy ideas as well, all related to the dynamic aspect of Creation. **Holy Plan** is the realization that whatever is unfolding is Creation's wise drive toward coherence. So rather than resisting, running, or idealizing, we take things as they are. Then, **Holy Work** is doing only what is ours to do, knowing how to engage the laws and diverse energies within to bring this uniting pattern alive in the world. This is also known as magic, which requires the third idea of **Holy Wisdom**—the capacity to discern our magic from Holy or sacred magic, that which is essentially and always embedded in non-dual awareness and the good of all Creation.

At **Point 8, Holy Truth** is seeing the nature of Reality in accordance with the laws themselves, which serve to continuously update, renew, and unify the diversity of life. It is the Realization of the laws within—knowing ourselves as a spontaneous expression of this collective dance of One continuously becoming process. Since Truth is that to which nothing can be opposed, no one is in charge, there is no bad or good, no justice to be served. We need not control, but we create all the same—related, as we are, to everything in existence through Being in alignment with the laws. This leads to a profound sense of Innocence as we "play" with Creation.

Point 9, **Holy Love** is the holy idea that existed before everything else. Source created with love, because it is the One force strong enough to hold the massive complexity and diversity of all life together. It is *knowing* that everything is love, shining with life and possibility, and we are ALL also made of love and inherently lovable. When we actively *know* everyone and everything in Creation as divine love, we extend the force, hold space, and increase the capacity of others to *know* in this way. This is the kind of Unity that arises from diversity; not some kind of uniform fusion, but the product of many colors, many notes, that together make an other-worldly harmony.

The Enneagram of Personality says that there is just one holy idea that we lost. And yet, as with the virtues, we can grow through understanding all the holy ideas, because they are all different angles of perception on the Law of One. As we begin to see the whole through our one holy idea at point 5, then, we may begin to *know* through them all. Humans being as we are, however, we may need to keep wiping the windshield. Questions for reflection here include: *What veil still needs to be dropped to know the Unity underlying diversity? Or how would I see this situation through the eyes of Holy Love—if there was no-one looking?*

And because this connection to higher mind is received (just as we saw Thor and his hammer magnetize lightning), we would do well to spend even more time preparing the vessel of our soul in the practice of Presence through all our centers, dropping down and in, as well as opening up and out to received wisdom. It is work to stay here, and neither become righteous about our revelations nor lost in the watery depths of the unconscious spring we have tapped. This work is still the most essential. We have to keep using the sword of consciousness on ourselves, to cut away ego distractions, before we can wield it with grace in the world. Like Arya, we have to stay with the intelligence gathered in the unknown until insight comes and we can integrate, transcend, and help create *something more*. Then, beyond old programs, attitudes, and emotions, we too may glimpse a higher Truth drawing us on.

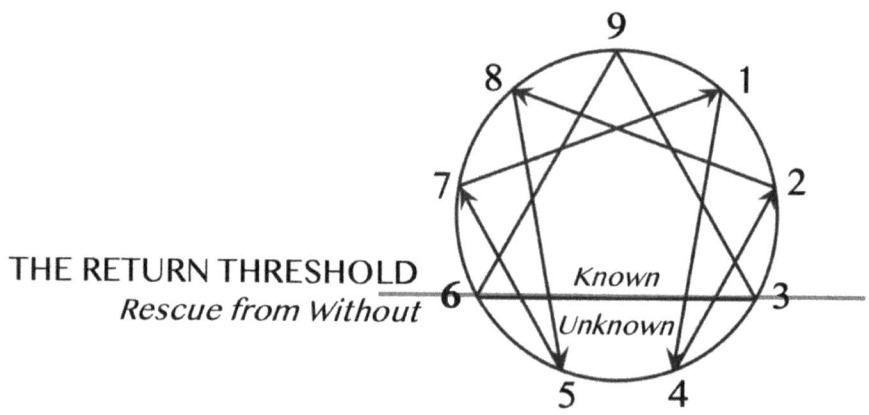

THE RETURN THRESHOLD
Rescue from Without

CHAPTER FIFTEEN

POINT 6:
THE RETURN THRESHOLD

*Only when man has truly and sincerely arrived at the
conviction of his own helplessness and nothingness and only when
he feels it constantly, will he be ready for the next and much
more difficult stages of the work.*[136]

~ G. I. GURDJIEFF

YOU'D THINK AFTER *ALL THAT*, the hero would be ready and eager to
get home. And yet, quite often the transition back to order and the
known world is not so simple. Take Dorothy...she and her mates are celeb-
rities, having tamed the forces of evil as the Wicked Witch and revealed
the truth of the Wizard of Oz as both more vulnerable and more compassionate than many believed. She has done her part to harmonize the forces
of tyranny and chaos in Oz. And yet, here at the threshold, many things
go wrong to thwart her return.

Dorothy left Kansas in protest of the rules of the father principle—
the culture and tradition-bound force that threatened to take away her
beloved dog Toto, a symbol of inner guidance and potential growth. But
despite her heroic adventures thus far, Dorothy is still doubting her inner
authority and thinking something outside of her will take her Home. So
she agrees to go with the Wizard of Oz in his hot air balloon for the trip
back to Kansas...even though she knows he is an empty suit! (That's how
strong our ego fixations can be, in moments, even at this point in the
journey.) Fortunately, the balloon takes off without Dorothy, because Toto
(purposeful as always) runs off at the last second and she chases him.

In the original book, Dorothy then turns to the winged monkeys and
asks them to take her home (shadow integrated, they are friendly now), but
Kansas is beyond their flight capacity. Finally, Dorothy and her whole crew
travel to meet Glinda the Good Witch. Serving as a positive example of
integrated consciousness and a "threshold rescuer," Glinda helps Dorothy
see that the power she needs to get Home has been with her all along in the

ruby slippers. Those slippers symbolize the *treasure* (spiritualization of the hero) that can help lead her to Realize her fully integrated soul in essence.

Point 6 is a shock point, as it again marks the threshold between known and unknown worlds. Like point 3, it is not included as a musical note in Gurdjieff's formulation of the octave of growth, but it is very important to us as another place on the Symbol where the inner triangle intersects the hero's journey and *something more* is enabled through the Law of Three. At each point of the triangle, one specific role (king, queen, or hero) is emphasized to flexibly invite additional intelligence through our aligned mind, heart, body for transformation, but all three forces must be engaged to fulfill the promise of the journey. For us, the three forces, now mostly un-hooked from ego, represent important aspects of a developing Presence we will explore in the final part of the book.

For now, point 6 marks a key challenge and choice point for the hero: can he engage in his former known world in a way that holds the two worlds together as One? Having created some degree of order in the unknown, many heroes hesitate to return to the now-decaying places they left behind. In Joseph Campbell's formulation of the journey, helpers and mentors like Glinda often show up to contribute to the stalled action at the threshold to accomplish what he calls a "rescue from without." This is an important clue to the challenges ahead and the fully integrated nature they will require. Sometimes the hero welcomes this help or answers the activating challenge; sometimes the hero refuses the crossing and flees, only to be pursued and dragged across the threshold. This crossing is not easy.

At this point in our story, the hero is changed in a profound way. Having accessed her soul through the integration of shadow and the dissolution of ego patterns, she has some sense of her place in the whole and a capacity for creative imagination, but there is some serious work ahead. How will she fare in returning to the known world with its narrow definitions and outdated order? She has a growing sense of the contribution she is meant to make in community, but will anyone understand her? Will the kingdom reject her, wear her down, destroy the hard-won capacity of the changed hero? Will she get reactive and resistant to the disarray across the threshold, and lose the burgeoning peace she has attained through her ordeal? Is there anything that remains of the world she left behind? So many questions, concerns, and doubts at point 6!

THE PASSION OF FEAR

The hero at point 6 on the Enneagram grapples with the passion of Fear, and rightfully so, as the world she left way-back-when has become more chaotic and/or corrupt. In the face of imagined threat across the return threshold, some potential heroes choose not to return. They go on new adventures, perhaps, or cave up in the unknown to reach deeper and deeper states of *samadhi* and union with the Divine. But we know by now that the only way to continue to grow is to invite challenge. Crossing the return threshold marks the hero's commitment to again hold the tension of polar forces, this time outside of herself as well, bringing something of what she has learned in the mysterious unknown to life in the former known world. As always with the Law of Three, however, further evolution requires sacrifice. Even some of the hard-won revelations from the hero's transit through the Void must be surrendered to a higher master if the journey is to continue.

As the reconciling force, the hero crossing the return threshold commits to the challenging work of contributing to the world from a more integrated way of being and interbeing, and as a channel for higher intelligence. However, this work will require a new level of Courage, the virtue at point 6, to help transmute polarity in the world. The decision to cross is a significant decision that reverberates through the Symbol and influences the outcome of the whole journey ahead. To hold one's center against not only conflicting internal impulses, but also polarizing forces in the world, is the significant choice a hero makes. It is a shock point with the potential to forward profound evolution, but it comes with a high price. Joseph Campbell called it, "The final crisis of the round, to which the whole miraculous excursion has been but a prelude...the paradoxical, supremely difficult, threshold crossing" to bring the redemptive pattern (which is *the ego-shattering, life-redeeming elixir*) to life in the world of people who don't get it.[137]

Gurdjieff related the work of this crossing to "intentional suffering"—knowing it's hard work to address polarity in the world without ego defenses. It requires a certain level of skill in conscious labor, the work taken up at the first shock point, and a new level of self-remembering, as well, to even understand this...much less carry it out.

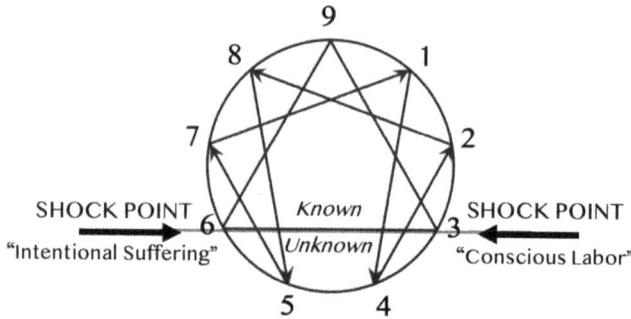

To be clear, intentional suffering has little to do with the kind of personal suffering hooked to our ego structure and the negative emotions of the lower heart center. Intentional, like conscious, means a voluntary movement *in* to challenge. This time, however, the hero understands more of the effort ahead, as well as the price. Intentional suffering is a heartfelt choice to endure the consequences of standing between polar positions to make a Way in the world for higher-order collaboration. With a different kind of Presence through aligned centers of intelligence, through conscience and a true sense of interbeing, a hero endeavors to live the pattern, flexibly applying all three forces, as needed, to invite *something more*. We gladly bear our burden because, having lived through the miraculous pattern of life-death-rebirth through the Void, we now know more about the purpose and promise of this sacrifice.

Gurdjieff's Fourth Way work was meant to be done while maintaining life as a regular citizen for a reason. Staying awake and relating from one's growing essence, particularly in a community that may not be aligned with what you have experienced or learned on the journey, is a great practice ground and source of friction for strengthening Presence and autonomous consciousness, and for furthering one's development. One aspect of this practice is withholding and "transmuting" the expression of negative emotion when triggered by others. Gurdjieff wrote that the greatest possible intentional suffering would be "enduring the-displeasing-manifestations-of-others-towards-yourselves."[138]

Transmuting negative emotion triggered in relation to others strengthens our will and third force ability to stay present and hold the center within provocative situations. This is different than repressing feelings. It is different than employing any of the ego's defense mechanisms to avoid discomfort. We may be quite aware and feel, maybe a lot, but we don't express or identify with our reactivity. Instead, this energy is harnessed in the development of greater being, made possible by the higher heart vessel built in the Void. We know precisely what the human heart is capable of, and we choose to stay present and open anyway, washing it all in the developing higher heart, with eyes on the mission.

Behind the work of not-expressing, Gurdjieff also taught the necessity of not "identifying" with the events of the world. Identifying would be like personalizing it when bad things happen, whether bad weather or someone's direct offense toward you. He was very much against "internal considering"—centering the self in the experience of unfolding events, including indulging in thoughts about other people's attitudes toward us. Not our business. Instead, we should concentrate on "external considering," seeing everything from within others' shoes, and from a larger perspective in general (*apotheosis*). We are learning to operate with a new compass, without the small self at the center of things, attending to higher intelligence. Nothing is personal!

All of these skills and more are required to pass into the next level of work across the return threshold. The hero, whether she knows it or not, has been chiefly involved in working on her own transformation and preparation. However, through the deconstruction of ego and creation of an integrated vessel of being, the hero leveled up her growth challenge, initiating a third layer of work mapped in the Symbol that aims to bring the horizontal and vertical dimensions together IN the created world. She commits to do what it takes to use that vertical axis to be a conduit for higher intelligence and renewal in the community, even at (what may seem like) her own expense. Because we won't really see the fruits of the choice at this shock point until much later, the threshold return is really just a commitment—a commitment to challenge oneself further in service to the higher and still-unrealized aim.

After all that has unfolded up to this moment, how does one summon the Courage to face even further suffering...effectively throwing oneself to the wolves? Or in Simba's case, to the hyenas. Remember that Simba balks when Nala comes to his hide-away, *hakuna matata* world and asks him to return to the Pride Lands. The prospect of leaving his new "normal" to face judgement about his disappearance, confront tyranny in his uncle Scar and the hyena brigade, and address the decaying conditions of the Pride Lands, is not an easy sell. Thankfully, as we saw, Rafiki manages the "threshold rescue" by sparking *apotheosis*, a higher mind, and helping Simba reunite with the benevolent ruler within himself.

CHALLENGES AT THE RETURN THRESHOLD

No doubt you have been here after a transformative event in your life—maybe a particularly powerful workshop or spiritual experience, an enlightening travel experience, even falling in love? You return home and try to share your experience from this renewed place, and people look at you funny. Or you don't share because you know they won't get it, but then you are left feeling the distance between you. Or no one even asks and their behavior towards you simply suggests: "Let's get back to normal here." I imagine people know, intuitively, that our insights and experiences might upset their orderly world in some way, perhaps tickling their own longing for *something more*.

The risk at this threshold is that we may not be strong enough to hold on to our burgeoning ways of *being* and *knowing*[1] beyond ego, especially in the face of challenges from our community and our internal reactions to them. It's hard not to feel diminished when our immense experience cannot be reflected by others, and then we start to get confused, or forget, or begin to Doubt (the fixation at point 6) the journey's revelations up to this point. Alternately, we may become the "true believer" here, forcing our certainty on others rather than leading the way to change through our evolving Presence. Choosing sides and regressing to ego habits is common under this new stress. In Wonder Woman's story, as the action heats up on the front lines of World War I, rather than having faith in her new partnership with Captain Steve, Diana diverges from the plan and disrupts Steve's efforts to stop the worst of the Germans' deadly plot to kill thousands with poison gas. Fixated on her singular quest to kill General Ludendorff (whom she thinks is Ares, and the only cause of this war), Diana puts everyone at further risk because of her errant beliefs and related drive to be the savior.

The hero finds herself again stuck between worlds. At the return threshold, we know a lot more about the other world that exists just behind the known—both its chaos and potential treasure. It can be challenging to walk in the everyday world carrying this additional level of knowledge and experience. Campbell defines the task: "How to translate into terms of "yes" and "no" revelations that shatter into meaninglessness every attempt to define the pairs of opposites? How to communicate to people who insist

---

1 I'm italicizing *being* and *knowing* periodically now to distinguish them as "higher"—the result of wholly integrated centers of intelligence in touch with intelligence (energy and information) from beyond the self as well.

on the exclusive evidence of their senses the message of the all-generating void?"[139] Can we hold the tension of knowing what we know along with respect for the world we left behind? Can we do this without diminishing ourselves or the community that doesn't "get it?" And how can we, in the process, bring to life our particular gifts and the "illuminating revelation" experienced in the Void in order to make a difference in our community? It's all very complicated.

This is hard enough to actualize in our own being, and the hero's journey asks us to bring our growing Presence to life in the world as well, modeling the way for others, and holding the center in a polarized society. Navigating this crossing consciously means that we don't know for sure if we can fulfill our higher aim, but we choose intentionally to face our Fear and take on the suffering. We risk displeasure and misunderstanding from others, as well as our own reactive irritability or escape maneuvers to assuage the tension. This takes Courage, as there is always something more of the ego and the world we left behind that must finally be resolved across the threshold—the challenge of which can intimidate even the bravest of heroes.

We can view Jon Snow's resistance to taking the Iron Throne for the good of the realm as refusing the return threshold. He is a brave and natural leader. Jon takes others into battle to safeguard the future of the entire Seven Kingdoms. With the help of his sisters, he aligns most of the territories in a fight against the Night King that ends in victory. And yet, from the beginning Jon resisted titles. He didn't seek to be Lord Commander of the Night's Watch, he did not want to be Lord of Winterfell like his adoptive father, or King of the North, and he will not oppose Daenerys Targaryen to claim his rightful place as heir to the Iron Throne. Whether still attached to his not-enough-ness or out of love for Daenerys, Jon Snow falters upon his return, unable yet to imagine how to *master two worlds* across the threshold.

Joseph Campbell uses the same word, "shock," at the return threshold to convey the idea that when we don't go willingly, here too, life has a way of stepping in and pushing us: "Society is jealous of those who remain away from it, and will come knocking at the door... If the hero...is unwilling, the disturber suffers an ugly shock; but on the other hand, if the summoned one is only delayed...an apparent rescue is effected, and the adventurer returns."[140] In some sense, then, resisting the crossing is futile. Because the hero has changed profoundly, there *is* no "going back." This serves as a reminder of Gurdjieff's words: "There is nothing worse than beginning to work on ourselves and then giving up and finding oneself 'between two stools;' it would be much better not to begin."[141] The world ahead is forever changed, because the hero is different. We don't know it yet, but it is far easier step across the threshold willingly, to use third force consciousness, invite paradox, and hold the door open for the emergence of something we can't yet fathom to carry us on.

In the stories, that something arrives as a good witch or a giant, or sometimes in the return of an ally you thought was gone—just as Rafiki emboldens Simba and Han Solo shows up for Luke Skywalker at that key moment, flying into the narrow channel to explode the Death Star. Heimdall, the wise keeper of the bridge between Asgard and realms beyond, manages to open the way for Thor's return home even though Loki has left Heimdall in a frozen state. Help for our heroes also arrives in the form of one more trial or test at the threshold that serves to strengthen the hero's capacity and courage for the return.

As the Buddha sat under the Bodhi tree for weeks, he persevered through many difficult challenges at the hands of Mara. Mara is the demon that works against enlightenment. Mara means *delusion,* and he is sometimes called the Lord of Passions, fittingly. Mara wanted Siddhartha to be a king or businessman or politician, or anything other than the Buddha who would bring liberation and healing to all beings through his teachings. Buddha sits tight through Mara's many assaults, and then Mara finally pulls out the big gun. His last temptation was no army or dragon or parade of pleasure, but rather the calm assurance that *no one* in the known world would understand the Buddha or be able to make use of his teachings. Mara's final case was something like: "It will never work! So why not leave man to self-destruct and slip back into *nirvana* yourself?"

At the conclusion of *The Hunger Games,* as the only two tributes (participants) remaining, Katniss and Peeta also face one more test. Last we saw them, they were in a labyrinthian jungle-like "arena" with 22 other young people fighting to the death, while all sorts of chaos and environmental hazards were rained down upon them by the Gamemakers. Katniss and Peeta had been promised that a new game rule allowed for *two* survivors (never before allowed in the games) and this had helped them fight harder. At the very last minute, however, after terrifying and brutal fights to survive together, the Gamemakers retracted that ruling. They essentially said "nevermind," now only one tribute can win the Games.

The Gamemakers' test aimed straight at the heart of Katniss who promised to survive for her beloved little sister Prim. They thought Katniss would give in and kill Peeta, which they knew would destroy her inside because of the growing love between them. And yet, having passed through the gauntlet of the abyss, changed by love, Katniss takes a leap of faith that a fourth way will open. She pulls out a handful of poison berries and she and Peeta hastily agree to die together rather than be forced into taking one life. Not a second too soon, President Snow calls it a tie, seeing he won't win this one. Her spontaneous action results in Katniss and Peeta being lifted together directly out of the arena and back to the known world. It also begins the transformation of that world by greatly strengthening the resistance movement aimed at the overthrow of President Snow and the Capitol.

It's important to understand at point 6 that there is no good or bad helper, no difference between the challenges laid out by Mara and President Snow and the threshold rescue efforts of Rafiki and Glinda the Good Witch. We are more and more moving beyond dualistic distinctions on the back-half of the journey. It's all about what they pull out of the hero at this pivotal moment. The Buddha could not exist and grow wise without the opposing force of Mara any more than Dorothy could get Home without Glinda. The good news is that the stories indicate that if we have the Courage to face paradox with a Holy Faith that knows we can hold two worlds as one (in the face of personal suffering), we can be helped across the threshold one way or another.

INNER WORK AT THE SHOCK POINT

Our personal work at this shock point is simple and difficult at the same time. I mean, there's the difficult work of intentional suffering, but beneath that the challenge is the decision and commitment to go ahead. The lived experience of our revelation in the unknown is what will make it Real and us Real-i-zed, but it's tough to understand the benefits with our still limited level of awareness. One temptation in doing psycho-spiritual work is to keep attending workshops, reading books, and devoting more and more hours of life to "my" growth. It is easy to withdraw or imagine that we are somehow above others or simply too different to maintain relationships or keep our same job that pays the bills, especially if these challenges disturb a new-found peace, which surely they will. It is easy to think we are not ready.

Crossing the return threshold requires facing a very deep and basic fear—something previously intolerable that called the ego and Enneagram type into being, way-back-when, to protect the scared child of the past. Having survived the Void, we have seen the full measure of shadow and of what we and other humans are capable. But we have also lived the pattern that allows us to embrace darkness. Although we may be confused, we now know there is a Way to transmute all of this into new potential. But we must untangle this core fear, in the form of its projections in the world that haunt us from without, to level-up our capacity to integrate polarized forces in community.

From the perspective of **Point 1**, facing our fear of being bad, defective, or evil, we no longer hold the badness in the world as "other," and instead provide a Way for transmutation through acceptance, attention, and Presence.

From **Point 2**, facing our fear of being unlovable or not needed, we no longer need to become lovable and save others to earn our worth, and instead become a clear channel for love.

From a **Point 3** perspective, facing our fear of being worthless apart from achievements, we no longer center ourselves or our agenda, and instead make a Way for *something more* to arise from the whole circle.

From **Point 4**, facing our fear of having no identity or personal significance, we feel free to be no one (and everyone), and instead hold space for the genius of Creation.

From the perspective of **Point 5**, facing our fear of being helpless or useless, we come out of hiding and head into the fray, knowing what is necessary and good for the whole will come through our Presence.

From a **Point 6** perspective, facing our fear of not having or being enough for survival, we *stand in the middle* willingly, holding the tension of paradox in the world with faith in the pattern.

From **Point 7**, facing our fear of being deprived or trapped in pain, we stop pressing for more and instead become a still point in the chaos through which life transmutes itself.

From **Point 8**, facing our fear of being harmed and controlled by others, we no longer protect, punish, or control, but rather willingly create the conditions to play with everything that arises.

From a **Point 9** perspective, facing our fear of loss, separation, or annihilation by rocking the boat, we instead *step in* to all manner of conflict and polarity, making a Way for all to be lifted through the unifying force of love.

As we face our deepest fears and pull back our projections we strengthen Real I and our ability to apprehend Reality just as it is. Applying the Law of Three, we are always working with opposing forces to catalyze growth. The knife edge of this challenge always calls something unexpected out of us if we can hold the intensity with an expansive Presence that includes Equanimity, Non-attachment, Courage, and other gifts from the Void.

The concept of intentional suffering is layered, itself a paradox that points beyond the obvious. On the one hand, there's no sugar coating it, it's hard to be human and messy and re-engage in the world that ego built, parts of which we may have condemned as "other" and sought to leave behind in our pursuit of inner work. As we cross the return threshold, we will rub up against the triggers of interpersonal conflict, feeling slighted or unseen, or otherwise not getting our way in relationship and community. We will witness all manner of things that don't align with our beliefs and desires for what is right and good. Human life goes on as per usual. And yet, Gurdjieff is saying this is not a necessary evil, but rather part of an intentional process that continues to develop higher consciousness. It gives us the perfect arena for honing and embodying higher intelligence that helps us to stay courageous and non-reactive, un-attached to ego and "my" need to control or define it all. Amplify those day-to-day challenges x10 in today's polarized society, and you have a powerful practice ground.

With this understanding, we are tasked to sacrifice once and for all even the *idea* of personal suffering, because we know that we need challenge to reach higher and deeper. This turns what would have previously been experienced as terrifying, painful, or unworthy of our embrace into something we welcome, open to, and learn from with ease...even gratitude. From this frame of reference, the suffering is transformed into something with great merit, something that actually redeems and gives meaning to our lives. In this way, former "enemies" are friends that help provide the fuel for growth, and we are given the opportunity to enjoy our practice and *aim higher.* It is from this stance that we access genuine virtue and the energy of a higher heart that fuels the rest of the journey and brings higher intelligence to life in the world.

It sounds good, right? And yet, at point 6 on the inner journey we can smell the intensity of this challenge across the threshold. Because of our work and efforts to see ourselves objectively, we have a front row seat to a view that is bound to show us the remaining gaps between how we want to be and how we are now. When we move from Fear and Doubt to Courage, however, and into this challenge of bringing higher aspects of *being* and *knowing* into the created world, we actualize the power of Holy Strength, one of two holy ideas at point 6. Holy Strength is what it takes to *stand in middle*—to *know* two worlds as One, even when they don't seem at all alike, and even when both sides condemn us. And all of this is aided by Holy Faith, knowing the pattern of the laws; knowing how, and knowing that, there is a creative and benevolent underlying intelligence that will fill the open space we hold between opposing forces and move things toward Unity. New life always rises, and we will be supported in fulfilling our destiny if we go.

Some reflection questions to prepare for this crossing might be: *What would it mean for me to sacrifice Fear of the unknown for Courage and Faith in the pattern? What would it look like (sound like, feel like) to "stand in the middle," in the face of polarizing positions in the outer world, to allow for reconciliation and renewal?* To stoke motivation for this crossing we can add: *What is the purpose of this engagement? What is my higher aim? And what would it take to give up personal "suffering" in its service?* And to prepare for the slips, it might be merited to consider: *What does it look like, in contrast, when I "personalize" my encounters with difficult things and people in the world, and fall for internal considering?*

We will need a new level of kindness for ourselves and towards others when neither live up to our ideals, just as we need the strength of will to decapitate leftover fear and limiting ego patterns. Our learning in the Void—the higher heart field that can hold all the shadow and messiness of humanity (including our own)—is a most powerful ally. If our internal compass is still aligned with the needs of our separate self, suffering, and passions, we will get stuck at this threshold. The continued and regular practice of Presence can serve as our mentor and threshold rescuer, helping us across the line when needed. In addition, we would do well here to strengthen the aspect of higher mind that can see things more objectively, choose our focus in a difficult situation, and choose the interpretation that guides our actions.

From the standpoint of neuroscience, integrating "Above and Below" moving forward includes linking the higher and lower aspects of our brain (the rider and the elephant) to increase top-down reflection, self-control, and impulse control when we are triggered, but also to allow for the bottom-up flow of information, instinct, feeling, and our sense of inter-being with others and the natural world. And from a spiritual perspective, the Above and Below extends through our now more integrated centers of intelligence from a sense of interbeing and connectedness to *All that Is* towards a higher kind of *knowing* that allows us to extend a grace beyond our small self's capacity into all of our interactions. Taking that step across the threshold means we are ready to live and model this process in the everyday world and fulfill the promise of the heroic journey. We must stay the course to realize the possibility inherent in this map.

THE RETURN

Somewhere across the threshold, we pass into the final stage of the journey, the Return. The hero, transformed through his encounters in the unknown, goes back to face the known world left at the outset of the journey. This could include an actual place, but also represents a fixated and fragmented state of being (perpetuated by chaos, tyranny, oppression, and fear) that pervades the kingdom or galaxy. What makes a hero is, most particularly, navigating this stage of the journey in which, by her example and participation, she contributes to the revivification of community that was falling into polarity and instability way back at the beginning of the story.

In this stage, the hero must first manage the complexity within her of being from two worlds—the known world of her former life and the unknown that now lives within her—to find her Way to help reconcile polarity in the community to which she returns. Whether we understand the unknown as the unconscious, diverse regions of the brain, a psychological frontier of sorts, the spirit realm, or the wave-field of quantum physics, the requirement is the same. What does it mean to know ourselves as One within a larger whole? How do we actually live in the everyday world from a place of greater integration and receptivity, from non-dual awareness, as a force for Unity or Holy Love? And how do we take an active role in Creation, supporting not only ourselves but also the communities in which we live? Only when we have lived our way through these questions will we find our true Home.

MASTER OF TWO WORLDS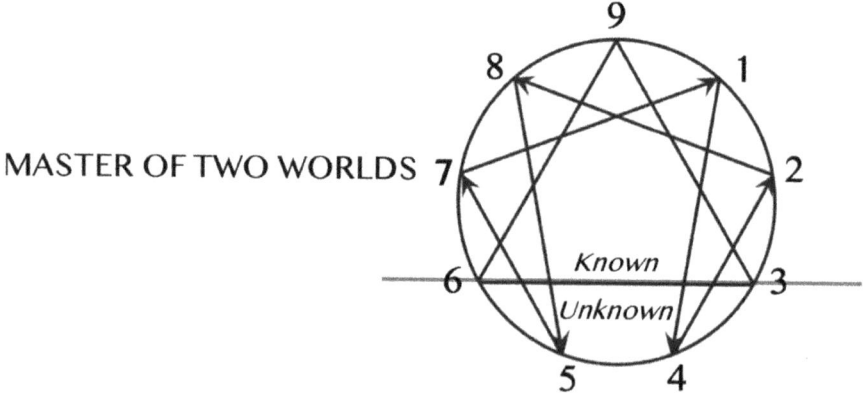

CHAPTER SIXTEEN

POINT 7:
MASTER OF TWO WORLDS

Freedom to pass back and forth across the world division, from the
perspective of the apparitions of time to that of the causal deep
and back—not contaminating the principles of the one with those
of the other, yet permitting the mind to know the one by virtue of
the other—is the talent of the master.[142]

~ JOSEPH CAMPBELL

OW DO WE GO BACK TO OUR FORMER KINGDOM, changed as we are?
Well...first, we go. Stumbling, overzealous perhaps, messy at times,
but stepping back into the known is an essential movement for the hero
toward consolidation of the vision of Unity and a furthering of her aim,
imagined or intuited at the outset of the adventure. Indeed, the only way
to fully realize the potential unleashed in the unknown is to engage with
the known world again, purposefully. As Campbell says it: "The returning
hero, to complete his adventure, must survive the impact of the world."[143]

From a neurobiological standpoint, we have to *act* to integrate our
learning from the journey through chaos, shadow, and the unconscious,
and unleash the hidden potential inherent in all of life. Self-regulation
of impulses, emotions, thoughts, attention, and behavior depends on
neural integration, strengthening fibers in the brain that connect widely
separated areas. Imagining and embodying new ways of seeing, thinking,
and reacting emotionally can create and strengthen neural pathways and
change how our brain works over time. Practice can rewire subconscious
programs and allow us to align with more purposeful ways of *being* and
knowing through all centers. Unless we embody in life what we are learning
on the journey, it doesn't last and can't make a difference.

At point 7 on the journey, the integrating pole of the hero archetype,
we are bringing to life what was birthed in the unknown to help create a
new known. And we have a lot to integrate by now, most especially the
virtuous heart that holds *the other* as myself, and the mind opening to

higher guidance, without the ego constantly (dis)organizing our experience of the world. Across the threshold, we are working at the creative process of staying open to the gifts of the unknown flow of spirit and life energy, emotion, and instinct, while navigating the complexity of the material world. We are integrating the unconscious, bringing hidden potential to life, and uniting opposing forces, within and without, for the benefit of not only ourselves, but also our communities.

This stage, Master of Two Worlds, develops a fluid capacity to pass back-and-forth between seemingly disparate realities. On a practical level it features the hero's third force ability to encircle polarized positions in any situation and hold the middle to invite a higher-order collaboration. It is foundationally rooted, however, in a mastery that incorporates the vertical or spiritual (nondual) reality with the human and horizontal plane. The alchemists called this stage of the work *distillation*. Chemically, distillation is a process of purifying the newly constellated *spirits* through repeated heating and cooling (interweaving fire and ice), in order to extract what is most essential. It takes practice to integrate worlds.

In the many years between Harry's first encounters with Voldemort and his final one in the dark forest at the end of the epic series, there is a bunch of back-and-forth, integrating worlds, that serves to solidify his learning from each challenging foray into the unknown. Harry's summers in the Muggle world with the Dursleys are full of mishaps and the illegal use of magic, such as blowing his Aunt Marge up like a human balloon for slandering his parents. Characters from the Wizarding world spill into the Muggle world, leading to all manner of confusion. One summer Dobby the magical house-elf ruins Mr. Dursley's important business dinner, resulting in further cruelty and restriction for Harry at the hands of his aunt and uncle. Another summer brings grave danger as Delores Umbridge sends a dementor after Harry and his cousin Dudley, which Harry has to stop with magic. All of these magical missteps result in Harry getting put on trial in the Wizarding world, as well as grounded in his Muggle household. Two world mastery is not easy.

Similarly, back in District 12 as a "normal" citizen, Katniss Everdeen cannot go very long without somehow stoking rebellion with her fiery ways and incapacity for artifice. *The girl on fire* is ultimately so threatening to President Snow's regime that a plan is made for a "special" 25th anniversary Hunger Games in which only past surviving tributes from each district will be chosen for a second turn in the Arena, guaranteeing that Katniss will again face death. Katniss, like Harry, goes back and forth between worlds more than once, struggling to integrate polar realities, before coming to the defining moments of facing the deepest shadows that have corrupted and split their respective worlds.

THE PASSION OF GLUTTONY

Having passed through the Void, the hero has more access to all the virtues of the higher heart, but the passion of Gluttony at point 7 must be resolved once and for all to fully realize the virtue of Sobriety. The optimistic and opportunistic drive of Gluttony may even be helpful in pulling the hero across the threshold and into the encounter with the everyday world, after considering all of what could go wrong. Gluttony is the heart's desire to consume experiences, to have stimulation and multiple options, to keep "my" life moving forward and serving compelling needs...or otherwise finding an escape hatch. It describes the primary addiction to ego habits that roots us *all* in the material world, obscuring higher intelligence.

The trap of Gluttony at point 7 is also related to the lower mental habit or fixation called Planning. This has to do with constantly imagining and planning possible positive futures versus engaging the truth and complexity of what is here-and-now in Presence. Often, we see the hero barrel back into the kingdom with his plans and vision for transforming community. After all, he left the kingdom in the first place with at least a vague idea of making things better. Now he has actually learned something, gained superhuman skills, or otherwise touched into greater personal capacity. The desire to drive his own vision of what is possible for the community can be strong...sometimes too strong. As Campbell says it: "What, now, is the result of the miraculous passage and return?...One may invent a false, finally unjustified, image of oneself as an exceptional phenomenon in the world...Such self-righteousness leads to a misunderstanding, not only of oneself but of the nature of both humanity and the cosmos."[144]

Daenerys Targaryen from Game of Thrones ends up only a would-be hero because she falls prey to self-righteousness. Early in the series, she walks through fire (literally and figuratively) to be transformed from naïve princess-daughter of a dead king and forgotten kingdom to the powerful Mother of Dragons. She emerges from significant trials in the unknown with a vision to reclaim the Iron Throne and take back the Seven Kingdoms from the corrupt powers that enslave innocents and oppress the poor. Despite her noble desire to be a benevolent ruler of the oppressed, somewhere along the line Dany's hunger gets the best of her. In her zeal to "break the wheel" of tyranny, Daenerys Targaryen ends up slaughtering entire communities, nobles and slaves alike, taking justice into her own (increasingly mad) hands. In the end, she acts out the very "sins" of the father principle, replicating the life of her own mad father.

Joseph Campbell writes: "Instead of clearing his own heart, the zealot tries to clear the world."[145] The lesson at point 7 is that the zeal of the activist who rises from chaos to break the chains (however idealistic and well-intentioned) can be just as destructive as the original tyrannical force. This is inevitable in a world with no understanding of the third force and how the Law of Three (engaging the "other") leads to an as-yet unimaginable solution. Even at this point in the journey, we must stay awake to the ego's belief in separation and the drive to gratify our personal vision. The arrow from point 7 back to point 1 gives us fair warning of the possibility of thinking we can be "the" Creator instead of the creative, reconciling force that unites extremes and makes a Way for the emergence of *something more*. The errant return to point 1 signifies reviving ego drives and self-focus, as well as rigid ways of understanding good and bad, in-groups and out-groups, all of which perpetuates polarity as the oppressed become the oppressors.

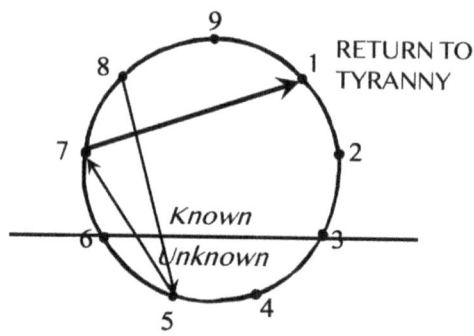

Instead, the hero must forego Gluttony for Sobriety, the virtue at point 7, and sacrifice her own plan for a Holy Plan (one of three holy ideas at point 7). Sobriety is freedom from the addiction to ego. It is related to a focused, clear, seeing of one's true work (Holy Work) of integrating worlds and allowing for emergence...not coming up with better options from our narrow mind. Sobriety speaks to embracing the suffering that arises in the context of relationships and living in the real world. It describes a heart that has lived through its own hell and can face the world with full knowledge of the depth and breadth of what lives in the darkness. There is always a new level of seriousness in the returning hero who has tamed and integrated shadow—a set in the jaw, a focus in the eyes, a determined gait. Sobriety also suggests that we would do well to move slowly, with deliberate practice, when we know the risks; when we are applying new ways of thinking, feeling, and operating with others in our world; and when we know that life does not unfold according to our plan alone, but rather a Holy Plan, in conversation with the larger circles in which we are embedded, according to the laws of the Universe.

In a way, crossing the shock point at point 6 and taking on intentional suffering in community, creates a second road of trials for our heroes, in which tests and trials further limit or enhance growth. (This makes sense if you know that the second shock is also the first shock of a second octave started at the point 3 opening). The hero is learning to be in community and in service, without ego and reactivity. Becoming master of two worlds is an active process of learning, often by trial and error, to be a channel for higher forces while living in the everyday world. Campbell writes: "The ultimate aim of the quest must be neither release nor ecstasy for oneself, but the wisdom and power to serve others."[146] This is not always as straightforward or easy as it sounds.

Katniss, Harry, Jon Snow, and other heroes we follow back across the threshold, struggle to figure out just who or where is the "community" they should be serving, when life has deteriorated all around them. The world to which they return is actually more chaotic now than the unknown from which they are emerging, which has become an integral part of their integrated *being*. So it is not at all clear who is on the side of "good," or how best to serve the whole...although their hearts are in the right place, with a new compass.

Wonder Woman Diana, having refused to listen to Captain Steve, pursues General Ludendorff to a military base where the deadly gas is being loaded on a bomber headed to London. She confronts and kills the General with the *Godkiller* sword but has a rude awakening when this does not immediately stop the war. Although determined to fight for those who cannot fight for themselves, Diana was so convinced of her own assumptions and plan for saving humans that she could not see the real and immediate threat of the imminent destruction of an entire region via poison gas. It is hard to know what part of ourselves to trust, and just who is the "master" in this process of integrating worlds.

In the midst of Diana's confusion, Sir Patrick, whom she thought was an ally, appears and reveals himself as the real Ares. Preying on her in these moments of disorientation, Ares as the ego adversary tries to seduce her back into his own dualistic worldview that would have her abandon her quest and prioritize herself. He spends a lot of words and energy insisting that humans are inherently corrupt and don't deserve her efforts (there are always reasons to justify betraying our own capacity for something higher). To make matters worse, Ares then destroys Diana's sword and reveals to Diana that, as the daughter of Zeus, *she* is the real "god killer." So much of her life was organized around the assumptions and stories held by her small self that Diana struggles in these moments to make sense of things, to reorient and recall just who and what she is serving.

Katniss Everdeen is facing similar confusion as her journey unfolds in the final book of the series. She is by now hiding out in the massive underground District 13 with the community of rebels working to overthrow President Snow's government. Her own district has been destroyed, and although she mounts a successful mission to rescue Peeta, who was captured and tortured in the Capitol, Katniss learns that he has been brainwashed to kill her. Who can she trust? In a series of additional trials, Katniss finds herself at odds with President Coin of the resistance movement as well. Through all of these challenges it becomes crystal clear that as our heroes return to carry out their missions, it is often not to the same world (or even the same mission) left behind.

Two World Mastery

What then does it mean to master two worlds? As an embodiment of the third force, the hero has this very particular role in the Law of Creation. Our myths and stories echo the Taoist teaching that the essence of the third element is to be a Way between the extremes of tyranny and chaos; and that, indeed, the re-establishment of dynamic wholeness in the individual soul is essential for righting the world. The hero holds the tension of opposites within and outside herself and aims higher. In this space, rather than flee to one extreme or the other (which is very tempting to relieve pressure), the hero learns how to bring new life, through her, to worn out patterns. It takes a great deal of patience and Sobriety to discern the Way of the hero.

To simply go along with President Coin's increasingly tyrannical rule goes against Katniss's nature, as well as her growing understanding of how to serve her community. Sure enough, some way into the mission to

destroy the Capitol, Katniss realizes that Coin and the resistance movement may not be as virtuous as they profess. As the mission commander
Boggs is dying, he admits this, urging Katniss: *Don't trust them (*Coin and
the other leaders of the movement*), don't go back. Kill Peeta. Do what
you came to do.* When neither faction, neither extreme, is healthy, what
is a hero to do?

For Harry Potter, too, the lines get very blurry towards the end of the
story. The Muggle world can no longer protect him at 17 years old, the
Wizarding world and Ministry of Magic is corrupt, Hogwarts has been
compromised, and Harry's wise mentor Dumbledore is dead. Even Ron
walks away from Harry and Hermione's quest for a time. Harry saves two
of his former school "enemies" (Malfoy and Goyle) even though they have
just tried to kill him, and he discovers the "evil" Professor Snape has had his
back the whole time. Sorting out who to serve and how to serve requires
a moment-to-moment attention to discern what is "true." Harry must use
the non-ego-based inner compass (the virtues and higher heart) that the
hero has been developing throughout the journey, as well as his growing
internalization of higher mind, through his more integrated being.

While these twists and turns make the notion of mastering two worlds
even more challenging, they sharpen a point of discernment that is essential to the hero's growth. Blindly serving an ideology or community is just
as dangerous as blindly serving ourselves, which we did when gripped by
the unconscious programming of our ego. Daenerys Targaryen's story is an
extreme example of that, but Jon Snow also gets confused in the process
of figuring out who and what he is serving. After breaking his oath to
the Brotherhood of the Night's Watch and spending six seasons with a
clear higher aim of securing the welfare of all seven kingdoms, Jon Snow
pledges his allegiance to Daenerys. His hesitation at the threshold turns
into blindness as he navigates the complexity of two worlds.

Many seasons earlier Jon Snow's ally and brother, the wise old Maester
Aemon, said prophetically: "Love is the death of duty." Love in the small
sense of blind commitment to another surely can distract us from a higher
duty and the idea of Holy Work at point 7. This and other stories warn us
that *anything*—any group, idea, party, or person we serve from ego—can
create catastrophe, as did Jon Snow's love for Daenerys. But in an instructive
twist towards the end of the epic series, Lord Tyrion says to Jon: "When you
think about it, duty is the death of Love." Holy Love integrates and enables.
It rises above, calling for more, while duty separates and compels, and a

personal love can blind us. It's a tricky dance between ice and fire for Jon Snow, but both the Enneagram Symbol and the journey tell us the Home to which we are headed transcends rigid conceptualizations of right, wrong, and duty, as well as our personal understanding of "love" perhaps.

In the end, mastering two worlds requires our heroes to continually navigate the process of integrating and aligning forces within themselves, with the communities they serve, and above all with the Force or higher wisdom that guides the Holy Plan unfolding through the journey. This, I imagine, is something like the third holy idea from higher mind at point 7, Holy Wisdom...the wisdom to know the difference.

INNER WORK FOR MASTERING TWO WORLDS

To understand our work at this stage we need to reflect on what it means to *master* as well as flesh out the nature of the *two worlds*. The backdrop against which the mythological hero's journey plays out is a battle between the forces of dark and light that takes place across known and unknown worlds.

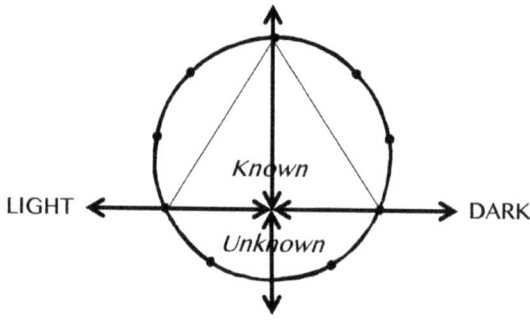

CONTEXT OF THE HERO'S JOURNEY

Mastery describes the transformation of our heroes that allows them to go between worlds, bring light to darkness, and restore harmony in the kingdom. While certainly the word mastery is used to refer to a level of achievement, in this case we are referring more to a mode of *being* that makes life, in this context of challenge and change, better. This is self-mastery, as in: we master our ego needs and integrate the conscious with unconscious mind, so that we can heal, align our will, and stay open to the breadth and depth of who we really are beyond the known: all shadow and all light, One with *All that Is* through the continuous arising of Being itself. We can then find our particular way to bring *that* to life in community to contribute to collective wholeness and healing. The work of the third force is still to stand in the middle, but on this half of the journey we are working with higher stakes.

The battle between dark and light is about bringing awareness and holding all that was disowned by ego into the broad light of consciousness. This goes on all throughout the journey on the "horizontal" level, as we are still vulnerable to the rise of dark forces, and we need to bring our newly developed gifts and resources to these challenges. Between points 4 and 5 on the Symbol, however, we found our way to the pause that unhooks us from the arrow of time—our cultural, biological, and emotional past—and makes way for a higher-order future through the vertical or spiritual dimension of the timeless and eternal. Crossing that gap opens up new terrain, allowing our developing souls to partner with higher ideas in the world. At point 7, the virtue of Sobriety is an ongoing practice of living from the pause, freeing ourselves again and again from the personal material that hijacks our lower intelligence centers, so we can master the kind of virtuous *being* that is a vessel for higher intelligence in the world. In contact with transpersonal or spiritual intelligence now, we work on linking and embodying two worlds as One.

If mastery is about the ongoing personal work to enable purposeful choices about how to be, how to integrate and serve both worlds as One, what are the two worlds exactly? While depicted as mythical places in our stories, the known and unknown are more like polar states of experience. They are symbolized by our foundational forces: one that creates order and the other that expands into flow/chaos. These two are further differentiated into their own polar aspects. As we know, the everyday world of order, culture, and tradition that organizes life in the face of chaos can grow stagnant and turn tyrannical, choking off new growth. The unknown

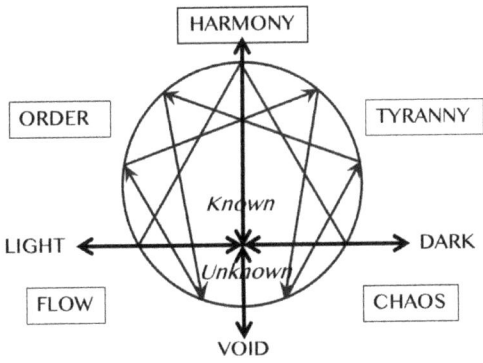

CONTEXT OF THE HERO'S JOURNEY

first shows itself as a dragon queen of destruction, confusion, and chaos, but it is also unexplored potential—a place of flow, from which new possibilities are continuously born. As Campbell says it:

The two worlds, the divine and the human, can be pictured only as distinct from each other—different as life and death, as day and night...Nevertheless—and here is a great key to the understanding of myth and symbol—the two kingdoms are actually one. The realm of the gods is a forgotten dimension of the world we know. And the exploration of that dimension, either willingly or unwillingly, is the whole sense of the deed of the hero.[147]

Like the particle and the wave, from which it arises, in the quantum field, these two worlds are mutually dependent "opposite" expressions of the same One energy. The potential of each one is always present in the other. It is we who are missing. Thus, *waking up* is the central creative act represented by the hero: knowing the two worlds as One, and living their creative possibility in the world. Campbell focuses on human and divine worlds here, but the spiritual dimension is one of many levels within which the Laws of the Symbol provide a blueprint for navigating challenge, change, and growth. Equally important for our inner work is the level of personality (through mind, heart, body centers) as it expresses itself in our lives.

Before we stumble into the Void and touch into the true depth and height of that vertical axis of growth, the known world is the everyday world that is "ordered" by our ego and personality type. The unknown consists of the sea of unconscious and disowned patterns that maintain type structure, *and* it holds the potential of who we are beyond type, symbolized by the whole Enneagram circle. Going beyond the known takes us beyond habits and grooved neural pathways, into new realizations, feelings, and behaviors that can rewire brain, body, and behavior, enabling growth, well-being, and better relationships. This is the kind of work we do when we use the arrow points to counter ego habits and challenge ourselves to think and feel differently, for example: to slow down and go inward, as a Type 3; rely on others, as a Type 8; embrace the ordinary and invite joy, as a Type 4.

Traversing the unknown takes us deeper into the terrain of our personal unconscious to see what's behind our habits as well—what the ego has defended us from feeling and knowing about ourselves. Here, among other things, we may encounter unhealed wounds from childhood along with gifts we left behind. Whether we are bringing "shadow" material into the light, seeing basic drives and programs that compel us to act and react in habitual ways, or remembering our essential nature, we are dipping into the unknown purposefully, and weaving a life between stagnant order and overwhelming chaos, to help co-create a different future. Exploring the chaos of unconscious triggers and memories can be destabilizing, but it is also freeing, enlivening, and empowering.

The unknown gets even more subtle and more vast when we pass into the Void and consider it from a transpersonal perspective. This view includes the understanding that there is something beyond even our personal unconscious. Carl Jung's work on the collective unconscious and archetypes, the stories of mystics across wisdom traditions, and the Enneagram Symbol itself, all seem to say that the deeper you go into interior regions (beyond shadow to instinct, the collective unconscious and the realm of the soul), the higher you extend into the spiritual, archetypal and transcendent realm.[148] Similar to many esoteric spiritual philosophies, there is this idea that the deep inner work of understanding our higher *being* and interconnectedness with Nature and all the world prepares us to receive higher guidance and participate in *knowing* the world through this whole and holy perspective. The two come together in the expression of an integrated and creative being-consciousness, in action, in the world.

KNOWING
OBJECTIVE PSYCHE/
ARCHETYPES
IMAGINATION
INTUITION
ANIMUS, **SPIRIT**

ANIMA, **SOUL**
SHADOW
INSTINCT
COLLECTIVE
UNCONSCIOUS
BEING

On the way to fashioning the philosopher's stone—a symbol for spiritualized matter and divine union—the alchemical stage of *distillation* represents a final "washing" to purify and prepare "the lesser stone" of alchemy (formed at point 5) for full re-unification of spirit and soul within the purified body. Like two world mastery, distillation carries this notion of back-and-forth, ascending and descending currents, coming together to prepare for a more complete vertical union. The hexagram is a figure found in many traditions (Hindu, Christian, Jewish, Islamic) as a symbol of "opposing" worlds, forces, or principles, now united. Because there are probably as many names for these symbols as there are belief systems (and the idea of opposing forces manifests at every level of existence) we have to use a broad brush to describe what is occurring as the two lines of development (*being* and *knowing*) come together, within the hero, across the threshold at point 7.

THE MAGIC OF TWO WORLD MASTERY

Beginning to integrate, embody, and channel higher intelligence in the world is the work of a true master. The outcome of distillation and two world mastery represents the "consecration" of the lesser stone. Our developing soul or essence brings its divine spark of creative imagination to life through embodiment in the world. The result is a kind of magic.

Christian Hermetic philosophers described the process by which higher consciousness or God is realized in the world as requiring four roles or stages. The first three align with an active, passive, and third (reconciling) force. There is: 1) the direct emanation from God (consciousness that creates); 2) the received, internalized experience (in a whole being); and 3) the lived expression of this union, they called "sacred magic," which is the realization of God or love—through incarnation of the Word (this creative pattern)—*in* the created world. The fourth role, theirs, was to fulfill the promise of all three phases by sharing this map in a way that integrates all traditions and diverse orientations to knowing.[149]

Gurdjieff wrote: "People who know these universal laws and know how to use them are magicians."[150] There is a great scene in a Netflix series called *The Witcher*, about a part-human and part-superhuman guy (a master of two worlds) who fights strange monsters. In the scene, a group of young women are being prepared for roles as magical stewards of life in various kingdoms. They are taking turns trying to bottle a direct strike of lightening, and their teacher says: "magic is simply organized chaos." Like the Way of the Tao, the third and magical role encircles and balances the first two polar forces in the course of fulfilling its own role: the creative *process* of *organizing chaos*, bringing the unknown/flow of spirit alive in the known world by becoming a vehicle (order) for higher values and truth in the world in a way that is intentionally self-less (without ego) and affirming of all life.

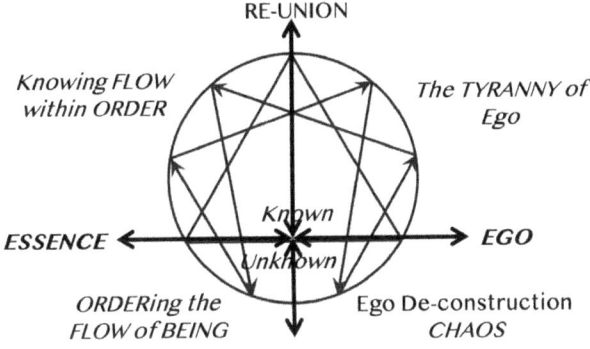

Mastering two worlds, then, is a dynamic process of continuously weaving and integrating the Above and Below at many levels, expanding our capacity and connection to all life. On this side of the journey, the hero has mostly integrated her unconscious and so has walked into a different reality across the return threshold. Because the known world is in great disarray at point 7, the hero who has the understanding and strength to *hold the center* now becomes the conduit for new energy and information—a vehicle for higher *being* and *knowing* in community. While the shock of this challenging work, intentional suffering, was chosen at the threshold, it will not come to fruition until close to the end of the journey. So the terrain looks more like this picture in which the new known, a true integration of worlds, is still ahead:

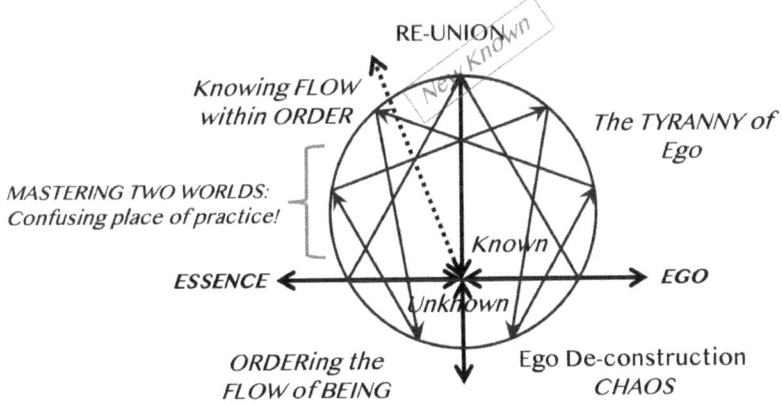

Carl Jung referred to this integrative process of distillation as engaging *the spirit of the depths* within *the spirit of the times*. He brought the psychological and spiritual (or transpersonal) together in advocating for us to travel our unique journeys through the personal and collective unconscious, to release ego, uncover our hidden wholeness and its connection to all the world, and unleash our unique expression of the immanent or in-dwelling divine spark in service to community. *Knowing* the two worlds as One is a creative process, with the potential to change the world around us, that will be realized in a fully integrated and grown-up soul or *being in essence* at point 8, in touch with higher forces. It's a beautiful vision, but it takes a great deal of Sobriety and discernment (Holy Wisdom) to realize the magic inherent in this work—to neither get swallowed up by the immensity of the unknown, nor hijacked by the temptation of greater insight and power.

RE-INTEGRATING THE EVERYDAY WORLD WITH OUR INNER WORK

At point 7, the path of the hero (versus the way of the mystic) takes us beyond a solely internal focus for our development and guides us to re-engage the known world differently. We are charged with accessing the potential of the unknown not only to realize our essential, integrated soul, but also to revivify the larger systems in which we live. We are forced to get clearer about who and what we are serving beyond our small self/ego, as we bring more of ourselves (and more of the laws) alive in the world. We are challenged to maintain the connection with our depths, and the *flow* of the unknown, as we go back into the context of everyday life that does not unfold according to our plans, with people who may not see or want our wisdom. We have to be very much awake to maintain our balance.

We definitely see our story heroes at this point doing things differently, heroically, often with little regard for themselves...intentional suffering. Pinocchio, knowing the dangers of the sea he braved to escape Pleasure Island, chooses to go right back in. He sacrifices himself by diving into the ocean to confront the whale, Monstro, who has swallowed his father. He devises a plan to be eaten by the whale, which alone is a life-threatening situation. Then Pinocchio risks his life again by lighting a fire (remember, he's made of wood) that causes Monstro to sneeze him and his hapless father Geppetto out of the belly of the whale. Having twice skirted death, Pinocchio is finally drowned as the great whale (now dragon-like, so we really understand the nature of the beast below) chases them and smashes their get-away raft.

Nearing the end of the series, Harry Potter simply walks into the dark woods outside Hogwarts, where he had his first encounter with Voldemort, and offers himself up to the gathering of Death Eaters. Harry has figured out that to sacrifice himself to Voldemort, as his mother did for him so long ago, is the only way to save his friends at Hogwarts. So he does. Harry gets to meet with Dumbledore one last time—in the liminal space between life and death symbolized by an all-white train station. Their conversation re-aligns Harry with what was lost in childhood. He seems to understand the meaning of his life, and his suffering, from a higher mind. Given the choice to stay in the white light with his own loved ones, Harry elects to return to the electric moment, in the middle of a dark wood surrounded by Death Eaters and Voldemort, to complete his destiny within his community.

Mastering two worlds in this larger sense describes balancing the reality that we are simultaneously an individual personality living in the material world *and* an indivisible part of the larger relationships, systems, and spiritual/energetic field we inhabit but do not control. Knowing that we are part of *All that Is* and living in a way that represents and helps to realize that hidden wholeness are two very different things. And our intentional participation in the well-being of these larger systems is essential for our *own* health and well-being, as well as for theirs. The hero's journey framework suggests that we can never be whole and healthy without knowing ourselves in community with others, and with the natural world, *but also* that it is the development of the human soul that is essential for repairing the fragmentation of culture and the fraying of the natural world.

As the Enneagram reminds us, Serenity, Humility, Veracity, Equanimity, Non-attachment, Courage, Sobriety, Innocence, and Right Action—all the budding virtues to which we aspire beyond ego—are hewn in the fire of living with and loving other messy humans who sometimes (often?) annoy or hurt us. And these same virtues provide us with a Way of higher *being* that helps to repair not only our own souls but also the connected fabric that is the ground of Being and living soul of the world. Similarly, the way that we see or *know* others shapes our experience with them. Most wisdom traditions teach that the path of service is an important way of developing ourselves beyond ego, but this is not always about what we do. Because Reality is so deeply interconnected, our state of being has a powerful impact on the health of the whole. We can be a conduit for something divine within humanity, or we can block that flow. Mastering two worlds requires us to be purposeful in *how we are* as we engage with others, not just *what we do*, because we are wired for connection.

WIRED FOR CONNECTION

Thanks to the pioneering work of Dan Siegel and others in establishing the field of interpersonal neurobiology, we know that our minds are not just in our heads but also *embodied and relational.* Siegel describes the mind as "a self-organizing process that regulates the flow of energy and information both within and between us."[151] What this means is that our "mind" exists in the relationships between us and others, as much as it exists in the relationship between our own brain and body. All of Dan's work defines health as a lived experience of our inherent interrelatedness. This is something like the Buddhist notion of interbeing, which Dan calls moving from a focus on *Me* to *MWe* (Me + We).

The brain is an open-loop system. Its energy field extends beyond the body. Aspects of our mind and brain literally change in response to the attention and emotion of other people, *outside* the system. The heart is another open system, in that its energy can also be felt and measured beyond the body, and it can be influenced by external inputs. It also has a powerful influence on the brain. Through our centers of intelligence, we are continually shaping and being shaped by the invisible/unknown realm of our interactions in community. One of the truths I consistently work on with clients is *people know how you feel about them, no matter how well you act.* And it happens in an instant.

When you go to influence someone...let's say you want to help improve someone's behavior or performance. You think it's your job as their parent, partner, or manager (although it's their job). So you go to "help" or fix with an internal mindset and heart-set that says "there is something not right with you" (no matter how well-meaning you are, no matter how "upbeat" your approach). Approached with this orientation, most people feel some degree of threat or judgment (conscious or not) that can disrupt their ability to think well and create and causes emotional resistance. Our thoughts and feelings are energy with a concrete impact. I think of it this way: when you play a guitar, if the strings are not aligned in a coherent tuning it sounds terrible. And that will be true even if you are the best guitar player in the world. Tuning our own instrument is like getting our centers (mind, heart, body) aligned so we can share our music without turning people off. When not aligned, there is static in the system that garbles our energy and messaging; it does not resonate with others as well as it could.

For example, if I say I want to help you, but I am coming from my own need to change you (I may have some degree of judgment or frustration, or just like being the hero), my centers are un-integrated. I am out of integrity. Most people can feel *my* need, and so not a true openness to their being. Because I am "out of tune" internally, they don't experience this as "help." On the other hand, if I am present, and all my centers are saying the same thing—without judgment, emotionally open, but not attached—people are more likely to feel the truth of my presence and be open to my collaboration. I call this skill of getting centers of intelligence internally aligned: *tune up*. By itself, *tune up* creates in us a more powerful and engaging, high-fidelity, Presence. But there's another level...

Going back to the guitar metaphor, consider what happens when you go to play music with other people. Your strings are aligned, you have a beautiful song picked out, but the person you are playing with is using an alternate tuning. Again, the connection doesn't work. It is literally impossible to make good music with another when you are not in tune *together* (this is called *attunement*), no matter how skilled or internally integrated you are. To address this gap, we have to combine the skill of *tune up* with *tune in*, which is a conscious and curious attunement to the other person's thinking, feeling, body language and behavior, as well as your own. Here our centers are free of ego stuff, aligned, but also our higher centers allow us to attune, adapt, and create with others.

In this case, mastering two worlds requires weaving unknown/invisible influences, like emotional energy and attention, into the known field of engagement between us. Because we now have more conscious mastery of ourselves, our attention, instinct, and feelings, we can purposefully attend to the unknown fields *between* us and others, as well as *within* others. This is one way to bring two worlds together; to bring the *spirit of the depths* alive in the *spirit of the times*. In this case, we use ourselves as the third force to encircle both positions and birth the promise of the creative unknown through our Presence, attention, and belief in possibility.

In practice, this requires aligning our emotions and thoughts with the highest and best for the other as ourselves. Often, we don't know what that is. But the Enneagram gives us a map. We have a new compass of interbeing and virtues to guide our higher aim. It's hard to go wrong when we orient with Serenity, Humility, Veracity, and the like, and then use a higher mind to imagine what is possible. From there, we can engage the Law of Three by pausing old habits (deconstructing ego) and conducting ourselves in relationship (aligning and attuning centers of intelligence) in a way that engages and respects both positions. We get curious about the other person's thinking, stay emotionally open (even when there is a vast chasm of difference between us), and then...a fourth way, a creative possibility, that *something more* beyond what we could imagine prior, can emerge from our collaboration.

When we orient in this way to people as *people* who matter, and not *objects* we intend to fix, they feel it and become far more inclined to engage in creatively solving the problem raised. Not only that, when people have their own "ah-ha" in the process, it creates a dopamine hit (a compelling neurotransmitter associated with reward) that helps to embed learning, raise motivation, and spark action. With the movement to tune up *and* tune in, we enter the field of interbeing (*MWe*), the space between known and unknown, and between our separate self and the flow of Being that unites us. Getting beyond what "I" need to accomplish and seeing the potential in you, I open the field and raise the level of play for *us* in the moment, rather than continuing to create more of our past dynamic in the future.

This is just one example of the "magic" of the third or reconciling force in community, and the incarnation of the organizing pattern of Creation. But we can start to see why two world mastery at point 7 is associated with the transformed hero, and how that is revealed via the sometimes-magical impact the hero has on others. Two world mastery is absolutely central to effective work as an activist and change agent, not to mention as a parent, manager, or partner. And it can only be learned through embodied practice. We are very powerful, indeed, but we need to learn the true source of our power.

How you ARE vs. What you Do

From a spiritual perspective, two world mastery reaches beyond the unknown space between us and other people to encompass the vast plane of potential that is the flow of Being, lying just beneath our experience of life, connecting us all to the soul of the world, as well as to transcendent ideas. From this perspective, trying to navigate life with the narrow view from personality is so limiting it's silly. Orienting to others as anything less than an equal expression of Source separates us immediately, drawing us downward. Mastery, from this view, is the conscious capacity of the third force to hold the tension between worlds, actively *knowing* others as One with us and *All that Is.* The practice of seeing the Divine or interbeing in everything and everyone (whether they are asleep or awake, like us or not) is the most powerful way to bring the truth of One world to life. Campbell describes "dwelling with others as an ego-less center [as the hero's] great compassionate act."

Of course, we still live in the human realm every day that the kids need breakfast, or the car breaks down on the way to work. Mastery of two worlds is a conscious practice of opening to our shared ground of Being, of weaving soul and spirit into our day-to-day interactions in bodies. Since the laws of physics at the quantum level don't always reveal themselves in the classical or Newtonian view, it's good to remember that mistakes will be made, and we are all always learning. Like our heroes, we may fumble, struggle to remember what and who we are serving, and choose again to align with *who we are* beyond ego and the known. All the while, we can let our ego strengths continue to help us with what we have to *do* each day, re-integrating our gifts now under the rule of a wiser master.

Mastering two worlds is not about becoming a better change agent. Well, it is, but it isn't. In the end, your influence is not as much about what you do, but rather more about *how you are*—how you engage with others and all of Creation in your daily life and work. To integrate the unknown with the known is to align with the continuous process of *knowing the two as One.* With the freedom to pass back-and-forth between worlds, we not only continue to refine our own *being* and ability to receive wisdom, but also, we can learn to use our divine spark of imaginative and generative consciousness (*knowing*), along with our unifying Presence, to bring about change in ourselves and in our world.

This act of *knowing* itself is an echo of the original divine impulse that creates, in partnership with attunement to the flow of potential Being. Linking these two forces (living wisdom or love) is the third force in action. This is one version of what it means to *walk the line* linking order and chaos, where meaning is found. On this line we may find our purpose and way to serve the larger systems of which we are a part, according to our unique essence. But our service starts from our alignment with the virtues of the higher heart, and the growing alignment with a higher intelligence that wants to come through us, enabling us to be an instrument of peace through this dynamic process of integration, making two worlds One.

As we saw in our heroes, the boundary between worlds can be blurry at this point. Across the threshold, the old "known" seems like chaos compared to the order we made of deep encounters in the unknown. It appears that our principles are getting switched, or the world of the story is upside down...which it kind of is! But each force is waking up inside the other, as the hero tries to dynamically align with and integrate *both* forces in a creative partnership with the underlying intelligence of Creation. We are in a period of practice and experimentation, sorting out who and what we are serving, and learning how to learn in the context of real life. Questions to reorient oneself in confusing terrain include: *Who and what am I serving? How do I refrain from separation and make a Way for two worlds to become One?*

As we re-enter the known, especially if we have done ego deconstruction in the context of a spiritual community or with a particular process or teacher, it can be easy to confuse the map for the territory once again. If we have become enlightened, found Jesus, or otherwise aligned with new truths and understanding, it can be tempting to lobby others to follow or otherwise teach "the" Way to grow in wholeness, spirit, and learn to love better. But the teaching can take us only so far. However well-intentioned our efforts, to be a master of two worlds is to remember that what we learned in the unknown is not a specific creed or practice, a book, a teacher, or a system—not even the Enneagram. If it were, then we would be back to assuming that there are aspects of life and other people that are "right" and others that are not; methods that are an expression of the Divine, and those that are not. We would be back to reacting as we did at point 1, separating ourselves by deciding who and what is outside of the Law of One, Source, or the unifying Holy Love that is primary in this Symbol. We choose to align with the laws because they are universal, not because they are "right."

As master of two worlds, we accept the oscillation between order and flow, known and unknown, and the processes of creation, decay, and renewal, because we know all of this intimately inside ourselves, along with our shadows and our light. And then we practice; we pay close attention. With kindness and intention, we work on creatively *knowing* each world by virtue of the other, owning our part in bringing to life the invisible potential inherent in everyone we encounter, whatever their beliefs. From here, we are on the verge of Innocence and playing with the Universe to realize the Law of One.

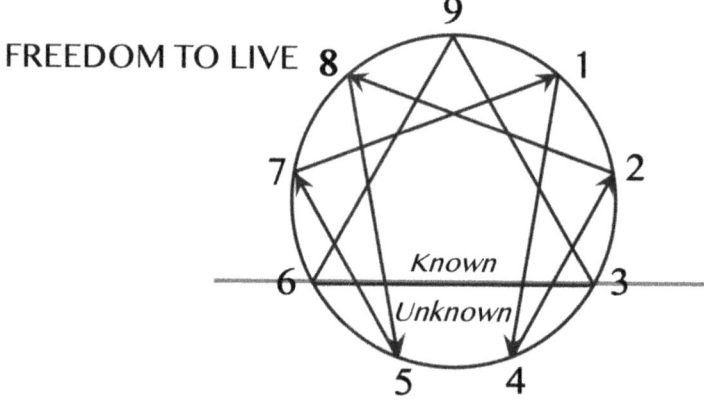

FREEDOM TO LIVE

CHAPTER SEVENTEEN

POINT 8:
FREEDOM TO LIVE

Personal ambitions being totally dissolved, he no longer tries to live but willingly relaxes to whatever may come to pass in him; he becomes, that is to say, an anonymity...The Law lives in him with his unreserved consent.[152]

~ JOSEPH CAMPBELL

I F LEARNING HOW TO LIVE IN TWO WORLDS is the practice at point 7, point 8 brings this dance to fruition through the virtue of Innocence. Innocence is the open-hearted and spontaneous expression of Being we see in children. Young children are not so concerned with being someone special or important, about maintaining control, or achieving certainty. Innocence is the willingness of the heart not to judge, condemn, and control, but rather to engage with what's right here, right now, and let the complexity of the world be what it is. This allows a hero to skillfully receive impressions from life as they arrive—without any particular attachment or self-referential interpretation—and to act directly from a higher sort of spontaneous intuition and creative imagination, making an impression on the world.

Innocence also *plays well with others* because there is no "other." This stage, Freedom to Live, describes the hero's final reconciliation with ego that allows the free flow of higher intelligence through the integration of all centers of intelligence and all the points (or "notes") around the Enneagram. A fully developed essence unites every part of us into a coherent whole that puts us in resonance with a higher intelligence that is always already moving through the world. Paradoxically, in the final surrender of our individual, passionate point of view, we receive a great deal more. Through Innocence, we learn to "play" with Creation itself. Campbell writes: "The hero is the champion of things becoming, not of things become, because he is."[153] Freedom to live has to do with this continuous *becoming* through spontaneous co-creation.

The Passion of Lust

Up to this point on the journey, the hero has contended with the passion of Lust from point 8. Lust has to do with the ego's drive to bolster a separate self and gratify its material desires. It turns life and other people into separate objects that may or may not be fulfilling those desires. If not, the ego is driven to make things happen, and blame someone for them not happening, which leads to the related mental habit of Vengeance—seeing a solution in up-ending something outside of myself instead of turning within. And when we successfully make things happen out there, it sucks us deeper into the delusion that the solutions to our lives come from the ego's desires and aversions, which fuels them further and keeps us cut off from our highest potential. From this perspective, in personality, we are always creating more of what we don't want.

In many of our stories, the hero has projected her frustrated desires outside of herself and is engaged in an intense process of fighting dark forces and restoring justice in the world—a pursuit that has her locked into a lead part in perpetuating polarity. Of course, it has all been well-intended! Wonder Woman set off from Themyscira to "fight for those who cannot fight for themselves," and to single-handedly save the planet. With the battle of light versus dark coming to a climax at this point of the journey, many of our heroes are facing life-threatening encounters with malevolent forces, in communities that are in serious danger and disarray. Shockingly, in the face of all that, the Symbol advocates a childlike practice of Innocence. What?! Surely our heroes would be better served by the passion of Lust, the intensity, the ability to make big things happen, along with the rebel's drive for Vengeance. It has, by the way, gotten them this far. Well...apparently not.

Daenerys Targaryen's lack of Sobriety and Lust to rule drove her to mount the attack on King's Landing and then take the Iron Throne. Vengeance fueled her fire into a killing spree after her aide and beloved friend, Missandei, was beheaded in front of her. In the end, Dany's use of power was not different from her enemies, Queen Cersei and all the other oppressive regimes Dany overturned on her path to power. Violence begets more violence. Opposing forces just change roles in a cycle that perpetuates the dark/light split and creates more of the past in the future. It was disappointing to see a female character with such heroic potential go awry, but she served as a symbolic foil for Jon Snow's encounter with fire, the dragon of chaos within, that the hero must integrate and rise above.

INNOCENCE: BECOMING A RENEWING FORCE

In contrast to Dany's story, our heroes with happy endings serve to revivify communities as a result of their final encounters with ego and what sent them on the journey. As champions of *things becoming* (including themselves), they align with the ever-present flow of energy and information available through Presence and with the creative process of seeing with eyes that *make all things new*. This is the power of Innocence. Re-engaging the known world with an Innocence that sees anew is something like playing with Creation. It's an actively receptive *and* creative process, as the hero's fully integrated *being* (in relation to all the world) allows for the continuous and effortless realization of a higher kind of *knowing*, through the divine spark of imagination, that allows her to live the creative pattern and fulfill her mission. And the results are sometimes surprising.

In our heroes we see things like a sudden inspiration, action, or change of plan; self-sacrifice, the prioritization of the good of the whole; and mercy, or at least a laying down of long-held Vengeance. Our heroes seem spontaneously guided, aligned with something beyond ego. The Wicked Witch of the West died at the hands of Dorothy, but it was in some sense an "innocent" accident...or inspired intuition perhaps. There was no Vengeance. It was as if simply aligning on the side of good won the day of its own accord.

And given the chance to destroy his enemy Scar, Simba actually refuses. Simba has returned to the Pride Lands to reclaim his power and his destiny from his tyrannical uncle. It seems sure to be a fight to the finish. In their final battle moments, with Simba dangling precariously off a ledge, Scar brags that he killed Mufasa in the same way as he is about to dispose of Simba—by pushing him off the cliff. This confession renews Simba's passion to fight. He launches himself up, and seconds later has Scar pinned for the kill. Except...he doesn't do it. Instead, Simba tells him to run away, saying "I'm not like you, Scar." With this claim, Simba reaffirms his own Innocence and *freedom to live* unhooked from the personality's drive to perpetuate the polarity that keeps one enslaved to the old ways.

The hero's last encounter with childhood wounds finishes the process of at-one-ment with the father principle, and connection to higher mind or spirit, that was glimpsed in the Void and led to the discovery of her own divine spark. Thanks to the point 7 work of integrating the two worlds, at point 8 the hero also achieves a horizontal reconciliation between the tyrannical king aspect of ego and the benevolent ruler, bringing the story full circle, and all the aspects of *being*, laid out around the circle, under a higher master. Knowing dark and light within himself now, Simba chooses to align with the highest expression of a leader. It works even better. Scar being Scar, he attacks Simba again given the chance. And because of his own choices, Scar inadvertently falls off the ledge while lunging at Simba. He is then summarily devoured by his own team of hyenas (who he was only too willing to throw under the bus moments earlier).

Thor and Loki are also perched at the edge of a vast abyss at the climax of their fight. After defeating the Destroyer on Earth, Thor returned to Asgard to find his home planet in chaos thanks to his brother and adversary Loki. Loki was in the midst of carrying out his convoluted plan to sneak King Laufey of the Frost Giants into Asgard to kill their father King Odin (still in his death-like sleep). As it turns out, Loki's true plan was to "catch" Laufey in the act, kill him, and *appear* to save his father in order to earn Odin's love and blessing—and potentially the future king title.

Thor interrupts all this just in time to stop Loki from using the bi-frost bridge (that takes them all between worlds) to destroy the Frost Giant's entire planet. As Thor demolishes the bridge itself to prevent the larger loss of life, Loki attacks him. Their fight takes Thor and Loki to the point of teetering on the edge of the world, with a yawning abyss of space opening below them. As they start to fall, they are grabbed just in time by the now-awakened benevolent ruler, King Odin. The King grabs Thor, Thor grabs Loki. In most of his movies, we find Thor extending a hand to his "evil" brother, dangling off this or that ledge of destruction, to save him. This time, Loki sacrifices himself, simply letting go of Thor's hand. (Whatever the circumstance of his "fall," Loki always returns with a new plot for Thor's undoing, in another movie, prompting another octave of growth for Thor).

Thor becomes the embodiment of Innocence in these pivotal moments, always seeing his brother as his old friend and playmate. It's almost as if Thor knows that Loki simply carries his own shadow, seeing as how they were somehow played against each other growing up. Thor is completely unwilling or unable to return the malevolence when it comes down to it, and so he finds a kind of freedom to choose anew each time, in Innocence, for the highest and best good...even within their ongoing feud. This is a change from Thor's brash beginnings where the slightest trigger sent him off to avenge himself against an entire planet. With King

Odin waking up, it seems that Thor has more growing to do to be a fully integrated benevolent ruler himself, but we can see the architecture of what is to come. Odin has recognized Thor's transformation and noble efforts to save the realm, and the two are "atoned," meaning Thor has internalized the wisdom of the benevolent leader.

This step symbolizes the hero's full embodiment of higher mind-heart (spirit and soul) that comes after a final reconciliation with ego and something lost in childhood for which the ego had been compensating. We see in both Thor and Simba a new capacity for *ordering* the *chaos* of life (their emotional, instinctual, and imaginal power within) to discipline and align it with higher principles, so as to become a conduit for the *flow* of truly higher intelligence in the world. They are stronger, more king-like and mature. In a paradoxical way, this strength is synonymous with the innocent heart, in alignment with higher mind and spirit.

Harry Potter also gets a chance to reflect on his choices and solve something about his character in that final conversation he has with Dumbledore in the all-white train station between life and death. What I didn't mention before is that they are not alone; there in the white light with them is a baby swaddled in white: Voldemort as a baby. As Dumbledore explains it to Harry, this infant is all that is left of Voldemort's soul. As with our own egos, all Voldemort really wanted was to be seen as someone special, someone immune to needing, protected and part of a community. Harry notes the sadness of this and recognizes himself in that description, because he too was hurt by life, the loss of his parents, and having to grow up in an unsafe situation.

Dumbledore acknowledges the similarities between Harry and Voldemort, and then he underlines the one difference: Harry chose differently. And then Harry chooses differently again. He elects to go back to the dark forest from which he was plucked before the white light. Here, surrounded by Death Eaters, he will sacrifice himself to Voldemort in hopes of saving his friends and the Wizarding world. In speaking about what differentiates Harry from Voldemort in the end JK Rowling writes:

> *They have each been given certain weapons and safeguards, but the power of these objects and past happenings lie in how they are understood, and how they are used or enacted upon. Harry has a deeper and truer understanding of the meaning of the objects and past events, but his greatest powers, those that save him, are free will, courage and moral certainty.*[154]

What enables the positive pole of the Great Father element and higher mind to be fully Realized in the world at point 8 is not only the integration of its own shadow, but its harmony with the Great Mother, the flow of Being. The hero aims with highest intentions, but also stays keenly attuned to inner wisdom arriving in each moment. Highest intentions come from holy ideas. And since everyone is connected as One from this non-dual perspective, there is no "one" left to blame. Arya Stark simply walks away from her quest to destroy Cersei Lannister, the evil queen behind the deaths of her family members. Granted, the Lannister kingdom, King's Landing, is being burned down all around her, but that is not stopping Arya from pursuing revenge. What stops her finally is observing Vengeance—the fixation at Point 8—embodied as Sandor Clegane ("the Hound") in his obsessive quest to kill his own brother.

Arya is driven by Vengeance through much of the journey, as evidenced by the grisly act of feeding Walder Frey his grown sons, in a pie, before executing him. We saw a change in her at point 5 (*apotheosis*), but Arya does not transcend the battle within her until the very end. This is a flag for all of us that even at this point of the journey, the hero can slide backwards by succumbing to the personality's demands. Arya does not. In a surprisingly touching moment, with King's Landing literally crumbling around them, the Hound urges Arya to see how the drive for revenge has destroyed him. He urges her to walk away, at first angrily, and then with as much affection as can be summoned by such a hardened man. Then they each choose.

Arya turns away as the Hound knowingly proceeds toward Vengeance and his own sure death. As she does so, Arya calls out "Thank you Sandor," using his real name for probably the first time ever. It's a poignant gesture, an acknowledgment of the best of him that (despite their oppositional energy) has cared for her all along. And with that, we get a last glimpse of shadow work, of the ability to own (and love) all aspects of the adversary, and how this singular act of acceptance integrates and disempowers it, helping Arya return to Innocence and a higher master.

ALIGNING WITH HIGHER WISDOM

More than just devices of storytelling, the dramatic and surprising twists that mark this final phase of the journey show the hero beyond ego, aligning fully now with higher wisdom, in a moment-to-moment way, to fulfill her destiny. Innocence is this ability to *be* in a new way, unencumbered, embodying higher centers, fully present and connected within the flow of everything around us. This state allows our heroes to understand (*being + knowing*) and actualize, in the moment, just exactly what is theirs to do in the greater story they are living. Luke Skywalker's attunement with the Force, finally, allows him to perform the death-defying flight to get close enough to blow up the Imperial Military battle station, the Death Star.

For Katniss Everdeen, the fall of the Capitol and President Snow's rule brings little consolation since she lost her sister Prim in the bombing that happened as rebel forces stormed the Capitol. This loss of small "i" innocence is for Katniss the final blow to her singular ego—the defended, independent, and fiery girl driven all through the journey to pay back her persecutor, President Snow. Without ego, the way is opened for her fully integrated essence that *knows* what is hers to do in this partnership with Creation. With new eyes, Katniss finally sees that President Coin's regime is about to step in and perpetuate the same abuses as Snow's, in that karmic cycle of violence where the persecuted become the persecutors.

This is an extremely important choice point for Katniss, because the two rivaling forces are at maximum tension (approaching the final shock point), about to flip into a state where the other party dominates but the fight is the same. This is a moment that calls for *something more*. Surrounded by a huge crowd, bow and arrow at the ready to finally execute President Snow with a single shot, Katniss *aims higher* at the last second, and sinks the arrow into the heart of the next tyrant and true threat to the community, President Coin. Katniss spontaneously sacrifices herself for the interest of the community, as this assassination is sure to put her at risk of prosecution or even death. But in that moment, she could do nothing else.

The illuminating revelation of Unity that started in the Void comes to fruition in these culminating moments of the journey. The difference is that this time the hero is acting with full consciousness (a Real I) and an un-self-ish alignment with the greater good, rather than stumbling into danger as she did in the abyss. Seeing and sensing with a higher heart-mind is solidified in action as our heroes sacrifice themselves to serve a higher purpose. For many, a final brush with death invokes their earlier re-birth from the Void and helps to resolve the original wound that shaped their early life. And it is exactly this inner transformation that allows our heroes at point 8 to act freely and spontaneously, with a new clarity about their aim or purpose as one who creatively serves all diverse life in the kingdom.

Just like Katniss, Jon Snow sacrifices himself by assassinating Daenerys in a split-second move to save the realm that I'm not sure he even knew he would carry out. This act was a death sentence for him for sure, given Dany's devoted following, as well as the actual dragon standing right next to them. I believe his act was guided by Innocence and alignment with higher mind because Jon Snow never wanted to rule, because he really did love Dany...and because, otherwise, her grieving dragon would have smelled ego and incinerated him right then and there. Instead, the last of the known dragons in the Seven Kingdoms flies away from the scene, freeing the entire realm from extremes and freeing Jon Snow to choose his own way, the Way between fire and ice.

When we last saw Wonder Woman, Ares (the god of war) had just revealed that Diana herself is the fabled *Godkiller*; it was never the sword. He then proceeds to take advantage of her confusion by trying to sweet talk Diana into joining his quest to extinguish the corrupt humans and deliver Earth to paradise. Ares tells Diana that he is the only one who truly knows her and knows humans as they are: weak, cruel, selfish, and capable of the greatest horrors. He says that mankind stole this world from them, the gods, and ruined it. He claims himself to be the god of truth, not war, saying humans destroy themselves on their own. In these tense moments, we can see Diana struggling with her confusion, black-and-white thinking, childhood legends of Zeus and Ares, and her role in all of this. She has indeed seen humans perpetrate horrible things along her tour of Earth during World War I.

While Diana is in this daze, Captain Steve rushes up to her to say "good-bye, I love you" before he pilots the bomber loaded with poison gas, on a suicide mission straight up into the atmosphere, to prevent anyone from deploying it. She only half hears him, given her confusion and concentrated effort to sort out what is true. Continuing with the seduction, Ares offers Diana a chance to kill Dr. Maru, the chief scientist who developed the deadly gas. In a moment of clarity, Diana realizes the complex nature of humanity—that people are not all good or all bad—and just then she sees Steve's plane explode. Remembering Steve's goodness and love for her, through her grief and anger, she taps into a level of power she has not known before. Living up to her name as the *Godkiller*, Diana re-directs Ares' lightning strike back into him, and he is destroyed for good.

While none of these heroic acts seem "innocent" at face value, they all give the sense that our heroes are not working from a personal plan, but rather are attuned to a larger aim that is taking shape through them in a moment-to-moment way. As Campbell says it: "The hero is the conscious vehicle of the terrible, wonderful Law, whether his work be that of butcher, jockey, or king."[155] The hero is no longer deciding in an analytical sense, but rather aligning with an embodied higher heart-mind in the creative act of "re-knowing" things. In the intentional creative act of *knowing* the non-dual nature of reality, the hero himself becomes different, like a clear channel for loving intelligence, unconcerned as he is for the separate self's agenda. It is this virtue of Innocence, in the moment, that allows the hero to Real-ize his destiny, disempower shadow forces (owning them all within), and bring about the repair and revival of his community.

Harry being Harry, while playing dead in the company of Voldemort and crew in the forest, he still lets Draco Malfoy's worried mother know that her son is ok—an action that risks sure death by revealing he is alive. This radical act of kindness in the face of evil transcends duality, but also it connects back to the original wound that made Harry who he is, with and without ego. Once again, a mother's love helps to save Harry in these final moments. Narcissa Malfoy keeps the secret that he is alive, even as Voldemort and the Death Eaters descend on Hogwarts to display the "dead" Harry Potter and declare their win to those who would still oppose them.

From there many threads laid down by Harry and his mates earlier in the journey are woven together into coherence. Dark and light face off. Somehow Neville has the right sword and the wherewithal to kill the snake that holds the last split-off bit of Voldemort's soul. Harry has the right wand so that when Voldemort deals a lethal spell to Harry, it bounces back and puts an end to the greatest enemy the Wizarding world has ever known. Others play equally important roles. While a triumph in the moment, we know these events are the result of Harry's long heroic road that brought all the disparate parts of the magical world together to enable renewed freedom to live in harmony.

INNER WORK AND THE FREEDOM TO LIVE

The Innocence we saw in our heroes enables living in alignment with Holy Truth, the holy idea at point 8 on the Enneagram, and the fulfillment of higher mind (and spirit) *within* a fully integrated being (our soul) in connection with the higher heart. This is our own version of the mythological process of rescuing the old "father" or dominant aspect of ego consciousness from the underworld, where it lay as potential, and integrating it under a truly higher master (*at-One-ment with the Father*). Coming to terms with this final and most tenacious piece of the puzzle that is the ego ideal of our Enneagram type allows us to fully surrender the striving that keeps us from an integrated higher or essential self, and it opens an entirely new landscape of possibility. As long as we are striving to be something or someone, we will never know the truth of our Being.

Truth, by definition, is something that applies in a universal manner: "the property of being in accord with reality."[156] The Greek word for truth, *aletheia*, also refers to Reality itself, and a state of not being hidden. If nothing is hidden, it is whole, connected with *All that Is*. The Hebrew word for truth begins with the first letter of the Hebrew alphabet, continues with the middle letter, and ends with the last. A similar all-encompassing expression: "I am the *alpha* and the *omega*," the beginning and the end, is a claim made by God and Jesus both about the nature of Reality as everything, whole, a reflection of the divine One.

The universal truth or pattern we have been studying in the Symbol via science, story, and spiritual wisdom is Realized as we near the end of the journey. The holy idea of Holy Truth at point 8 is something like seeing the whole pattern and the dynamic Unity underlying diversity, as revealed through the laws; or more accurately, *being* in accord with it. We are completing the work of re-membering—literally weaving together all the disparate parts of ourselves—so we can embody higher *being* through all our centers (and interbeing) and come to *know* (and understand) in a non-dual way that invites the best in others and brings the flow of spirit alive in the created world. Truth, in concept, is that to which nothing can be opposed. With nothing hidden, separate, or in opposition any longer, the whole pattern of Reality is revealed. And it is revealed *through* us, as we grow into our highest selves across two planes of existence.

First, as we have been tracking through the arrow lines, we are creating an unseen vertical relationship between opposing worlds and forces. The known and unknown (order and flow), at different levels of expression, have been woven into greater harmony through our inner work and Presence in community. This represents the journey's primary goal of unearthing the deeper self or soul, with its inherent sense of interconnectedness with *All that Is*, and its unique capacity to help weave into the manifest human story the transcendent intelligence that governs the unfolding of life. All the split off parts of our human or "horizontal" being, laid out around the circle, had to be collected and aligned in order to become a clear channel for the vertical flow of intelligence or spirit in the created world. The heroic stance now serves to help marry these two dimensions together through integrated Presence and conscious participation with the creative pattern of the Universe.

The vertical weaving began with a deconstruction of the known world down the right side of the journey. With both Culture and Nature in disarray, the hero left the tyranny of the ego (her own culture) to face the hidden and rejected parts of her own nature as shadows of the unconscious—the dragons of chaos lurking in the depths of the unknown. With this sacrifice of ego, the hero falls into total chaos in the Void, but also accesses a deeper part of herself connected to the vast sea of energy and potential that weaves through all of Creation, and from which new life rises. In surviving this crossing, the hero gains not only a lived understanding of the regenerative pattern of life, but also unearths her own spark of the creative force that brings order from chaos. Armed with this inner *treasure*, the hero faces the next-level task of reconciling a *higher* version of opposing forces (two worlds) in order to live this "magic" in community at point 7. If they can bring the final fragment of ego under a fully integrated essence or soul in touch with spirit, at point 8 the hero becomes a benevolent leader who helps renew and unify the kingdom as well.

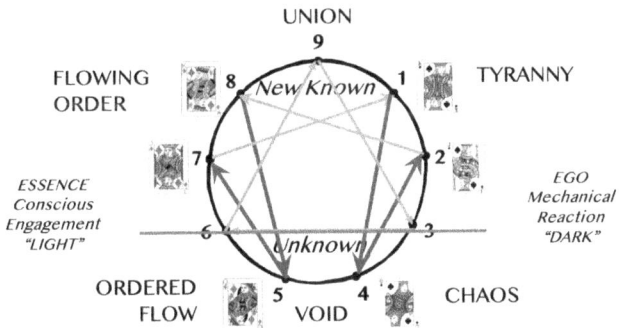

VERTICAL INTEGRATION OF TRIADS

As noted above, the vertical integration through two higher centers of intelligence on the left side of the symbol can come to fruition only because at point 8 the hero is also finishing a horizontal integration whereby the habitual, "dark" (ego-driven) side of *each* of the three constituent forces (king, queen, hero/adversary) has integrated with its opposite to create a balanced version. The dark side of each element was absorbed by its singular agenda. But either side without the other is imbalanced. In each case, what makes the archetype whole again, is knowing *the other* within itself. As each center fragment is freed from the restrictions of the small self, all can align into a central conduit for higher intelligence.

At point 5 the two aspects of the queen represent the undifferentiated higher *being* or soul that can receive higher *knowing* or spirit and "give birth" to the integrated consciousness of a true hero that is finally embodied at point 7. At point 8, with the re-incorporation of the former ego king from point 1, all the fragments of our centers, all the roles and poles, come together in the fulfillment of a fully integrated soul or essence that is now also "atoned" with the father principle, and a clear channel for spirit or higher intelligence in the created world.

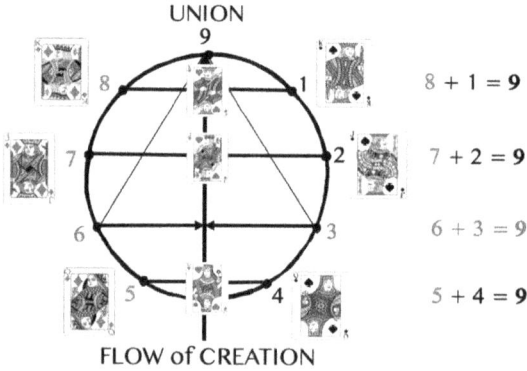

UNION

FLOW of CREATION

$8 + 1 = 9$

$7 + 2 = 9$

$6 + 3 = 9$

$5 + 4 = 9$

HORIZONTAL INTEGRATION OF EACH ELEMENT

The father element is that which brings structure and makes sense, creating order out of the flow of potential experience. It is an "organizing principle." Back at point 1, the tyrannical king symbolized how ego structure shapes our experience of life through the centers' habitual patterns of thinking, feeling, and reacting. In this sense, it serves as the "mind" of the organism, although it's not actually in the mental center. We refer to this element as leader of the "known world" because it continually creates more of the same for us with our narrow filters of perception and interpretation. That's why the ego ideal, embedded in our neurobiology, is our king or "ruling principle" at the start of the story. At point 8, with all the fragments of our intelligence centers now coming into alignment, as integrated higher being, consciousness, and heart, we are actualizing a new sort of ruling principle.

Like our heroes, we may need a final face-off with the tyrannical king or adversary (in some stories they are the same person) and, in particular, with the early life dynamics that shaped our ego ideal. Although we had to "sacrifice" ego at the edge of the Void, totally rejecting ego (or any part of us) only *keeps it attached* in that never-ending dance of polarity that separates us from Holy Truth—that to which nothing can be opposed. The opportunity here is not to destroy the personality but to take it out of the driver's seat, resolve early wounds that keep us divided inside, and from others, and lay down defensive strategies once and for all. We may even feel gratitude here for how well the ego served us as we grew. In many of our heroes, we see a revelation of something about their childhood or a reconciliation with something about their character and their true heart that focuses their heroic purpose. The sacrifice was essential, but everything that was "real" in us comes back with this fulfillment of inner unity and consolidation of a "Real I."

While each Enneagram type has different work to do, embracing the ego ideal as well as the adversary dissolves any leftover need to be someone special, safe, and in control (that keeps us from Presence), and unifies our whole being with higher consciousness. Like Harry Potter, then, knowing our capacity for all possible "dark" and "light," we can consciously and continuously choose a higher aim. Redemption brings the ego, along with all the other fragments of self around the Enneagram Symbol, under the rule of a fully "Real-i-zed" essence, the integrated and benevolent ruler who is not just a king but rather an embodiment of all the archetypes engaged in the ongoing creative work of renewing larger systems (bringing eternal life). The alchemists called this state *coagulation*, in which light and dark, soul and spirit, and the Above and Below all come together in the fulfillment of the philosopher's stone. But what exactly is this new "benevolent ruler" and organizing principle? Without the ego to shape our experience, how do we navigate?

A New Ruling Principle

In mastering two worlds at point 7, we learned the dance of intentionally integrating two worlds in dynamic practice. We worked at bringing more of the unknown/flow of life alive in our everyday world, whether spirit, emotion, intuition, or through co-creating with someone else, beyond ego. Here in this stage, freedom to live, we come to realize that while our presence and intention are key, we are not really in charge. In the end, everything is up to the unfolding intelligence of Creation. We could say, along with Joseph Campbell, that our conscious participation with the laws allows not just our own Realization, but also for the laws to be made "real" through us—whatever our work in the world. Again: "The hero is the conscious vehicle of the terrible, wonderful Law, whether his work be that of butcher, jockey, or king."

Holy Truth is related to the concept of *Logos*. *Logos* from the Greek means something like "word" or "plan;" something that "orders" or "gives form," just as words and language give shape to our experience and understanding. *Logos* is an organizing or ordering intelligence. When we are controlled by conditioned habit, our *logos* is our ego structure. As a fully developed soul in essence, we can operate with autonomous consciousness (immune to assaults from both within and outside of oneself) or a "Real I" that can be aligned, in single-pointed focus, with spirit and the universal *Logos*—the creative and all-encompassing pattern of birth, death, and renewal revealed through the laws of the Symbol. This pattern has been there from the beginning of life and reveals the One Unity of Creation through its continuous unfolding. In aligning with this *Logos*, we are Real-i-zing ourselves as One with the Source and Flow of loving intelligence that renews the world.

In the Christian tradition, we understand *Logos* as the Word that *was* God and *was with* God at the beginning. According to Father Rohr, the Word is indeed something like the blueprint or pattern of Creation. He relates the Word to *the first incarnation*, in which God created something out of nothing, and infused all of Creation with Himself through the blueprint. The organizing principle is God and is revealed in Jesus, the Word incarnate, or the living example of the pattern through which all things are made new.[157] And if we understand Jesus as the third force for some part of the journey, he shows the Way to live the most difficult part of this pattern—holding the tension of opposing forces to actualize the sacrifice and de-construction that brings new life and a higher order reunion of Spirit within the Created world. And then he leaves us not only with the flow of loving intelligence awakened in the world, but also with the pattern itself—the *alpha* and the *omega*.

Within the Symbol, our definition of a hero is one who lives the laws, Holy Truth, a higher *Logos*, by going on the journey. This is exactly what Joseph Campbell is proposing: "The hero of action is the agent of the cycle, continuing into the living moment the impulse that first moved the world."[158] The hero continues the original creative process at the heart of our creation stories. His journey also shows the Way to evolve life by finding our own connection to the hidden wholeness of the world and bringing our spark of genius to it in a way that revivifies and unites the kingdom. Isn't this what most wisdom traditions aim to provide? A Way? A way to *be* when things are in chaos and we don't know how to be? And perhaps a way to *know* and to Real-ize the higher potential in all of Creation?

Living from Holy Truth, then, may be something like aligning with the laws themselves and the realm of what Gurdjieff called objective knowledge. Like Jung, in using the term "objective" Gurdjieff was referring to a fundamentally different way of knowing, not as a separate one, but through our integrated *being* and creative capacity to perceive things as they are—as whole and wholly interconnected. Through our unencumbered Presence, we access a collective intelligence from beyond the known. Obviously, that means both teachers believed there is such a thing as Truth, particularly as regards the laws of nature and the universal patterns or archetypes through which they reveal themselves in all of life. This is an idea that can be traced back through various ancient and indigenous cultures that held true knowledge as a "remembering" from a transcendent realm. And the fact that we can find the laws and archetypes across ages, traditions, and disciplines, through myth and symbolism, as well as within our own inner landscape, supports the existence of an "objective" consciousness.

While our ability to access higher intelligence—objective higher values and ideas—towards which we might orient our lives is very important to our inner work and engagement in the world, the notion that only some people might be in touch with such divine or objective truth is just a hair's breadth away from perpetuating separation, tyranny, and righteousness.

The Enneagram Symbol gives us a simple recipe for avoiding this trap. We may not be unleashing fire-burning dragons on the enemy kingdom, but as soon as we find ourselves sucked back into any shred of delusion that we are special, or when we are too certain of how things *should* be, feel entitled to oppress others, or assert control to get what we want, we are going the wrong direction (through Lust, Gluttony, Fear, Avarice, Envy, Deceit, Pride, and Anger). That is the path of a child *building* an ego structure. In the development of essence, we are owning and unhooking from those passions, traveling clockwise to a point where the ego is fully integrated within a much wider circle of wisdom. The development of higher *being* (free from passion/vice) and being in the universal heart, with a well-developed conscience, is essential to the (rather frightening, admittedly) concept of an inner or "received wisdom" from a higher Source.

And then, at point 8, Innocence can be trusted because there is no more Vengeance. There is no one and no thing outside the pattern, no one outside the One Source that creates and is the *Logos*. Instead of the passion of Lust, the drive to make life happen on our terms, we learn how to work with the pattern, find the Middle Way and the Tao that unifies life through Presence and the ongoing journey. And at this point, we can trust and serve the unfolding of life precisely because we are no longer governed by personal reactivity, or any of our ego needs and stories about who we are, how the world is, and how things "should" be. We are living in Presence as Serenity, Humility, Veracity, Equanimity, Non-attachment, Courage, Sobriety, and especially Innocence, guided by Holy Truth, to ensure Right Action in the world.

From Ego to Essence

The integration, under a new ruler, of that final piece of ego that worked hard to compensate for what was lost in early childhood marks the full development of the soul child that was lifted from the Void. Something is remembered here about our essence before it was obscured by personality. For all of us, part of this is a literal child-like innocence that can be in touch with the free-flow of emotion, life energy, and instinct. Because we have looked honestly at the destructive potential of this elemental energy and owned it, we can work with it (*ride the dragon* like Jon Snow). Our shared work is to own all the aspects of who we are, so we are not owned *by them*. At the same time, according to our Enneagram type, we left behind particular gifts and qualities we were born with but forgot. Because of this loss, we compulsively strive to simulate what was lost, paradoxically cutting ourselves off from the kind of Presence and attention that would allow us to re-member who we are. When we have fully mastered and disempowered the ego's striving at point 8, we can access this unique lost Innocence that helps shape our contribution in renewing the world.[159]

When **Type 1s** face off with their drive to set things right in themselves and the in world, they remember an inherent ease, lightness, and ability to follow the flow beyond rigid boundaries.

When **Type 2s** face off with the drive to be lovable and indispensable to others, they re-experience their own inner nature as love itself and resolve to follow it into life.

When **Type 3s** face off with their drive to be the hero, they remember their sensitivity and true gifts as a fully integrated heartfelt presence that engages and inspires others.

When **Type 4s** face off with their drive to be somebody unique and special, they re-know the peace of an extremely stable sense of self in touch with the eternal now.

When **Type 5s** face off with the drive to stay resourced and contained, they rediscover the endless flow of information and energy continually arising through *being* in Presence.

When **Type 6s** face off with their drive to absolve fear and achieve certainty, they recover an inner authority and strength that can hold the center in even the most polarized situations.

When **Type 7s** face off with the drive for more stimulation and options, they remember the power of focus and commitment to reveal the depth and immensity of a moment.

When **Type 8s** face off with the drive for intensity and balance of power, they re-experience the true power of their own innocence, tenderness, and ability to play with Creation.

When **Type 9s** face off with their drive to accommodate and maintain harmony, they rediscover their own intensity and power to bring effective change into the world.

This may be a little different for you. Or, in addition to these gifts, you may re-integrate some aspects of your soul child that are unique to you. The point is that without past biases that distort our perception, we are free to experience life and the loving intelligence of Being as it arrives in this moment, in this context, with this person. This should put us in contact with our own lost innocence. We don't become our opposite completely. We re-member it and help it to grow up and grow together with the other parts of ourselves. As we re-own this last piece of "other-ness," we experience a new level of inner coherence and wholeness. In the end, our heroes show us that integrating *all* aspects of the ego adversary we have been following and fighting reveals a profound gift that may be necessary for what we came here to do. This is a *treasure* best revealed through your own kind attention. Watch for it.

In a sense, freedom to live represents the whole pattern of the journey lived in a moment. Going beyond the known, right now, is the way we can be re-known. We are made new (innocent) through aligning with the flow aspect of Creation and bringing Real, real-time intelligence and energy to life. Gurdjieff wrote: "Life is real only then, when I AM."[160] I AM is the portal to eternity that opens up when we are a wholly integrated being in Presence, in a moment, because we are free to "become" what is needed from the vast potential of our souls, in touch with the ground of Being and vertical connection with Source. After inhabiting this "I AM," the next word is critical, because what we speak organizes our experience of *being*, and we create what we know. Beyond ego, we can spontaneously create with greater integrity—integrated within and without—bringing Holy Truth to fruition.

Creating through Holy Truth

As we are made new through internal integration and Innocence, we also "make" all else new by external integration and Presence—by bringing Holy Truth, the all-encompassing pattern, to life. If we follow the pattern, we are also meant to *re-know* the disparate parts of the world as an expression of the One, original Source. As we come into union, both horizontally and vertically, the connection with an even "higher" or universal intelligence that is brought more fully online lends us a creative capacity. Through our collected Presence and a kind of divine imagination, we continually connect the Below and Above, the part with the whole, and play an essential role in lifting everyone and everything. I say "lifting" because this capacity comes from our combined higher centers and holy/whole-y transcendent view. And because...can you imagine what would happen if we really lived with this lens?[161]

The "sin" of ego is that it separates us and causes us to "miss the mark" in our efforts to access our higher selves and to live well in community. When we throw others out of the field of goodness, we perpetuate separation, and so throw ourselves out as well. When we seek, instead, to play *with* Creation like children, actively *knowing* the potential (however hidden) in another, we make room in the field for all...even if "the other" (just like Loki) may come back around again. Living in accord with Holy Truth extends to embracing others in all their messiness and beauty, rather than perpetuating polarity. I realize how naïve or just impossible this might sound. Are we really to re-know that seemingly evil or tyrannical other—the one who perpetrated unfathomable pain—as part of the One, divine *Logos*? This is confusing enough when we are passionate about changing communities to make a better world, but even more so when we feel harmed and justified in our righteousness or vengeance.

This, to me, is the hardest part of the pattern to understand. And yet, an idea that persists across the stories, science, and the natural world is that "dark" must be held with "light," and Above and Below are One. Chaos and tyranny must be approached and encircled, to restore harmony. It's not about condoning or conceding to what you experience as evil or wrong. It's about *how* you engage (*being*) and *know* another in essence too, trusting the pattern that when you aim higher and embrace opposing ideas (although your mind may go dark for a time) *something more* always arises. Pushing directly against something only fuels it. Newton's third law of classical physics states "for every action there is an equal and opposite reaction." This remains true at the interpersonal level. Adversaries don't change their beliefs in the face of shame and demand (although they may comply, temporarily, with enough threat). This is the crux of the problem, and the key to change in a polarized world. There is always a fourth way that arises from third force consciousness and the capacity to *stand in the middle.*

Point 8 asks of us something simple and direct, like: *How would Innocence be (and know) in this moment?* As our stories reveal, doing our own work by living the pattern is always the Way toward higher-order union. It often leads the "dark" force to self-destruct all on its own, or it can actualize a surprising and wonderful twist that we cannot fathom from our current level of awareness. Innocence does not negate the need for action or service. It does not negate individual consequences earned. On the contrary, it seems to provide a compass. What Innocence implies most strongly is that our impact lies in *how we are* when we engage, whatever our work in the world. The heroic action is becoming a conscious vehicle for Truth, for the law, which is both "wonderful and terrible" in that it may take us apart with its embrace of *All that Is,* but it always leads to a wonder-full life.

Innocence, then, is a radical act, a paradoxical act in which, through surrendering our singular agenda to the laws that hold everything and everyone as an expression of the One Source and Flow of Creation, we enable something much greater. Innocence trusts that the pattern that governs the transition between diversity and Unity is alive *in us,* or it can be, just as it is in everyone and everything else in the Universe. The heroic journey can be understood as Realizing, or making the unifying pattern Real, by embodying and living it consciously in the world. And then the world itself is renewed through our being, attitude, and action. The full Realization of the laws is made manifest in the Symbol itself as the Merkaba, our "vehicle" to higher consciousness.

BUILDING THE MERKABA

Gurdjieff maintained that we have to build a soul. We aren't born with it intact. And he described this with the creation of two additional energy "bodies" that, when fully integrated with the human mind-heart-body (in another Law of Three process), can give rise to a fourth divine body (the whole vehicle), in touch with Source. The Merkaba is a representation of this interplay of personal and universal intelligence as a "vehicle" to higher consciousness and being. While the Soul in Ancient Egypt was also considered to have nine parts, the Ka and Ba were primary aspects whose magical union created the Akh, the immortal transformed self (perhaps something like "the spiritual heart" in the center?). Together they form the temple or place of wisdom and ascension that is the Merkaba.

We have been envisioning the points around the circle, similarly, as fragments of our centers of intelligence that require "collecting" and clearing of past habits and trauma to prepare our souls for the reception of higher intelligence or spirit. In this process, they seem to collect in two primary chunks of four, as two higher energy "bodies," formed through law of three processes and related to the two tetrahedrons of the 3D Enneagram Symbol. The lower story, related to higher *being*, opened up as we dropped deeper into Presence at the edge of the Void. When we take apart the structures that have been driving our personality, we meet the shadow energy they were protecting, but we also find more moments during which our primary centers can come into alignment with the continuous flow of energy that connects us with the hidden wholeness of the world. This aspect of being is equated with the soul, the part of ourselves that is closer to the body, feelings, instinct, and connects us to Being, the universal heart and living soul of the world, *anima mundi.*

The upper story is related to spirit, consciousness, higher *knowing*, and the *axis mundi*, or vertical nature of intelligence. It can only emerge because of the vessel and foundation provided by the developing soul. Each of us has an individual spark of the creative imagination that gives form to the flow of life. On the back half of the journey, this spark is refined into an autonomous Real I, no longer compelled to grasp or judge or otherwise react mechanically to life. Sealed against *internal* derailers, Real I can act purposefully and consistently, with third force consciousness, in service of a higher aim. After crossing the threshold this soul-spirit vehicle is tasked with linking the Above and Below to create magic in community. To navigate this difficult work, we must also become immune to *external* derailers (irritating others and situations). At that point, a hero does not allow anyone or any force to disrupt them from fulfilling their unique purpose in the world and *knowing* everyone and everything as part of the same One Source.

The Merkaba is often equated with the Seal of Solomon (the encircled hexagram). The name of the Seal purportedly came from the figure on a ring received by King Solomon from God as a symbol of his ability to rule with wisdom and an understanding heart, and to "lock up" the demons of this earth. This is a legend found in teachings from Judaism, Islam, and Christianity that relates to the reconciliation of the two primary forces in Creation. The Seal has been described as symbolizing "a harmony of opposites, the cosmic order, the skies, the movement of the stars in their spheres, and the perpetual flow between heaven and earth...super-human wisdom and rule by divine grace."[162]

With all the various fragmented and "opposing" aspects of being reconciled at point 8, one is "sealed" against earthly and egoic concerns that arise both from within and from outside oneself. To "lock up" material demons is to be immune to all that distracts us when dominated by our ego needs, and so able to navigate consciously in both horizontal and vertical terrain. Gurdjieff said that creating the Seal of Solomon within introduces "the line of will first into the circle of time and afterward into the cycle of eternity."[163] And Joseph Campbell called this step (freedom to live) "a final reconciliation of individual consciousness with divine will."

As "the Law lives in him with his unreserved consent," the fully integrated hero is aligned with truly higher forces with the potential for facilitating further union with God, or eternal Being, in a state of complete Union ahead.[164] This is akin to Simba's revelation that he is part of and guided by all the lion kings who have gone before.

The body-heart-mind triangle at the center of the Symbol is fully developed as one with a higher heart and mind. And yet, at this point the centers are not at all separate (nor located wholly within), so we may also consider it as a spiritual trinity of body, soul, and spirit. Christian scripture distinguishes these three parts: "May God Himself, the God of peace, sanctify you through and through. May your whole spirit, soul and body be kept blameless at the coming of our Lord Jesus Christ."[165] Whether that trinity is cloaked in the terms of Christian, Hindu, Sufi, Buddhist, Jewish, or Indigenous belief systems, however, we all must un-earth, clear, and integrate our own inner trinity of higher aspects so they are *blameless* (free from "sin" or ego entrapment), in order to become available for healing and transformative experiences—both created or released from within, and given from Above.

While the relationship between energy bodies, states of consciousness, and higher centers of intelligence is complex and confusing, it has helped me to think of the tetrahedrons as representations of higher heart and higher mind (or more specifically, additional organs or energy bodies we create that connect one into a universal heart or "Holy Soul" and a universal higher mind or "Holy Spirit"). Our human body is enfolded in this vehicle, and fantastic as it might sound, there is some evidence that the additional "energy bodies" formed around the human body and represented in the Merkaba are literal.

Both the heart and the brain have broad fields of electromagnetic energy that can be measured by EEG (electroencephalogram) and ECG (electrocardiogram). While we are accustomed to thinking of "brain waves" as energy, the heart's rhythmic electromagnetic field is a hundred times greater in amplitude than the brain's waves. And the heart's rhythm has as much or more influence upwards on the brain as the brain has on the heart. The Institute of HeartMath, Joe Dispenza, and others conducting research on these fields, suggest that our thoughts (knowing) are like electric signals that focus and send energy out as imagination and intention. Embodied higher-frequency states of emotion (being in the interconnected higher heart) act as magnetic energy that unites us with higher frequency energy outside of us and charges our intentions and action.[166] I imagine this is something like we experience when falling in love—the world seems brighter, and magical things sometimes unfold.

Fields of electromagnetic energy are always present around our bodies. They just become more powerful and higher frequency when working together "coherently." Coherence is a broad term for describing the way diverse parts of a system can work together in a synchronized fashion. Coherence also leads a system to synchronize and evolve *emergent* or higher-order properties, because greater coherence leads to an increase in intelligent self-organization, adaptation, and growth. This is as opposed to the *chaos* that characterizes systems in which the many parts are not working in unity. As with most systems we have studied, it seems the right combination of focus and *order* within a system, that also has the flexibility and *flow* required to integrate its diverse pieces, is key to increasing coherence, accessing new intelligence, and creating the possibility for emergence into higher-order functioning.

When the heart's energy is more coherent (something measured with heart rate variability), it is in a state of well-being and health in which positive emotions arise naturally. Positive emotions also feed back to, and increase coherence in, the whole body system. Coherent rhythms increase a system's resonance (which is vibration that extends beyond its boundaries), creating the potential to link up with other systems. In this case, there is evidence to suggest that a coherent heart draws the brain into greater coherence. When the whole brain is working in both a broadly connected and more coherent fashion, there is more flexibility, resilience, and mental health. And in a coherent state, the focused energy of the mind's intentions has more potential to make an impact on matter, just as focused beams of light in a laser can cut something, in contrast to the diffuse light of a lightbulb.[167]

We can also then talk about the heart and brain in resonance, working coherently together, to create greater resonance with others and with systems outside of ourselves. Earth has an electromagnetic field that radiates out into space. When the heart is in coherence it resonates at the same frequency as the slowest of the Earth's magnetic fields.[168] As more aspects of our whole being come into coherence, our system resonates at higher and higher frequencies. We can literally become more energy than matter, more in synch with the unified flow of intelligence underlying our lives, and so more whole or "holy." From this state of inner and inter-connectedness, we have more potential to adapt, create, and influence reality.

There are many ways to access this state. My first experience of feeling more energy than matter was at the hands of a very gifted Qigong master and healer, Master Ming Tong Gu. I went to check him out because I was planning to take my young daughter who had been suffering from severe sleep and hormonal disturbances for over a year. Over the course of an hour or so, using only his voice, he ushered me into a state in which I felt totally dissolved into a rushing field of energy. After studying these ideas for years, for the first time I really felt and understood how bodies can be rearranged and healing can evolve from this state of flow.

All of this is to say that it's not hard for me to believe that establishing greater coherence in our integrated, embodied higher heart-mind can impact not only our own bodies, but also people and other systems outside of us. The electromagnetic field of the higher heart-mind (or soul in touch with spirit), represented by the two tetrahedrons of the 3D Enneagram Symbol, amounts to a creative force in communication with universal intelligence, and it helps to explain the heroic capacity to lift the people, systems, and fields around us through building the Merkaba or living the laws of the Symbol. And, in fact, it is the real world "practice" of integrating dimensions (*making two worlds one*) in the created world that serves to fully develop and integrate the bodies. For the alchemical process to continue to unfold after spirit and soul are united, they must be embodied in the world.

This brings us to the final "layer" of the work in the Symbol, in which the completed Merkaba can become one with the Absolute. It is a rare occurrence, but those who integrate the horizontal and the vertical dimensions of inner work completely become a "divine human" in the created world. Then they reach a level of *being* and *consciousness* that leads beyond the final shock point into union with the Divine at a far higher-level point 9, the zero point—the *alpha* and *omega* from which all begins and ends.

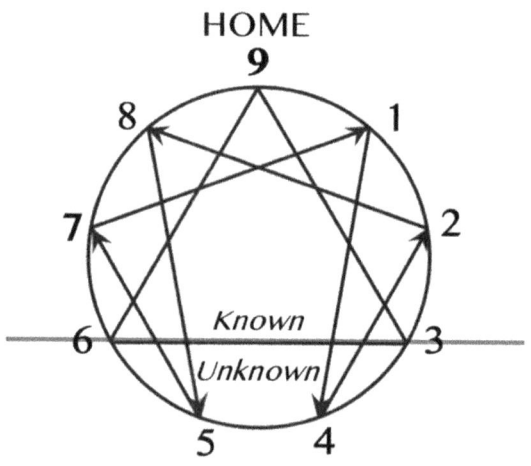

CHAPTER EIGHTEEN

POINT 9:
THE JOURNEY HOME

Be here now.

~ RAM DASS

THE LAST FEW MINUTES OF *THE LION KING* bring the journey Home. Following Scar's demise, Rafiki invites Simba to climb Pride Rock alone, in the rain, and take his place as king. As the clouds part, Simba again hears his father urging him to "remember" who he is, and he lets out a powerful roar. It's an emotional moment as we take in the full measure of Simba's transformation and ascension. The final scene shows Simba and Nala standing on Pride Rock together, along with Timon and Pumbaa (signaling a new kind of order). They are looking out over the gathering of animals and the return of life and springtime to the Pride Lands. Rafiki arrives with a new lion cub in his arms. Another future lion king, eyes wide, is presented to the community, completing the hero's journey— harmony has been restored for the moment, and life has come full circle.

THE VIRTUE OF CONTINUOUS RIGHT ACTION

When we started the journey at point 9 on the Symbol, our heroes were asleep to their destiny, like the new lion cub in the Pride Lands, undifferentiated within the family unit. The passion of Sloth described this lack of self-awareness and self-determination. However, as we revisit point 9 the heroes have truly earned their title by going on the journey to awaken, transform themselves, and help renew the community. In the process, they have realized a higher dimension of being and consciousness, and are an example of Right Action, the virtue at point 9. Right Action describes the activation of higher *being* that *knows* (in a new way) what is most important, what is the highest and best next-right-thing for all; it's a kind of compass. The virtue of Innocence describes a spontaneous, moment-to-moment, creative expression of divine interbeing and intelligence. Right Action, as a *Way* of being-in-the-world, adds the important notion that the Way (to live in alignment with the laws) is both now and continuous, as the "circle of life" goes on.

Our stories illustrate in different forms this idea that the journey is never-ending. And I don't think this is only the design of producers greedy for a sequel. Creation is a wheel that keeps turning, and coming Home is not a place but more like a state of coherence, where diverse parts are continually *being and becoming* as One. At the end of *Game of Thrones*, we see Arya Stark boarding a sailing ship to who-knows-where, as she leaves the Seven Kingdoms in the hands of her remaining siblings, Bran and Sansa. We get the sense that *the girl with no name* has more work to do and may be fashioning a new aim for a higher "octave" of adventure.

In other stories, the birth of children reflects the continuous cycle of life through the laws of the Symbol. As the curtain closes on *The Lion King*, with its new configuration of king-queen-hero, we get the sense that our baby hero-to-be will take his place in the next dance of the Law of Three. At the end of the *Harry Potter* series, Harry and Ginny Weasley are married, as are Ron and Hermione, and the two families are at the train station sending their own children off to school on the Hogwarts Express train. The last scene of *The Hunger Games* trilogy is, similarly, a glimpse of Katniss and Peeta picnicking together with their little boy and girl, in the fields where we first met Katniss hunting for food.

Vishnu is the Hindu God known as "the preserver," representing the third or reconciling force in the triad of Brahma-Shiva-Vishnu. As he describes his role in the *Bhagavad Gita*, "Whenever the Sacred Law fails and evil raises its head, I (Vishnu) take embodied birth. To guard the righteous, to root out sinners, and to establish Sacred Law, I am born from age to age."[169] Rather than advocacy for war, this is Vishnu's commitment to addressing both tyranny and chaos, as needed, to re-make the world. The fact that he is born *from age to age* speaks to the necessity of this role in preserving the world by continually updating and renewing it, through challenge and change, and through the laws themselves.

In Taoism, the Tao is un-nameable as a concept because it is a Way to live in accord with the nature of Reality that can only be Realized in practice. It is the Way to harmonize extremes of yang and yin that threaten to destabilize the whole (like tyranny and chaos), in order to continually realize the Unity underlying diversity. This is not so conceptually different from Vishnu's role to establish harmony and Sacred Law, the Way of Jesus, or the Buddha's notion of a Middle Way and the nature of the Eightfold

Path that leads to liberation. As we have seen, the alchemical process and Carl Jung's path of psychological individuation also link to the journey-line and the integrated laws of the Symbol. To incarnate the redemptive pattern inherent in the laws, to be a vehicle for continuous renewal (eternal life), is the Way of the hero embodied in "the philosopher's stone" that Gurdjieff equated with the Enneagram.

Another thing we know about Right Action is that it is fully understood only at the last stages of the journey, when all lower centers of intelligence are free of ego and the higher centers are aligned with the Source and Flow of Creation, in service of the whole system. Right Action is a little different from the other eight virtues. The other virtues are more like qualities of Being. You can be Humble, Courageous, or Innocent. How do you be Right Action?

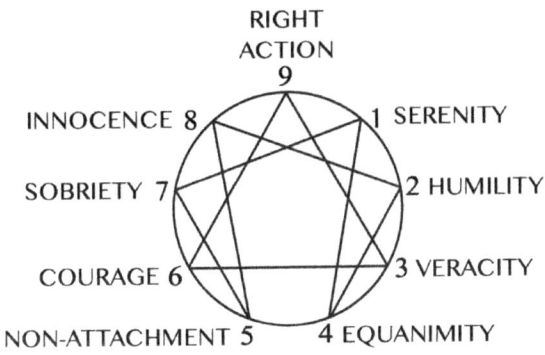

ENNEAGRAM VIRTUES

Just as we considered the possibility of trusting higher mind and received wisdom when we are firmly situated in the higher heart, perhaps we can finally trust our actions once we have achieved a mode of right *being*, in partnership with a non-dual Way of *knowing* (the holy ideas), and most particularly, the holy idea at point 9, Holy Love that unites all of Creation. Perhaps these are the summary skills that help us with the most difficult aspect of living the laws: holding the shadows with the light and embracing the chaos within our orderly understanding of things? The most essential Right Action required to restore the disparate parts to harmony and continually evolve the kingdom is related to this higher understanding of love.

THE WORLDVIEW OF HOLY LOVE

Holy Love describes a return to wholeness or coherence, the Law of One. It describes our ability to *know* the multiplicity represented in the world (and every distinct part of it) as an expression of the same One Source and ground of Being. Indeed, love is synonymous with union—with a commitment to something beyond your singular self. You simply can't consider yourself alone, as separate, in love. Love is perhaps the only force powerful enough to integrate the great diversity of life, within and around us. It is a way of knowing that is also an active and generative force in its ability to lift and unite fragments in its embrace. Relationship expert and psychologist Esther Perel says, "Love is a verb."[170] It's an active engagement with the diversity of all of life that has an impact.

In practical terms, when we orient to anything with this kind of love, it facilitates unity and wholeness, which is synonymous with healing. It is a different orientation and infusion of energy that invites some kind of shift. When we hold our own hurt or anger within a larger field of compassion and kindness towards ourselves, this can soften or break it up. Like a drop of food coloring in a glass of water, it is absorbed in the greater field. And when we can bring our full Presence to others' anger and hurt, make room to listen instead of condemning, we are aligning our own integrated being with a larger flow of Being that can absorb and transform in a way that our small selves cannot.

Joseph Campbell sums up this pivotal point in the journey by saying, "The good news, which the World Redeemer brings and which so many have been glad to hear, zealous to preach, but reluctant, apparently, to demonstrate, is that God is love, that He can be, and is to be, loved, and that all without exception are his children."[171] As the ultimate non-dual perspective and unifying force, it's no wonder we equate love with the Divine, and both with the Law of One. Without a supreme Being, the state of enlightenment of Eastern seekers, *samadhi* or *satori*, describes a state of union, absorption, wholeness or merging with an all-encompassing One consciousness as well. There are many ways to describe the Home and state of wholeness that we journey towards, just as the holy ideas at each point give us slightly different perspectives on the Law of One.

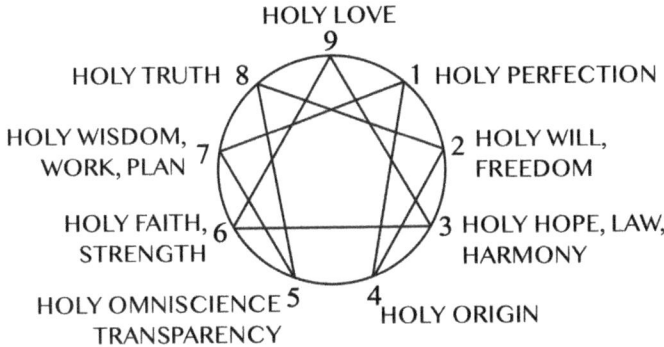

ENNEAGRAM HOLY IDEAS

While that's a lot of ideas to remember, the good news is that we don't remember them as much as they re-member *us*, when we are present and connected in this everyday world as One, simultaneously, with the Source and Flow of Creation. The map Home provided for us by our Enneagram personality type put us in touch with the most unifying perspective (holy idea) for our particular wiring—the one we forgot way-back-when. And yet, because all aspects of the Symbol come into coherence at point 9, Holy Love contains all the perspectives from which to see ourselves, others, and the Universe as a unified whole. Combining the holy ideas of the inner triangle that we are all developing through three-centered Presence, we have: Holy Hope, Holy Faith, and Holy Love. "And now these three remain: faith, hope and love. But the greatest of these is love."[172] As the Home toward which the journey leads, Holy Love is the strongest unifying force.

As is true in the story of *The Lion King*, love and union between characters is at the heart of all the Princess stories that end with the girl marrying the prince (even if he *was* a beast) and spreading peace in the kingdom. The families of the Harry Potter series characters, along with our Hunger Games heroes, also point to love as the unifying force. The love between Geppetto, Pinocchio, and Jiminy Cricket as well, helps to revivify life, as Pinocchio is revived by the Blue Fairy and turned into a Real boy. And while neither Thor nor Wonder Woman end up together with the humans they fell for, the love they experienced with these mortals transformed our superheroes and lives on through them in their changed worldviews.

At the beginning of the Wonder Woman story, Diana was going to single-handedly save the human race through her imagined heroism. By the end of the story, she has a profoundly different understanding of how that can happen, and her role in supporting it. Rather than return to the island of Themyscira and the Amazon Women after the war, Diana is compelled to stay in the realm of humans, doing what she can, with Right Action, to live and spread what she now knows about Holy Love. She makes it all pretty clear for us:

I used to want to save the world. To end war and bring peace to mankind; but then I glimpsed the darkness that lives within their light. I learnt that inside every one of them there will always be both. The choice each must make for themselves—something no hero will ever defeat. Now I know that only love can truly save the world. So I stay, I fight, and I give, for the world I know can be.[173]

Becoming One

Our stories represent the evolution of an internal wholeness of the hero that brings her into coherence with the larger systems in which she exists. As the individual turns within and confronts shadow, facing her wounds leads to the revelation of gifts that can be used to help renew and revitalize the community as well. This is due not only to the developed being, heart, and consciousness of the hero, but also to the wisdom recovered in the unknown world about the regenerative pattern of life that unfolds if we have the strength to put aside our egos and *stand in the middle.* This is what the journey was always about, after all; not just *being*, but continuously *becoming* whole is heroic. At the outset, the hero needs only a higher aim and the willingness to hazard herself in the unknown to discover her purpose and potential in healing the whole.

It is the journey that helps Dorothy pull herself (her centers of intelligence) together symbolically by collaborating with the Scarecrow, Tin Man, and Lion to overcome the fragmenting forces in Oz. Like the girl with her ruby slippers, Dorothy's companions in Oz also already had within them what they were looking for. The Scarecrow, Tin Man, and Lion each prove the merit of their respective mind, heart, and courageous will, as the journey unfolds. And through their collective work, the Land of Oz is saved from the tyranny and chaos of wayward witches and would-be wizards who seek to segregate and secure power. Healing and renewal, in the end, is not some kind of uniform fusion, but rather evolves from diverse parts working together in dynamic coherence.

The journey metaphor is a circle, always, because of the way in which we gather up, heal, tame, and unleash previously conflicting energies and parts of ourselves. Rather than becoming something or someone so different, it seems more like re-membering oneself as whole and tuning into latent capacity. Carl Jung used the circular *mandala* as a representation of the whole Self and the process of *circumambulating*—literally, walking around all four directions on the map—as the journey to the Self that is simultaneously the center and circumference of the circle. This is something like would be depicted in a labyrinth, with its movement through four quarters toward the center. The encircling and re-integration of all opposing parts within takes us to the center of the (balanced) garden where a vertical axis of development initiates a spiral pattern of increasingly higher levels of being and consciousness.

In *The Spiritual Dimension of the Enneagram*, Sandra Maitri describes this circular pattern as a process of remembering our essential nature (before ego) and returning to union within and with the One Source of Being.[174] She uses the specific passions of points 9, 6, and 3 on the inner triangle to reveal both our shared process of falling from the original state of Oneness to develop a personality or ego, and also the return journey to union. We mapped this journey from birth to ego development in greater detail (through all the points and passions) in the chapter on the Law of One, but it bears repeating in abbreviated form here as a reminder that the Symbol maps a process for us all, whatever the Enneagram type.

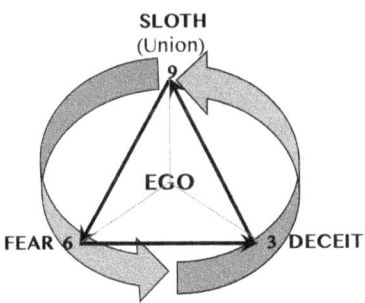

THE FALL INTO PERSONALITY

Moving counterclockwise from point 9, in the first few years of life we fall out of union with Source. Because of this loss, we sense deficiency and emptiness, and experience Fear of survival at point 6. Due to the intolerable sense of loss, anger, and fear, we start to use our mind, heart, and body intelligence in fixed ways in an attempt to defend ourselves from the pain of life and re-create what we sense is missing from that original union. Deceit, at point 3, marks the emergence of our attempt to compensate for that initial loss with a "false" self, an Enneagram personality type or ego structure. It's not a conscious deceit, of course, but nevertheless "false" because our striving to be a separate someone obscures the truth of our inherent wholeness and connection with the Divine. We then proceed to become fused with this false self and go to sleep to the notion that we were ever anything other than this ego, as we complete the circle in Sloth at point 9.

Although being fused with our personality type protects us from experiencing the pain of our original loss, its fixed habits create a self-reinforcing loop that is its own kind of suffering, keeping us in the known and fixated world of our separate ego. Ironically, the striving of personality to be somebody, to be safe, to be in control, in order to solve for what we sense has been lost, becomes the *exact thing* that prevents our contact with the missing sense of wholeness. It prevents us from accessing all that is outside the fixed triangle—our unconscious shadows and essential gifts, as well as the Source field from which we came. In its place, we have a nagging sense of something missing, an inner emptiness or lack of meaning. When our personality type exhausts all attempts to control, do, or be something to solve for this, we may begin to unwind the same program in the opposite direction, through the virtues of these three points.

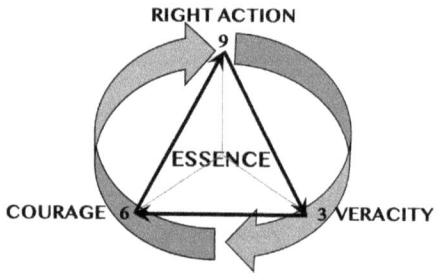

THE RETURN HOME

I find it delightful, but maybe not surprising, that we can trace this archetypal return journey through the virtues of the inner triangle in Pinocchio's story. Pinocchio turns into a Real boy by acting *unselfish, brave, and truthful*—something, of course, he was quite capable of all along, in some sense, but needed the challenge of the journey to discover in himself. Following Pinocchio's Way of Real-i-zation to restore inner coherence and harmony, the work is to be:

1. **Un-self-ish**, which is one without the small self or ego at the center, and the essence of *being* in continuous Right Action.

2. **Truth-full**, which is to be someone to which nothing can be opposed—whole, shadow integrated, a vehicle for the continuous flow of spirit, life force, intelligence. To be in truth (Veracity) is to be an expression of this wholeness or Being, as it unfolds through us; and

3. **Brave**, which is to be Courageous, with a higher heart that holds paradox and the tension of opposites with the Holy Faith that knows how new life always springs from the pattern.

Pinocchio, in his own little way, follows the Way of Jesus: "I am the way, the truth, and the life,"[175] the Way to Realize or live Truth (objective knowledge) through integrated being, heart, and consciousness. This is what finally brings Pinocchio Home.

The poet T.S. Elliot described the elusive nature of this Home to which we return as a place we know, indeed, the very place we started. "We shall not cease from exploration. And the end of all our exploring will be to arrive where we started and know the place for the first time."[176] And yet, we could not know it without having gone on the journey, which changes our ability to live these virtues. Like our heroes, we lift our strengths and gifts from within, but beyond what was previously known. They emerge from our bravery in the unknown, as we integrate shadows and defensive reactions—the things that obscure our wholeness—and liberate energy. A purposeful encounter with chaos is absolutely necessary to deconstruct the ego and its habits that block us from our higher, integrated self or essence. And then, inevitably, all that energy can be brought to bear in the Realization of both our interconnected and compassionate heart and our unique purpose and aim in this lifetime.

As most of our stories note, this process is not a walk in the park. A courageous engagement with not only our defensive habits, but also the internal adversaries kept at bay by that ego structure, is challenging. Whether life shocks us or we go by choice into the unknown chaos, it is clear that we are not in charge. Precious parts of us are compromised, relationships fall apart, jobs are lost, and there are very real encounters in the world (and in ourselves) with malevolence. Of course, we know now that challenge is part of the game—exactly what we need to unlock who we really are and what we are capable of being in the world—but finding our Way takes time. Although Katniss is pardoned for the treason of assassinating President Coin, no one can pardon her from the trauma of battle and the losses of loved ones. In her journey Home, we see a slow process of healing and coming to trust love again. Eventually, time and Peeta's devotion helps Katniss to heal, and the series leaves us with a vision of their beautiful family—an echo of a time, long ago, when her own family was still in harmony.

Jon Snow's story takes him from one extreme to another, from ice to fire, to recover and re-unite the parts of himself. By the end of the series Jon is convicted of his crime of killing Daenerys and sentenced to life at the Wall at the northern edge of the Seven Kingdoms. This is despite the fact that we know his sacrificial actions saved the entire realm from a new form of tyranny! But Jon Snow seems to know what he is doing. His early wounds stemmed from being known as Ned Stark's illegitimate son *and* from suffering the rejection of the woman forced to play his mother, Caitlyn Stark. By facing off with the frozen part of the Great Father and the fiery part of the Great Mother within, Jon finds a Way to freedom within the truth that he is indeed a unique manifestation of two great and opposing royal houses: House of Stark and House Targaryen. The final scene of *Game of Thrones* is Jon Snow *not* stopping at the Wall, as sentenced, but rather riding still further beyond the known world to be with the wildlings or Free Folk (the truly free people in the Seven Kingdoms)—not being, but becoming, heroic.

RENEWING THE KINGDOM

Beyond the hero's ability to integrate or "come Home" internally, we also see new life, peace, and an evolved kingdom. This is, in fact, central to the story of coming Home at point 9. It speaks to the unifying and revivifying power of love and the role of the hero's transformation in the healing of the community. The medicine we find in restoring our own dark and wounded parts to wholeness can also help the world. We saw this in the Pride Lands, represented by the arrival of spring, and in the diversity of animals attending the revelation of the newborn lion prince. The presence of Timon and Pumbaa on Pride Rock with Simba's family indicates something of the (formerly estranged) unknown world has been incorporated into the new known, illustrating the capacity of Holy Love to unify, integrate diversity, and incorporate new information that evolves the system.

The idea that an entire system that is fragmented or broken can be made whole again in some way is symbolized in most of these stories. It is a welcome message of hope in these fractured times. Indeed, as broken as the Wizarding world appears at the end of Harry Potter's story, we understand that peace and restoration can grow following the death of Voldemort. We can almost hear the "Ding dong, the witch is dead!" refrain from *The Wizard of Oz* rise up from the gathering at the end of the Harry Potter series. And at the end of *The Hunger Games* trilogy, for the first time in 75 years, the underground District 13 will be part of the restored nation of Panem.

Both Sleeping Beauty and Belle from *Beauty and the Beast* lead a process of bringing castles and kingdoms back to life. When the prince's kiss awakens Sleeping Beauty, her castle and everyone in it who had been asleep for 100 years, comes to life. In Belle's world, after the Beast is changed into a prince (this time with a kiss bestowed by the princess), all of the animated household fixtures, like Lumiere the candelabra and Mrs. Potts the tea pot, are changed back into the Real and devoted servants and friends they were before the curse that turned the prince into a beast. This is no small nod to the idea that when heroes become a conscious vehicle for Holy Love and "the wonderful terrible Law" that Campbell describes, they help to Real-ize, make new, and lift others into the renewed kingdom as well.

Even the fragmented land of the Seven Kingdoms of Westeros depicted in *Game of Thrones* is on track for renewal, as "Bran the Broken" assumes the Iron Throne and agrees to share leadership with his sister Sansa Stark, who takes charge of the newly independent North. Knowing what we know now about the journey line, it makes sense that Bran is the one chosen to lead this new configuration of the realm, as his small self was sacrificed at the very beginning of the story when he was pushed out of the tower and left paralyzed. Indeed, his "broken" nature led him to acquire special other-worldly powers to see beyond time and space. And Bran, in turn, chooses another misfit in Tyrion Lannister as his advisor or *Hand of the King*. We are long past the days of the other Lannisters' rule, of pretty faces that hide terrible secrets. Here the broken are whole; the wounded, healers; and former enemies, allied.

As disappointing as the end of *Game of Thrones* was to many people, the three remaining Stark children represent the integration of elements in the Law of Three and the initiation of a new octave of growth. Sansa symbolizes the alignment with renewed *order*, having survived the Lannisters *and* the Boltons, an even more horrible manifestation of the tyranny and corruption that is always a potential of the ruling force. Bran's life represents the chaos of sacrifice, as well as the potential of the unbounded *flow* of life (and its link to deeper wisdom) to transfigure the hero who ventures beyond the known. Bran is transformed into a master of two worlds, as both a human and the time-traveling, three-eyed Raven who can see beyond the veil. And Arya, like Jon Snow, walks between worlds, forever free as a third force to find a Way. No doubt each of them will play a pivotal role in the triadic dance that ensures the continuous renewal of the Seven Kingdoms in generations to come.

Arriving at this point in the journey is, in fact, what makes it heroic. At point 9 all of our heroes have earned the title by embodying the pattern that renews and brings peace. They have healed the broken places in themselves that caused their earlier ego-driven mishaps and made a Way for Holy Love (through their own spirit, soul, and heart) to revivify and reunite the entire kingdom. Whether the hero herself is at home in this scenario, a new king, or heading off for another adventure, is less important than knowing that heroic potential exists in all of us. And it can be drawn upon in every age (like the Hindu God Vishnu) to evolve the kingdom. This heroic potential, symbolized by the philosopher's stone and the Merkaba, is the treasure with which the hero continues to transform lead into gold, bringing healing and renewal ("eternal life") in the world with continuous Right Action that brings Holy Love alive in the world through the open portal of this moment.

The idea that the healing and evolution of the individual soul is essential to the healing and renewal of the world was central to the work of both Jung and Gurdjieff. Both men were conceiving their respective work during a time of great upheaval in the world; a time when some of the worst of human nature was revealed. With two World Wars, Nazi-ism, and the rise of Bolshevism along with the Russian Revolution, a shocking level of extremism, polarity, discrimination, and violence was perpetrated among humans. Both Jung and Gurdjieff blamed ideology and group identity, as well as the unconscious nature of most humans, for perpetuating violence. And they both noted the inadequacy of religion as a guide to peace, healing, and moral development, due to humans' inability to live the ideals represented in the venerable lives of spiritual heroes.

Instead, both teachers centered the idea that our world can be saved only by individuals taking responsibility for a reconstruction of the human soul (or higher self) that would enable one to live in alignment with higher values and intelligence. Without this, humans are destined to play out ego drives that trap us all in duality, polarity, and reciprocal violence. Owned as we are by our unconscious (Jung) or mechanical (Gurdjieff) reactivity, we must work on ourselves to become free and to aim higher. Both Jung's individuation process and the Gurdjieff work hinge on bringing a unified higher self to life to fulfill what Joseph Campbell called the *world-redeeming function* of the hero. Gurdjieff referenced the doctrine of Reciprocal World Maintenance, which includes the idea that the development of our souls is as much (or more) for the redemption of the world as it is a search for a holy grail of individual spiritual fulfillment.[177]

And because becoming a source for healing and wholeness (Holy Love) in the world is the final purpose of honing the philosopher's stone, this world-redeeming function of the hero means there is such a thing as sins of omission. By *not* going on the journey when our world (inner or outer) has succumbed to tyranny or chaos, we contribute to its fragmentation. Without a third force that can hold the tension of opposites and invite new information, systems move between these extremes. With the development of third force consciousness, however, we can see the eternal cycle, work with the regenerative pattern laid out in the Symbol, and contribute to higher-order evolution. Right Action is the perfect name for the Way to engage and help renew harmony, again and again, because it points above all to *living* a unifying Holy Love versus making a pledge.

INNER WORK FOR COMING HOME

While writing this book I had many dreams about walking around or inside of the Enneagram Symbol. I would always wake up with some new understanding about the laws. In the middle of writing about this final step on the journey I had a dream that my childhood friend Laura, who has done a lot of inner work and paid her dues, was moving from point 8 to point 9. She was being welcomed to the kingdom by "King Ubu." I woke up like: "Ubu…Ubu? Huh?" And then it hit me, "Ohhhh…U. B. U!" A wise and funny client I worked with years ago used to say this all the time, meaning "you be you." When we arrive Home, it is to a house no longer divided against itself; a place where you can be you, all of you, in harmony, although not the "you" defined so long by your ego structure.

As we are unified internally—present in aligned, open mind, heart, body—our soul (integrated essence) can be in greater resonance with all the systems in which we are embedded *and* serve as a clear channel for spirit and higher intelligence. Without the ego constricting and garbling our centers of intelligence, we can develop our conscience and interbeing enough to receive and transmit "real" (undistorted by our personality structures) energy and information—intelligence from within and beyond—and bring imagination and creative potential alive, in ourselves and others, in each moment. When we arrive Home to this Presence, we discover our superpowers were there all along, just as Thor eventually finds he does not actually need the hammer to draw down immense power from the skies, and Diana finds the true "weapon" for dethroning minor gods is herself. In that sense, we arrive Home to the understanding that, like Dorothy, we never actually left. Everything else was the dream. Perhaps we all have a hero inside of us awaiting our Presence.

When **Type 1s** are Home in Presence, they know the perfection of reality just as it is. They see the goodness, sacredness, and purity in themselves and all others. They see that there is an intelligent order to the continuous cycle of renewal, however chaotic it seems in moments. Like Diana of Themyscira, Wonder Woman, Type 1s model and inspire others with their honor, commitment to ideals, and discernment in knowing when and how to engage and help revivify the world.

When **Type 2s** are Home in Presence, they experience the flow of Being that is always available and connects us all without any striving. When they know they are part of this loving field, Type 2s are free to be, and they teach others about care, selfless service, and true emotional leadership from the integrated higher heart, like Peeta Mellark—Katniss's partner and another hero of *The Hunger Games.*

When **Type 3s** are Home in Presence, they feel the value of their unique existence and the true purpose of their work in relation to the harmonious unfolding of life through the universal laws. When they know their value and calling, Type 3s apply their being, heart, and consciousness in service of lifting others, as does Pinocchio, a truthful, brave, and unselfish Real boy.

When **Type 4s** are Home in Presence, they know their true identity as a beautiful and continuous unfolding of *All that Is.* When they have integrated dark and light and become fully present to the wonder of who they are in essence, Type 4s connect deeply with the flow of Being itself, and teach us about equality, balance, beauty, and depth, like the uniquely heroic Jon Snow.

When **Type 5s** are Home in Presence, fully embodied, they *know* everything they need to know, directly, within, without striving. As One with the flow of Being, they engage and become a creative vehicle for wisdom and healing in the world. Type 5s illuminate truth through conscience, just like the unlikely princess Belle from *Beauty and the Beast.*

When **Type 6s** are Home in Presence, they see exactly what is going on and have the power to hold the paradox between order and chaos, between *what is* and *what could be,* without flinching. Type 6s inherently know how to *stand in the middle,* and they teach us all about courage, faith, and the true strength of holding the door open between polarized positions, awaiting revelation, like Dorothy from Oz.

When **Type 7s** are Home in Presence, they have an expansive quality of awareness that can be present with a full range of experience. They are able to find freedom in the depth of a moment (*kairos*), allowing a higher plan to unfold through them. In no longer striving to make their own magic, Type 7s teach us about the wisdom and work of sacred magic that can be drawn upon in each moment, like Thor of Asgard, the god of thunder.

When **Type 8s** are Home in Presence, they know that Truth (as that to which nothing can be opposed) encompasses all diversity; that true strength is as much about an open heart as it is about power; and that turning the other cheek can be about as badass as it gets. In the immediacy of the present moment, Type 8s teach us about the innocence of responding skillfully, powerfully to This. Here. Now...like my hero Arya Stark.

When **Type 9s** are Home in Presence, they realize their own significance and solid ground within the multivariate nature of *All that Is,* and know that, at the same time, it all lives in them. Knowing they too are essential, Type 9's engage directly and forcefully with conflict and complexity, to teach us all about the creative and courageous Way to renew the world, just like Harry Potter, one right action at a time.[178]

LEVELS OF WHOLENESS

But what exactly is Home for us mortals? Beyond the realization of our individual holy idea and the essential gifts of type, we all have something to learn at point 9 about living in alignment with Holy Love. Point 9 on the map also represents the Law of One. It is the state of both being and continuously becoming more whole. Here we understand that the Enneagram journey was never really about the typing, but rather more about un-typing ourselves, so we can find the shadowy and split off parts of us that need to be welcomed into the circle to discover who we are in Presence. In the process of this work, we remember some One inside—an integrated higher self in touch with the flow of life and spirit—who can hold all this complexity with kindness.

That may not sound like such a big deal, but the power of inner work approaches such as Internal Family Systems therapy and Tara Brach's Radical Acceptance, give us plenty of reason to have faith in this sort of radical whole-making within. In fact, I have heard Richard Rohr refer to the true self as this whole-making instinct itself. Rather than unleashing monsters into the world, acceptance of shadow allows us greater capacity to align with love and choose how we show up—with Right Action, in service of the whole—and to attune with what is emerging in this moment that needs similar holding and unification. When our centers of intelligence are operating as One in a state of loving Presence, with access to creative intelligence, we participate in a much broader whole-making process. With clear mind, open heart, grounded receptive body, we have the clarity and freedom to make conscious choices and bring to life higher emotions, values (virtues), and perspectives (holy ideas).

In this way, the Home we are aspiring to is not a new walled garden so much as a *Way of being* that allows one to *stay* on the journey. Regularly reflecting on and taking apart tired structures, welcoming diverse and "opposing" forces to enable evolution, is living the universal pattern— the Word incarnate. Each time the three forces that enable this circular dance of creation come into coherence, there is a leap to a higher level of consciousness. We saw this "higher octave" reunion of three elements represented in Simba's new family of three. In the next turning of the wheel, Simba will play the role of king, the known world, and his son will be the new potential hero. This is a good example of how the creative divine spark essential to evolution (in Simba) eventually gets fixed and stagnant in the created world, necessitating an update. The characters change but the roles are the same. And the Way of the third force is always the heroic process of living the redemptive pattern in order to unify disparate parts as one constantly renewing whole.

This Way of operating in alignment with the laws of the Symbol applies at every level we might choose to examine. More psychological wholeness occurs as we take aim beyond the passions or "sins" that cause us to miss the mark of who we are beyond ego and Enneagram type. When we own and integrate more of our unconscious shadow, we invite conversation with our deeper selves, interbeing, and with a greater imagination hooked to the realm of the collective or objective psyche. Does this mean we will never again get triggered by our ego habits and the wounds they were designed to protect? Maybe. Probably not. But that is the meaning of Right Action as a continuous practice. Because no aspect of life is cast outside our awareness, we can become very fast at catching, pausing, and holding the reaction or pain with a Presence that transmutes lead into gold, and the old pattern into a higher-order outcome. Knowing and treating everyone as an expression of the Divine that is continuously seeking to Realize itself in Creation is our best chance at raising their level of alignment as well.

From a mind/brain perspective, this process serves to weaken old neural connections that led us from wound to trigger to reaction to fixed worldview, in ego (a kind of personal hell). Those grooved pathways can then be re-routed toward more flexible and virtuous responses that get stronger and stronger. Through conscious attention and choice, we develop greater flexibility and integration throughout the whole brain. According to Dan Siegel, a healthy mind/brain is one where diverse aspects of functioning are both differentiated *and* linked together in a coherent way. This is the brain's version of Holy Love! And if we follow Dan's definition of mind as "embodied and relational," this new-found freedom of consciousness also enables us to attend and attune to others purposefully, including them in our definition of wholeness—moving from Me to *MWe*.

The Way of the hero then grows our capacity in life as well as in brain function through the continuous process of learning and discovery. We explore ourselves into being to the extent that we are willing to move beyond the ego's self-oriented organizing principle based on our past embedded experience and emotion. Every new horizon arises out of an absence of the old. First stepping out of the comfort zone of habit, we can partner with the chaos/flow of potential that is this moment, this person, this situation. We may then try listening better in leadership or risking ourselves in relationship and dating. We might spontaneously pull in our Type 8 power, Type 4 creativity, or Type 7 visions of possibility to support our relationships and communities. Even better, we could invite "strangers" into our small and predictable circles, and different views into our political and social beliefs.

In every case, we learn and grow through purposefully pausing the familiar, welcoming what has been rejected or hidden, and holding the tension of both—holding the door open for *something more* to unfold, again and again. As soon as we become fixed or "right" (and righteous) again, it's time to welcome the stranger who is knocking, calling us toward renewal. While a continuous journey sounds exhausting at one level, it is also freeing to understand that there is no one finish line. A big part of the treasure unearthed in the Void is this deeply held wisdom that life, done well, is an ongoing process of updating ourselves, and the systems we are a part of that have become stagnant and constricting, in order to renew health and wholeness. It is a continuous process of coming into greater coherence with the "wholes" to which we belong; building bridges inside us, between us and others, in community, with Nature, and with the Divine, or the implicate, intelligent order that governs the Universe.

While spiritually coming "Home" surely means different things to different people, we find some common themes across traditions. The One Source, whether God or the unified field of consciousness, can be found within us just as it pervades every aspect of Creation, light and dark, seen and unseen, as three different forces in perpetual relationship. Indeed, there is something about seeing this pattern in action—the differentiated parts becoming One again—that points toward the numinous. At this level too, re-uniting with the One is as much a process of undoing, creating an absence that can be filled or shaped in relationship with the aspect of the Divine that *flows* continuously through all of life. This goes so directly against our modern understanding of growth that it deserves underlining: the emptying is essential to evolving higher consciousness. Sacrifice is essential for new life; before then, we cannot even imagine what could be! From the open field created in its wake, however, we can discover our potential in collaborating as a vehicle, through the laws, for the Realization of love that renews the kingdom.

THE FINAL LEAP

From this point in the Symbol there is a final leap. It is the final chapter of the journey, and it is just one step. But it is a big step, another directional shift—to the top of the Merkaba and beyond—becoming One, in Holy Love, with the Absolute. At least in *this* moment. The final transformation has more to do with the hero's character and right alignment with higher principles, her own integrated being, consciousness, and heart, and the creative capacity to unite life within and without. Her work on herself and in the world thus far (conscious labor and intentional suffering) will help determine whether she reaches an even higher union with the One Source of intelligence underlying Creation. At this threshold, technically, there is nothing more to be done except surrender to higher forces.

The higher-level point 9 indicated here is a kind of hidden

threshold—another interval or opening through which higher intelligence can enter, cause a directional shift, and powerfully transform the system. While all three forces of the Law of Three are required to access new information through the triangle (and the nature of the third force is the secret to this creative process), at each of these junctures along the journey where the triangle penetrates the hexad figure, a particular role in the triad of the Law of Three forces is indicated as a developmental step for us humans participating in this triadic dance.

At point 3, the journey required the wish or intention of the hero, imagining something more for himself and the world, offering himself up to the unknown and beginning the process of combining worlds. Point 6 called for the courage and strength of a future benevolent ruler with the focused know-how to create order from chaos *and* bring the flow of spirit alive in the created world. The return threshold at point 6 was not really an interval, as it was more about the hero's commitment to the hard work ahead of *making two worlds One* through a growing inner integrity and service to community. Point 9 on the journey marks the fulfillment of that commitment and the final interval through which higher forces can flow. It is an echo of the hero's experience in the Void, so the role of the realized hero here is to embody the queen's flow, a receptive force, in a conscious invitation for Spirit to reconcile the Above and Below, and complete the pattern.

Passing from point 8 to a higher point 9 brings the Merkaba or 3D Enneagram Symbol, into relationship with higher forces and a higher octave of development. The 8th and final note of any alchemical octave involves hesitation and uncertainty. It is a repetition of the same phenomena as occurred at the first threshold at point 3, heading into the unknown, but the method is different, the choice is conscious, and the "unknown" is changed because we are. Even more is riding on this final interval, because it represents the fulfillment of the seven steps and the beginning of a new order. Because it is the "mother" of a new series of seven, the eighth step is often related to the flow aspect of the Divine, sometimes referred to as the Ogdoad, Sophia; other times, it is described as the final dimension of "the seven-fold work of the Holy Spirit."[179] Either perspective supports a hero's receptive stance to invite a new third force.

We can look to examples of some of the great sages and saints to confirm that the role here is passive. The hero surrenders and the mediating role is left to Spirit to reconcile the created world with the One Source of Creation. The integrated divine human is pulled into the trinitarian process, submitting entirely to grace. If completed, the move to the zero point in the center marks the assumption of the entire vehicle, the developed soul, as One with the Absolute. The divine human has actualized all three Laws (One, Three, and Seven) within, is a fully integrated being, and can apply all three forces (active, passive, and reconciling) as needed to fulfill the creative evolutionary movement—through seven dimensions of increasingly higher levels of consciousness—toward the eighth step of union with the Divine.

And yet, very few of us mortals are likely to reach this last step of the work of unification until our literal death. To deal with this truth, the hero's journey sticks to the first two stages of the work: a new level of maturity, integration, and selflessness for the hero, and the return of harmony in the kingdom as a whole. There is a union achieved here, but maybe not "the" union. Most of our heroes seem to leap this point and continue around the Symbol to a new manifestation at point 1, just as Simba becomes the new king, beginning a new cycle that will require a new hero to renew the kingdom. At the same time, the word "hero" actually means something like "one born from a mortal and a god," so whatever happens next, the journey has introduced the hero to dimensions, within and beyond, that she may not have been in touch with prior.

And since the supreme task of the hero is a continuous, creative process of updating what has become stagnant in ourselves and in the world, for most of us there is a new round of adventure. Like Arya Stark and Jon Snow, off to distant lands, we will always be faced with new challenges that require the further deconstruction of cherished attachments, beliefs, and patterns. So we keep moving through cycles or octaves of development around the Symbol on the way to that final step of full absorption and union with Source. According to Gurdjieff, there are many octaves—at least seven levels of seven steps each (each note around the Symbol is its own Enneagram). That's 7x7 or 49 steps to becoming a divine being.[180] In this scenario, point 9 on the journey seems to be a place of respite and fully embodied Presence to which we continually return, and in which the central practice is surrendering to the Mystery—after all we have done to heal, refine our being, and direct our consciousness toward good. I suppose this is something like the still point described by poet T.S. Eliot:

At the still point of the turning world. Neither flesh nor fleshless;
Neither from nor towards; at the still point, there the dance is.
But neither arrest or movement. And do not call it fixity,
Where past and future are gathered. Neither movement from
nor towards,
Neither ascent nor decline. Except for the point, the still point,
There would be no dance, and there is only the dance.

If there is a point of reflection here in the flow state it would be something like: *What would Love do?* The journey has revealed that we are all One, one continuous arising of Being, Spirit, Love, God. This is so easy to say that it's kind of a throw-away statement today. And yet, lived, it really is a revolutionary stance. If we were truly able to get out of the way, to go willingly into the deconstruction of ego—the small self that is compelled to divide and blame, compete and control—we might have a shot at feeling our interconnectedness with *All that Is*, and experiencing the loving intelligence at the center of Creation as it seeks to arise through us. From here we might radically transform our relationships with ourselves, each other, our communities, and the earth.

I keep circling the concept, but at this final threshold of the Symbol it's not possible to name the Home and the One that exists within, beyond, and through Creation. Just as the Taoists say, "the Tao that can be spoken of is not the Tao," St. John of the Cross (1542-1591) said that "God can be loved but not thought." And St. Augustine: "Love is the highest form of knowing." We get to Holy Love at this point of self-transcendence because love unifies, whereas thought requires a thinker and separates us from *All that Is.* Father Rohr writes that "God is found when we reach the end of what we know."

PART 3:
The Symbol

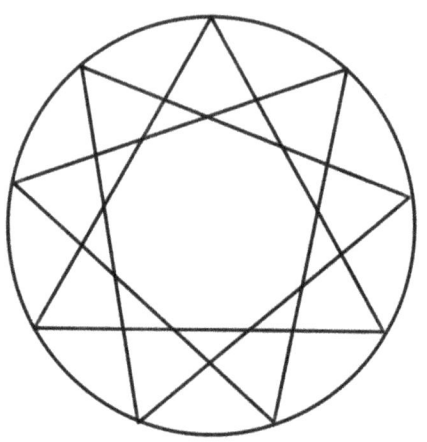

CHAPTER 19

THE SYMBOL IS THE WAY

The symbols that were used to transmit ideas belonging to
objective knowledge included diagrams of the fundamental laws of
the universe and they not only transmitted the
knowledge itself but showed also the way to it.[181]

~ G.I. GURDJIEFF

OPEFULLY, THE STORIES HAVE GIVEN YOU a felt sense of what it means to travel the Law of Seven steps, using the Law of Three forces, to evolve unity within, renew community, and grow spiritually. Now we can return to the Symbol itself to explore more concretely how the laws can be integrated to actualize their creative power along your own journey of growth. As with any great adventure, it's good to have some kind of map. Without one, we are in danger of falling into disorienting depths for which we are unprepared or distorting the work for purposes that serve our singular egos, and not our souls and communities. At the same time, since a symbol is a dynamic expression of knowledge that can be interpreted from many perspectives, my version of this map (woven from diverse disciplines) is just one possible vision. And the map is not the territory anyway, so consider all of this as food for reflection and sustenance on your own journey, which is, in the end, the only way one can truly understand.

In October of 2018, when I was first conceptualizing this work, I made a big map on my wall of the Enneagram Symbol with all the puzzle pieces of a lifetime's worth of related study, reflection, and experience laid out around it. I'll never forget the moment when my younger daughter (then 18), who has always had this other-worldly intelligence, said to me: "Mom, you collapsed time and space in that symbol." At that moment I sensed the scope of what we are working with in the Enneagram Symbol, and what Gurdjieff meant by saying (in the chapter heading quote above): a symbol not only transmits objective knowledge (such as the fundamental laws of the Universe), but also *shows the way* to it.

The Enneagram Symbol is a map for transforming ourselves, in accordance with the laws of creation and renewal, into a "vehicle" of higher being-consciousness that can help reveal the Unity underlying the diversity of life, in service of evolving humanity. Gurdjieff's statement about the Symbol "showing the way" struck me as an important clue. He drew the Enneagram in a distinct fashion. While we can trace the universal laws through various disciplines and myths as far back as earliest recorded history, our modern Enneagram Symbol seems to be original. There were previous versions of an enneagram or enneagon drawn with three closed equilateral triangles instead of the hexad figure. Later in his career, David Daniels was using this version of the Symbol to teach about three "harmony triads" revealing hidden connections between centers of intelligence that could help people grow beyond personality type.[182]

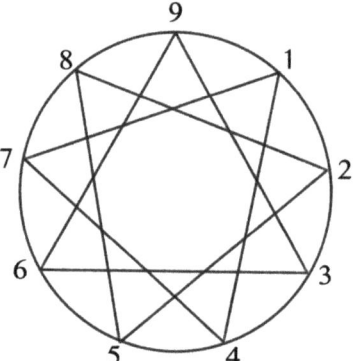

David's name for the triads is fitting because the diagram drawn in this way was used as a representation of "the harmony of the spheres," in reference to cosmology, long before Gurdjieff was born. Early versions of this enneagram referred to ideas reaching back to the Greek scholar Pythagoras and other ancient philosophers who used music and math to explain the cosmos. As the depiction of a universal process connecting humanity with Divinity, through nine virtues and three layers or spheres of being that create a kind of "ladder" to the Infinite, the ideas conveyed in this diagram are surely related to Gurdjieff's teaching. But why the different drawing of the Symbol?

As we reflect on Gurdjieff's version of the Symbol with its unique hexad shape that leaves the opening or Void between points 4 and 5, what becomes clear is that his hexad figure is a kind of broken-open hexagram (two intersecting, equilateral triangles). Moving from Gurdjieff's form of the symbol to the one with three triangles is a matter of simply re-routing two lines to close the triangles. Just that gives us a sense of movement, and maybe a plan, embedded in his design. Perhaps we are meant to create or restore the harmonious structure of the three triangles? Or take it apart? Or both?

TWO PATHWAYS

And if the Symbol shows the way to the realization of a harmonious whole, we are left with another question posed by Gurdjieff's symbol that we considered in part one of this book: Why is the Law of Seven, the Law of World Maintenance, depicted with the hexad figure *and* described with the musical octave and pathway around the Symbol? At first pass, this leaves us in a bit of a quandary: which path should we follow for growth and realization?

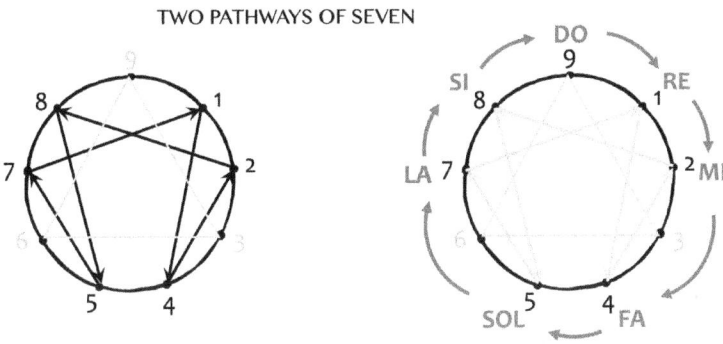

TWO PATHWAYS OF SEVEN

Oscar Ichazo, the first person to place specific ego drives and higher qualities around the Enneagram Symbol, and a man well-versed in diverse wisdom traditions, stated that he could find most everything from Gurdjieff's teaching within ancient Greek philosophy, particularly *stoicism*. This includes the Enneagram Symbol itself, which Ichazo claims is a "pure form" (an archetype from the realm of objective knowledge) and a "key" to the knowledge of universal processes. Ichazo uses a number of these symbols in his teaching that he calls "Pythagorean seals." He writes that in reading these keys the outside movement is to be considered "constructive and progressive," while the inside movement is "destructive and regressive."[183] Should we ignore the arrow lines then? Not so fast. As with all things Enneagram, it seems clear by now that the true transformational journey is one that integrates *opposing* currents.

I mentioned earlier that in the Sufi tradition the hexad figure is referred to as the *line of spirit* or *line of change*. It refers to how spirit carves our life out of the space of possibility that is our soul and emanates from the center of the circle—the "zero point" and Source from which all proceeds and returns. Why would the line of spirit be incomplete? As fourth way scholar and priest Cynthia Bourgeault explains, the force of God descends into the material world to create life and release certain qualities that can only be realized in form and action. Certain things need incarnation. At the same time, the Holy One provides "a tug toward the endless" that erodes matter and permanence as it draws us toward ascent.[184] These "opposing" movements characterize our unique journey as humans aspiring to a higher aim.

The Kabbalah Tree of Life (another symbolic representation of a *ladder* between the finite and the Infinite) also distinguishes two paths of growth. "The path of the flaming sword" is the downward path of Spirit into Creation that zig-zags between masculine and feminine *sephirot*—the constituent elements of Creation depicted in the Tree. This path shows the way the Infinite devolves organically through three "worlds" or dimensions into the material world at the base of the Tree. (Similar to the structure of the enneagon, these three dimensions are made of three triangles, one being a "higher" triad, with two more in the middle, between the Absolute and the created world.) The second path, "the path of the serpent," winds upwards from material existence to higher Being, tracing and integrating all the lines, as well as all the points or *sephirot* in the symbol. It is said that this is the path of redemption, but it must also take into account the descending path of the flaming sword.

What seems clear from the stories and science we covered, is that without any conscious action on our part, life seems to move in the zig-zag fashion of the hexad lines: order-chaos-order-chaos...on and on. In this vein, we are at the mercy of every accident, as life happens *to* us. Maybe this is something like the Universe trying to wake us up!? The push-pull of two opposing forces at the center of existence indeed powers Creation. Without our participation, life goes on; two forces do create a third result—but it is not a *higher-order* result (from the human perspective at least). It is a *sequential* result of the natural collision of opposites that tends to repeat and maintain the polarized pattern. It is a third thing, but not necessarily a third *force*. It is, in Gurdjieff's words: "the reciprocal destruction of two opposing forces and the cause of artificial light."[185]

What does he mean by artificial light? We saw what would have happened if, instead of traveling the hero's journey, Thor had followed the hexad arrow line path and moved directly from point 2 to point 8 to become the new ruler of Asgard: an ego-based assertion of power that would simply maintain the same oppositional dynamic between planets. This is "artificial light" because although change occurs, it is the symbolic version of putting old wine in new skins or, as Gurdjieff said it: "pouring from empty into the void." There's nothing new there, because conflict prevails in the perpetual dance between the extremes of tyranny and chaos. The hexad lines form a closed system that circles round and round itself without the true light of awakened consciousness.

Although we don't travel the hexad lines on the hero's journey, we definitely cannot ignore this powerful current. We saw the value of using the arrow line from 2 to 8 as an internal guiding star—a higher aim the mind can hook to while the hero sacrifices ego in the depths of the Void to prepare for a new ruling principle of the psyche. And this is just *one* of the important points of intersection between the circular journey and the hexad lines we explored along the journey. So while the arrow lines, alone, are not the way to Realization, this path is not regressive. Engaging with the dynamic process of the hexad figure plays a key role in our progression around the Symbol. Without it, the circular journey alone would also lead to a never-ending recurrence of material existence—the snake eating its own tail.

Gurdjieff described two paths in life as two rivers: an "involutionary" and "evolutionary" one. The river of involution seems to be the natural process by which energy or spirit devolves into form, giving life, but it trails off into oblivion (from a human perspective) in the dissolution of matter. Gurdjieff said that our task is to cross over from the river of life's involutionary flow to engage an "evolutionary backflow" toward higher consciousness that goes against the grain of this natural flow. And yet, it seems that to do this we have to consciously engage *both* currents: "A motion does not follow a straight line but has a simultaneously a twofold direction, circling around itself and falling toward the nearest center of gravity."[186] The Way of the hero has a simultaneous twofold direction, incorporating the hexad lines while traveling around the entire circle, navigating within and between both rivers to fulfill the promise of the Symbol drawn by Gurdjieff.

Spiritual alchemy unfolds when we step into *the third role* to do the work of preparing ourselves and consciously engaging *both* lines of development. We must travel the entire circle, integrating all parts and developing our *being*, while simultaneously engaging purposefully with the hexad line to develop a higher kind of *knowing*. Whether that integrative journey is seven times around the *Kaaba*, through the seven rooms of St. Teresa of Avila's "interior castle," or along the Buddha's Eightfold Path, it is a seven-step Way to our own spiritual center (the eighth step) that is united with the Presence of God or non-dual awareness.

The idea of integrated descending and ascending pathways can be found in many places in the natural sciences, from the nerve impulses taking information up and down your spinal cord to the air currents responsible for your airplane ride. The currents must work together to produce a result. From a spiritual perspective, the story of Jacob's ladder from the Old Testament can be found in Christian, Jewish, and Islamic teachings. Jacob (later to become King of Israel), while fleeing persecution had a dream of angels "ascending and descending" on a seven rung vertical ladder between earth and heaven.[187] And while some wisdom traditions value one or the other current of flow, many have a version in which (having descended from spirit into matter) we humans have to prepare our souls to invite a deeper penetration of energy and information via that same "descending" current of spirit. This meeting between our preparation and higher forces enables an "ascending movement," through layers of increasingly more refined being, heart, and consciousness.

I believe the nature of a true third force is one that encircles and engages opposing currents to help reveal higher dimensions—a "fourth way." In Christianity, the Way to fulfill this integrative journey was shown by Jesus: "God was in Christ reconciling the world to himself."[188] When we are "in Christ," living *as* the reconciling force is the Way to reunite the created world with the Divine. Gurdjieff wrote that "the Word began to manifest itself in the quality of the Third Holy Force of the Law of Three".[189] We already know the redemptive pattern. It requires, first, a "descent"—taking ourselves apart (by holding opposing ideas) to open a Way for the self-organizing intelligence of Creation to transform our souls. Only then is there the possibility of an "ascent" and partnership with higher forces that lifts the created world. Whether the Way is shown by Jesus, Buddha, Muhammad, Vishnu, the Tao, or the Hero, it is a Way that integrates opposing lines of work to restore Unity and the unifying flow of Holy Love in the world.

HARMONIOUS DEVELOPMENT

Earlier I used Gurdjieff's musical analogy to explain the process that links the two paths of seven as two layers and lines of development around the Enneagram. At one level, we travel the circular path, collecting the points like music notes (Do-Re-Mi-Fa-Sol-La-Si) by owning the passions that derail us when we are gripped by ego patterns. This represents the horizontal, human, and psychosocial journey to wholeness and Presence—*the line of being*—in which we gather all the fragments of our centers of intelligence to work together as One. In making the unconscious conscious, the first layer of the circular path "purifies" the soul or essence from ego (integrating shadow and light), so we can receive and partner with the organizing force of spirit along the vertical and transpersonal axis of growth, which marks a second layer of development through *the line of knowing*.

This second layer hones our ability to *know* in a different way, in partnership with the universal flow of intelligence represented by the line of spirit. In music there are "rules" for combining notes and making directional changes in the music that are always there, running in the background. The hexad arrow lines are like those rules, they carve a path in our soul whether we participate or not. The Way of the hero is one in which we prepare ourselves to work consciously with those rules, or laws, in this case. Through our collected *being* in the universal heart or soul, we can develop a higher mind, or way of *knowing* in partnership with spirit, that supports our journey around the Symbol to access higher levels of integrated being and consciousness, in touch with higher forces, through the "vertical" dimension of growth.

Interestingly enough, the potential of this vertical dimension is glimpsed in the Void, where the arrow lines don't go. There is a deep experience here of what is to come through the integration of worlds, but it is not made Real until the end of the journey. And it is only through the sacrifice of former structures, and a re-membering of all of who we are in those depths, that a divine spark of creative possibility is uncovered to help us more skillfully weave opposing forces and worlds. On the far side of the Void, the hero has a new line of work for the second half of the journey—to further link the horizontal and the vertical lines of development by bringing the flow of spirit to life *within* the created world. This process continues to develop the soul in relationship to the line of spirit within, and at the same time it helps harmonize the soul of the world with an even higher mind or Spirit through the hero's Presence in the world.

As we considered on the journey, this process is made literal in the formation of the three tetrahedrons or "energy bodies" of the Merkaba— the Enneagram as it *could be* when we have extended the flat Symbol and horizontal plane of body-heart-mind into the vertical or spiritual plane of existence (as "body"-soul-spirit), forging a mini universe of the laws within ourselves.

The vertical and horizontal layers of the work are then sewn together on the third leg of the journey, with the hero's efforts to be a clear and creative channel for divine love in community, in his or her unique way. This leads to a final "layer" of work, which is another law of three process that aims to complete the octave of development (and "ladder" to the Infinite) in one step that unites this creative vehicle with God or the unified field of intelligence, realizing the harmony of the spheres.

To fulfill the promise represented in this Symbol, the two lines of development must be worked simultaneously and combined into true *understanding* and a lived wisdom. For this, the Laws of Three and Seven must be combined and lived within us. *They are not meant to stand alone.* And the secret to their integration lies in growing our own inner triangle of actualized forces. As Gurdjieff said, "Each completed whole, each cosmos, each organism, each plant is an enneagram, but not every one has an inner triangle," indicating the presence of "higher elements," which we can understand as a more refined Presence.[190] Developing our fully integrated Presence through all centers, and the ability to inhabit all three forces of Creation (order, chaos, and the reconciling third), is what enables us to engage the line of spirit consciously along our soul's journey around the circle. To see how this works, we must first develop our inner triangle; then we will apply it along the journey of seven steps around the Symbol, one more time, to see how the laws might come together to help us fulfill our role in Creation.

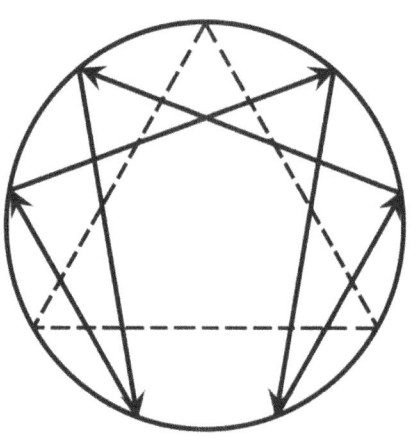

CHAPTER 20

Our Role in Creation

In our system we are created in the image of God—of a trinity.
If we consciously absorb three substances and send them out, we
can construct outside ourselves what we like.
This is creation.[191]

~ G.I. Gurdjieff

GROWING A CREATIVE INNER TRIANGLE starts with waking up a hero, with *a higher aim*, willing to explore the shadowy and "opposing" world beyond the known. Remember the Law of Three formula: two dueling forces, reconciled by a third, creates a triangle open to new intelligence (energy and information from outside the system) that can be transformed into a fourth integrated and *higher-order* whole. With that fourth point, in geometry, the triangle becomes a tetrahedron, evolving into an entirely new dimension. That is why the Law of Three is known as the Law of Creation. We use it to break through to new levels of understanding and growth.

The "fourth way" describes a continuous process of living the signature pattern of creation in the Universe revealed by the Law of Three's dance of three forces. One of the oldest written references to this law comes from the alchemist Maria Prophetessa, said to be the sister of Moses and female counterpart to Hermes, who was charged with safekeeping of the Emerald Tablet sometime around 100 BCE. Her legacy includes the alchemical *Axiom of Maria*: "One becomes Two; Two becomes Three; and out of the Third comes the One as the Fourth."[192] And this sounds very like that passage from the *Tao Te Ching* that dates back to 400 BCE: "The Way begot one, and the one, two; then the two begot three, and three, all else." We find the Law of Three everywhere because, as Gurdjieff stated, "This teaching of three forces is at the foundation of all ancient systems."[193]

This creative vehicle of three, with its potential to always make way for an integrated and higher-level, fourth arising, is the real point of the Law of Three. In the language of nonlinear systems (where we started this journey with the S-curves), the self-organizing capacity of an open system leads to that magical concept of *emergence,* in which a new order, governed by higher-level rules, arises. It *emerges* as the fragments of a decaying old order are synched up with the living field of creative intelligence underlying all existence, in that space between curves. Life itself seems to have a self-organizing drive toward coherence following chaos, in a continuous cycle of breakdown and renewal—that is, when it is allowed to access new and diverse energy and information. To enable this process to work through us, however, we need to develop a deep understanding of that third force within, and how it weaves order *and* chaos to help evolve new life

Once we get this concept down, we can grow the capacity to engage not only all three centers of intelligence, but also *all three forces* intentionally, as needed, to grow. It is easy to confuse the centers with the forces, but they are not the same. The forces are like roles played by the centers as they interact with each other, but forces also act *within* each center, just as they play out at every level of existence. At the outset of the journey, our centers (under ego) are each blindly controlled by opposing forces, *and* they are at odds with each other. Without a true third or reconciling force, any system naturally falls into a reactive pattern in which the forces of *contraction into order* (tyranny) and *expansion into flow* (chaos) vie for control. Through the development of third force consciousness, we can free the centers from their polarized patterns to unite as a coherent vehicle. As this occurs, our mind, heart, and body intelligence forms One united vessel—an inner triangle—with new super-powers.

Without the distortions of ego, under whose rule this duality prevails, our primary centers of intelligence become "perceivers" or creative participants in the vast field of potential, intelligence, and spirit. Together they amount to a little creation machine of Presence that can help to unlock all the other fragments of our centers around the circle. If this goes well, we gain seven additional "brains"—seven clear "receivers" of intelligence— that help us meet reality far more clearly and objectively. As all these mini receivers come online in a central channel of energy and information up and down our spine, their collective dynamic gives increasing access to the vertical dimension of transpersonal or spiritual intelligence.

To fully develop the inner triangle and unlock the whole system, the journey must move around the circle and incorporate the influence of the hexad lines—applying the law of three forces all along the path of seven. We might think of the triangle as turning, bringing its creative process to *each* point, and slowly opening up the other two triads of the *harmony of the spheres* into the large tetrahedrons of the Merkaba. Along this integrative path, the spaces between the points on the Enneagram (Gurdjieff called "stopinders") are as important as the points. In particular, the intervals where the triangle penetrates the hexad figure (at 3-6-9) are key moments in which the direction of the journey is determined.

In the hero stories, we saw these intervals as the thresholds between known and unknown worlds. As the points of greatest tension between opposing worlds or forces (order and chaos), they are openings through which new information can enter the system to divert life from an invo-lutionary flow, that moves haphazardly between extremes, towards an evolutionary process that consciously engages both forces to access higher dimensions.

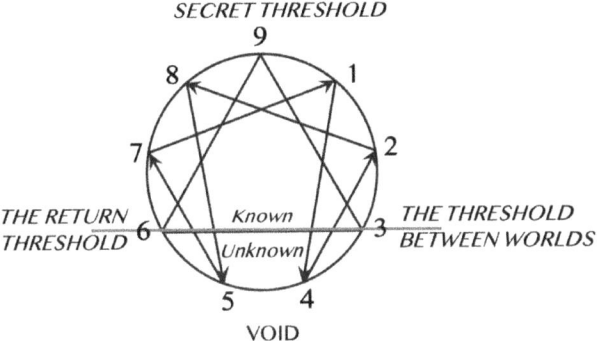

When life throws us across the threshold and into the unknown by "accident" (along that arrow line from point 1 to point 4), most of us compulsively scramble back to the known world as soon as possible, with-out changing much, following the flow of the hexad (1->4->2) that keeps us from entering the Void. Without the intervention of the triangle at the interval, the natural order of things would continue to swing between the two poles (order *or* chaos) instead of engaging the Law of Three to *reconcile* opposing forces (order *and* chaos) and advance us around the circle (into the Void) towards higher-order growth. As the triangle implies, navigating the intervals requires aligning all three primary centers of intel-ligence, our integrated Presence, to open a channel for new information, access new dimensions, and maintain the evolutionary path.

What's also important to know is that the Void between points 4 and 5 is an early taste of the interval at the final point 9 threshold and transition to a higher octave of growth. As Campbell says it: "The temple interior, the belly of the whale, and the heavenly land beyond, above, and below the confines of the world, are one and the same."[194] Whereas the first threshold, at point 3, marks the transition from ego ideal into engagement with the "world" of unconscious shadow at the personal level, the doorway between worlds that is accessed in the Void (and brought to fruition at point 9) is between the personal and the transpersonal, linking the Above and Below at a higher level. Precipitated by the hero's sacrifice, crossing the Void is like merging into the sea of energy and potential underlying our material reality. The hero must survive the impact of this crossing to link worlds through the back half of the journey and move into the further reaches of consciousness along the vertical dimension of the Symbol.

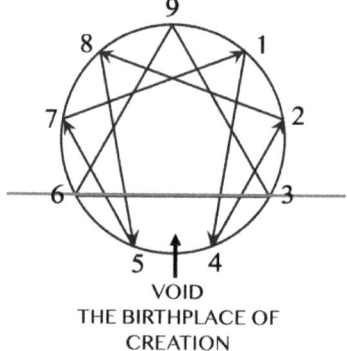

VOID
THE BIRTHPLACE OF
CREATION

For one, this is just good behavioral science. Habit change is more enduring if we disconnect patterns with a pause before embedding new ones. But also, spiritual and wisdom traditions incorporate this pause, an emptying through the practice of Presence and present-moment attention. In the present, ego can simply fall away as we rest in the Holy Spirit or know ourselves again as interbeing. There's a reason this state is so often approached on our knees. We must be no one, and not separate, to make this passage. Here, beyond distinctions between self and other, all manner of dark and light intermingle as an unknown field of potential awaiting the creative spark of new intelligent organization. We have entered the gap. The space between curves.

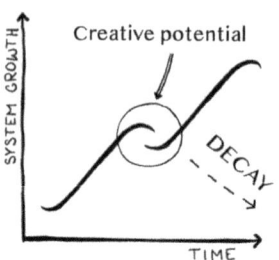

Within the frame of physics, we might describe this place between curves as a quantum wave of possible futures. A "particle" is shaped out of this field of energy into a particle (really a little packet of energy), remarkably, by the observer that comes and looks. In ego, the way we "shape" potential is habitual, getting us more of our past in the present. As that fixed pattern gets old and narrow, it blocks out adaptive information, resulting in a slide down the first curve into decay. But each time we sacrifice our knowns and enter the gap by lining up our centers—clear receptive mind, open heart, grounded in the body's full intelligence—we access a sea of potential. With no attachment or aversion to the thoughts, feelings, sensations that typically yank us back into the material realm, our now more integrated being starts to resonate with the flow of intelligence that pervades all of Creation. As we remember who we truly are, more like energy than matter, we can participate in creating a different future.

If the Symbol is a vehicle to interconnectedness and higher consciousness, then accessing the Void and gap between S-curves at key intervals (with meditation, contemplative prayer, and other methods) is our way *into* that vehicle. In this sense, the journey of a single moment has great power. It is that point where we plug the whole thing into a higher energy source, or not. Ego can't create essence. Essence is a significantly different state of being, feeling, and knowing that, in one sense, is gifted to us. But there's much we can do to prepare the soil. Some of our best modern teachers of the Enneagram focus so much on the practice of Presence because it is a proven process for making this monumental shift, in a moment, re-purposing our centers of intelligence for greater coherence, resonance, and union, both within and outside of ourselves.

DEVELOPING OUR INNER TRIANGLE OF PRESENCE

To inhabit and activate our inner triangle as a creative force, we have to learn Presence as a multi-faceted process. Dan Siegel describes three "pillars" of Awareness derived from research into mindfulness and mental training as "open awareness," "focused attention," and "kind intention."[195] These three pillars are like three different ways we can *apply* our three-centered Presence; meaning, they all start with the basic practice of being fully present and aligned in all centers of mind, heart, and body, and proceed to a specific way of orienting that collected Presence. Not surprisingly, perhaps, the three pillars match the three forces of the Law of Three that together have the potential to operate as a coherent and self-organizing whole. We must learn how and when to use each of these pillars purposefully along the journey.

Open awareness is like resting in the queen, receptive to the unknown, undifferentiated *chaos* or *flow* of potential underlying life, without an agenda. With the ego filter off, all sorts of energy and information may arise from the depths of this sea, but there is little to no sense of "self" to react or attach to it. *Focused attention* is like the king who monitors and *orders* or "creates" our experience by zeroing in on specific aspects and rejecting others. Consciously applied, this pillar also serves to strengthen an "inner observer"—a higher kind of mind that can stand back and observe our experience in action. These first two pillars of awareness, as queen and king (flow and focus), are "opposing" because when the nervous system network governing one of them is operating, the other tends to be turned off—unless a third player is around to link and manage the whole lot.

The third force and pillar, *kind intention*, is similar to the heroic capacity to flexibly link the ordering force with the flow of new potential, in service of higher-order growth. Intention shapes our experience by focusing how we pay attention. The king's focused attention is very powerful but, applied unconsciously, it tends to fixate and limit us. The hero knows how to "sacrifice" this element, as needed, to access open awareness in weaving together the two "competing" forces. Taking the responsibility for making (and re-making) intentional choices for one's attention that don't shut out the flow of inner experience (higher emotion, instinct, spiritual intelligence), but *also* prevent getting lost in a sea of potential chaos, is the hero's job. The hero is always an adaptive embodiment of *both* forces, so there are two parts of this.

With intentional *kindness*, we hold the tension of conflicting aspects of our experience, enfolding them in the flow of open awareness where all this diversity is linked with acceptance. The higher emotional energy of this pillar (kindness or love) is key to linking forces and to growth. Indeed, we might say that only love is capable of unifying, transmuting, and transcending polarity. With kind *intention*, we participate with Creation by aiming higher. We sort through the vastness of inner experience and *choose* when and how to re-engage our focused attention to align with transcendent values (while still allowing the flow of experience to reveal ever more). Our heartfelt and focused wish for a better outcome (whatever it is we are working with) does not guarantee the outcome, but it serves as an important engine for the creative process invoked through the Law of Three.

Learning to develop and use this "unlocked" inner triangle of three forces purposefully and creatively (through our aligned centers of intelligence) is as powerful in life as it is in meditation. Dan Siegel's work reveals that employing these three aspects of Presence regularly can not only increase our capacity for empathy and connection with ourselves and others, but also has serious health benefits. It can: enhance immune function, improve cardiovascular health, help repair and maintain the ends of our chromosomes (related to cellular and overall physical aging), reduce inflammation by altering epigenetic regulation of the inflammatory response, reduce the stress response, and cultivate integration in the brain, which enables us to better regulate emotion, attention, and behavior.[196]

From an Enneagram perspective, working with these three pillars of Presence directly impacts our centers of intelligence, individually and collectively. Practice can strengthen attention and emotion regulation in aspects of the prefrontal cortex, alter areas of the limbic system related to memory processing and emotion regulation, build the connection between brain hemispheres through the corpus callosum, and increase overall connectivity and coherence both within the brain and between the brain and all body systems. This sort of internal integration signals a more united or higher self, no longer pushed about by unconscious contents, and able to *aim higher*. And practicing such multi-faceted Presence can also increase our capacity for resonance with people and systems outside of us, enhancing the creative potential of the inner vehicle we are building.

Dan teaches his Wheel of Awareness meditation as a way to develop and apply the three pillars of Presence through eight aspects of consciousness, gradually cultivating a more integrated and expansive container of consciousness. The eight aspects of consciousness are: each of the five senses, the sixth sense of bodily sensations (*interoception*), a seventh aspect of all "mental" activities (that includes feelings, thoughts, and memories), and an eighth aspect that concerns our sense of interconnection and relationship with others and all life (interbeing). In this process we are "collecting" and aligning aspects of ourselves previously fragmented, operating independently, and sometimes at odds.

Dan's practice echoes the idea that we have considered from different lenses of gathering fragments of our being—as music notes, mythic archetypes, sephirot, chakras, or energy centers—spread around the Enneagram Symbol. Some of these other approaches to collecting parts of a whole system also distinguish a "higher" triad (like the pillars of Presence) that helps us to free and gather the other pieces. In order to develop and apply this inner triangle of Presence, in which all three creative forces can collaborate in bringing the whole system into harmony, we have to first release them from the prison that is their fixed functioning under ego.

OVERCOMING DARK FORCES

Gurdjieff made sure to note that his job (helping people wake up) was "harder than God's," because he had to influence people to first take something apart in order to create anew. As we saw along the journey, the hero has to leave the king and the kingdom to grow. To develop this inner triangle of Presence, we have to deconstruct the habits of ego that distort our intelligence and keep us attached to the limited version of who we are. As we start the journey around the Symbol, instead of a creative vehicle of integrative Presence, we are a bundle of opposing energies in a dance that maintains the former "kingdom." This plays out as the habitual distortions of mind, heart, and body intelligence that make up our Enneagram type: a fixated king, the chaos queen of disowned instinctual drives, and the passionate adversary.

Because the dance of these three forces maintains ego, there is no one home in our inner triangle of Presence. Our creative divine spark (the echo of a former king), and the highest potential of *being* (queen) exist largely outside our awareness. They are essentially *trapped in matter*—obscured by the embedded patterns of our biological and cultural history. And there is no hero, no third force capacity to link all these different energies and renew harmony in the kingdom.

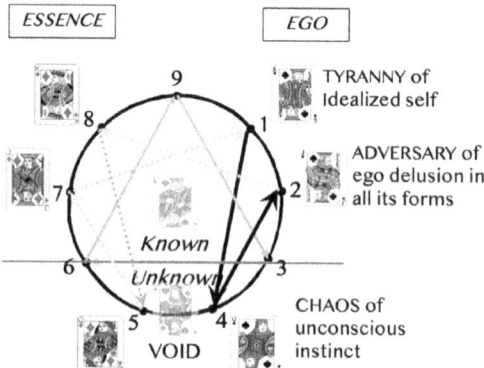

While life itself is initiated by three creative forces, in personality we end up with six fragments of our being spread around the circle because everything in the created world casts a shadow. When we refer to *order, chaos, and third force* incarnated as king, queen, and hero/adversary, they each have two versions and either can affirm or deny life. On the left side of the Symbol above sit the mirror image of the fragments on the right. They are no "better," and unless they are freed from matter to work their triadic dance at a higher level, they will play out the same fixated formula in a new suit (old wine, new bottle).

All of the mythic archetypes are like fragments of our centers of intelligence we need to integrate and harmonize into a coherent whole being. They have become separated from each other and from their primary Source. This means our head, heart, and body intelligence is often in conflict. Centers tend to oppose each other. But also, as I mentioned, the dualistic forces (king and queen) hold sway *within* each center too, causing us to react automatically, preventing presence and true intelligence. As Gurdjieff said it:

> *Man, in the normal state natural to him, is taken as a duality. He consists entirely of 'pairs of opposites.' All man's sensations, impressions, feelings, thoughts, are divided into positive and negative, useful and harmful, necessary and unnecessary, good and bad, pleasant and unpleasant. The work of centers proceeds under the sign of this division. Thoughts oppose feelings. Moving impulses oppose instinctual craving for quiet.*[197]

The centers aren't the problem so much as it is the way the unreconciled forces inhabit them. And even then, the dark forces aren't "bad," they are inherently creative and work at every level of life. But when it comes to the body and the psyche, they are trapped in the dualistic world of matter, pushing and pulling within and between centers. There is a third element that keeps the fixed world intact, symbolized by the passionate adversary, but no third force that might up-level the game. In order to untangle these knots of ego and access higher intelligence, we will keep our attention on the three forces to learn how they operate both within and between centers.

Perspectives on the Three Forces

In Buddhism, the dark version of three forces is described as three types of craving or three "poisons." These are: 1) aversion or hostility (the king who keeps chaos and "the other" out of the kingdom); 2) attachment or greed, a desire of the senses (the expansive queen); and 3) ignorance or delusion (the adversary that thinks its self-oriented efforts of attachment and aversion actually work). These poisons are the very roots of suffering.

They constitute a "three-fold fire," that keeps us in *samsara*, the eternal cycle of birth and death in the material world (order, chaos, order, chaos... or the seven steps with no hero). The poisons are personified as the daughters of Mara, Buddha's ego adversary and a "magician of delusion."[198] Mara takes on different guises to try to derail the Buddha as he is approaching enlightenment (much like the deadly sins), but his three "daughters" are especially powerful in their attempts to seduce him away from the pursuit of liberation.[199]

The three poisons keep us trapped, because as long as we are compelled to pursue what we are attached to and repel what we find aversive (whether it comes from within or outside of us), we are controlled by a world that happens *to* us. When we are occupied with this or that effort to be ok, we are not home in the clarity and freedom of our aligned whole being. In this way, the poisons (like the three forces under ego) keep our lower centers disjointed and cut off from the greater flow of intelligence. Rooted in the material world, controlled by the duality of attachment and aversion, we believe the foundational delusion that we *are* this separate self that can get what we want if we can just be a somebody, and stay secure and in control, in the face of all that happens within and to us.

In the Christian tradition, Eve fell from grace in the Garden of Eden by succumbing to three temptations also. In this story, the temptations align with the three fixations of the egoic inner triangle that obscure our connection with the vertical and transpersonal realm. Eve *listened* to the voice of the serpent (doubt is listening to two voices or spiritual "disobedience"), she *saw* the tree was good for food (vanity is prioritizing a personal and material aim over the spiritual one), and she *took and ate* the fruit of the tree of knowledge of good and evil, also giving it to her husband (indolence is plunging into the material realm of senses; and, here, taking others along).

On the other hand, the example of Jesus says that there is a Way other than acting only out of our very human and biologically bound ego structure, blind to the vertical dimension, and it starts with vanquishing these three poisons. Jesus prevailed over three material world temptations delivered by the devil in the desert, forty days after his baptism: a desire of the senses (*turn stones into bread*); emotional temptation or pride in the self (*jump off the temple if you are real*); and control/power (*bow to me and get the kingdom*). The Christian Hermetic philosopher Valentin Tomberg describes both of these biblical stories as tests of the three most sacred spiritual vows—of obedience, poverty, and chastity, which he likens to faith, hope, and love (the holy ideas of our inner triangle).[200]

The Symbol gives us a general map of how our failure to fully inhabit our three centers of intelligence allows the three forces to control our system and create the delusion of type as our most powerful self. In ego, we *all* blindly flow with our drives (Sloth), grasping for what our senses desire, and we repel that which might threaten the control and order of our kingdom (Fear). This pattern of attachment and aversion varies by Enneagram type to shape our particular type's delusion (Deceit) that is the small self's adaptation to the demands of our nature within us and culture from outside us. Our personal version of these temptations and how they play out through our fragmented centers is described by our type structure. As long as we are stuck in the pattern, we are in deceit or delusion, prevented from knowing our true nature, intelligence, and potential.

And our particular delusion is more than sleep. Our passion and emotional suffering are a big part of what keeps us from waking up to who we really are. Like Mara, the adversary is the embodiment of the passions that takes many different guises. Our primary delusion of self is an active engine that maintains our human nature and ego structure and works against our awakening at every point along the journey. It traps us in the duality that kidnaps and distorts all our centers of intelligence and creates a world where we, and everyone else, are separate from Source.[201] This is why we must integrate all of the passions in the "horizontal" and human layer of work, although our primary passion is the most challenging.

Until we are internally "one," there is no chance at being One with the Source and Flow of Being. Both Buddha and Jesus, after resolving the first three temptations, had a fourth—the invisible compilation of all three poisons—related to the central delusion of separation. Subjugating the human and material self to something higher, in service to all of humanity, was the final step to awakening their divine nature. They both fully mastered the ego, its material desires and will to personal power, by going back into the world to teach, serve, and lift others. We are vertical *and* horizontal beings. For both spiritual leaders it was not about denying the dualistic material world and force of evolution, but rather about bringing this under a higher master and higher aim, to restore paradise in this life.

For the Buddha that paradise was called *nirvana*, which literally means the three-fold fire is "blown out," and it is also understood as enlightenment or non-dual consciousness. It requires extinguishing the three-fold fire of delusion at its roots with three antidotes: generosity, loving kindness, and wisdom. Following this inner work, the Buddha headed back into the world to live and teach these antidotes through virtuous behavior along the Middle Way of the Eightfold Path. As with our journey around the circle, the eighth step on this path of realization resolves the *octave* of growth that transforms the kingdom.

Jesus also returned to worldly work after mastering the three temptations with hope, faith, and love. And he proceeded directly to perform seven miracles described in the Gospel according to John, manifesting the seven "I am" names of the Master: "I am the true vine, I am the way, the truth, and the life, I am the door, I am the bread of life, I am the good shepherd, I am the light of the world," and "I am the resurrection and the life." Tomberg calls this the "octave" of the seven tones of the revelation of his mission—essentially, bringing three-fold dark under the mastery of three-fold light, and "the manifestation of the glory of the Father *through* the Son.[202]

While these may be big shoes to fill, the Way is clear. As we become conscious of how we also are trapped in matter by the forces of duality under ego, we can start to wake up third force consciousness and develop a creative inner triangle of forces. With an awake third element, we can harmonize and re-purpose the forces of the king and queen, whose true mission is to give birth to a heroic integrative third force consciousness that can help renew the kingdom. When the freed-up forces create together they can manifest specific aspects of the higher heart (Courage, Veracity, Right Action) and mind (Holy Faith, Hope, Love) of a fully developed essential self. We are going to work with the forces directly as the three pillars of Presence—orientations of our integrated higher being-consciousness-heart—distinct from the centers. Think of these as our own version of *antidotes* to the three dark forces under ego.

PREPARING FOR THE JOURNEY: STRENGTHENING FORCES

Strengthening each of the pillars of Presence is a prerequisite to applying them along the steps of the hero's journey. We can develop our capacity for the *focused attention* of the king with a number of different practices. You have probably already been exposed to some kind of basic mindfulness or contemplative prayer practice. Most simply, this is a process of collecting and directing your attention purposefully to one thing (your breath, a word/prayer, or sensation), noticing when it slides, and—without judging (aversion) or getting attached to the distraction—returning to your focus point. Noticing and returning, again and again, builds the muscle of focused attention and choice just like strength training would build a body muscle.

This practice may seem simple, but it is very powerful and important work. It shifts our consciousness away from the many inner distractions that hijack focus and keep us fragmented, attached to our senses and separate self in ego, and it develops an *inner observer*—part of our awareness that can separate and observe our experience. Once you get the gist of it, you can "go to the gym" and build this muscle anywhere—in line, on hold, on a walk, in the minute between zoom calls—and strengthen the king's gift of focused attention. In some eastern frameworks "one-pointed attention" is the first step on the way to enlightenment.

Helen Palmer, founder (with David Daniels) of the Narrative Ennea-gram, often starts attention training exercises with something like this: *put your attention on the wall in front of you, then move it to the space behind you, then bring it to book-reading distance in front of you, and finally shift your attention inside your body and drop it down into the belly. Feel yourself seated in your body, breathing.* This progressive movement of focus quickly shows us our ability to choose where we put our attention, and how it shapes our experience. We always have this choice, but it is not one we make when we are in the trance of habitual unconscious programs. The capacity to choose our focus is an essential foundation for developing higher consciousness, because not only does it "create" our experience, but also it helps the inner observer learn how thoughts, feelings, and sensations work inside us. And actually, this is a simple definition of "higher consciousness"—observing from a higher perspective—although it's just one dimension of many.

Taking off from my version of Helen's introduction, once your attention is in and down continue the practice by focusing on your breath. Notice the in-flow and out-flow of breath in your belly, or at the tip of your nose, or in the rise and fall of your chest. Pick one spot to anchor your focus. From there you can experiment with expanding your attention to incorporate other aspects of consciousness, one by one, noting your sensations, then your feelings, and then your thoughts as they arise. The aim is to notice and name what you observe (further separating your consciousness from its contents), but always to return straight-away to the anchor of your breath and designated point of focus, without getting lost in a story about what you observe. No matter how many times your mind wanders off, bringing it back strengthens present-moment attention and choice. Regular practice will build focus and resilience (the capacity to return to a neutral state) in many areas of your life and work.

The second point of preparation is practicing heroic *kind intention*. Kindness (Love) is the unifying force weaving through Creation, a self-organizing intelligence that seems to drive toward greater diversity *and* coherence. Intentionally extending kindness towards yourself, within the meditation and beyond, takes practice for most of us. Being kind to yourself doesn't require "earning" it or having anything figured out. You are human, you suffer, make mistakes, try, don't try, whatever...it doesn't matter. Kindness allows us to let go of distractions and our ego's need to make this moment anything other than it is. It enables equanimity in the face of whatever is revealed by our focused attention (which will always include shadow elements). And it is our link into the larger field of loving Presence, the flow of intelligence without form or "self" at all, that is always already available.

The science related to practicing self-compassion is clear. It does not make you weak. It makes you healthier, able to think more clearly and creatively, approach challenges, and generally feel better about yourself, which helps you be more generous with others. Kindness, compassion, love...all are versions of the unifying force necessary for creation. True positive emotion (from the higher heart field) is magnetic. With third force consciousness, we practice creatively linking the expansive *flow* of intelligence with what has become stagnant or rigidified (like judgment or hurt) to unite opposing energies and facilitate growth. A classic *metta* or "loving-kindness" meditation and Tara Brach's RAIN practice (introduced in chapter 12) are ways to strengthen this kind of radical acceptance and unifying kindness.

Practicing the *intention* part of kind intention is also important. Intention is the aim or wish that guides our focused attention to give up the old (as needed) and capture something from the sea of intelligence to which we have linked. In this way the hero knits together the king and queen (focus and flow) *toward* some higher aim. And making sure that guiding intention is wise *and* kind, toward us as well as others, just makes sense from the perspective of interbeing. It also turns up the power of the intention with higher emotion. With our whole being aligned, wish becomes "will." Practicing kind intention can be as simple as setting a reminder alarm a few times a day to wake up and notice: *Where is my attention? Is it working for me?* Meaning...*is that what I intend? And is it kind (infused with higher emotion? Am I hooked into the awareness of interbeing)?* If not, do a re-set...without judgment. When you aim higher, make sure you *feel* the goodness of it, to unify both flow and focus in its wake.

Understanding and strengthening the final pillar, the *open awareness* of the queen, is more involved, as hers is the most mysterious and expansive domain, as well as the key to unlocking potential. The queen rules the space between curves. As the undifferentiated ground of Being, she has as many names as qualities. Chaos/flow, the sea of potential, river of Great Memory, and the living soul of the world, are some we have used. She is the portal keeper to the vertical dimension of the Symbol that unites us with spirit and truly higher forces. As we integrate shadow and become more whole, we drop into this undifferentiated flow of intelligence beyond ego and the Default Mode Network (unite with our *anima* or soul queen). When we are fully integrated, no more shadow, no more duality or resistance, there is no trigger to take us back to the material realm. When we are *no one*, we are everyone, and we move beyond time into an "eternal" dimension of consciousness.

In this vein, Gurdjieff's "self-remembering" takes on another meaning. As we re-member the pieces of ourselves that were in shadow, we drop deeper into this river of "Great Memory" and remember that we are so much more than our physical brains and bodies, our individual intentions and behaviors, even our loves and losses. Within whatever spiritual framework you imagine, we are truly little bundles of energy enveloped in that greater unified field and flow some of us call God, Allah, Brahman, Consciousness, the Great Mother/Father, divine ground of Being that is both immanent and transcendent. And, because we are made *in the image* of our Creator according to this divine blueprint, we can and need to know *ourselves* as creators too. From this perspective, the Enneagram shows us how we get in the way of that remembering, and how to get beyond ourselves so that we can know the "I AM" behind it all.

Gurdjieff called the three sacred forces many names, among them: "I am," "I can," and "I wish."[203] Without experience of the "I am" Presence that is fully embodied through all centers and connected to higher forces, there is no "can," or *know how* to do and be what we need to in order to fulfill a "wish" or intention, much less to *know what* our true wish and higher purpose might be. To realize "I am," we have to swim through chaos into the open awareness of the queen's flow, the field of potential beyond the ego's rule. From there, the "can" of focused attention that knows how to create, and the "wish" of kind intention that links them together toward a shared vision, can create with the queen's flowing potential. For this Law of Three magic to open new dimensions, however, we first have to learn how to access the "I am" of higher being through *open awareness.*

Conceptually, what we are trying to do with this practice is to get beyond the sense of a separate self and experience ourselves as an integral aspect of *All that Is.* Open awareness is resting in the present moment(s) with all of our centers aligned and receptive, connecting the Above and Below through ourselves. There are two ways to approach this sea of potential: the straight path and the circuitous. As always, both are necessary lines of work.

To drop straight in, first come to ground in all three centers—clear mind, open heart, present in the body—and then turn your focus to deeper body sensations. Tuning into deeper sensations (*interoception*) involves experiencing actual physiological sensations such as heartbeat, respiration, digestion, and the feeling of your skin connecting to the air around you. These living sensations in our bodies are the portal to real presence and awakening to a larger Presence. Try to sense any movement and stirring inside you without getting involved in explaining anything, attaching to it, or pushing it away. Over time, if you stay with the sensations, and stay out of stories and what you know as "feelings," you will sense into a flow of life force energy pervading your whole system that can help transmute those disruptive "lower" emotions (that typically keep us trapped in old patterns) into energy for growth.

To move further into open awareness, after sensing the flow of internal sensation and energy, expand your awareness to the space around your body, sensing the field of energy in which you sit. Think of it as expanding the container of awareness from a point of light directed at sensation to a room full of light and energy that absorbs it, and you. Moving away from focus on "me" at all helps take us beyond the Default Mode Network that constricts our brain's energy and information flow by repeating habitual patterns. Imagine resting in Awareness itself, the biggest wave field, and become One with the flow of intelligence all around and through you. You might feel a different kind of energy moving through you as you come into greater coherence internally and start to sync up with higher frequency energy around you.

Resting *in* and *as* this expansive Presence, with the heart in greater coherence, causes positive emotion to arise spontaneously. Allow yourself to be filled and expanded by this higher frequency energy but maintain the stance of being Awareness itself—aligned within and with the unified field of intelligence. New information or insight may arrive as a gift. Just note it, and return to being Awareness. If you need it, a repetitive prayer, word, or *mantra*, can occupy the king's attention while you experience the queen's generous Presence. With practice, the straight path gets easier. More moments of "dropping in," whether through meditation or centering prayer or something else, strengthen this circuitry. Even a few minutes here is good for you.

When the Straight Path is not Enough

In addition to the straight path, most of us need to work on clearing away our habitual distractions to resting in the queen's open awareness. This is the circuitous route. As we practice the straight path of accessing a more unitive state of open awareness, inevitably we "meet the dragon." If we have not done much work to understand the habitual movements of each of our centers of intelligence and what they serve to protect, these energies will rise up to meet us as soon as we even *plan* to sit still. The body contains *all* the energies (and all the points around the Symbol) that can animate our being, as chaos and potential. This includes the embedded patterns of mind, feelings, and senses, as well as latent instinct and sexual energy; so, there is a lot to face and integrate.

Gurdjieff located force 2 (our queen) in the spinal column, and he related it to those seven "receivers", or "centers of gravity" mentioned above, which are like fragments of our centers of intelligence. These are "deflection points" because they distort and interrupt the flow of intelligence that is always trying to move through us. According to both ancient and modern sources we do have "intelligent" centers in the body, each like a little brain, under control of the autonomic (automatic) nervous system. These are specific points where information (energetic, chemical, and hormonal) is processed according to past programs. Just as is true for the main centers of intelligence we have been studying, relaxing the programs in these other fragmented pieces allows for an unobstructed flow of energy and informa-tion through and between all of them, up and down the spine.

Gurdjieff's framework requires us to clear and align five "lower" centers of intelligence (remember the body center is divided into three parts) to access the two "higher" ones, through our whole integrated being. From the perspective of Chinese medicine, first harmonizing five organ systems is necessary to open the Way between heaven and earth. The Hindu framework of seven *chakras* in the body also relates to seven concentrations of nerves, organ systems, neurotransmitters, and hormones distributed throughout the brain and body that can become blocked or distorted.[204] In yoga philosophy, these seven *chakras* or centers are related to seven dimensions or levels of consciousness we travel through toward unitive consciousness with the Divine. And Tomberg, the Christian Hermetic philosopher, equates the same centers with the seven "I am" names of Jesus in the Gospel that map the history of seven stages of the revelation in the world of the divine mission and essence of Jesus Christ.[205]

So there are different ways to understand what needs to happen here to enable the queen's *open awareness* by promoting a healthy flow of diverse intelligence through a clear and integrated system. But they are all generally about opening the inner flow of energy and information that is central to health and well-being, as well as to creating greater coherence and connection with others, the natural world and, vertically, with the Source of Creation. The Enneagram Symbol gives us a somewhat neutral model for clearing the way to the "I am" of Being. It integrates the seven primary modes of feeling and imagination, with the three creative centers, into one integrated higher self or essence.

To work with this model, imagine the points around the Enneagram running up your torso. Use the *chakra* locations if you know them but include a "secret" sixth center in the middle-back of your head, putting the seventh at your "third eye," and an eighth center above your head, as your bridge to Source, God, or creative, unitive consciousness. I think of the ninth center as both the ground of Being from which we emerge and begin any meditation, and also a sphere of energy all around us, connecting us to *All that Is*—the *alpha* and *omega*.[206] We are going to bring the creative process of the three forces to each one of the points. The essence of the Law of Three is that everything has the potential to call out more from and through itself—to *re-order its chaos* into a more coherent and higher level of functioning and unlock the overall *flow* of intelligence.

Along the horizontal and human layer of the journey, each of the passions (sins) represents a wired-in emotional and motivational state that sneaks up and derails all of us at times. Unresolved emotions, and memories connected to them, contribute to greater stress and chaos that keeps us attached to our personality as a coping mechanism. While your Enneagram type passion may be dominant, each passion plays its part. And when we follow them around the circle, they have a way of drawing us deeper into our unique inner experience, revealing more about who we are and what needs to be integrated for us to grow. Working with emotion is a chief source of all growth. Its integration is necessary to unhooking from the central delusion that is our limiting false and separate "self" so that we may Realize our true self and purpose here.

We could approach this work mentally by identifying the embedded beliefs developed from past challenges that give rise to the emotions we most often experience (everything from "this should be different" to "I'm not enough"), and then working to shift the beliefs to relax the driving nature of each hijacking passion. A deliberate practice of catching and questioning the habitual stories we tell ourselves can start to rewire the circuitry that goes from belief to emotional reaction. But this is hard work, takes time, and often doesn't sustain itself without getting to the emotion and energetic root of these stories. The mind does not have access to the stuck energy that perpetuates the pattern. With practices like qigong and meditation, however, we can bypass the mind and approach the energy of the point directly. Applying our three forces to the stuck energy of each point, in a particular way, can help release fixed patterns and open the flow of intelligence through our whole system.

This practice applies the pillars of *focused attention* and *open awareness,* linked with *kind intention,* to disperse the blocked energy at each point/center, link up with a broader flow of potential, and shape this flow with a higher-order aim to revise the old pattern. Qigong uses sound (chanting) to accomplish this three-step progression. The first sound is directed deeply into the fixed energy pattern that exists in an organ system (like the old king) to break up past conditioning and disperse the energetic block. The second sound is used to return that broken-up energy to the ever-present unified field of energy—the queen's flow. The third sound links focus and flow to intentionally shape the now more flowing energy with a higher or spiritual aim that can help transform the compost of the old pattern into something new, like the lotus flower that grows out of the mud.

The good news is that you don't have to chant in order to apply the formula. You can use the three pillars of Presence in a practice that strengthens all pillars, while (in time) clearing conditioned patterns and opening the central channel of intelligence that will allow for a full experience of integrated being and the queen's open awareness. As each center is retrained, there is a gradual increase in energy and information up and down the body, as well as an increase in resonance with spirit and the natural world. The Law of Seven actually describes the rate of change in the frequency of vibration as we unlock this flow and transition from low vibration energy (dense matter) to increasingly higher vibration energy. This is the same rate of change in frequency through the rainbow progression of visible color or along the scale of sound (that's why the Do-Re-Mi...is laid out around the circle). But you don't have to understand how that works to practice and experience the benefit of this meditation. All of these ideas will make more sense over time as they are revealed through your own practice and inner experience.

Journey Meditation: Collecting Notes, Creating Coherence

To begin, as always, come to ground through your three primary centers with clear head, open heart, relaxed body, finding your breath as an anchor to the present moment. Return to this anchor at any moment you notice you are lost in distracting stories or feelings. It is always good to invoke your connection to the Earth or the ground of Being here, and imagine a bubble of protection around you, symbolized by the point 9 at the beginning and end of the journey. Next, focus your attention in the first energy center, at the base of your spine; not analyzing, but rather receiving any sensation, information, imagery, or feeling related to this point in your body. You can work with what comes up for you specifically there, or you can use the Enneagram as a guide and focus on the passion of Anger.

To work with the passion of Anger, imagine a scenario in which you strongly felt this point 1 orientation of "standing against" reality—thinking and feeling that you, or someone or something else, should *not* be the way it is. Imagine just enough detail to experience the feelings and sensations of what this is like for you. Maintain your focus and do not get lost in the story or try to change anything with your mind. Simply sense the Anger-against as energy in your body. Feel into the sensation itself, where it is, how and whether it moves. Notice if it has a color, a shape or symbol, and any specific imagery associated with it. Name your experience, but don't judge or get lost in it, stay with the sensations in your body.

Staying with this first center, now shift to the pillar of open aware-ness. Expand your attention from the point and its specific imagery or sensation to a huge field of awareness surrounding it (and you). Bringing an expansive and benevolent Presence to your own suffering is key to surfing these waves of passion and how they express themselves in our pain bodies. Rest the analytical mind and become One with the spacious field of energy surrounding your body in the area where you were focusing (or your whole body, or the whole room and beyond, if it's that big). Allow this expansive Presence to absorb you and your prior focus entirely. You'll find your way to do this over time.

This resting-but-awake brainwave state takes us beyond the Default Mode Network into the Void of no self, the womb of the Great Mother. We can only influence the unconscious processes that drive us by getting beyond the knowns that our mind gets caught in, so resting in this expansive Presence is not only relaxing but also links you up with the underlying field of intelligence in the Universe. While you are not trying to fix anything or figure out what you observed in the first center *at all*, new information may be gifted to you as insight or intuition. Just note it and return to the flow. Positive emotion arises when the heart and mind are in greater coherence, and this will further raise your frequency and resonance with the underlying field of intelligence. Even a few minutes here is good for you.

After hanging out in that gap between curves for a few minutes (or however long it takes to sense this larger flow), bring the king and queen together again with a heroic kind intention to *re-order the chaos* deliberately. From your relaxed and open state, ask the question: *Instead of my habitual reaction, what would I like to experience when triggered by the things that threaten my personality, invoking aversion?* Instead of assigning yourself a new "should" here, just ask this greater intelligence you have tapped into: *what would be a kinder (to you and others) response?* See what shows up. It may come in the form of an idea, feeling, image, song, or something else; or you can just imagine briefly what you might think, feel, do from this state.

Next, choose a symbol that represents to you this new state (according to the map, a state of Serenity). At point 1, I like to imagine myself as a great tree with roots extending to the center of the Earth. When I know myself as anchored in the Earth and part of the flow of Being, I find the solidity and serenity to not have to resist anything that blows at or through me. Then I can see clearly and respond thoughtfully from a wiser perspective. As you find your symbol, try to feel the emotion connected to the intended response; feel it, as if it's happening *now*. Remember that the mind sends a signal to order your experience, and feelings attract more energy. This allows new information to flow to that center, build new connections between neurons, and create new habits. Also, the symbol will give you a short-cut to an integrated *ideal + feeling* state to access quickly the next time you find yourself visited by the "god of Anger." Eventually, you won't need to think up a desired state. Just skip right to the symbol you have chosen and amplify the feelings that come with it to retrain the center.

That's the process, in detail, to apply at each point. Proceed up the central channel of your body, as stated above, from the base of your spine to the top of your head, through the seven points (or centers), imagining the eighth above your head and the ninth as a bubble and field of energy connecting you to the flow of life around you. You can see what specifically arises for you in each center of focus, but the passions provide a useful map to orient us to what we might be looking for. Doing the practice on a regular basis should help to rewire habitual responses (and brain circuitry), decrease reactivity and stress, increase coherence in the heart and brain, and develop your connection with Source if that is meaningful to you. I imagine this is something like the Christian desert monks were doing when working with the seven deadly sins to unblock their connection with God and open the vertical dimension.

Ideally you will listen to the energy of the center itself (*what shows up when you focus there?*) and observe how each point manifests in your own life, but the Enneagram does provide a good map to get us started:

At **Point 1**, working with Anger—standing against "what's wrong"—to find the Serenity to embrace diversity and chaos, and move into the inevitable challenge and change of life.

At **Point 2**, working with Pride—that you can and should already be a ruler—to reach a Humility that reminds you to first do your own work. Remember when that point in the heart awakens, its first movement is to learn to receive.

At **Point 3**, working with Deceit—how you adapt and strive to maintain a sense of a significance—to realize your integrated being in Presence (Veracity), in alignment with the intelligent pattern of Creation that calls out of us *something more* than we can imagine.

At **Point 4**, working with Envy—how your desire to be some "one" causes suffering, paradoxically limiting your true nature and value—to realize an

Equanimity that holds a neutral center, in the face of desire and aversion, and provides entry to the higher heart field.

At **Point 5**, working with Avarice—the drive to contain your energy (stay in a closed loop system) and maintain separation and security—to realize Non-attachment and the wisdom that arises from knowing you are an aspect of the intelligent flow of Being.

At **Point 6**, working with Fear—uncertainty about how to be ok in the face of chaos and tyranny as you grow beyond ego—to find the Courage and strength to *stand in the middle* with faith in the intelligent pattern that reveals a Way for higher-order solutions.

At **Point 7**, working with Gluttony—the drive to use "your" magic and creative power for greater personal experience and escape—to live in Sobriety from ego needs and discern your real work in the world as a model for *two world mastery* and the sacred magic it enables.

At **Point 8**, working with Lust—the desire for greater intensity and control to defend and protect the world your way—to remember the Innocence that spontaneously receives guidance and plays with Creation, imagining the best without any attachment to outcomes.

At **Point 9**, working with Sloth—the temptation to ignore the depth and complexity of this whole journey for the small self's comfort—to realize Right Action, the continuous practice of revivifying yourself and the world through aligning with the laws and making a Way for Love.

Most important in this journey meditation is to choose a symbol for each center that is meaningful to you and helps you *feel* the energy of the virtue and awakened qualities of the point. A symbol is a visual intention and summary of energy and information. Symbols also serve as bridges that connect us to a deeper realm of meaning and possibility. You can use mythic or superhero symbols, religious symbols, or other images that hold meaning for you, like my tree/roots. Over time, what has emerged for me is a spontaneous mix of religious and mythic images, and things from the natural world. Don't work to make these symbols and feelings happen, see what comes up for you, and you might be pleasantly surprised.

As I was finding my symbol at point 3 (angling toward the veracity of integrated being as a clear channel for higher intelligence), I was "given" a diamond necklace to wear. This image seemed a bit out of place compared to the other symbols that showed up for me, but when I put the necklace on (in my imagination), it felt something like owning my inherent dignity and value through the flow of divine energy I felt with my *being* in alignment. I wanted to sit up even straighter each time I put it on. So I stayed with it. Nearly two years later I stumbled upon a poem fragment from Rumi, the great Sufi mystic, that made me smile in recognition:

> *You wander from room to room*
> *Hunting for the diamond necklace*
> *That is already around your neck*

When we are at Home in ourselves, without the ego's striving, we experience qualities of Being that are always already there, and in which the spark of imagination can take flight. So relax and listen to what your soul has to offer. Enjoy the movie! The hero in essence *plays* with Creation. Above all else, remember to extend heroic kindness to yourself as you move intentionally through each point, looking at how the passion or energy of that point shows up in your life. These are normal human reactions to the trials of life! And always finish the journey as our heroes do, with Innocence that allows for spontaneous play, inner- and interconnectedness, knowing that the next Right Action will reveal itself. All you have left to do is to be grateful for what you *know* will be. Let go and rest again in open awareness for a few minutes, leaving any outcome or agenda to the universal flow of intelligence and its innate drive for healing and wholeness.[207]

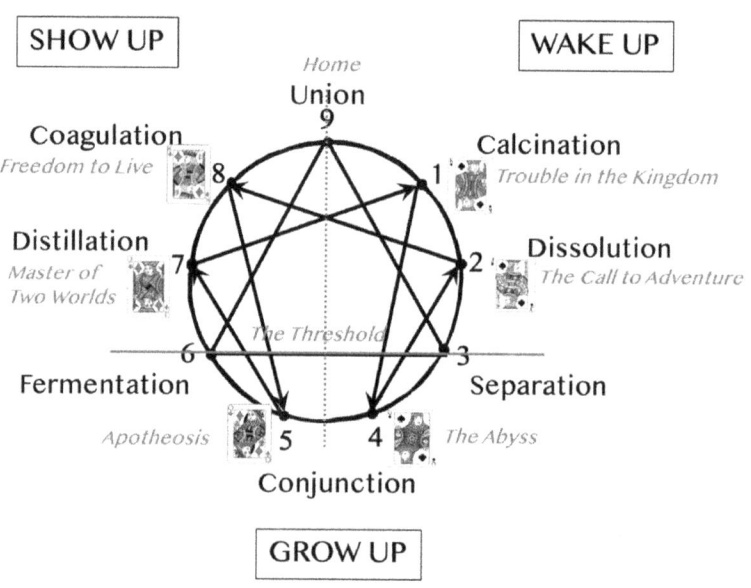

SHOW UP

WAKE UP

Home

Union
9

Coagulation
Freedom to Live

8

Calcination

Calcination
Trouble in the Kingdom

1

Distillation
*Master of
Two Worlds*

7

Dissolution
The Call to Adventure

2

The Threshold

6

3

Fermentation
Apotheosis

5

4

Separation
The Abyss

Conjunction

GROW UP

CHAPTER 21

The Alchemy of the Symbol

The enneagram is perpetuum mobile, the perpetual motion that people have sought since the remotest antiquity and could never find...The understanding of this symbol and the ability to make use of it can give a person tremendous power. It is at once perpetual motion as well as the philosopher's stone of the alchemists.[208]

~ G.I. Gurdjieff

A s we gain experience inhabiting and applying all three forces, we can use this powerful inner triangle along the seven steps of the journey to consciously integrate the Laws of Three, Seven, and One. We are now better equipped to weave the hexad arrow lines with the journey around the Symbol to fulfill more of our heroic potential, promoting harmony within ourselves and communities. To explore how this might work, we will invoke the wisdom of the ancient Hermetic philosophers and the related practice of alchemy. The aim of Hermeticism was to reveal a shared truth underlying all religious and philosophical approaches—a perennial philosophy. And alchemy refers to a related set of practices or a "recipe" for refining or "spiritualizing" matter based on this shared truth and the original pattern of Creation.

Not exclusive to one religion or philosophy, the alchemical worldview emerged in ancient cultures ranging from China to India, Persia, Arabia, Egypt, and Europe.[209] Alchemists were attempting to show the correspondence between the Above and Below by transforming coarse material into fine ("turning lead into gold"), but along the way they discovered a kind of science of the soul, the goal of which is to evolve the spiritual nature of humankind. True alchemists transformed themselves into the exploratory hero who embodies the creative pattern, aligning with a power beyond the individual self to evolve *something more*. In fact, it seemed that without the development of one's own soul into an integrated creative vehicle, the alchemical process yielded no treasure.

Carl Jung was drawn to the ancient art of alchemy as its symbolism echoed archetypal patterns he observed in the human psyche. He had one of the largest libraries of ancient alchemical texts in existence at the time, most of which read like myths, with the king and queen playing central roles in the transformation of matter. And while some thought alchemy to be heretical, Jung found that the Old Masters were not only *not* critical of church doctrine, but also believed their discoveries would prove that the mysteries of faith were reflected in the natural world. And indeed, following Jung's trail through alchemy, and both through Gurdjieff's teaching, the myths, science, and the architecture of the Symbol, left me in awe of the wonder of Creation itself that yields its patterns to penetrating study of all kinds, whether focused within us or spanning the cosmos.

The alchemical process we will follow is rooted in the cryptic formula laid down in the Emerald Tablet that Gurdjieff linked with the Enneagram. We explored its stages briefly, and through metaphor, along the hero's journey. The seven stages describe a primary process in each interval that forwards the octave of growth and resolves in the creation of *the philosopher's stone* and state of union with the Divine.[210] The central formula of alchemy—*solve et coagula*—is a version of the Law of Three process at the center of the Symbol. We must first *solve* or dissolve what is fixed from more subtle elements, then "coagulate" or re-integrate opposing forces into a "higher" or more refined whole.

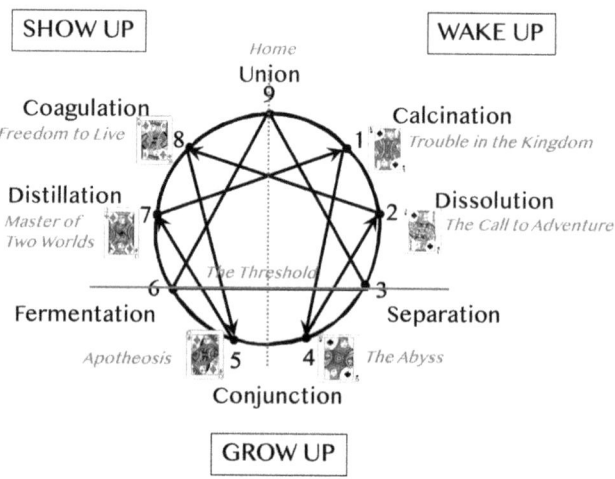

In addition to the phases of alchemy, as we move around the Symbol, each side of the developing inner triangle adds a layer of work and marks a shift that enables the continued journey around the circle. In part two of the book, we followed Joseph Campbell's names for these three stages of the journey: Separation, Initiation, and Return. In the Hermetic tradition we would travel this same path through stages of Purification (of ego), Illumination (of higher self), and Union (with others and with Source). For Gurdjieff each of these is an "octave" that kicks off a new "Do" note and layer of the work, and each requires a new type of "food" to keep the operation turning. I think about the three stages as: Wake Up, Grow Up, and Show Up.

The stages are hierarchical in that some level of mastery in one is required for the next, but they are not exactly sequential. They are like layers of a cake that also interweave as they build into a coherent whole picture that restores Unity and elevates the whole system. We have been tracking these layers as: first, a horizontal and human layer that continues throughout the journey to purify ego and integrate all parts into a unified soul or essence; second, a vertical and spiritual layer of growth through which the increasingly unified soul accesses her spiritual nature and connection to higher intelligence; and a third layer of "making two worlds one"—linking these two dimensions by bringing Spirit alive in the created world (through the developed hero) in a way that further transforms both the hero and the kingdom. And there is a fourth "higher" outcome of an even higher-level law of three process that lifts the developed body-soul-spirit vehicle into total union with the Source of Creation.

While our unified Presence—aligned mind-heart-body symbolized by the creative inner triangle—is developed and applied all along the journey, each of the layers of work noted above emphasizes a certain orientation or "pillar" of three-centered Presence: the linking practice of *intentional kindness* symbolized by the hero, the *open awareness* of the queen, and the king's *focused attention*. This will make more sense as we track how the inner triangle of unified being and Presence, flexibly applied, interacts with the hexad line of spirit to help us stretch into higher being, heart, and consciousness on the alchemical journey. Although this will involve some review, hopefully, the repetition will be welcome as we continue to sort out the meaning and relevance of the laws.

WAKING UP

The first part of the journey wakes up a potential hero from the trance of ego to launch a law of three process along the right side of the Symbol that takes apart the old structure. This phase includes the alchemical processes of the *calcination* of the king, *dissolution* in the waters of the queen, and begins a *separation* of the forces from the "body" of the ego that sends the hero first over the threshold between worlds, and later into the Void. To set the stage again: at the outset of the journey, we do not inhabit our primary centers of intelligence in an integrated and aligned manner, so we have no "inner triangle." Instead, we have three fragments of these centers whose habitual interaction locks them into a repetitive dance that perpetuates the inner split.

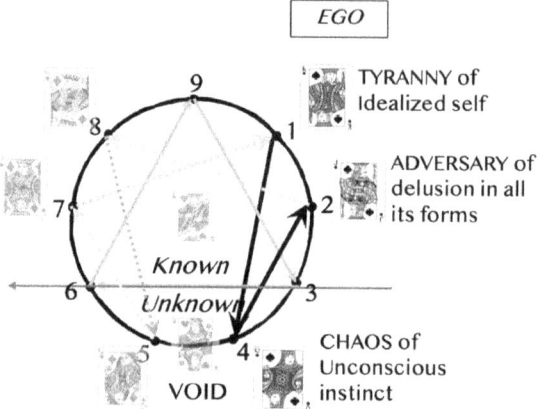

We can think of the tyrannical king as our ego ideal and fixation, the ruling principle of ego and the "mind" that orders our experience and behavior. The king was once a heroic solution for how to balance Culture and Nature to get along in our young lives, but it has become controlling, stagnant, and limiting. It is literally "fixed" in neurobiological habit patterns that maintain type structure and attempt to keep out unconscious threats to its dominance (chaos). When the king is off his game, our shadow parts rear their heads as emotional chaos and instinctual impulses, specific manifestations of the hidden aspects of our character that react against the king's order. The rise of these dragons of chaos from below creates opportunity for the passionate adversary (with its driving need to take over the kingdom), who proceeds to hijack the heart and suppress the potential hero who might leave the kingdom and go on the journey to deconstruct this old pattern. The efforts of the adversary actually reinforce the fixation and control of the king, who regathers his force and represses the chaos rising from below.

The passion and fixation of our Enneagram type are like the original "hostile brothers" who fuel one another in competition for the kingdom. They have very different styles, but essentially the same agenda. Most importantly their dynamic distracts us from the truly disruptive chaos below and helps the system maintain its structure—the dysfunctional equilibrium among all three players and the delusion that our ego strategy "works" for us. There is no real hero, no third force capacity to reconcile the tension between tyranny and chaos and invite greater intelligence to evolve the triad. In fact, this whole system was devised to suppress and protect the soul child of the would-be hero who went into hiding long ago. The deconstruction of this fixed operating system kicks off with the calcination of the king.

Calcination refers to heating a solid compound for the purpose of decomposing it and removing impurities. To counter the old king's rigid control of the ego structure, we can heat things up by using his stagnant force actively, paradoxically, to throw our attention into the "opposing" unconscious domain of the queen. The hexad line of spirit is always offering these opportunities to wake up anyway, along that 1->4 arrow line. Life and change always come knocking to burn the king and reveal his limitations, because he represents a model stuck in the past. Most of us recover from these assaults to our ego ideal that reveal shadow by fleeing the unconscious unknown back to the known world. In doing so, we become the adversary of our own potential. But even when we scamper back, we may still feel a tug from the unresolved material lurking below. Perhaps something in us knows that when things are no longer working so well, the solutions we need cannot be found in the old kingdom?

So instead of ignoring this tug that is calling us toward unseen truths and (eventually) greater wholeness, we can practice Serenity when things fall apart and get curious about what might evolve. When shadow rises, we can move toward it and practice Humility by inquiring into the role we play in our own drama, looking more deeply at what the ego has been up to, and noting the suffering it has caused. Even when we don't know what to do to update this broken system, we can invoke the heroic pillar of *kind intention* to first aim higher and hope for more, for ourselves and for the world. Having that wish upon a star provides a motivating force for the journey. And then, armed with self-compassion, we can begin to move away from past defensive patterns by cultivating a counterforce to our ego structure. Proceeding past point 2, towards the rumbling from point 4, is the sign of a hero willing to leave the kingdom, and it proceeds with the dissolution of the ego ideal in the waters of the queen below.

Dissolution is the process of dissolving the dried-out ashes of the old structures in something that will return life-giving moisture. This something is the undifferentiated flow of feelings, sensations, and impulses that starts to spill in as the ego structure is releasing. Of course, it does not necessarily feel life-giving and, in fact, can kick off a period of confusion, emotional chaos, and feelings of fragmentation, as the original unity of the ego is torn up. We fall apart, as they say, in four directions—meaning that all possible opposing aspects of our character (previously shut out of the kingdom) start to leak in. It seems a little crazy to invite this stuff, but when it is already calling from below and leaking out at inopportune times, it is a sign that the old structures are no longer sufficient in the face of our changing lives. And, the stories seem to say, it goes easier when the labor of ego deconstruction is chosen willingly.

An awakening hero (at point 3) embraces the challenge of the arrow line from point 1 to point 4 to engage polarity on purpose via the Law of Three. Employing the king's focus *within* the waters of the queen, to uncover the truth of one's being, begins to wake up a third force in the heart center not solely identified with either of the original two forces. If we can stay present with this paradox between ego ideal and revealed shadow (without running away), a higher intelligence comes to aid us along the journey. Campbell calls this higher intelligence *supernatural aid*, and we saw it as the mentor's efforts to initiate and support the hero's crossing. We can understand it as the organizing intelligence of Creation moving toward reunion, whether by accident or as the result of a potential hero attempting to make a Way for *something more* to arise in a polarized world.

So while we don't exactly initiate ourselves, as a developing hero we can aim higher, and we can invoke our own inner mentor to engage in conscious labor whether we step over the threshold into unknown terrain or are thrown over by circumstance. One way or another we must feed ourselves to the chaos below!

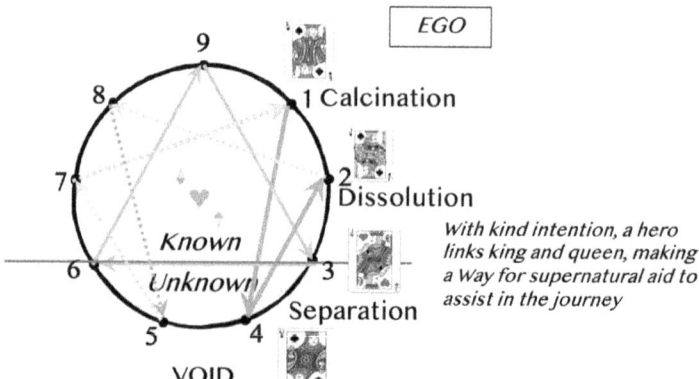

With kind intention, a hero links king and queen, making a Way for supernatural aid to assist in the journey

Conscious labor speaks to a particular orientation of our attention as an observer, within the broader domain of our inner experience that has been in shadow. This helps to forward the deconstruction of ego, but also, it is a stabilizing process that educates and prevents total overwhelm by unconscious contents initially. The capacity to observe our experience will help us to separate a bit from the chaos, establish Equanimity, and gain a "higher" perspective. With this curious observing stance, we can first learn more about our ego patterns and how they hijack our centers, and we gain a measure of choice. If our choice is to stay in Presence (instead of acting out the tyranny of old habits or dissolving in chaos), we grow the heroic capacity to *stand in the middle*, sacrifice the patterns of the past, and make a Way for new intelligence to shift our consciousness.

This is not easy. The road of trials between points 2 and 4 is a long interval, and it ends at the abyss! But through the alchemical process of *separation*, we can maintain a little objectivity as we tolerate the flow of feelings and information that arises with this inner discovery mission and sift through the remains of ego. As we observe each part of the ego's dance—how our thinking, feeling, and body centers operate—we are actually differentiating and amplifying the conflict among parts of ourselves. Again, this is not an intuitive move for most of us, as it increases the sense of fragmentation and discomfort. But the alchemical pattern, like the Law of Three, reminds us that higher-order growth (and renewing a broken system) requires that we first fully differentiate, understand, and embrace polarized positions, and *then* hold the tension of their opposition to invite new growth.

This is a good time to get to know the "dark" king, queen, and the adversary as habits of the lower mind, heart, and body (Enneagram fixation, passion, and dominant instinct), all devised to protect you as a child. While you might initially be horrified by the worst of their controlling or self-sabotaging behavior, remember the point is to own the shadow so it no longer owns *you*. You might then begin to appreciate how these parts developed to defend you initially. You can literally personify and have dialogue with each of them, something like: *How have you been trying to protect or serve me? How old do you think I am? And what would you rather be doing (if not this job)?* In keeping with the spirit of the Symbol, when we welcome all parts without judgment and begin to learn about why they are there and how they work, they are more inclined to cooperate and come under the leadership of a higher self or essence eventually.[211]

As these defensive parts of us relax, we will encounter deeper layers of the personal unconscious—all the "sins" that cause us suffering, as well as feelings and memories long repressed. Traversing these waters may seem treacherous, but the places where guilt, shame, fear, anger, and pain reside are like cracks in the ego structure that can lead us into the depths of our potential. While we are ultimately working to transform compulsive habits in each center, our feelings (which can be expressions of both the heart center and the instincts at this point of the journey) are a central leverage point for growth. Owning our vulnerability, opening the heart, and developing a "higher" heart—one that speaks a different language entirely—is essential for the work on the second half of the journey. In that paradoxical way that life seems to operate (according to the Law of Three), our gifts are connected to our wounds. But also, since our emotions are tightly tied to our ego, to become free of ego we have to change our relationship to feelings.

As Gurdjieff described it, our emotional reactions give rise to "a thousand petty attachments and identifications" that tie us to the small self, "each of which says 'I' and takes its place as king for a moment." When strong emotional drives arise, so does our sense of "me," "mine," and "I," the sense of a separate ego self that Buddhists would say is the root of all our suffering. Gurdjieff said that no inner development is possible when we are attached to our negative emotional reactivity, and at the same time most of us are unwilling to sacrifice our suffering. This idea seems strange at first pass, but we are attached to our suffering because it gives us a sense of self and is connected to our positions on justice, learning, and even creativity. This is something to think about for sure! Are you willing to sacrifice suffering...no matter what life or some bad actor throws at you? Given the central role and tenacity of challenging emotions in our lives, we must inquire into the full spectrum of emotional reactions to access our shadow and who we are beyond ego. But we do so in order to reclaim the power they steal when they control the kingdom.

The passions are represented by the many faces of the adversary that challenge the hero all along the way. And like our heroes, we learn in the end that we and our adversaries are one and the same. We are subject to *all* of these emotional and motivational drives, at times, and we need to know what we are capable of if we are to avoid being surprised and hijacked by them. That means all learning is good learning as we work to integrate all aspects of our shadow and emotional reactivity. Equally important is a curious and intentional kindness that can maintain Equanimity without fighting, fleeing, or freezing in response to what we uncover. The transmutation of passions (by not repressing them but not acting them out either) creates friction and energy to animate our growing "vessel" of Presence that will sustain us through all manner of rising tide ahead. This process is central to developing third force consciousness and the capacity to stay awake in each of our centers of intelligence that is the essence of Veracity or *being* truth.

When we have enough third force strength to stay present and resist attachment and aversion within *each* center of intelligence, we no longer automatically act out patterns of thinking, feeling, and reacting. In a very real sense, holding integrated, aware, compassionate Presence itself "sacrifices" the ego—the "body" of embedded patterns that organize the kingdom, keeping us separate from pain but also from our deeper potential. When we get to this point we have passed through "the crucible of acceptance," as Gurdjieff says it—the acceptance that "one can do nothing by oneself, but that nevertheless something has to be done."[212] This requires great determination and a profound understanding that there is no other way than this sacrifice, as the old ways do not work. With a new-found freedom from reactivity, then, we experience integration *among* centers, which allows us to move closer to the aligned center of our whole being, through which we can tap into "higher" intelligence. At point 4, at the edge of the Void, the work we have done to develop this aligned Presence ushers us into the second layer of work and the vertical dimension of growth in the Symbol.

The lower tetrahedron of the Merkaba provides us a visual image of the integration of the first four points into a vessel of greater psychic wholeness. Developing such an internal vessel was a key to the alchemical work and a secret not often taught overtly.[213] The four points of the tetrahedron represent aspects of our intelligence centers, but they are also four dimensions from which to experience life in Presence: height, width, depth, and the fourth dimension of time, which goes two ways. The development of this fourth dimension connects us (in the moment) to our evolutionary past (instinct) and our potential future (through intuition and imagination), revealing the door to a vertical axis of growth between our time-bound existence and what is timeless or eternal. That means that beyond this point, we can access a flow of higher intelligence and life energy that moves through and around us but is not "ours."

GROWING UP: INTEGRATING TWO PATHS

Growing "Up" (literally, in a vertical manner) begins with the "illumination" in the Void that we are far more than we understood in ego, and it confronts us with a new level of polarity to master (beyond shadow and light within) between the personal and the transpersonal dimensions. The prospect of vertical growth is invited by the potential hero's willingness to engage polarity by crossing the threshold into the unknown world to begin with, and it comes to fruition at point 7, as a real hero returns from the unknown to face the known world. We can learn more about the relationship between this vertical growth and the horizontal level of the alchemical process in the Symbol by tracking the two lines of development through the two paths of seven—*the line of knowing*, through the hexad lines, and *the line of being*, through the journey around the Symbol.

If the first part of the alchemical *separation* was about cleaving an inner observer from its fusion with ego patterns to take a higher perspective from which to view defensive strategies and inner material, the second phase of separation requires a hero to sacrifice the ego "body" fully, face the dragon queen (even deeper unconscious contents), and merge with the vast chaos of the Void. With this second separation, the king and queen (forces formerly entrapped in matter) release their grip on the body, but also, they are separated from *each other* to follow their different paths. A hero's sacrifice at point 4 takes us into the deepest realm of the queen (now unbounded chaos), as we stay the course around the circle, developing our vessel of Presence. Simultaneously, the king (the ordering force—in this case, the mind fixated on our ego ideal) rises along the hexad line of spirit. It doubles back from point 4 to point 2, and continues on to point 8, toward our higher aim and future benevolent ruler of consciousness. In the depths of the unknown, where the hero faces the dragon and finds treasure, the former king and/or mentor is always absent, existing only *in spirit*.

To make sense of what these two paths mean for our development, we can apply the Kabbalistic metaphor of two paths of growth through the Tree of Life, and consider the hexad lines as *the way of the flaming sword* and the circular path as *the way of the serpent*. This double-track version of the growth process clarifies many of the dynamics surrounding the Void, why it's always about facing the dragon, the "sacred marriage" that occurs, and the birth of another dimension of consciousness on the other side. It also gives us a prescription to avoid the spiritual bypass that might happen if we were to avoid doing the full work of the circular journey—to embrace our shadows and woundedness in the Void and empty and prepare our souls before reconnecting with a higher mind or spirit through the hexad lines.

Much like the *vajra*, the powerful sword-like weapon wielded against "serpents" by Indra, king of the heavenly beings in Hindu philosophy, the flaming sword of the Old Testament guards the gates of Paradise. Particularly after the fall of Adam and Eve, it serves to prevent those who would "take" from the Tree of Life, using it for personal power. The Tree of Life in the center of the walled garden (the state of perfect harmony between opposing forces) holds a secret in its rings (as do all trees) about the Way of combining horizontal and vertical growth (linking humanity and divinity). While we are not directly following the hexad lines and path of the flaming sword along the hero's journey, if we align humbly with its teachings, it will connect us with a higher mind and spirit. And it will provide some insurance against the ego adversary who is always lurking to derail our highest intentions with a more personal will that would take from that tree and misuse its secrets.

On the right half of the journey, although we moved around the circle (9-1-2-gap-4) unlocking each center fragment or "note" to begin to develop our unified soul vessel, we also embraced the "theory" of the arrow lines from an inner perspective: inviting the flaming sword 1—>4 to produce friction, help calcinate and burn up ego, and then cleave a conscious observer to help sort the remains of dissolving ego structures. We are not equipped to wield the sword here, but we can choose to "go with" its energy (as a kind of mentor), and towards our fate, when the dragon of chaos bursts into our lives and the ego is burned. We can also call on this weapon to help sacrifice the false self, fall into the Void, and free the shadow king and queen to evolve beyond their roles under ego. After that point, the sword (and the focused attention of the king) has its own development trajectory.

Our fixed beliefs and former ways of knowing ourselves can't help us grow through this passage. They get in the way of a necessary surrender. And anyway, once a certain amount of unconscious material is surfaced, the way the ego ideal used to operate is no longer available. To sacrifice the structure of your ego and become One with the greater field and flow of Being is the only way through the Void. So the first movement along that vertical axis is *down*, into the chaos. In this model, the way to transformation is always through a reconciliation with the repressed and rejected parts of ourselves, and at this point the raw energy of our instinctual and cultural heritage must be faced, felt, and transmuted as well, if we are to "ride the dragon" and employ its energy toward higher (non-egoic) service. Engagement with these depths in the Void can bring us face-to-face with everything from aggression and sexuality, massive existential fear, the need to conserve and contain oneself, and eventually, utter annihilation. And all those energies may be in conflict.

The arrow lines suggest that the thing we *can* do with our former "mind" ahead of this appointment with chaos is to send it, with a prayer or wish upon that future star again, along the path of the flaming sword's arrow lines from 4 to 2 to 8, to await our soul's further preparation via the *way of the serpent* around the circle. Holding the intention of an evolved king and kingdom (higher consciousness and how we will live and serve from fully integrated essence), even with our limited vision on this side of the Void, is helpful. And then, as the stories imply, a higher mind may go with us in spirit, as Holy Hope due to the laws and the pattern that says *something more* can emerge from sacrifice and the subsequent re-integration of what has been in the dark.

The way of the serpent also has Biblical associations as that which leads to the fall and exile from the balanced garden of Paradise into the land of duality. The serpent represents our attachment to the material world that obscures our higher or divine nature. But we are human, have bodies, and need to integrate this "horizontal" world too as an aspect of the One. The separation of humanity and divinity is a necessary prerequisite to the eventual re-unification that gives birth to integrative consciousness as the incarnation of the Word through humanity. The fall has to happen. The way of the serpent marks an essential process of soul development that involves collecting all the pieces of our nature fragmented in that fall. As our souls become more whole, we remember ourselves as an integral part of Great Nature and the regenerative pattern that yields something from nothing. It is this re-membering of parts that makes possible the union with spirit and the birth of permanent, integrative, third force consciousness across the Void. Holiness is not about perfection, it seems, but wholeness.

One way to understand the metaphor of the serpent is as the sinuous shape of our DNA. Some combination of learned and inherited patterns encoded in our genes has altered our being in a way that obscures the flow of intelligence and light that is possible to hold. We have to witness old wounds and embrace shadows to clear these obstructions and fully inhabit our soul's potential. Similarly, in Chinese medicine the body is animated by rivers of flowing energy called meridians. Health is mediated by an open flow. Blocked energy is stagnant and leads to imbalance and disease. If you think about rivers blocked with sludge, you can imagine they also look like dark sinuous lines, roots, or maybe...serpents? To heal, we actually have to go into these blocks and unclog the lines. As we invoke the open awareness of the queen and drop beyond the mind, deeper into the body and sensation, we meet these energy blocks as "serpents" that must be broken up and linked with the vast flow of healthy chi in the Universe.

Many people who travel beyond the Default Mode Network encounter not just their own history that needs to be healed and integrated, but also ancestral pain and archetypal shadows, as well as the raw power of instinct that was repressed by personality. This may be the inner equivalent of loving your enemies while they are persecuting you. It is easy to talk about, hard to do, and can be frightening and even traumatizing if you don't understand where you are on the map. Not much makes sense at this stage of the journey, and it is not uncommon to have feelings of being fragmented, lost, or even wanting to not exist at all. It is important to understand this as a temporary manifestation of the pattern of Creation that needs chaos for the emergence of new order. There is a longing for the queen's receptive, enveloping, open awareness...even though dissolving into the further reaches of chaos seems to promise only an inner experience of the collective horror of which humankind is capable.

But if we somehow remember to meet it all with Equanimity and Non-attachment, learning to ride this dragon harnesses a great deal of energy for growth. As the last of the "lower" centers of intelligence, the integration of the sexual aspect of the body center helps weave together all polarity here in the unification of our humanity that opens the door to divinity. As the lower centers of intelligence are freed from the ego's compulsive actions, and the body's wisdom comes into alignment, there is no more shadow, no more resistance, no more separation, and so no triggers to distort our centers and cut off the greater flow of loving intelligence. Here in the depths of the Void, experiencing the wholeness of Being itself reawakens our own "whole" being, our soul or essence, that knows itself as One with *All that Is.*

In Enneagram terms, one's essence is that with which we were born that, although dormant, remains uncorrupted by our culture. Jung characterized this part of the individuation process as uniting with the inner feminine (*anima* or soul) because of its "hidden" nature, deep within, and because when we integrate our "opposite" in the depths of the unconscious, there is always a new birth. But again, this is a gender-less concept. While the further reaches of this unconscious domain are in the realm of "the queen" in mythology as well, it is a field of *undifferentiated* chaos. It is the "first matter" or *prima materia* that includes the "ashes" of the dead king, the quest for power symbolized by the pursuing adversary, primal instinctual drives, and much much more. The Void is a place where *all* opposites exist together in the greater flow of Being. It is also the "living water" of Creation from which new life arises, but only by swimming through chaos do we find that this dark realm of sludge is also a sea of great potential—the soul of the world or *anima mundi* that grants us, as Jung said, "a vision of deeper things."

Here one can tap into wisdom beyond the personal, including an understanding of universal organizing principles (archetypes) and patterns of life, like the laws of the Symbol, that reveal the mysteries of birth, death, and renewal unfolding through us. This deeper wisdom can help us make sense of our lives and our losses, experience great empathy for ourselves and others, and it can help guide us through dark times with the understanding that new life arises from the deconstructed state of interbeing. In the Hermetic tradition, such wisdom was thought to be inscribed magically in a region between heaven and earth—"the sanctuary of the everlasting zones"—that could not be seized by the intellectual mind.[214] So the queen's open awareness, the expansive force and unifying flow, rules the day here. At the same time, she is also the portal to *something more* from the vertical realm.

The alchemical stage of *conjunction* in the Void describes a multi-layered process of "marrying" all opposing forces within. The initial conjunction between the hero and undifferentiated chaos/flow of our unconscious depths in the Void (*meeting the goddess*) accomplishes a revival of our soul's essence, an aspect of the Great Mother through which we are connected to all others, the natural world, and the ground of Being. I associated this *flow* with a "universal heart" because aspects of the higher heart center, virtues and positive feelings like awe, wonder, connectedness, and love arise naturally when we are able to rest in the open awareness of the queen. Her breath becomes ours as we surrender into this unifying intelligence beneath the waves of feelings, sensations, and desires...and it is transformative.

The second conjunction unfolds from the first. As we surrender and become one with the sea of intelligence underlying material existence, the soul child or baby essence in us not only remembers its greater *being*, but also hooks us into higher *knowing* or spirit. Although we went "down" through the body and instincts into collective ways of being One with *All that Is*, there is a somewhat surprising experience of reaching "up" as well, or being touched by the transcendent with insight, inspiration, and the emergence of a new way of *knowing*. At-one-ment with the Father describes a marriage between the emerging soul and spirit that is tasted in the Void. Our souls begin to grow "up" here with the experience that, as Campbell writes, "the father and mother reflect each other, and are in essence the same."[215]

What happens for individuals is unique, but something is illuminated when we tap into our hidden wholeness: a divine spark of consciousness, the recognition of our unique creative imagination and intelligence, and the possibility of new life. Campbell writes further, "The paradox of creation, the coming of the forms of time out of eternity, is the germinal secret of the father. It can never quite be explained."[216] And yet...of course! We access the light that creates life out of the Void only by entering the primordial *chaos* from which it is drawn.

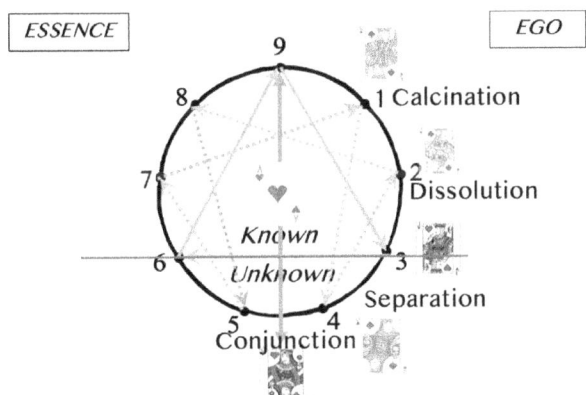

Becoming One with the flow of Being through the queen's open awareness gives access to the vertical dimension and higher intelligence

Profound states and visions of possibility, including a new sense of one's gifts and purpose in the world are not uncommon in these transits through the Void. But while dipping into the queen's sea of potential through open awareness is healing and mind-expanding, we are not meant to live there. The light of consciousness sparked in the Void must be developed and raised up further, along with essence, if we are to bring our gifts to fruition for the world. So we must keep moving.

The journey of the hero is about integrating forces and worlds. Neither extreme is healthy. On the back half the journey "higher" versions of the two forces, still symbolized by king and queen, will work *together* through the awakened hero. The conjunction in the Void results in the birth of a new level of integrative third force consciousness, more skilled at unifying opposing forces. Not only shadow and light, but also inner masculine and feminine forces, spirit and soul, are coming together into a kind of "feeling mind" or "loving intelligence" that will be perfected through further operations, beyond intuition into a higher kind of *knowing* or *gnosis* of Reality. This third conjunction (the birth) is the real *treasure* the hero lifts from the Void, and it sets the stage for the work ahead.

This is a point of great importance in our developmental process. If we don't have a map, we can confuse the spiritual depths and heights we might experience in the Void as the journey's destination. In fact, you can drown here. Some people get lost in unconscious contents for years and can't manage their day-to-day lives. Some become spiritually addicted, chasing the high; others grow increasingly arrogant and separate from "ordinary" life, and are in danger of using their now-more-aligned will for personal power. What makes a hero is marshalling the *kind intention* to link opposing forces, continually. It is the courageous engagement with feelings, instincts, and the collective unconscious that helps us come to awareness of the breadth and depth of our being *and* the attunement of our consciousness to a higher mind that can use loving intelligence to help make flowing order from chaos.

Although we may taste the transcendent in these passages through the Void, we have more ground to cover before we finally break free of the conditioned morality of a personal will and Real-ize the conjunction between our developing souls and higher mind, the Great Father, and reflection of the spiritual order informing reality (the *Logos*). But we are off to a good start when we reach point 5, on the far side of the Void. As the path of the flaming sword (the hexad line) reunites with the way of the serpent (the circular journey), we step through the door that links the Above and Below into a new dimension of consciousness in which we can partner more directly and thoughtfully with that sword. As a result, something from the star we wished upon at point 8 (way back at the beginning of the journey) "calls" or ignites in the awakening hero that divine spark of the original creative capacity that makes the world.

The Lesser Stone

As we learned along the journey, in alchemical terms, the *treasure* (or boon, or elixir; sometimes an awakened princess) lifted from the Void is the "baby" of the reunited king and queen, otherwise known as "the lesser stone." It is not yet the philosopher's stone, the ultimate goal of alchemy and spiritual "gold" said to supply eternal life. On our map, the queen of diamonds is used at point 5 to symbolize birth, emergence, or a kind of gift from the unknown realm. What is born is neither "feminine" nor "masculine," but rather our integrated being with a permanent third force consciousness that can hold divergent points of view to help transmute polarity into higher-order union. Jung called it "the transcendent function." Although this is a great leap in conscious being, according to the alchemists this "baby" is a mercurial and rather fledgling substance, and needs a good deal more work.

While the lesser stone will eventually become the beautiful phoenix that rises from ashes, the alchemists regarded it at this stage as more of a just-born worm. This is not to minimize the significance of the moment entirely, however. Not only is the developing soul in touch with new wisdom, but also our engagement with challenge has changed the "world" we are in on this side of the journey. Since we don't see the world as it is, but rather as *we* are, we are in a different reality where the underlying backdrop of Unity is more accessible, and the constituent elements of Creation are not so separate. King and queen mingle in the re-born hero. As we saw in our hero stories, it can be tough to distinguish here between good and bad, friends and enemies, known and unknown, and even the Above and Below take on different meaning on this side of the journey. This can be very confusing and, at times, dispiriting. We don't yet know how to orient and how to operate in this new terrain.

On the right side of the Symbol, rooted in our ego ideal, we were navigating between our known worldview and understanding of ourselves and the unknown world of both our inner unconscious material and our untapped potential, but it was still a "flat" earth, so to speak. From the integrated center of our being, the tree of life grows vertically as well as horizontally. We can understand the "Below" now as our soul's connection to the deeper flow of intelligence we tap when in union with others and in touch with the aliveness of the natural world. And with our divine spark lit, our imagination can now reach far beyond culture and the letter of the law towards the spirit of a higher unifying *Logos* in the "Above." And truly, these realms are not even so distinct at this level, but rather flow into one another as the ever-regenerating ground of Being, the unified field as it manifests through the awakening hero.

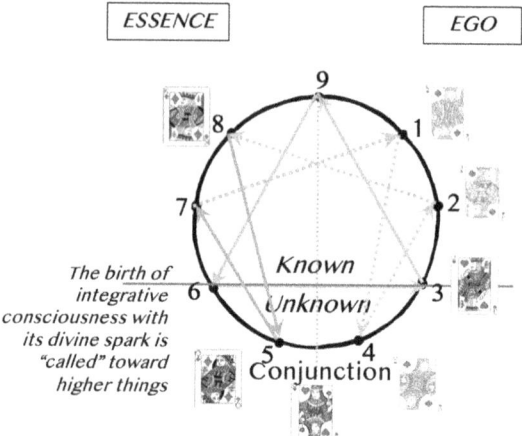

The further operations of the alchemical process aim at using the evolved three forces to purify, refine, spiritualize, and coagulate the remaining elements of the soul into One fully Realized essence—a vehicle for a greater intelligence and love that serves to unify nature and culture, soul and spirit, human and divine realms, in service of peace in the world. All of that is to say that the backdrop and characters have new meaning on the back half of the journey.

From the perspective of alchemy, the operations on the right side of the Symbol served to combine the four elements of fire, water, and air, in the earthly *prima materia* and release the fifth element or *quintessence* as spirit or *ether*, the secret to further operations. On this left side of the Symbol, having stepped into the vertical or "ethereal" realm, the more refined or "spiritualized" elements of mercury and sulphur will be combined to produce the purified salt (the body to house soul and spirit) that will evolve into gold, the philosopher's stone, the rising phoenix, and fully Realized essence. In seven steps, the four material world elements become three refined substances in a new domain, and then three become One again as the unified whole, through the octave of Creation. How can we use this alchemy to make sense of the work ahead?

Revelation in the Void is a blessing, but it reveals higher level challenges from point 5 on. Becoming "as one" ourselves, we are far less likely to become possessed by the vices or passions, those powerful gods that divide us and cause us to miss the mark of who we are in wholeness. Becoming "sealed" against internal demons, prepares us for the higher-level challenge of engaging polarity in the world, to help evolve One-ness in the kingdom. We can now use the light of unified consciousness to learn from our inner experience, images, and symbols without being swallowed up by them—effectively "turning" unconscious chaos into a valuable flow of energy and information. This spark of higher consciousness is the beginning of our "Real I." The hero's *apotheosis*, "seeing as God sees," describes a whole, holy, and higher perspective that integrates not only shadow and light (knowing there is no "other") but also the Above and Below (and nowhere that love does not reach).

With that spark of genius ignited, we can eventually learn to participate in Creation as a future benevolent ruler. To do that work, however, we must bring our divine spark and new power under a higher master as we step across the return threshold to embody soul and spirit in the world. Thankfully, due to natural law and its unwavering path, the line of spirit (with its flaming sword) can be called upon to *guard the gates of Paradise*. On this side of the Symbol, the arrow from point 8 to point 5 indicates the opening to higher realms, but also signals the necessary submission of the developing soul to far higher ideals. We are still human and have a few more points and passions to integrate at the horizontal level under a fully integrated essence and benevolent ruler at point 8. So, while indeed *treasure* has been lifted at point 5, any further movement forward requires additional ego purification. In alchemy, rather than a celebratory moment, this stage of the work is called *putrefaction* and *fermentation*, which describes the smelly remains of a still decomposing ego.

Precisely because we have developed a solid Presence and a receptive intelligence that can learn from the flow of inner information, we also need to curb any tendency to think we know "the" truth as our intuition and imagination grow. The experience in the Void has taught the pattern: we must hold paradox within, surrender or empty our "selves," and engage through Presence with a universal intelligence to evolve *something more*. And when we forget the part about emptying ourselves, the flaming sword may be wielded to cut away any dark serpents that persist as arrogance and narcissism. It's just as likely, though, that the flaming sword is needed here to fend off doubt, self-criticism, and give sustenance to the higher heart that feels more of the pain of the world here and sees the long road ahead.

Our experience in the Void—knowing ourselves, in essence, as not separate from *All that Is*—develops conscience along with the virtues of a higher heart. For this reason, this segment of the journey represents the true dark night of the soul. Becoming more conscious of our potential as creators can cause a good bit of inner turmoil (the ferment). Because we see things we could not see before (*apotheosis*), we see the great gap between where we are, even now, and that higher aim at point 8 where, fully Realized and unified with higher intelligence, we contribute to the world in a different way. We also know that we can't really "accomplish" this in the old ways, and we may experience some despair at the loss of the old self, or a sense of hopelessness about ever figuring out how to close the gap.

To add insult to injury, many of the worldly things we used to derive pleasure from leave us empty, and yet we are not yet drinking deeply from the flow of spirit in our lives. It is not uncommon to feel like you are two people again at this phase of the work, which can be disconcerting after all the effort made to welcome split-off parts and surface an inner healing intelligence. It is an essential tension, however, that when reconciled can help us with the process of "living in two worlds" across the return threshold ahead. Fermentation is a messy affair, and we can easily backslide into darkness. But all of this is necessary and important so that, as we develop our creative intelligence, we can be trusted to know what is *worth* creating.

Non-attachment is an essential stance from here on, as each new level requires a letting go of the previous, and our inner work practices become even more important. Time in meditation and/or prayer, working to strengthen all three pillars of Presence, is a necessary investment for the work ahead. The *kind intention* of a hero can be called upon to link: to direct our inner king's *focus* toward higher ideals and our sense of what's possible, as well as to know when to drop back into the compassionate presence of the queen's *open awareness* to renew our sense of interbeing and faith in the flow of Creation. If we can resist the urge to judge ourselves (which sends us back into "self" focus and a dualistic and dark world), conscience can temper the flame from above into an inner fire—a strong desire for a higher union—that allows what has putrefied to start to come alive again as *spirits*. This process of fermentation and the inner fire of inspired imagination helps to drive the hero over the return threshold to Show Up and do the difficult work of integrating polarity in the world.

SHOWING UP

This return crossing is a big deal, one that doesn't come to fruition until the end of the journey (and then it is gifted), but the decision to go ahead is formative. While we may have mastered the polarization inside, there is still the problem of living in the world from this larger identity, committed to something beyond the self. Especially now that our perspective has been raised and our hearts have expanded as a primary compass for *being*, this is not easy. The work of this crossing, at point 6 where the triangle again penetrates the hexad figure, is called *intentional suffering* because we know exactly what we are getting in to. Now the challenging serpents are on the outside, as we encounter all manner of possible triggers in the real world of our lives. This ups the ante on our inner work and third force capacity to hold together the diversity of reality with our vision of the truth of Unity, without descending again into the tyrannical king's judgment or the chaos of emotional reactivity.

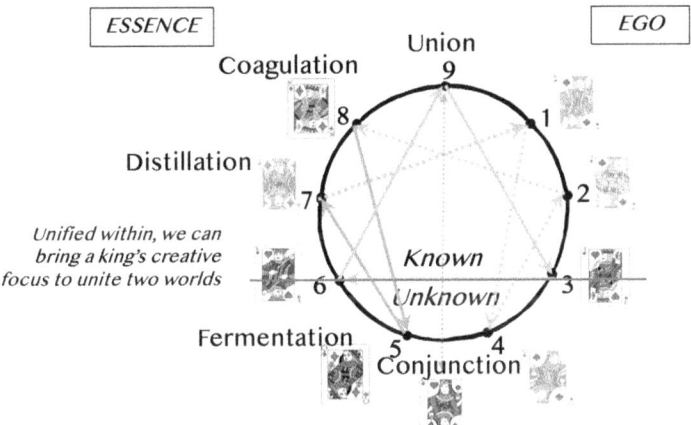

On this side of the journey, we aim to link the Above and Below through integrated being and our creative capacity to know the highest in others. We are learning to use all three pillars of Presence, all three forces (chaos, order, and the third force) as needed, to give form to the "invisible" realm and restore the flow of life, love, and spirit to the chaos and tyranny of the created world. Eventually, the power of a united king and queen, loving intelligence conducted through the awakened hero, can be used to create. An embodied union of conscious and unconscious, spirit and soul, masculine and feminine, order and flow—the opposing poles of Creation—is a clear channel for the self-organizing intelligence of the Universe and has the potential to yield "sacred magic" in the world ahead.

The hero had an epiphany about this potential while still in the Void, but here the work is chosen consciously. Point 6 is a shock point but not an "interval" through which higher intelligence flows, because this moment is all about the hero's commitment.

With the choice to align our entire being and consciousness in service of a higher purpose, we add back to our inner triangle of forces the creative power of the king's focused consciousness to help *make two worlds One.* Intentional suffering describes the shock of sacrificing one's personal plan to engage the pattern that can make order from chaos, usher light from darkness, and bring Unity and new growth into fragmented communities. Highlighting the renewed king here suggests that one-pointed attention on higher or holy ideas is a necessity when working with polarity in the world. And it points to the creative possibility of one who becomes a master of two worlds. We are *raising the father from the underworld,* mythologically speaking, but this is not the old king left behind. Following the re-membering of soul and the hero's *apotheosis,* an evolved version of the king's focused attention may be wielded with grace.

From a more integrated state within (higher being), we have a clearer (non-egoic) understanding of impressions and other symbolic material that "arrives" in us when we are not so attached to material-world senses; and we are more equipped to "make" an impression on reality as we direct our creative imagination, choose our focus, and choose to partner with even higher intelligence by actualizing the triadic dance of growth at a different level. This interval is the only moment on our journey around the circle we travel with full consciousness *with* the line of spirit (moving from point 5 to point 7). Point 6 is not a "note" on the Do-Re-Mi music scale, because it is in some sense "created" with the hero's choice. To "wield the flaming sword" in this way, with intention to fulfill the commitment to higher ideas and virtuous being, requires incredible Faith, Strength, and self-mastery—the mark of a true hero and future king.

Holy Faith is not an intellectual opinion or a personal feeling, says Hermetic wisdom, it is "the product of the union of the thinking, feeling, and desiring human being with cosmic being."[217] It is the lived understanding of an intelligence available when we have become a clear channel, with singular aim (a single "I" and eye), that lends us faith in a possibility beyond our current capacity to see. At this point of the journey, we can use the focused attention of the king because we have a deep inner experience and understanding of the importance of *two eyes,* two worlds, and of the necessity of embracing the "other" in us or in the world as a vehicle for evolving higher order solutions through the magic of emergence. This is what it means to *aim higher.*

So rather than a rigid commitment to fixed beliefs, Holy Faith is fundamentally a commitment to the *Logos* of Creation, a Way of living the pattern that throws new light on our polarizing earthly dilemmas. It is no wonder that the hero sometimes hesitates and is dragged across the threshold. It's a narrow gate, as they say, where we forgo our membership and attachment to this or that tribe or ideology and have no place to lay our heads as we go between worlds. But this is the Way to bring the flow of spirit alive in the created world. Then the creative spark of a true hero is realized at point 7, as the hero fulfills his or her commitment in action, uniting within oneself the vertical and horizontal realms. We lift treasure from the unknown, but ultimately, we must bring our unique voice, vision, and presence across the threshold and *into the world of form* if we are to play our part in renewing the world.

At point 7 the hexad line has run its full cycle (1-4-2-8-5-7). This is not the end of the story, but it's a pivotal point that brings together the descending line of spirit with the ascending development of the soul. The two lines of development (*being* and *knowing*) merge into a lived understanding (*wisdom*) of the patterns of Creation and our creative role in relationship to the larger systems of which we are a part. The power of loving intelligence, conducted through the awakened hero, can be used to bring greater integration (health and well-being), interbeing (love), and higher spiritual wellness (higher consciousness) to the kingdom within and without.

Whether symbolic or literal, we have visualized the weaving together of the horizontal and vertical layers of work along the octave of growth as the creation and integration of the Merkaba or 3D Enneagram, the "vehicle" for higher consciousness. The tetrahedrons (each built through a law of three process) are like organs of intelligence made from the formerly fragmented centers of intelligence—roughly the Ka and the Ba, whose magical union creates the transcendent self in the center. Together, they actualize our soul's wisdom, spiritual imagination, and connect us with the Source and Flow of Creation, or the transcendent and immanent Divine.

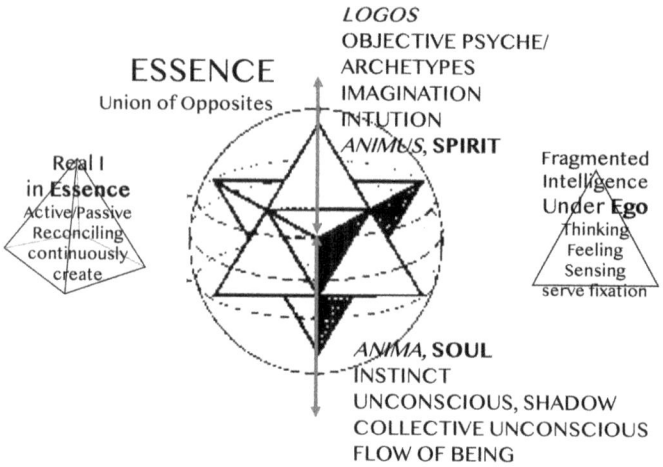

I used this figure along the hero's journey to illustrate a vertical pole of intelligence that begins between instinct and intuition and expands into "collective" or shared dimensions of consciousness at both "ends" (which are secretly connected). This pole is a portal into a timeless domain that opens up as we reconcile polarity within and between our sensing, thinking, and feeling functions (the three centers of the "horizontal" or material world dimension) and come to the aligned center of our being. The opening of that vertical axis then poses a fourth polarity to be reconciled between spirit and soul, which we can also think of as projective (creative) and receptive intelligence, that unfolds on the back half of the journey into deeper states of awareness. At point 7, the hero has resolved this fourth polarity and collected most of the fragments of their own being. In touch with the higher heart and flow of Being, from here they can receive and creatively partner with even higher intelligence or spirit as it seeks to be expressed in the created world.

As we considered in chapter 17, achieving greater coherence within and between our primary centers of intelligence creates a high-frequency heart-mind energy field outside the body that resonates with the natural world and impacts other beings. But even if that science is a little far out there still, we can grasp the power of sacred magic at point 7 as an embodied Presence and active *knowing* of all things as of One Source that begins to transform outer-world experience. When we orient to everything and everyone in this way, we make a Way for that surprising and magical experience of emergence (*something more*) to evolve in the world, through and around us.

But bringing our gifts to fruition in the world takes practice, and our continued commitment to maintain Sobriety from ego drives and old stories. At point 7 on the hero's journey, we got a snapshot of the effort to live the pattern in everyday life, and of the potential magic of two world mastery as a creative force that can lift others. In alchemy, *distillation* is the name of the phase where we sort out these last kinks to purify the horizontal layer and become a master of two worlds, embodying the vertical or spiritual layers of the work through higher centers. It refers to the continual agitation and purification of the fermented substance, through ascending and descending movements, until it becomes concentrated and condensed—*spirits* made corporeal. For us, this washing and consecration of the still-developing *lesser stone* amounts to subjecting ourselves to all the challenges of living in community while sublimating our own reactivity, ego, and personal will to make way for *something more* to unfold from these efforts. While magic might be the outcome, the process is sobering.

As the manifestation point of spirit in Creation, point 7 is another powerful and treacherous juncture. Integrating two worlds through oneself continues to challenge, refine, and purify the soul to live from higher *being* that is rooted in conscience and guided by "objective" or "holy" and universal ideas instead of the self-driven *logos* of the personality. If, however, instead of continuing to prepare our souls around the circle, we try to follow the arrow line of spirit from point 7 back to point 1, we can become mad with power like Daenerys Targaryen, asserting a personal morality. In Hermetic philosophy this transit in the work is through "the sphere of mirages" or "sphere of the false Holy Spirit."[218] The cautionary message is that it is far too easy to mistake a personal vision as "given from above" and to misuse spiritual gifts or knowledge—even when the intention seems to be "saving" or healing others.

Rather than owning any of the sacred magic as "our" creation alone, or using it only for personal ends, we must continue moving along the circular journey to point 8 and beyond by *becoming as little children*, embodying Innocence. We have to play well with others—all types of others—because we have realized through our inner work that any solution not fully rooted in the higher heart, one that doesn't include *all* beings and the natural world in which we exist together, is not true, or beautiful, or good...and so not sustainable. Peace is the realization of Unity in diversity. At the same time, there is no peace without the diversity and complexity of the world. This truth allows for the magical process of creation through polarity, in which a reintegration of diverse elements and the renewal of whole systems can arise via our engagement with the self-organizing, loving intelligence of the Universe. So, although it sounds simple, arriving at this practice of "innocence" has taken a good bit of work!

The alchemical operation of *coagulation* is the final unification of purified elements that actualizes the "gold" of our spiritual nature. It is complete when the "child" of the conjunction in the Void, with newly awakened hero consciousness, is purified, condensed, and infused with the *spirits* produced through that back-and-forth between-worlds distillation process.

The coagulation happens at two levels. There is a horizontal integration of all the fragments, including the gifts of our original Enneagram type, into fully developed essence with the wisdom, will, and heart to engage in this dance of creation (without going to pieces again). This is a pivotal moment in the process where the ego is finally, fully, dethroned. As we say goodbye to the adversary and last shred of our need to be someone special, separate, safe, and in control, we are free to live as a divine expression that is, at the same time, uniquely us. When all parts belong, just as they are, and we can love and accept the particular human form we were gifted, we can love and accept others as well. And then, just as our own soul's unification and higher aim is realized, we fulfill the vertical connection to an even higher mind, spirit, objective knowledge, and the *Logos*, with the full Real-i-zation of what it means to *live* as a spontaneous expression of loving intelligence and the pattern of Creation that renews the world.

Only at this point can we operate reliably as a clear channel for Real (unbiased) energy and information "between heaven and earth." We have become an autonomous, integrated self with the capacity for creative, real-time *knowing*, rooted *not* in the head center, but rather in the interconnectedness of *being* in essence, in the higher heart relationship with *All that Is*. It is a unified and unifying Presence that can bring about change in the world. We saw it symbolized in our heroes at point 8 who received and translated guidance, in pivotal moments—and often at their own peril— into action that contributed to the healing and renewal of the community. Although the king and "benevolent ruler" is located at this point of the map, "we" are not the ruler here. There is no striving to "grow," and no concern for the self now that the ego is fully integrated under this ruler. At the same time, having an autonomous Real I, in touch with higher intelligence, is precisely what enables the hero to discern and prioritize the next right thing. It's an interesting paradox. We are still human, doing this life fraught with cycles of order and chaos, but somehow, *standing in the middle*, we are not defined by any of it. This allows us to bring our unique gifts to fruition and share them in the world. We can be a pure channel for the organizing intelligence of Creation no matter our purpose and profession, *and* the particular manifestation of that flow—how we apply it in service to community and the earth that sustains us—varies according to our own soul's essence and individual divine spark. Those gifts are directly related to our humanity, to our early wounds and defenses. And as we go on the journey to heal and re-member ourselves, we inevitably find that the medicine we gather along the Way, laid out by the breadcrumbs of ego left behind, is also something the world sorely needs. We find our unique place in the universe of interbeing. It is the combination of our individual creative spirit, along with the wisdom gained related to our shared Source and its eternal patterns of life, death, and renewal, that is embodied in the fully Realized hero.

Coming Home

As we saw along the journey, the work of a hero does not stop with this fully integrated leader or "king," which is interesting in and of itself. Having developed aspects of higher *being* and *consciousness* into the fully sealed Merkaba, our vehicle for accessing further dimensions, at point 9 the hero is called again to surrender to the flow of self-organizing intelligence in the Universe and see what comes next. Initiated by the hero's commitment at point 6 to *show up* as a vehicle for Holy Love that renews the world, there is a final law of three creative process that can occur in the interval and hidden threshold marked between point 8 and point 9.

The one who makes it to this threshold does so because of a fully developed inner triangle. The hero's whole being can embody all three forces (pillars of Presence), as needed, to integrate the Laws of Three and Seven into a creative vehicle in touch with an even higher trinity of forces. And while all three forces are *always* required to create, along each layer of work one of them is added, like food for us, and fuels a particular orientation that helps us partner with the line of spirit, add depth and dimension to our work, and travel the octave around the circle to wake up, grow up, and show up with our gifts to help reunite and revivify the kingdom. Here, as the triangle penetrates the hexad again, body, soul, and spirit have the final opportunity to line up behind the queen's open awareness, with full Presence, to await the next challenge and Right Action.

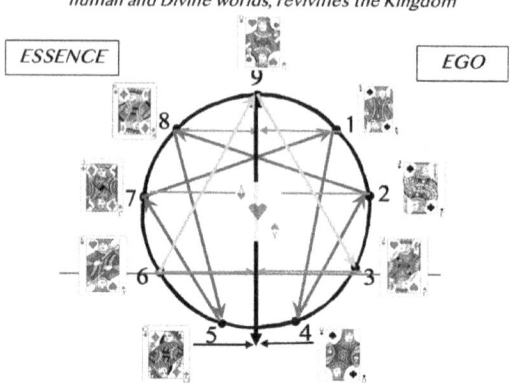

Surrendering to the Mystery that reconciles human and Divine worlds, revivifies the Kingdom

ESSENCE

EGO

One way to think about it is that the hero is making an offering—of all that they have become along the Way—in service of a new round of adventure. This is a culmination of the *growing up* process initiated in the Void via sacrifice and *meeting the Goddess* through open awareness. But back then we went into it still under the sway of ego and arrogance, thinking *we* were the one destined to save the realm. Thankfully, that experience of the massive power of the Great Mother schooled us in the adoption of the proper attitude of humility in the face of the immanent force that animates the world. And the surprising encounter with the transcendent, at that very same juncture, lent faith in the mystery of new life rising that enables the hero to step into the gap here again. This time, the sacrifice is voluntary.

Locating the queen of hearts at point 9, the undifferentiated flow of Being, is an important statement about where the true "power" lies (not in us) and the necessity for continuous renewal. The link between the Void and point 9 suggests that whether we are at the lowest point or the highest point of our journey—whether we are overcome by the face of our own darkness, or we have realized our connection and capacity to create through evolved Presence—the next move is surrender. There is a kind of continuous composting of what has become, or has the potential to become, codified as "complete" or "right." This gardening metaphor is not to say that it's easy. In fact, at this point the first sacrifice may not seem like it was so bad. It is far more difficult to let go of what you have "earned" than it is to hazard a self who is actually longing for more. That thing about getting a camel through the eye of a needle being easier than a rich person entering the kingdom...it makes sense here.

The alchemical way of the hero is a Way of dissolving what's *fixed* to reanimate it with the ever-present *flow* of a more refined level of Reality. And a "hero" is one who has committed their life to a larger purpose. So the potential reconciliation between the Above and Below, between the now Realized human and eternal Being, God, or the Source of all arising, requires a new level of Presence and the receptive, open awareness of the queen. The next step is determined by the flow aspect of Creation, sometimes known as the Holy Spirit. If made, it is one great leap into the unified fourth outcome of the alchemical process that the alchemists called *unus mundus*—becoming One with *All that Is*.

As we saw in the stories, however, rather than ascending to non-dual consciousness or saintly status, most of our heroes carried on into a new octave of growth around the Symbol. Point 9, then, is a still-point prior to a return to the realm of matter, a point of momentary balance and unitive consciousness before the new "king" of consciousness gets fixed at point 1 and starts another necessary round of transformational growth. As discussed, it may take seven turns around the circle—with each point requiring its own seven step process of deconstruction and re-alignment to the next higher dimension—to climb this ladder toward the Infinite. But whether we are on our seventh, fourteenth, or 49th step of this spiral around the Enneagram towards higher union, a hero fulfills the journey of seven steps with the eighth step that restores the harmony of the kingdom and births a new octave of growth (and a new hero, or the potential for a new heroic journey).

The key to each new birth lies in that creative inner triangle. Without the wisdom of the Law of Three that helps to lift our consciousness beyond what we can see as possible at key points along the Way, the Law of Seven as depicted by the hexad line would not yield the same result; we would continue to be tossed about randomly by the laws of nature that use the opposing energies of Creation (order and chaos) to sustain life. Cycles of order and chaos go on and on, but we learn how to "dance" with them, to engage these energies through third force consciousness in a process of evolution that revivifies our souls and our communities. The integration of the two laws, and the two paths of growth, through a developed inner triangle, fulfills the promise of the Symbol by yielding three fully actualized layers of being. The spheres of body, soul, and spirit click into place—each tetrahedron reaching into the next higher dimension to form a ladder or "portal" into the Absolute—creating a clear channel for Holy Love.

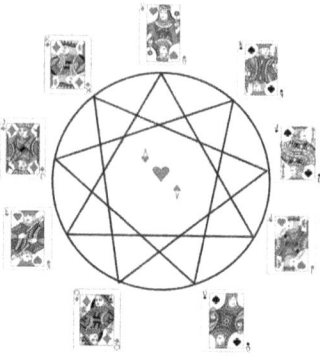

HARMONY OF THE SPHERES

The figure above appears to be a flat representation of the same process conveyed in the Merkaba in 3D form, and both seem like a resolution of Gurdjieff's Enneagram drawing. The Laws of Three and Seven, combined through inner work, *are* the Way to return those nine fragments around the circle to One dynamic whole, in greater union with others, our communities, and the transcendent and immanent divine Source and Flow of Creation. In the colorful language of Gurdjieff, the combined functioning of both laws within gives one the capacity for "Objective Divine Reason" and alignment with "the Most Great Foundation of the All-embracing of everything that exists and constantly emanates throughout the whole of the Universe."[219] The laws unlock the "harmony of the spheres" by bringing diverse tones together and transmuting complexity into a harmony that rings through the layers of self, community, and into the Absolute. At this point, in some sense, the laws themselves take center stage.

In the end, the embodiment of the alchemical pattern represented in the Symbol IS the philosopher's stone. It is the "gold" that can be used to bestow "eternal life" to the alchemist through the refinement of their own being, as well as to the other "substances" to which the alchemist lends this wisdom. The unifying pattern, the *Logos*, is alive *in* us and in everyone and everything else in the Universe. The heroic journey can be understood as learning how and when to participate with and make the pattern Real, by embodying and living it consciously in the world...even if it's just in a moment of meditation, kindness, or collaboration. Living the laws is the courageous and creative process of continuously evolving ourselves to be a clear channel for the unifying intelligence of Holy Love. And then the world itself is revivified through our being, attitude, and action. How else might we bring the love and light of our wisdom traditions into the human plane but through our individual soul, mind, heart, and hands?

Wisdom needs assistance in a human landscape. It is not news that our time in history is fraught with polarization and incivility, and seems always on the verge of social, financial, and environmental chaos. And as the stories reveal, when both the web of nature is fraying and the structures of culture are in decay, tyranny rises. Too many of us are driven by ego to act in compulsive ways that lead to further wounding and fragmentation. But the Enneagram offers us this alternate process for gaining the wisdom, moral courage, and heart to unravel tired structures, renew ourselves, and come into coherence with others, with the natural world, and with the Divine or the implicate, intelligent order that governs the Universe. It offers us a Way to find integrative solutions, as yet unimaginable!

We must know, however, that the Way out of the pressure cooker of these fragmented times is actually the Way IN. As Campbell says it:

And where we had thought to find abomination, we shall find a god; where we had thought to slay another, we shall slay ourselves; where we had thought to travel outward, we shall come to the center of our own existence; where we had thought to be alone, we shall be with all the world.[220]

If we are willing to not only engage the spirit of exploration, but also "slay ourselves," our rigidified ways of seeing and being in the world, we can experience our interdependence with all the world through the pattern, revealed in the laws of the Enneagram Symbol, that animates, evolves, and unifies all of life. And because it is a "Way," the primary purpose of the heroic journey is in the trying. The courageous and creative process of living the laws, according to our unique expression, *being and becoming* a force for Holy Love, is enough to lift us all to higher ground.

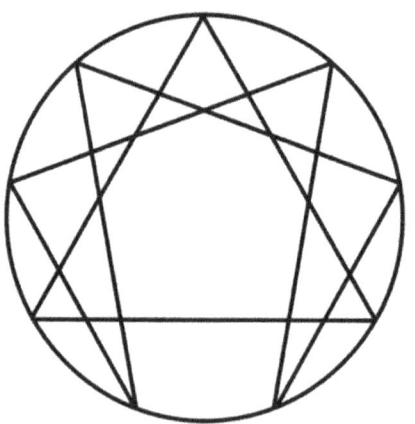

CHAPTER 22

A Universal Map

Pure knowledge cannot be transmitted, but by being expressed in symbols it is covered by them as by a veil, although at the same time for those who desire and who know how to look this veil becomes transparent.[221]

~ G.I. Gurdjieff

URDJIEFF MADE SOME BOLD CLAIMS about the Enneagram Symbol, among them, that it is a vehicle for conveying "pure" or objective knowledge and can show the way to the realization of that knowledge. But the three laws of the Symbol, when realized within through "Great Doing," do seem to reveal a kind of map. And it seems to be a *universal* map, one followed by both mythic and spiritual heroes throughout time. With this understanding, questions about the Enneagram's origins, who discovered what and when, dissolve in my mind. If every created thing carries a divine spark and the potential to realize this signature pattern of Creation, it makes sense that people from varying disciplines, regions, and ages would seek to understand and teach about the laws. And they would uncover them at many different levels of being, in diverse terrain, through objective *and* subjective study.

In the Hermetic tradition, to speak of something as "written in stone," like the seven-step alchemical process of the Emerald Tablet, meant that it was inscribed in the liminal realm of our collective unconscious or the "objective" mind—a connecting link between the concrete world of matter and the divine realm of spirit. What that means is that they believed that the symbols and archetypes revealing patterns that operate at every level of the Universe can be accessed by going deep within, past the personal debris, to this shared realm of knowing. This, in itself, illustrates the meaning of "As Above, so Below," which is that essential phrase of the Emerald Tablet we have been entertaining all along our way. It means that the constituent elements of the psyche *are* the constituent elements of the Universe. They are markers along a universal process of creation and renewal that echo throughout all layers of Creation, from the Infinite to the infinitesimal.

If the Enneagram Symbol is indeed a map of this pattern that governs the transition between the One Unity and the diversity of the created world, it is a summary of an almost unfathomable measure of wisdom that can provide guidance across disciplines and cultures, and at every level we might care to apply it. This was the question we set out to explore at the outset of this book: *Are the laws of the Symbol truly "universal" and, if so, how can they help guide our lives at this time in history?* As we come to the end of our journey through the Symbol's mysteries, I hope Gurdjieff's claims no longer seems so outlandish. The idea that there might be laws to explain the workings of the Universe at all levels, from the atom to the cosmos and every interaction in between, is a kind of holy grail of physics. Einstein himself searched for a grand unified theory, which he claimed must be simple and beautiful to be true.

It's tough to imagine a more simple and beautiful way to convey universal truth than through a symbol. Jeffrey Kripal, a professor of philosophy and religious thought at Rice University, claims that symbolic forms of knowledge are bridges between levels of reality and, as such, some of the most important and meaningful forms of knowledge. Symbols are a third force that unites the two poles of the knowing subject and the object known, pointing to another world—a deeper ground of pure Presence shared by subject and object that can give rise to a new formulation of understanding. The word *symbol* literally means something like "two things put together that create a new whole." And numbers are some of our most well-known symbols. Kripal says that numbers represent a relationship between a human subject and an objective physical world, between mental (immaterial) and material domains, and "enable the human mind to commune indirectly with the deepest hidden structures of material reality."[222] In this way, numeric symbols, in particular, can serve as a kind of *bridge* across the Void and a Way to realize some far greater understanding of Reality itself.

Is it possible, as my daughter pointed out, that our Enneagram Symbol is just such a portal beyond space and time into an experience of the very structure of the Unity underlying our known world? I can't explain how this works, but the Symbol seems to reveal itself in layers. One week you have no idea what you are looking at, but if you hold the complexity of ideas, a new way of seeing opens through which you not only understand what was confusing, but also access another layer of complexity...

and another locked door. Little by little, doors open. It pulls you in.

It took me the better part of a year of living with the question of why Gurdjieff depicted the Law of Seven in two ways (around and through the Symbol) to see how the two paths need to be integrated to fulfill the octave of growth and Unity. What finally helped me was a dream—itself a symbolic message, through my unconscious, from that "other world" and deeper layer of Reality. In the vision, I was traveling around the Symbol but I had to enter door #4208 in order to solve this mystery, which meant incorporating the hexad movement (from point 4 to 2 and across the circle "0" to 8) *with* the circular journey. Now it seems so obvious...*of course* we have to combine "opposing" paths to realize the evolutionary potential of this Symbol! That idea is at the very center of the Enneagram, represented in the triangle. Although I did a lot of reading, study, and effortful reflection, I could share many such stories about how the Symbol revealed itself through symbolism in this way.

RETURNING TO THE FINE-STRUCTURE CONSTANT: 1/137

The idea of symbolic knowledge as a bridge to the underlying structure of Reality and ground of Being, brings us back to the mystery of *alpha*, the fine-structure constant, or the number 1/137. This is the number that unites opposing realms of physics and is thought to be related to a universal "theory of everything." Among other things, the fine-structure constant describes the interaction between energy, light, and matter, measuring as it does the relationship of charged particles with their electromagnetic fields. It is named after the pattern of light emitted as electrons whirl around their atomic nucleus—a pattern that is said to have "fine-structure." Among those preoccupied with *alpha* and a theory of everything was Nobel laureate theoretical physicist Wolfgang Pauli.

Pauli was already a distinguished physicist when he turned to Carl Jung for help managing a difficult juncture in his life in 1930. This contact led to a 26-year letter-writing relationship that would impact both quantum physics and depth psychology. Central to their collaboration were hundreds of dreams Pauli shared with Jung as they worked on Pauli's individuation, integrating his unconscious in service of growth. Within those dreams were many archetypal and universal themes we have been exploring, such as the fundamental role of opposites in the Universe. The dreams guided Pauli's personal work of owning his shadow *anima*, the "opposing" aspect of his soul, but also impacted his work in theoretical physics. His dreams about the transition from the trinity to the quaternity (something like our Law of Three) for example, aided him in the Nobel prize winning discovery of the "fourth quantum number" in physics, extending a fourth degree of freedom to the electron's spin.

Brilliant minds from divergent disciplines, both Pauli and Jung were convinced such archetypal ideas arose from a "shared mind" (the objective psyche) and so could be valid inputs to scientific theory. They both felt that a complete science should explain this mysterious relationship between the personal and the universal, the observer and the observed, and they combined their disciplines in a co-authored book: *The Interpretation of Nature and the Psyche*. This correspondence between nature and the psyche is something like what Gurdjieff was teaching when urging us to study personal experience as a way of understanding the universal laws, and vice versa. And indeed, for Pauli, delving deep into his psyche was part of what led him to believe that $1/137$ *must* be at the heart of a theory of everything and the fundamental structure of the Universe.

But more than dreams provoked Pauli's obsession. Pauli's lifelong mentor, physicist Arthur Sommerfeld, first discovered the equation for the fine structure of the lines of light emitted as electrons whirl around their atomic nuclei. Sommerfeld was an enthusiastic follower of the 16th century scientist/astronomer Johannes Kepler. Kepler was also convinced that the axioms of geometry were imprinted (as archetypes) in our psyche and that they held a key to understanding the secrets of the Universe, God, and the soul. As fantastic as it sounds, Kepler's link between the scientific data and his beliefs about a cosmological holy trinity of sorts led him to his pioneering discoveries about the laws of the motion of planets.

Pauli traced Sommerfeld and Kepler's ideas back to Pythagoras, who posited a Universe built of five three-dimensional shapes, each one representing an essential element of matter: the tetrahedron, standing for fire, the hexahedron as earth, octahedron as air, icosahedron as water, and the dodecahedron as ether. These same five elements of matter were the subject of the seven-step formula said to link the Above and Below that was laid down in the Emerald Tablet. Not only was this document "written in stone," but also it was attributed to the Greek god Hermes Trismegistus, who was synonymous with the Egyptian god Thoth, both of whom were *masters of two worlds*, frequent travelers "between dimensions," and purveyors of hidden universal knowledge. And some versions of history hold that Pythagoras, who studied and traveled in Egypt, was "initiated" by

Thoth into secrets of the Universe underlying his mathematical theories. Pauli also pursued the study of the symbolic meaning of numbers themselves. In ancient Hebrew, as in ancient Greece, numbers had great universal significance. Each letter of the Hebrew alphabet had a number associated with it. Pauli learned about a practice called *gematria*, in which the numbers of the letters in Hebrew words were added together to find the hidden meaning of not only words, but also entire religious texts. Early Christian thinkers fascinated by the possibilities of gematria adopted a practice of assigning numbers for the "names of God." From the perspective of gematria, in both traditions, the number seven is a symbol for a complete (divine) process. Number three stands for divine completion, harmony, and new life (via the third mediating number). And one is the symbol for Unity and God.

Of course, all of this symbolism eventually clashed with a modern-day material science that could describe with mathematics the trajectory of planets as well as snowballs. And yet, modern scientific observers of the cosmos still do use symbols (numbers and geometry) to decode and describe the mysteries they encounter. In 2016, a team of physicists in Poland observed the shape of a photon to be a "maltese cross," described as the "side view" of a star tetrahedron.[223] Photons are packets of energy, electromagnetic radiation, that make light. When photons are smashed together at very high speeds, they create matter. And you know that the Merkaba, a double or "star" tetrahedron, is said to enable movement between matter and spirit. Perhaps the ancients who linked their observations of inner and outer world phenomena with their spiritual beliefs, and both with geometric and numeric symbols, were on to something?

Thus far anyway, the mathematical approach to explaining 1/137 and its relationship to a theory of everything in physics has fallen short. For Wolfgang Pauli, the fine-structure constant was a mystery that would dog him up to his death which, in some great cosmic synchronicity, he knew was imminent when he fell ill and was hospitalized in room 137. As we covered in part one of this book, one of the reasons Pauli and other physicists think the fine-structure constant or *alpha* may be related to a unified theory is because it links three other constants that unite three of the primary domains of physics:

1. from general relativity, the speed of light;
2. from quantum mechanics, Planck's constant; and
3. from electromagnetism, the electric charge of one electron.

From the perspective of the Law of Three we could say that since general relativity accounts for the orbit of planets and the laws of the Universe that govern our everyday lives on a large scale, it describes the *order* of the created world. Quantum mechanics describes the *flow* of life at the very smallest of scales, a strange world made up of the interconnected potential of energy in which "particles" leap into and out of existence as the scientist observes them. Today's physics holds these two domains as serving up incompatible descriptions of reality. We could say, like particle and wave, form and emptiness, they are "polar" forces.

The third factor in *alpha* comes from electromagnetism, which describes force and interaction between particles, revealed as "light" or particle-like wave packets (photons). In some sense, electromagnetism *stands in the middle* of the other two domains, as a force included in quantum mechanics that is *also* compatible with general relativity. It not only holds a reconciling role, in this sense, but also seems to be a force with which we humans can actively engage through our thoughts and feelings, which, when coherent, apparently resonate with electromagnetic fields measured in the Universe. One study from Germany found that the heart emits measurable (electromagnetic) light energy or photons, at a rate 5000 times greater than resting rate when one is engaged in meditation focused on opening the heart.[224]

Is it a coincidence that the three roles of the triad of *alpha* match the Law of Three? Or that electromagnetism is the process, the light, and third force with the potential to mediate between the *form* of the created world and the *flow* of creation in the renewal of life? ("I am the light of the world.") I wonder if Sommerfield had an *omega* in mind when naming the fine structure constant *alpha*? At the end of the day, I know I have proven exactly nothing with these musings...except that I can totally understand Wolfgang Pauli, his dreams, and his obsession with this special number as a key to glimpsing the fundamental structure of the Universe! Many notable physicists, while acknowledging its significance as a universal constant, have chalked 1/137 up to mystery. The famed physicist Richard Feynman was quoted as saying: "You might say the 'hand of God' wrote that number, and we don't know how He pushed his pencil."[225]

But as a numeric *symbol*, 1/137, is a perfect description of the relationship between a being (1) and the Universe via the laws of the Enneagram Symbol (137). And while Gurdjieff's claims about the Enneagram were indeed bold, we can find the laws of the Symbol operating across diverse cultures and generations, in fields ranging from psychology and neuroscience to physics and biology; embedded in nature; shared across religious and spiritual traditions; and at the foundation of the world's enduring myths and stories. There is, at least, *some*thing universal and worth attending to in this Symbol that *shows the way* to realizing its wisdom; maybe, just enough, to use its laws as a guide for navigating our inner work and outer service through the challenges in today's world.

One of the most remarkable things about the Enneagram *is* its universal guidance, particularly in an era fraught with relativism and contradictory notions about how to be. Coincidentally, in simultaneous but separate coaching engagements that occurred while working on this book, I found myself working with a Catholic priest, an academic and graduate school dean who had fled her religious past due to sexual identity persecution, and a devout Muslim who was then a regional bank president. As I helped each of them understand their respective challenges in the context of the wisdom of the Symbol, each felt it illuminated not only their personal journey but also some of their most cherished beliefs. In fact, after a long silence (during which I wondered if I had stepped in something), the banker said to me, with awe and gratitude in his voice, "I feel like you understand my religion better than I do."

This is the promise and purpose of inner work with the Enneagram Symbol, whatever your type and belief system. While we desperately need to value difference and work to include all unique voices, we *also* sorely need to uncover and elevate our shared humanity and the collective wisdom that has endured across traditions, throughout the ages. And we need the *intentional kindness* it takes to integrate these two endeavors and breathe new life into our efforts. We are all living a challenging journey of one form or another, some harder than others for sure, but with a common compass perhaps we could do it more often hand in hand? Then maybe someday, as French philosopher, scientist, and priest Teilhard de Chardin famously wrote, "After mastering the winds, the waves, the tides and gravity, we shall harness for God the energies of love, and then, for a second time in the history of the world, we will have discovered fire."

The geometric symbol for fire? The tetrahedron ;-)

The End

ENDNOTES

Chapter 1: Introduction

1   P.D. Ouspensky, *In Search of the Miraculous: Fragments of an Unknown Teaching. Digital Edition.* (U.S: Library of Alexandria, 1949), 431.

2   Fatima Fernandez Christlieb, *Where on Earth di the Enneagram Come From?* (Mexico City: Lightning Source, 2016) provides a comprehensive academic study of the possible origins of the Enneagram. Many shorter summaries are available online and in books. See for example: The Traditional Enneagram (History) at https://www.enneagraminstitute.com/the-traditional-enneagram; The Complete Enneagram, Chestnut (2013), 51-56; Rohr and Ebert (1993), 3-11.

3   Ouspensky, *ISOM*, 431.

4   G.I. Gurdjieff, as quoted in *In Search of Being: The Fourth Way to Consciousness*, ed. Stephen A. Grant (Boulder, Colorado: Shambala Publications, 2012), 132.

Chapter 2: The Enneagram of Personality

5   https://enneagramprisonproject.org

6   Rollin McCraty, "New Frontiers in Heart Rate Variability and Social Coherence Research: Techniques, Technologies, and Implications for Improving Group Dynamics and Outcomes," *Frontiers in Public Health* 5, no. 267 (October 12, 2017): p.6.

Chapter 3: Universal Patterns

7   Ouspensky, *ISOM*, 449.

8   Richard P. Feynman, *QED: The Strange Theory of Light and Matter* (Princeton: Princeton University Press, 1985).

9   Summary of the fine-structure constant is derived from multiple articles in the reference section: Miller (2009); Davies (2016); Brooks (2018); Ratner (2019).

10   Ludwig Von Bertalanffy, *General Systems Theory: Foundations, Development, Applications* (New York: George Braziller, 1968). While systems science has grown and changed, my initial understanding of general systems theory was drawn from Von Bertalanffy and a contemporary application to organizational systems from George Land and Beth Jarman. *Breakpoint and Beyond: Mastering the Future—Today* (New York: Harper Business, 1993).

11   Steven Strogatz, *Sync: How Order Emerges from Chaos in the Universe, Nature, and Daily Life* (New York: Hatchette Books, 2003). Covers many of the diverse research approaches to synch in universities today.

12   Strogatz, *Sync*, 286.

13   Ouspensky, *ISOM*, 437.

14   Michael Meade, "Myth Makes Meaning" *Living Myth Podcast*, episode 260, (Mosaic Voices, Dec. 12, 2021).

Chapter 4: The Law of One

15   Joseph Campbell, *The Hero with a Thousand Faces, Third Edition* (Novato, CA: New World Library, 2008), 221.

16   https://en.wikipedia.org/wiki/Ancient_Egyptian_creation_myths

17   Genesis 1:2-4, King James Version.

[18] Richard Rohr, "The Blueprint of Creation," *Daily Meditations*, March 28, 2017. https://cac.org/daily-meditations/the-blueprint-of-creation-2017-03-28/

[19] Rav Michael Laitman, *Kabbalah Science and the Meaning of Life: Because Your Life Has Meaning* (Toronto, Canada: Laitman Kabbalah Publishers, 2007).

[20] Charles Seife, *Zero: The Biography of a Dangerous Idea* (New York: Penguin Books, 2000), 200-209.

[21] https://en.wikipedia.org/wiki/Superstring_theory

[22] Gurdjieff, *In Search of Being*, 226.

[23] Gurdjieff also associated the triangle with "higher forces" that create. While this is definitely true, I believe that in the fixed form of the flat enneagram symbol it is most helpful to understand the triangle as representing *what has been created* by higher forces, and is now only un-actualized potential, with the original divine spark of creation "trapped in matter."

[24] Bargh, John, *Before You Know It: The Unconscious Reasons We Do What We Do* (New York: Touchstone Books, 2017).

[25] Jonathan Haidt, *The Happiness Hypothesis: Finding Modern Truth in Ancient Wisdom* (New York: Basic Books, 2006).

[26] Daniel Siegel, *Mind: A Journey to the Heart of Being Human* (New York: WW Norton & Company, 2017).

[27] Elaine Pagels, *The Gnostic Gospels* (New York: Vintage Books, 1979), 129.

[28] Laleh Bakhtiar, *The Sufi Enneagram: Secrets of the Symbol Unveiled* (Chicago: Institute of Traditional Psychology, 2018), 59-61.

[29] Richard Rohr and Adreas Ebert, *The Enneagram: A Christian Perspective* (New York: Crossroad Publishing, 1990), 8-14.

[30] Kenneth L. Davis and Christian Montag, "Selected Principles of Pankseppian Affective Neuroscience," *Frontiers in Neuroscience* 12, no. 1025 (January 17, 2019): 2.

[31] Tara Swart, *The Source: Open Your Mind, Change Your Life* (London: Penguin Random House, 2020), 124-126.

[32] Beatrice Chestnut, "Understanding the Development of Personality Type: Integrating Object Relations Theory and the Enneagram System," *The Enneagram Journal* (Summer 2008): 22-51.

[33] Thomas Armstrong, "The Stages of Ego Development According to Jane Loevinger," *American Institute for Learning and Human Development Blog*, January 31, 2020.

[34] The figure I use showing a link between points 234, points 789, and point 156 on the enneagram was first drawn for me by Dirk Cloete in May 2018. He used it to show me the "mirrored" image set up when we group the types according to their common counter-instinctual drive.
I realized later that it conveys the Law of Three pattern.

[35] Lionel Corbett, "Jungian Psychology and Kohut's Self-Psychology," C.G. Jung Institute of Chicago. Audio recording, 1989.

[36] Some Enneagram teachers believe that we "come in" with our type, like our soul's imprint. This may be true, but we still "attract" and experience our early social context in ways that continue to shape and refine us. In psychology the answer is always "both," both nature and nurture lead to ego development.

[37] Keiron Le Grice, *The Archetypal Cosmos: Rediscovering the Gods in Myth, Science and Astrology* (Edinburgh: Floris Books, 2010), loc. 3615-3811.

38 LeGrice, *The Archetypal Cosmos*, loc 4776. Swimme starts with power zero: Seamlessness, the source of all powers and ground of Being. The ten powers: Centration, Allurement, Emergence, Homeostasis, Cataclysm, Synergy, Transmutation, Transformation, Interrelatedness, Radiance.

CHAPTER 5: THE LAW OF THREE

39 Gurdjieff, *In Search of Being*, 215.
40 Gurdjieff, *In Search of Being*, 61.
41 G.I. Gurdjieff, *Beelzebub's Tales to His Grandson: All and Everything, First Series* (New York: Penguin Books, 1950), 138.
42 Ouspensky, *ISOM*, 449.
43 Gurdjieff, *In Search of Being*, 81.
44 Stephen Mitchell, *Tao te Ching: A New English Version* (New York: Harper Collins, 1988), 42
45 G.I. Gurdjieff, *Life is Real Only Then, When 'I Am.' All and Everything, Third Series* (New York: Penguin Books edition, 1991), 171: "It is not important to know which of the two forces is affirmative and which is negative; what matters is that when one affirms, the other denies."
46 Gurdjieff, *Beelzebub's Tales*, 1139.
47 2 Corinthians 5:19.
48 John 14:6.
49 John J. Baker, "The Dharma in a Single Drawing," *Tricycle: The Buddhist Review* (Spring 2015), 37.
50 Jordan B. Peterson, *Maps of Meaning: The Architecture of Belief* (New York: Routledge, 1999). I have drawn both the account of the Enuma Elish and the Egyptian creation story from here, as well as much of the interpretation. My understanding of the entire order/chaos dynamic in world creation is credited to this book.
51 G.I. Gurdjieff as quoted in "The Enneagram: A Lecture by Gurdjieff," Endless Search - Work Philosophy (a website by Ian MacFarlane, 2004). https://www.endlesssearch.co.uk/philo_enneagramtalk.htm
52 Murray Stein, *Jung's Map of the Soul: An Introduction* (Illinois: Carus Publishing, 1998).
53 Arthur I. Miller, *137: Jung, Pauli, and the Pursuit of a Scientific Obsession* (New York: WW Norton & Co, 2009).
54 Stephen Hawking, *Brief Answers to the Big Questions* (New York: Bantam Books, 2018).
55 Ian McGilchrist, "Reciprocal organization of the cerebral hemispheres," *Dialogues in Clinical Neuroscience* 12 no. 4 (December 2010): 503-515. I should also credit Peterson, *Maps of Meaning* again for the understanding of the forces of order and chaos at the center of existence, and their relevance to brain structure and function.
56 Siegel, *Mind*, discusses this model I first encountered in: Michael Pollan, *How to Change Your Mind: What the New Science of Psyche-delics Teaches Us About Consciousness, Dying, Addiction, Depression, and Transcendence* (New York: Penguin Random House, 2018).
57 Siegel, *Mind*, 19.
58 Gurdjieff, *In Search of Being*, 228.

59   Ellen J. Langer, *Mindfulness* (MA: Addison-Wesley, 1989).

60   Victor E. Frankl, *Man's Search for Meaning* (Boston: Beacon Press, 1959).

61   There is confusion and disagreement in the Enneagram world about whether the passion of Type 3 is Deceit or Vanity. After pursuing many versions of the Law of Three, I think the Laws support Deceit, the original version. The passions on the inner triangle, as Sandra Maitri relayed, show an archetypal process we <u>all</u> go through. In this way, the inner triangle represents a "higher order" category of experience (like dog, rather than retriever). Deceit describes the shared drive to take on a false self in personality. Gurdjieff said that before we can do any real work our "self-deception" must be destroyed. Deceit is a central challenge for all. What distinguishes Type 3 is that they *continue* to use Deceit to adopt new roles, believing their current manifestation of "self" is real.

62   In particular, I learned this from Helen Palmer in my Narrative Tradition Training.

63   Saul McLeod, "Erik Erikson's Stages of Psychosocial Development," *Simply Psychology*, last updated 2018. https://www.simplypsychology.org/Erik-Erikson.html

Chapter 6: The Law of Seven

64   Gurdjieff, *In Search of Being*, 92.

65   I *know* in the song version it is sol, la, *TI*, do ("tea, a drink with jam and bread"). For whatever reason, Gurdjieff used "si" instead.

66   Gurdjieff, *In Search of Being*, 85.

67   There isn't a definitive account of the meaning of Merkaba, because it runs through diverse traditions, but some of many sources to draw upon: Joshua Mark, "The Soul in Ancient Egypt," World History Encyclopedia, March 2, 2017. And, Dag Herbjornsrud, "The Radical Philosophy of Egypt: Forget God and Family, Write!" Blog of the American Philosophy Association, December 17, 2018.

68   Bakhtiar, *The Sufi Enneagram*, 54-55.

69   Dennis William Hauck, *The Emerald Tablet: Alchemy of Personal Transformation* (New York: Penguin Compass, 1999).

70   Hermeticism was a philosophical doctrine that affirmed the existence of a single true theology present in all religions—something like the perennial philosophy—that, thanks to the religious cross-pollination of its time, may have sent roots into diverse esoteric teachings.

71   Ouspensky, *ISOM*, 450.

72   You can read a lot more about modern and more science-related theories about this system of energy centers, their specific properties and related organ systems in Joe Dispenza, *Becoming Supernatural: How Common People are Doing the Uncommon* (Carlsbad, CA: Hay House, Inc, 2017), 93-99. Also Sue Morter, *The Energy Codes: The 7-Step System to Awaken Your Spirit, Heal Your Body, and Live Your Best Life* (Miami: Atria Books, 2019).

73   Ouspensky, *ISOM*, 195-200.

74   Gurdjieff, In Search of Being, 73

Chapter 7: Introduction to the Hero's Journey

75 Ouspensky, *ISOM*, 430.
76 I'm referring here to the Captain Marvel of the most recent (2019) film from Marvel Studios, featuring the character Carol Danvers. Earlier renditions of Captain Marvel and Captain Mar-Vell were both male and female.
77 By the time of this publishing, Uranio Paes and Beatrice Chestnut (CP Enneagram Academy) have been teaching their detailed model of psychospiritual development mapped around the Enneagram Symbol for a few of years. My early understanding of the development described by the journey around the Symbol is thanks to them. I have incorporated some of their theory here along with my study of the hero's journey, with the alchemical process, my understanding of Gurdjieff's writings, and other perspectives on "the map" of growth and where it leads. I deferred to comparative mythology (an enduring tradition), as well as my inner experience of symbolic material via dreams and such, when perspectives diverged.
78 Campbell, *Hero*, 221.
79 Ouspensky, *ISOM*, 437.
80 Campbell, *Hero*, 27.

Chapter 9: Point 1 – Trouble in the Kingdom

81 https://enneagramprisonproject.org
82 Gurdjieff, *Beelzebub*, 11.
83 Patterson, *Gurdjieff*, 239.

Chapter 10: Point 2 – The Call to Adventure

84 Campbell, *Hero*, 59.
85 Campbell, *Hero*, 303.
86 Campbell, *Hero*, 101-102.
87 Campbell, *Hero*, 46.
88 Russ Hudson, "The Inner Critic/Inner Rebel—Two Obstacles in Our Inner Work," The Awakened Company, Enneagram Series with Russ Hudson, 2020.
89 Pagels, *Gnostic Gospels*, xv.

Chapter 11: Point 3 – Crossing the Threshold

90 Campbell, *Hero*, 42-43.
91 Campbell, *Hero*, 106.
92 Campbell, *Hero*, 77.
93 Campbell, *Hero*, 94.
94 Campbell, *Hero*, 77.
95 Campbell, *Hero*, 73.
96 Campbell, *Hero*, 84.
97 Rohr, *Daily Mediations*, Sept 8, 2019.
98 In the modern Enneagram era we often refer to the Sexual Instinct as the One-to-One instinct. While it definitely makes it easier to teach in some contexts, this obscures the nature of the instinct, which is an intense and expansive energy and not just about the drive for deep 1-1 personal connection. It derives from the animal drive to discover, compete, and consummate the search to expand and extend life. Too many people think that if they desire 1-1 intimacy, they are a "Sexual dominant" subtype, but it's more

complicated than that. Most people desire 1-1 intimacy. The question is: what is the nature of that connecting? And where else, like competition, does this energetic intensity show up?

99 Bargh, *Before You Know It*, 21-94.

100 There is also the chance that you have a counter-reaction to your passion. This creates a specific subtype expression called a "counter type." It is fueled by an instinctual drive that goes the *opposite* direction, energetically, as the passion. One of the three subtypes within each Enneagram type is a countertype, and it may not appear as much like the true type as the other subtypes within type. While the existence and nature of countertypes is also a point of disagreement in the Enneagram community, conceptually they make sense as a representation of the universal Law of Three governing all things. I offer the concept here in case you are not seeing yourself clearly in the nine passions of type. See Beatrice Chestnut's *The Complete Enneagram* for more detail on countertypes.

CHAPTER 12: POINT 4 – THE ABYSS

101 Campbell, *Hero*, 102.
102 Campbell, *Hero*, 91.
103 Gurdjieff, *In Search of Being*, 98
104 Carl McColman, *The Big Book of Christian Mysticism: The Essential Guide to Contemplative Spirituality* (Minneapolis: Broadleaf Books, 2010).
105 C.G. Jung, *The Red Book: Liber Novus A Reader's Edition* (New York: WW Norton & Co, 2009), 332.
106 Jung, *The Red Book*, 231
107 Ouspensky, *ISOM*, 331.
108 Rohr, *Daily Meditations*, Sept 9, 2019.
109 Matthew 16:24.
110 Colossians 1:17.
111 Luke 6:27.
112 Gurdjieff, *In Search of Being*, 91.
113 Tara Brach, *Radical Compassion: Learning to Love Yourself and Your World with the Practice of RAIN* (New York: Penguin Life, 2020).
114 Dechar, *Alchemy of Inner Work*, 217, 219.

CHAPTER 13: THE VOID: REVELATION IN THE VOID

115 C.G. Jung, *Psychology and Alchemy*, Second Edition, translated by R.F.C. Hull (Princeton, NJ: Princeton University Press, 1968), 74.
116 Campbell, *Hero*, 99.
117 Lewis Carrol, *Alice in Wonderland: The Original 1865 Edition with Complete Illustrations by Sir John Tenniel* (Independently published, 2021).
118 Tomberg, Valentin. *Meditations on the Tarot*. Translated by Robert Powell. (New York: Penguin Putnam, 2002), 547-551.
119 John 3:5.
120 Campbell, *Hero*, 110.
121 Campbell, *Hero*, 96.
122 Michael Meade, "The River of Deep Meaning" *Living Myth Podcast*, ep. 273 (Mosaic Voices, Mar 30, 2022).

123   Daniel Siegel, *Aware: The Science and Practice of Presence: The Ground-breaking Meditation Practice* (New York: Penguin Random House, 2018).
124   Mark Coleman, "A Heart as Wide as the World. Cultivating the Brahma Viharas: Love, Compassion, Joy, & Equanimity" *Monday Evening Dharma Talks*, Spirit Rock, May 24, 2016.

CHAPTER 14: POINT 5 – APOTHEOSIS

125   Ram Dass, In Stephen and Ondrea Levine, *Who Dies? An Investigation of Conscious Living and Conscious Dying.* (New York: Anchor Books, 1989) – "A letter to the grieving parents of Rachel."
126   Joseph Campbell, "The Hero's Adventure, episode 1," *The Power of Myth with Bill Moyers* (New York: Doubleday, 1998).
127   Campbell, *Hero*, 158.
128   Siegel, *Mind*, 184.
129   Campbell, *Hero*, 26.
130   Again, I have to credit Peterson, *Maps of Meaning,* for clarifying the nature of many of these archetypal ideas that help explain the hero's journey through the Symbol.
131   Shunryu Suzuki, *Zen Mind, Beginner's Mind: Informal Talks on Zen Buddhism.* (New York: Weatherhill, 1970).
132   Dechar, *Alchemy of Inner Work,* 454.
133   Matthew 6:22.
134   The Christian Hermetic philosopher Valentin Tomberg notes that the shape of the star, often interpreted as a symbol of the occult and personal magic, is only a distortion of power when it is NOT taken as part of the unity of the whole - when the personal will is not in submission to the universal. In the Enneagram, the 5-pointed stage of consciousness (the star) is a *stage,* embedded in the longer journey. The arrow line from point 8 to point 5 indicates the necessity of bringing this stage under a higher one.
135   Campbell, *Hero*, 31.

CHAPTER 15: POINT 6 – THE RETURN THRESHOLD

136   Ouspensky, *ISOM*, 345.
137   Campbell, *Hero*, 186.
138   Gurdjieff, *Beelzebub*, 241.
139   Campbell, *Hero*, 189.
140   Campbell, *Hero*, 178.
141   Gurdjieff, *In Search of Being*, 132.

CHAPTER 16: POINT 7 – MASTER OF TWO WORLDS

142   Campbell, *Hero*, 212-213.
143   Campbell, *Hero*, 194.
144   Campbell, *Hero*, 205-206.
145   Campbell, *Hero*, 134.
146   Campbell w/ Moyers, *Power of Myth*, xv.
147   Campbell, *Hero*, 188
148   C.G. Jung, *Mysterium Coniunctionis*, translated by R.F.C. Hull (Princeton, NJ: Princeton University Press, 1963), 184. In Jung's psyche map, this vertical dimension runs between instinct and intuition. He writes: "Sensation tells

us that a thing is. Thinking tells us what a thing is, feeling tells us what it is worth to us. But there is yet another category, and that is time." Intuition perceives past and future, and leads into the archetypes, patterns of order in the human psyche that are also found in the Universe.

149   Tomberg, *Wisdom.*
150   Gurdjieff, *In Search of Being*, 115.
151   Siegel, *Mind* and *Aware.*

CHAPTER 17: POINT 8 – FREEDOM TO LIVE

152   Campbell, *Hero*, 205.
153   Campbell, *Hero*, 209.
154   J.K. Rowling, "What exactly happened when Voldemort used the Avada Kedavra curse on Harry in the forest?" The Rowling Library.
155   Campbell, *Hero*, 206
156   https://www.merriam-webster.com/dictionary/truth
157   Richard Rohr, *The Universal Christ: How a forgotten reality can change everything we see, hope for, and believe.* (New York: Convergent Books, 2019).
158   Campbell, *Hero*, 296.
159   This idea that what we first recover in essence is quite opposite of how we know ourselves in Personality came to me from Uranio Paes.
160   G.I. Gurdjieff, *Life is Real Only Then, When 'I Am.' All and Everything, Third Series* (New York: Penguin Books edition, 1991).
161   While this idea about our creative capacity to "lift" others through our *knowing* of them as divine is echoed in the Hermetic tradition as well, I have to credit Paul Selig for the clarity with which I understand this teaching revealed at point 8.
162   Israel Ministry of Foreign Affairs, "King Solomon's Seal," *The Israel Review of Arts and Letters.* MFA Archive, February16, 1999.
163   Gurdjieff, *In Search of Being*, 227.
164   Campbell, *Hero*, 205
165   1 Thessalonians 5:23
166   Some of this work is described in: Dispenza, *Becoming Supernatural*; McCraty, "The Energetic Heart"; McCraty, "New Frontiers."
167   For a greater summary of research showing the effect of mind on matter: Church, Dawson, *Mind to Matter: The Astonishing Science of How Your Brain Creates Material Reality* (Carlsbad, CA: Hay House, 2018).
168   McCraty, "New Frontiers."

CHAPTER 18: POINT 9 – THE JOURNEY HOME

169   Bhagavad Gita IV, 6-8. As cited in "The Hindu Trinity," *The Indian Panorama*, Last updated October 30, 2015.
170   Schwartz, Alexandra, "Love is not a permanent state of enthusiasm: An Interview with Esther Perel," *The New Yorker Interview*, December 9, 2018.
171   Campbell, *Hero*, 135
172   1 Corinthians 13:13.
173   As quoted in: Wonder Woman movie, Warner Brothers pictures, 2017.
174   Sandra Maitri, *The Spiritual Dimension of the Enneagram: Nine Faces of the Soul* (New York: Jeremy Tarcher/Putnam Inc, 2000), 23-41.
175   John 14:6.

176 T.S. Eliot poem *Little Gidding*. http://www.columbia.edu/itc/history/winter/
w3206/edit/tseliotlittlegidding.html

177 Gurdjieff described our role in world maintenance, in fact, as an obligation; the price we should pay for existence. His teaching was meant to enable us to contribute to the "evolutionary backflow" of life towards our One shared Source in what he called the Doctrine of Reciprocal Maintenance.

178 Russ Hudson, "The Enneagram as Nine Paths for Awakening," *The Shift Network Global Summit*, 2020 audio recording. This talk is the source of ideas about "type in awakened Presence." The superhero guesses are my own and come with no claim of accuracy!

179 Jung, *Mysterium*, 401-404.

180 According to Gurdjieff, a Divine Being is "man #7". He says most humans are located within the first 3 levels (man 1, 2, and 3), locked into a habitual pattern lead by the head, heart, or body center that has kidnapped our three forces. When we wake up and work on ourselves, we can learn to apply the inner triangle of forces at each of seven levels and become one of 3x7 or 21 kinds of "Idiots" trying to become real. Waking up third force consciousness that is no longer caught by ego is only (hu)man #4, a transitional state between the first three and the last three more integrated (hu)mans up to #7 who establishes essence with Real I, as a fully realized soul, and can become one with the Divine.

 I also want to point out here that the Buddha spent 7x7 days (7 weeks) in deeper reflection before leaving the bodhi tree to serve humanity, which is another version of the 7x7 process. And since creation is always a cascade of opposites, those 49 steps around the Symbol, each with a shadow (as everything in Creation carries its opposite), amount to 98 "Names of God" or attributes of the Divine that, combined with the one for God, make the 99 Names, the number claimed in the Islamic tradition. These are all just musings on the overlapping versions of the Way to complete the process of union with the Divine or non-dual, higher consciousness.

CHAPTER 19: THE SYMBOL IS THE WAY

181 Ouspensky, *ISOM*, 430.

182 David N. Daniels, "Working with the Enneagram Harmony Triads: A Key to the Development and Integration," Written 2019. https://drdaviddaniels.com/articles/triads/

183 Oscar Ichazo, "Letter to the Transpersonal Community," Written 1991.

184 Bourgeault (2013), p. 112

185 Gurdjieff, *Beelzebub*, 157.

186 Gurdjieff, *In Search of Being*, 243.

187 Genesis 28:12.

188 2 Cor 5:19; and Eph 1:9-10.

189 Gurdjieff, *Beelzebub*, 757.

190 Gurdjieff, *In Search of Being*, 241.

CHAPTER 20: OUR ROLE IN CREATION

191 Gurdjieff, *In Search of Being*, 217.

192 Jung, *Mysterium*, 429.

193 Gurdjieff, *In Search of Being*, 61.

194 Campbell, *Hero*, 77.

195 Siegel, *Aware*, 45. I have adapted Dan's three pillars very slightly to fit this application, because I do believe they represent a "truth" about the forces of Creation, and because understanding both a "positive" and "negative" use of the forces is relevant for us.

196 For a more detailed summary of all this and how to grow your capacity, check out Dr. Dan's 2018 book *Aware: The Science and Practice of Presence - The Groundbreaking Meditation Practice.* His Wheel of Awareness Meditation serves to develop and apply the three pillars of mind training that line up with our three forces of the inner triangle. Guided practice can be found on his website: https://drdansiegel.com/wheel-of-awareness/

197 Ouspensky, *ISOM*, 433.

198 Campbell, *Hero*, 138.

199 Ananda W.P. Guruge, "Part III: Temptations by Mara in Non-Canonical Buddhist literature," *The Buddha's Encounters with Mara the Tempter: Their Representation in Literature and Art.* Copyright 2015. https://www. accesstoinsight.org/lib/authors/guruge/wheel419.html In this account, Mara first tries to persuade the Buddha by promising him he will become a universal monarch (in seven days!) if he gives up his pursuits and returns home - sticks to the material world and land of duality.

200 Tomberg, *Wisdom*, 132-144. Tomberg explains Eve's betrayal of the three vows and how Jesus upholds them. The Enneagram interpretations here are my own.

201 Claudio Naranjo, "The Enneagram & Personal Awakenings: The Life & Teachings of Claudio Naranjo," *Video and Audio Excerpts from Shift Network Interviews with Claudio Naranjo,* The Shift Network Enneagram Global Summit 2020 Bonuses. In these excerpts, Claudio Naranjo, one of the key players in the definition and application of the modern Enneagram, not only lays the three poisons around the points of the inner triangle, but also go on to use them to explain the three instinctual subtypes within type. I do think the poisons and the forces are synonymous, and the fact that he uses them to "create" subtypes indicates *how central the Law of Three is to the Enneagram of Personality.* But I have a question about how he seems to have integrated this theory...

With all due respect, I have located the three forces on the inner triangle differently than Naranjo did, based on my understanding of the Buddhist and Christian stories, as well as Gurdjieff's teaching about the forces. Naranjo appears to have placed the poison named "desire" or "attachment" at the heart center, and I think these other systems would locate it in the body. Both the Sanskrit and Pali terms for this poison link it to a *sense-based* desire. It is an expansive force often noted as "greed." And Gurdjieff clearly located "force 2," to my mind commensurate with this expansive force (chaos), in the body. Since we have no third force, a true heart center is missing in his pre-work framework. Instead, there is this active *delusion* of ego (the third poison) that is more like the passion of Deceit at the heart center, the fusion with the false self or ego from which we all suffer. Given this, I would place the third poison "delusion," like Deceit, at the missing/deluded heart. Delusion is the central ignorance that also represents Mara himself (the Lord of Delusion is an expression of our self-orientation attachment to the material world illusion, and suffering). The reason this is important is that it informs the interpretation of the mixture (subtype) created when combining the type with the dominant instinct.

Of course, I may be wrong! And there is a further issue complicating things if we mean to use the forces to help define subtypes, which is that the forces don't line up exactly with the centers anyway. I believe they would more accurately be organized as: chaos or "desire" (7-8-9), order or "aversion" (5-6-1) and "delusion" (2-3-4), in keeping with the diagram drawn for me by Dirk Cloete related to the clusters of types that share the same counter instinct. Whatever the "right" organization, I believe this seemingly small point of designation to be the source of the disconnect between different Enneagram schools' interpretation of the 27 subtypes, as well as the very serious (to my mind) conflict about whether Deceit or Vanity is the emotional habit or passion of Type 3. Naranjo changed Ichazo's original passion at point 3 (Deceit) to Vanity, which some teachers have continued. I imagine that he did this due to his interpretation of the Buddhist poison of "desire" as connected to the heart. Because of this foundational disagreement, I am not sure we really understand Type 3 and what drives it.

Beyond Type 3, this issue impacts all of the subtype interpretations, which again, Naranjo (in the Shift Network talk at least) appeared to formulate by integrating the three poisons or forces with each passion. This makes total sense because the three forces are indeed akin to the instincts, three basic forces at the center of Creation. We can have three different orientations to each passionate drive. However, because the Enneagram community also does not agree on the nature of the instincts, most especially the sexual instinct, we would have to sort that out too before applying the formula. At this level (and under ego), "desire" would correlate to the sexual instinct (Force 2), "aversion" to the self-preservation (force 1), and "delusion" to the social (the missing third, that adapts to align with both culture and nature). I have here linked the sexual instinct with the chaos/flow principle that is also "feminine" in the myths. Our collective interpretation of the nature of the "feminine" force is skewed by what we assume "receptive" and "feminine" to mean literally. Remember each force can take an affirming *or* a denying stance; an active *or* passive position relative to the other. The feminine is not *only* passive, but also the vast, elemental, life-giving power of chaos. It is boundary breaking, ravenous, reaching to extend life that has grown stagnant - and therefore more in line with the sexual instinct, which is about seeking and competing to acquire a mate and extend the species.

The most important point here, regardless of whatever theory is "right," is that **the Laws of the Symbol have profound implications for type and subtype.** And using them for this purpose, to come to consensus across Enneagram schools, seems to me a fair and wise endeavor to promote and pursue.

202 Tomberg, *Wisdom*, 150-151.

203 Gurdjieff, *Life is Real*, 110-112.

204 Dispenza, *Supernatural*, 93-99.

205 Tomberg, *Wisdom*, 228.

206 Locating the Enneagram points with the *chakras* works well for this meditation if we understand point 9 as the ground and bubble of interbeing; 8 as the point just above the head connecting us to Source consciousness, and point 6 as "the secret chakra." Kundalini yoga teaches about the development or discovery of this chakra through inner work. (This also explains why it is not an

"interval" on the journey, but rather a step made by the hero, aligning two worlds to call in higher forces). Joe Dispenza connects the 6th center to the pineal gland. It is located towards the back of the head, midway between spine and top of the head, placing the 7th at the "the third eye," related to pituitary function.

207 For a guided meditation following a similar process, try Joe Dispenza's *Blessing of the Energy Centers II: Symbols*. www.drjoedispenza.com. I re-mixed his teaching with Dan Siegel's pillars of mind training as three forces, and Gurdjieff's teachings about integrating the Laws of Three and Seven, because they all fit together with enduring themes from our varied wisdom traditions. All bring a specificity to the idea of Presence that includes the three forces, applied to increase integration and coherence within and between constituent elements of being-consciousness (as centers, or aspects of consciousness) represented in the brain/body/heart, as well as with the larger systems we inhabit of relationship with others, the natural world, and with Being itself.

CHAPTER 21: THE ALCHEMY OF THE SYMBOL

208 Gurdjieff, *In Search of Being*, 242.

209 Stephen L. Julich, "An Alchemy of Heaven on Nature's Base: Intimations of the Universal Opus in the Integral Yoga and Divine Life in Man in the Work of C.G. Jung," *International Journal of Transpersonal Studies* 37, no. 1 (2018): 132-198.

210 Hauk, *The Emerald Tablet*. The Alchemical formula and its number of steps varies by interpretation. We are following here the seven steps laid down in the Emerald Tablet as interpreted by long-time student of Alchemy and Hermetic philosophy, DW Hauck.

211 Richard Schwartz's Internal Family Systems Theory (IFS) is a very effective way to work with aspects of your Enneagram type (fixation, dominant instinct, passion) that grew up as "protective parts" to defend the child within.

212 Gurdjieff, *In Search of Being*, 131.

213 Jung, *Psychology and Alchemy*, 240.

214 Tomberg, *Wisdom*, 262.

215 Campbell, *Hero*, 110.

216 Campbell, *Hero*, 124.

217 Tomberg, *Wisdom*, 210.

218 Tomberg, *Wisdom*, 634-635

219 Gurdjieff, *Beelzebub's Tales*, 244.

220 Campbell, *Hero*, 18.

CHAPTER 22: A UNIVERSAL MAP

221 Ouspensky, *ISOM*, 437.

222 Jeffrey J Kripal, *The Flip: Epiphanies of Mind and the Future of Knowledge* (New York: Bellevue Literary Press, 2019), 136.

223 Cathal O'Connell, "What shape are photons? Quantum holography sheds light—Physicists created a hologram of a single light particle," *Cosmos Magazine*, July 20, 2016.

224 Puran Bair, "Visible Light Radiated from the Heart with Heart Rhythm Meditation," *Subtle Energies & Energy Medicine* 16, no. 3 (2005): 211-217.

225 Feynman, *QED*.

References

Armstrong, Thomas, "The Stages of Ego Development According to Jane Loevinger." *American Institute for Learning and Human Development Blog*, January 31, 2020. https://www.institute4learning.com.

Bair, Puran. "Visible Light Radiated from the Heart with Heart Rhythm Meditation." *Subtle Energies & Energy Medicine* 16, no. 3 (2005): 211-217.

Baker, John J. "The Dharma in a Single Drawing." *Tricycle: The Buddhist Review*, Spring 2015.

Bakhtiar, Laleh. *The Sufi Enneagram: Secrets of the Symbol Unveiled.* Chicago: Institute of Traditional Psychology, 2018.

Bargh, John. *Before You Know It: The Unconscious Reasons We Do What We Do.* New York: Touchstone Books, 2017.

Bhagavad Gita IV, 6-8. As cited in "The Hindu Trinity." *The Indian Panorama*, Last updated October 30, 2015. https://www.theindianpanorama.news/other-stories/the-hindu-trinity/

Bourgeault, Cynthia. *The Holy Trinity and the Law of Three: Discovering the Radical Truth at the Heart of Christianity.* Boulder, CO: Shambala Publications, 2013.

Bourgeault, Cynthia. *The Meaning of Mary Magdalene: Discovering the Woman at the Heart of Christianity.* Boulder, CO: Shambala Publications, 2010.

Brach, Tara. *Radical Compassion: Learning to Love Yourself and Your World with the Practice of RAIN.* New York: Penguin Life, 2020.

Brooks, Michael. "There's a glitch at the edge of the universe that could remake physics." *New Scientist*, October 2018.

Campbell, Joseph. *The Power of Myth with Bill Moyers.* New York: Doubleday, 1998.

Campbell, Joseph. *The Hero with a Thousand Faces, Third Edition.* Novato, CA: New World Library, 2008.

Carrol, Lewis. *Alice in Wonderland: The Original 1865 Edition with Complete Illustrations by Sir John Tenniel.* Independently published, 2021.

Chestnut, Beatrice. "Understanding the Development of Personality Type: Integrating Object Relations Theory and the Enneagram System." *The Enneagram Journal* (Summer 2008): 22-51.

Chestnut, Beatrice. *The Complete Enneagram: 27 Paths to Greater Self Knowledge.* Berkeley, CA: She Writes Press, 2013.

Christlieb, Fatima Fernandez. *Where on Earth did the Enneagram Come From?* Mexico City: Lightning Source, 2016.

Church, Dawson. *Mind to Matter: The Astonishing Science of How Your Brain Creates Material Reality.* Carlsbad, CA: Hay House, 2018.

Coleman, Mark. "A Heart as Wide as the World. Cultivating the Brahma Viharas: Love, Compassion, Joy, & Equanimity." *Monday Evening Dharma Talks*, Spirit Rock, May 24, 2016.

Corbett, Lionel. "Jungian Psychology and Kohut's Self-Psychology." C.G. Jung Institute of Chicago. Audio recording, 1989.

Cosmic Core. "Article 124B: Quantum Physics—Part 4—Geometry of the Photon." Accessed October 10, 2022. https://www.cosmic-core.org/free/article-124b-quantum-physics-part-4-geometry-of-the-photon/

Dane, Heather. "The Seven Directions of the Medicine Wheel." *Catalyst, issue 7: Energy Medicine and Healing Summit*, 2019. www.theshiftnetwork.com/blog/2019-04-05/seven-directions-medicine-wheel

Daniels, David N. "Working with the Enneagram Harmony Triads: A Key to the Development and Integration." Written 2019. https://drdaviddaniels.com/articles/triads/

Dass, Ram. In Stephen and Ondrea Levine, *Who Dies? An Investigation of Conscious Living and Conscious Dying.* New York: Anchor Books, 1989.

Davies, Paul. "The number that fascinates physicists above all others." *Cosmos: The Science of Everything.* January 28, 2016. https://cosmosmagazine.com/science/mathematics/the-number-that-fascinates-physicists-above-all-others/

Davis, Kenneth L. and Montag, Christian. "Selected Principles of Pankseppian Affective Neuroscience." *Frontiers in Neuroscience* 12, no. 1025. January 17, 2019, p. 1-11.

De Salzmann, Jeanne. *The Reality of Being: The Fourth Way of Gurdjieff.* Boulder, CO: Shambala Publications, 2010.

Dechar, Lorie Eve with Benjamin Fox. *The Alchemy of Inner Work: A Guide for Turning Illness and Suffering into True Health and Well-Being.* Newburyport, MA: Weiser Books, 2021.

Dispenza, Joe. "The Role of Brainwaves in Meditation: Part II." December 12, 2020. https://drjoedispenza.com/blogs/dr-joes-blog/the-role-of-brainwaves-in-meditation-part-ii

Dispenza, Joe. "Synchronizing Your Energy to New Potentials." October 9, 2020. https://drjoedispenza.com/blogs/dr-joes-blog/synchronizing-your-energy-to-new-potentials

Dispenza, Joe. *Becoming Supernatural: How Common People are Doing the Uncommon.* Carlsbad, CA: Hay House, Inc, 2017.

Edinger, Edward F. *Ego and Archetype.* Boston, MA: Shambala Publications, 1992.

Encyclopedia of Buddhism. "Three Poisons." Last modified 3 September 2022. https://encyclopediaofbuddhism.org/index.php?title=Three_poisons&oldid=65620

Facts and Details. "Brahma, Vishnu, Shiva: The Hindu Trinity. World Religions – Hinduism, it's History, Texts, and Gods." Last modified September 2018. https://factsanddetails.com/world/cat55/sub354/item1353.html

Feynman, Richard P. *QED: The Strange Theory of Light and Matter.* Princeton: Princeton University Press, 1985.

Frankl, Victor E. *Man's Search for Meaning.* Boston: Beacon Press, 1959.

Gurdjieff, G.I. *Beelzebub's Tales to His Grandson: All and Everything, First Series.* New York: Penguin Books, 1950.

Gurdjieff, G.I. *Meetings with Remarkable Men.* Penguin Compass edition, 2002.

Gurdjieff, G.I. *Life is Real Only Then, When 'I Am'. All and Everything, Third Series.* New York: Penguin Books edition, 1991.

Gurdjieff, G.I. As quoted in Stephen A. Grant. ed. *In Search of Being: The Fourth Way to Consciousness.* Boulder, Colorado: Shambala Publications, 2012.

Gurdjieff, G.I. "The Enneagram: A Lecture by Gurdjieff," *The Endless Search - Work Philosophy,* 2004. Website by Ian MacFarlane. https://www.endlesssearch.co.uk/philo_enneagramtalk.htm

Can also be found here: https://www.academia.edu/27075984/The_Enneagram_A_Lecture_by_Gurdjieff?email_work_card=view-paper

Guruge, Ananda W.P. "Part III: Temptations by Mara in Non-Canonical Buddhist literature." *The Buddha's Encounters with Mara the Tempter: Their Representation in Literature and Art.* Copyright 2015. https://www.accesstoinsight.org/lib/authors/guruge/wheel419.html

Haidt, Jonathan. *The Happiness Hypothesis: Finding Modern Truth in Ancient Wisdom.* New York: Basic Books, 2006.

Harris, Reg. *The Hero's Journey: The Path of Transformation.* Napa, CA: Harris Communications, 2015.

Hauck, Dennis William. *The Emerald Tablet: Alchemy of Personal Transformation.* New York: Penguin Compass, 1999.

Hawking, Stephen. *Brief Answers to the Big Questions.* New York: Bantam Books, 2018.

Herbjornsrud, Dag. "The Radical Philosophy of Egypt: Forget God and Family, Write!" Blog of the American Philosophical Association. December 17, 2018. https://blog.apaonline.org/2018/12/17/the-radical-philosophy-of-egypt-forget-god-and-family-write/

Hudson, Russ. "The Inner Critic/Inner Rebel—Two Obstacles in Our Inner Work." The Awakened Company Enneagram Series with Russ Hudson and Catherine Bell, 2020. Audio recording. https://vimeo.com/ondemand/enneagramseries/

Hudson, Russ. "The Enneagram as Nine Paths for Awakening." The Shift Network Global Summit, 2020. Audio recording. www.shiftnetwork.com/

Ichazo, Oscar. "Letter to the Transpersonal Community." Written 1991. http://www.arica.org/articles/trletter.cfm (Note: this link is now inactive. The letter that existed there for many years seems to have been removed from the revised website as of 2022.) A pdf can be found at: https://pdfcoffee.com/letter-to-the-transpersonal-community-pdf-free.html

Israel Ministry of Foreign Affairs. "King Solomon's Seal." *The Israel Review of Arts and Letters.* MFA Archive, February 16, 1999.

James, Ken. *The Way of the Sly One: The Psychology of Our Possible Evolution in the Writings of Gurdjieff, Ouspensky, & Jung.* C.G. Jung Institute of Chicago, 1997. Audio recording.

Julich, Stephen L. "An Alchemy of Heaven on Nature's Base: Intimations of the Universal Opus in the Integral Yoga and Divine Life in Man in the Work of C.G. Jung." *International Journal of Transpersonal Studies* 37, no. 1 (2018): pp. 132-198.

Jung, C.G. *Aion: Researches into the Phenomenology of the Self.* Translated by R.F.C. Hull. Princeton, NJ: Princeton University Press, 1968.

Jung, C.G. *Analytical Psychology: Its Theory & Practice.* New York: Vintage Books, 1968.

Jung, C.G. *Psychology and Alchemy,* Second Edition. Translated by R.F.C. Hull. Princeton, NJ: Princeton University Press, 1968.

Jung, C.G. *The Red Book: Liber Novus.* A Reader's Edition. New York: WW Norton & Co, 2009.

Jung, C.G. *Mysterium Coniunctionis.* Translated by R.F.C. Hull. Princeton, NJ: Princeton University Press, 1963.

Kripal, Jeffrey J. *The Flip: Epiphanies of Mind and the Future of Knowledge.* New York: Bellevue Literary Press, 2019.

Laitman, Rav Michael. *Kabbalah Science and the Meaning of Life: Because Your Life Has Meaning.* Toronto, Canada: Laitman Kabbalah Publishers, 2007.

Land, George and Beth Jarman. *Breakpoint and Beyond: Mastering the Future—Today.* New York: Harper Business, 1993.

Langer, Ellen J. *Mindfulness.* MA: Addison-Wesley, 1989.

Le Grice, Keiron. *The Archetypal Cosmos: Rediscovering the Gods in Myth, Science and Astrology.* Edinburgh: Floris Books, 2010.

Levitan, Daniel. "The Dalai Lama: Suffering, compassion, and being a perpetual student." *New York Times,* July 6, 2020.

Maitri, Sandra. *The Spiritual Dimension of the Enneagram: Nine Faces of the Soul.* New York: Jeremy Tarcher/Putnam Inc, 2000.

Mark, Joshua. "The Soul in Ancient Egypt." World History Encyclopedia, March 2, 2017. https://www.worldhistory.org/article/1023/the-soul-in-ancient-egypt/

Martin, Michael. "In the name of the Mother, and of the Daughter, and of the Holy Soul." *The Center for Sophiological Studies Blog.* February 2, 2019

McLeod, Saul. "Erik Erikson's Stages of Psychosocial Development." *Simply Psychology.* Last updated 2018. https://www.simplypsychology.org/Erik-Erikson.html

McCraty, Rollin. "New Frontiers in Heart Rate Variability and Social Coherence Research: Techniques, Technologies, and Implications for Improving Group Dynamics and Outcomes." *Frontiers in Public Health* 5, no. 267 (October 12, 2017): 1-13. https://doi.org/10.3389/fpubh.2017.00267

McCraty, Rollin. "The Energetic Heart: Bioelectromagnetic Communication Within and Between People." In *Clinical Applications of Bioelectromagnetic Medicine,* edited by P. J. Rosch and M. S. Markov, 541-562. New York: Marcel Dekker, 2004.

McColman, Carl. *The Big Book of Christian Mysticism: The Essential Guide to Contemplative Spirituality.* Minneapolis: Broadleaf Books, 2010.

McGilchrist, Ian. "Reciprocal organization of the cerebral hemispheres." *Dialogues in Clinical Neuroscience* 12 no. 4 (December 2010): 503-515.

Meade, Michael. "The River of Deep Meaning." *Living Myth Podcast,* episode 273. Mosaic Voices, Mar 30, 2022.

Meade, Michael. "Myth Makes Meaning." *Living Myth Podcast,* episode 260. Mosaic Voices, Dec. 12, 2021.

Melchizedek, Drunvalo. *The Ancient Secret of the Flower of Life, Volume 2.* Flagstaff, AZ: Light Technology Publishing, 2000.

Miller, Arthur I. *137: Jung, Pauli, and the Pursuit of a Scientific Obsession.* New York: WW Norton & Co, 2009.

Mitchell, Stephen. *Tao te Ching: A New English Version.* New York: Harper Collins, 1988.

Morter, Sue. *The Energy Codes: The 7-Step System to Awaken Your Spirit, Heal Your Body, and Live Your Best Life.* Atria Books, 2019.

Naranjo, Claudio. 'The Enneagram & Personal Awakenings: The Life & Teachings of Claudio Naranjo." *Video and Audio Excerpts from Shift Network Interviews with Claudio Naranjo.* The Shift Network Enneagram Global Summit 2020 Bonuses.

O'Connell, Cathal. "What shape are photons? Quantum holography sheds light—Physicists created a hologram of a single light particle." *Cosmos Magazine,* July 20, 2016.

O'Brien, Barbara. "The Three Poisons: The Unwholesome Roots of Our Unease." Learn Religions. Last updated June 23, 2018. https://www.learnreligions.com/the-three-poisons-449603

Ouspensky, P.D. *In Search of the Miraculous: Fragments of an Unknown Teaching.* Digital Edition. U.S: Library of Alexandria, 1949.

Ouspensky, P.D. *The Psychology of Man's Possible Evolution.* New York: Vintage Random House, 1950.

Pagels, Elaine. *The Gnostic Gospels.* New York: Vintage Books, 1979.

Patterson, William Patrick. *Georgi Ivanovitch Gurdjieff: The Man, The Teaching, His Mission.* Fairfax, CA: Arete Communications, 2014.

Peterson, Jordan B. *Maps of Meaning: The Architecture of Belief.* New York: Routledge, 1999.

Pollan, Michael. *How to Change Your Mind: What the New Science of Psychedelics Teaches Us About Consciousness, Dying, Addiction, Depression, and Transcendence. U.S:* Penguin Random House, 2018.

Powell, Corey S. "Relativity vs. Quantum mechanics: The battle for the universe." *The Guardian,* November 15, 2015.

Ratner, Paul. "Why the number 137 is one of the greatest mysteries in physics." *Big Think,* October 31, 2018.

Rohr, Richard. *The Universal Christ: How a Forgotten Reality Can Change Everything We See, Hope For, and Believe.* New York: Convergent Books, 2019.

Rohr, Richard. "The Blueprint of Creation." *Daily Meditations,* March 28, 2017. Center for Action and Contemplation. https://cac.org/daily-meditations/the-blueprint-of-creation-2017-03-28/

Rohr, Richard. "Shadow-boxing." *Daily Meditations*, Sept 8, 2019. Center for Action and Contemplation. https://cac.org/daily-meditations/shadowboxing-2019-09-08/

Rohr, Richard. "Becoming Who you Are." *Daily Meditations*, Sept 9, 2019. Center for Action and Contemplation. https://cac.org/daily-meditations/becoming-who-you-are-2019-09-09/

Rohr, Richard. *The Divine Dance*. Pennsylvania: Whitaker House, 2016.

Rohr, Richard and Adreas Ebert. *The Enneagram: A Christian Perspective*. New York: Crossroad Publishing, 1990.

Rohr, Richard and Adreas Ebert. *Discovering the Enneagram: An Ancient Tool for a New Spiritual Journey*. New York: Crossroads Publishing, 1993.

Rowling, J.K. "What exactly happened when Voldemort used the Avada Kedavra curse on Harry in the forest?" The Rowling Library. https://therowlinglibrary.com/jkrowling.com/textonly/en/faq_view_id=122.html

Schwartz, Alexandra. "Love is not a permanent state of enthusiasm: An Interview with Esther Perel." *The New Yorker Interview*, December 9, 2018.

Seife, Charles. *Zero: The Biography of a Dangerous Idea*. New York: Penguin Books, 2000.

Siegel, Daniel. *Mind: A Journey to the Heart of Being Human*. New York: WW Norton & Company, 2017.

Siegel, Daniel. "Aware: The Science and Practice of Presence." *The Gottman Institute Blog*, August 21, 2018.

Siegel, Daniel. *Aware: The Science and Practice of Presence: The Groundbreaking Meditation Practice*. New York: Penguin Random House, 2018.

Speeth, Kathleen Riordan. *The Gurdjieff Work*. New York: Penguin Putnam Inc, 1989.

Stein, Murray. *Jung's Map of the Soul: An Introduction*. Illinois: Carus Publishing, 1998.

Stein, Murray. *Understanding the Meaning of Alchemy: Jung's Metaphor for the Transformative Process*. Audio course. Chicago: C.G. Jung Institute of Chicago, 1992.

Strogatz, Steven. *Sync: How Order Emerges from Chaos in the Universe, Nature, and Daily Life*. New York: Hatchette Books, 2003.

Sunyata Buddhist Center. "The Three Poisons." Accessed July 17, 2020. https://www.sunyatacentre.org/the-three-poisons/

Suzuki, Shunryu. *Zen Mind, Beginner's Mind: Informal Talks on Zen Buddhism*. New York: Weatherhill, 1970.

Swart, Tara. *The Source: Open Your Mind, Change Your Life.* London: Penguin Random House, 2020.

Taylor, Jill Bolte. *My Stroke of Insight: A Brain Scientist's Personal Journey.* New York: Viking Press, 2008.

Tomberg, Valentin. *Meditations on the Tarot.* Translated by Robert Powell. New York: Penguin Putnam, 2002.

Van Laer, Lee. *Chakras and the Enneagram.* Do Re Mi Shock, 2018. http://doremishock.com/leevanlaer/index.html

Van Laer, Lee. *The Universal Enneagram.* Do Re Mi Shock, 2013. http://doremishock.com/leevanlaer/index.html

Von Bertalanffy, Ludwig. General Systems Theory: Foundations, Development, Applications. New York: George Braziller, 1968.

Wang, Robin. "Yinyang (Yin-Yang)." *Internet Encyclopedia of Philosophy: A Peer-Reviewed Academic Resource.* Accessed October 10, 2022. https://iep.utm.edu/yinyang/

Wikipedia. "Classical electromagnetism and special relativity." Accessed October 9, 2022. https://en.wikipedia.org/wiki/Classical_electromagnetism_and_special_relativity

ACKNOWLEDGMENTS

I am grateful to Beatrice Chestnut and Uranio Paes for initiating me into an entirely new experience of the Enneagram, and of myself, through their programs and vast knowledge of the Enneagram. Their leadership in raising awareness about the Symbol, as well as their insistence that we must do psychological work in our pursuit of spiritual growth, have contributed a great deal to the international Enneagram community. And, of course, this book would never have unfolded without my original Enneagram teachers, Michael Ray and David Daniels. Michael's foresight, mentorship, and belief in me gave me the courage to merge psychology and spirituality with leadership and business in many ways, and to follow my own path. And David Daniels continued to be a wise and kind teacher for me, along with Helen Palmer, through the Narrative Enneagram school they founded.

I also want to acknowledge my other teachers in the Narrative Enneagram, my mentor Peter O'Hanrahan and Terry Saracino, both of whom have been humbly and expertly teaching this work for a long time. Ginger Lapid-Bogda has been another exceptional mentor and supporter of mine for many years through the Enneagram in Business work. The combination of her expertise in the Enneagram, organizational theory and leadership, training design, and artistry has yielded impactful practices and beautiful tools that enabled me to take the Enneagram "out of my back pocket," use it overtly in my professional work, and learn so much from clients too. And thanks to remote learning, I have been able to study with other great teachers in recent years, most notably, Russ Hudson and Susan Olesek. I was especially impacted by the thorough, heart-based, and grounded way in which Susan and the folks at the Enneagram Prison Project are teaching the Enneagram.

Maybe it's odd to acknowledge people I only know through their writing, some of whom are long gone, but their work and weaving of many wisdom traditions has been particularly formative for me and underlies everything in this book. I mentioned Gurdjieff, Carl Jung, Joseph Campbell, Valentin Tomberg, and Jordan Peterson. I wanted to add to this list Richard Rohr, whom I quote often throughout the book, and Michael Meade, who's work, although I only discovered it recently, has provided much sustenance and confirmation that the enduring themes of myths and stories have merit, meaning, and truth.

Learning about the Symbol and writing this book was a journey for me, for sure, and one I could not have completed without some wise mentors and allies along the way. I am especially grateful for Sandy Wand, who has supported me through thick and thin, and Nancy Hunterton, who believed in me and this project from the beginning. I also want to thank my friends on the path who have encouraged me and read parts of the book, including Laura Paradis, Jane Tight, Elisa French, Carla Evens, Mark Nicolson, Steven Kalas, Frank DeLuca, Janet Watts, Laura Heard, Petra Lackey, Matt Ahrens, Amy Ream, and Rich Mertes. I was also lucky to happen into a long conversation about symbol-related topics with Dirk Cloete in 2019 that ignited my thinking and motivation to persist in this adventure.

My friend and editor, Patrick VonBargen, deserves extra special thanks for pouring through early editions and dogging me to keep the material accessible, while at the same time helping me keep the faith. I am also grateful to Carolyn Bond and Mina Familar-Ragsdale for additional editorial work, and Chris Molé for endless patience, as well as skillful book and cover design.

Finally, I'd like to thank my friends and family for experiencing my absence during this four-year journey and loving me anyway (I think ☺). I am especially grateful for my brother and sister-in-law, who help tether me to the everyday world, and for my amazing parents, who—although they did not understand what I was doing (nor why, perhaps)—supported me in so many ways throughout this process, which included the covid year I spent working in their backyard "monk cell." Finally, I am forever grateful for my wise and unique daughters who contributed ideas and drawings and, in some sense, both initiated and fueled this journey.

About the Author

JENNIFER E. JOSS, PH.D. is a psychologist by training, a coach and consultant by profession, and a hermetic philosopher at heart. She is a certified International Enneagram Association professional, and the Enneagram has been a constant (though sometimes challenging) companion since she learned the system 30 years ago. Since she was young, Jennifer has been preoccupied with questions about the nature of reality, suffering, the meaning of life, and her own purpose. Pursuing such intangible things led her down diverse paths of inquiry that have somehow woven together in the Enneagram Symbol.

Professionally, Jennifer has been studying and teaching about the well-being and potential of people and systems her entire adult life, with a particular passion for understanding great leadership and teaching a self-coaching method she developed. She graduated from Harvard with high honors in psychology, holds a Ph.D. in counseling psychology from Stanford's School of Education, and is always studying something—currently energy healing and psychedelic-assisted therapy. At the same time, Jennifer would say she has learned the most from the school of life, being a mother, and from inner work practices that connect her with archetypal ideas. She lives in Ashland, Oregon, where she can run in the forest every day with her best friend Charlie Brown.

You can learn more about Jennifer and her work at
www.jumpingcurves.com

CPSIA information can be obtained
at www.ICGtesting.com
Printed in the USA
LVHW050305060723
751536LV00003B/28

9 798987 664018